*Se(*

The
# Public Administrator's Companion
## A Practical Guide

Sandra Emerson
Kathy Van Ness
Georgianna Streeter
Linda-Marie Sundstrom
Parker G. Emerson

WAVELAND
PRESS, INC.
Long Grove, Illinois

For information about this book, contact:
Waveland Press, Inc.
4180 IL Route 83, Suite 101
Long Grove, IL 60047-9580
(847) 634-0081
info@waveland.com
www.waveland.com

10-digit ISBN 1-4786-4950-X
13-digit ISBN 978-1-4786-4950-2

Printed in the United States of America

7   6   5   4   3   2   1

*This text is dedicated to the men and women in public service and administration who work tirelessly to serve the public interest.*

—The Authors

# Contents

## SECTION 1
## The Public Administrator's World

## SECTION 2
## Planning and Analysis

## SECTION 3
## Human Resources, Planning and Risk Management

## SECTION 4
## Financial Resources

## SECTION 5
# Performance and Leadership

## APPENDICES

# Preface

Welcome to the second edition of *The Public Administrator's Companion: A Practical Guide*. The modern discipline of public administration in the United States dates to the Progressives of the early twentieth century. Texts in the discipline focus on planning, organizing, employee relations, coordinating, reporting, and budgeting. The profession and discipline have evolved over the past 80 years, and significant changes have resulted, such as nontraditional modes of citizen participation, significant challenges to public funding and accountability, the redesign of public organizations as less hierarchical, extensive intergovernmental grant arrangements, and contracting services to nonprofit organizations to name just a few. These evolving demands call upon today's public administrator to use decision-making tools that facilitate strategic and tactical approaches to implementing public policies and programs. While the current role of a public administrator encompasses new challenges, the administrator is still called upon to handle their traditional responsibilities. Therefore, this text discusses not only the fundamental aspects of public administration, including governmental structure, human resources, and public funding, but it also describes how today's administrators conduct public administration as a practical art, delineating the steps administrators take in such areas as strategic planning, consensus building, budget development, and performance measurement. The text also seeks to supplement academic and traditional material with discussions reflecting circumstances that professionals in the field face as they assume responsibilities associated with defining, implementing, and assessing public policy.

The newest elements of this edition include a chapter on nonprofits, one on organizational leadership, and an appendix on preparing and making presentations. We revised the appendix on getting a job in government to include hiring and interviewing from both the agency and applicant perspective. We have also added an Instructor Guide for faculty with sections for each chapter.

Real-world examples and cases from the local, state, and federal level reinforce key topics. To make the book as user friendly as possible to students of public administration, each chapter ends with a "Practicing Public Administration" section that provides useful exercises for building the skills described earlier in the chapter. Each chapter has its own bibliography which provides some of the source materials used in developing the chapter and also provides additional readings, sometimes contradictory, which help broaden the reader's knowledge of the chapter's topics.

This work is a collaborative effort among scholars and working professionals in the field. Authors are Sandra Emerson, Kathy Van Ness, Georgianna Streeter, Linda-Marie Sundstrom, and Parker G. Emerson. We are also very appreciative of the work of Royce Menkus on the first edition of this book.

Our academic and professional colleagues generously provided assistance to our effort. They have augmented our knowledge with information and examples, read and commented on early drafts of chapters, and contributed topics for discussion. The first edition benefitted from the comments of several employees of the city of Los Angeles (Patricia Canfield, Richard Dickinson, Susan McTigue, Margaret Whelan, and Barbara Yamamoto); academic colleagues (Thomas Tan, co-chair of the Masters in Public Administration Advisory Council, Charles Gossett and David Speak of the political science department, and Don Adams of the philosophy department at California State Polytechnic University, Pomona); and students (Rebecca Ramirez, Nuala Gasser, and Tim Johnson). David Speak also assisted with the second edition. In addition, Chief Mark Kling of the Rialto, California, Police Department provided significant support in describing collaborative efforts with a nonprofit organization in our updated edition. We acknowledge Deborah Caruso's assistance with our updated chapters on leadership and human resources.

Finally, we are thankful for the support from Waveland Press. This project has received encouragement and guidance from Neil Rowe and his staff.

While there has been significant input from many friends, family members, and professional and academic colleagues, we take full responsibility for the material contained in this text and any shortcomings therein.

—The Authors

# About the Authors

**Sandra Emerson** is member of the university's Office of Undergraduate Research and former director of the Masters in Public Administration program for the political science department at California State Polytechnic University, Pomona (CPP). In addition to teaching courses in public policy and public administration at CPP, the University of La Verne, and the University of Southern California, Emerson held positions in this field in the private and public sectors, including program administrator for Medicare Part B, consultant with Southern California Edison, and budget and program analyst with the City of Norfolk, Virginia. She has a PhD and Master's degree in Public Administration from USC as well as a BA and MA from Temple University.

**Kathy Van Ness** served as a strategic planning, budget, financial systems, and audit manager during her 30 years with the City of Los Angeles. She also worked as a manager with the City of Long Beach, as a planner and manager in health care, and as a researcher with The Brookings Institution. She has a PhD in Urban Planning from the University of California, Los Angeles.

**Georgianna Streeter** is an internal auditor with the Los Angeles World Airports, where she has held positions in the Audit, Ethics, and the Environmental Programs Group and helped establish a new ethics program and code of ethics department. She teaches public service ethics at California State Polytechnic University, Pomona, and has taught ethics and critical thinking at Mount St. Mary's University, Loyola Marymount University, and California State University, Los Angeles. Streeter has held senior budget positions at the New York City Office of

Management and Budget, the Manhattan Borough President's Office, and the Mayor's Office in Los Angeles. She has an MA in Philosophy from Loyola Marymount University, an MA in Public Policy and Administration from Fordham University, and a BA in philosophy from Smith College.

**Linda-Marie Sundstrom** worked in local government in Southern California as a Senior Analyst serving the Board of Supervisors. She then worked for a decade as a grant writing consultant for various government agencies, universities, nonprofit organizations, and tribal governments. She has spent the last 20 years teaching in Master of Public Administration (MPA) programs and is currently the MPA Director at California Baptist University. Dr. Sundstrom was a Fulbright Scholar and taught bachelors, masters and doctorate students in public administration under the Office of the President in Ukraine and has published numerous articles in the fields of education, nonprofit management and criminal justice. Linda-Marie earned her PhD in Public Administration at the University of La Verne, a Masters of Public Administration at California State University, San Bernardino, and a BS in International Business and Marketing at California State Polytechnic University, Pomona.

**Parker G. Emerson** has started, operated, and sold several successful companies, including management consulting, grant writing, and sheet music publishing and retailing. He has also taught speaking and presentation techniques to graduate and undergraduate students and revised and taught electronics courses to U.S. Naval personnel. He developed and implemented in-house technical training, management development, and quality assurance programs for most positions in a major alarm and patrol services company. Mr. Emerson served 10 years in the U.S. Navy, primarily responsible for the operation of the navigation center on a nuclear missile submarine. He earned his MBA from the University of Southern California, emphasizing entrepreneurship and venture management, and his B.S. in Business Administration from Old Dominion University, Norfolk, VA, majoring in production control and inventory management.

# SECTION
# 1

# The Public
# Administrator's World

The American Republic began in March 1789 with the adoption of the U.S. Constitution and has evolved over the past 230 years from an experiment in self-government by thirteen sovereign states into a nation that is a world power. Along the way the scope of what the public sector is, what government does, and government's responsibilities and relationships with citizens has changed significantly. The expectation of the public that government should reflect the community's ideals and ethical norms has evolved as well. Today the historic norms, legal structure, and public's participation and expectations constitute the public administrator's world.

Section 1 of this text discusses the administrator's world. The supreme law of the land is the U.S. Constitution which provides for a federal government, 50 state governments, and the District of Columbia. This federal system affords the public with opportunities for self-government or liberty. Today in the United States there are more than 90,000 governments: state, local, regional, and special districts. Chapter 1 invites the reader into the complex and interconnected world of government in a federal system. Chapter 2 discusses the functions of the various levels of government and explores some of the organizational and managerial concepts utilized by various agencies. Chapter 3 discusses non-profit organizations, sometimes called *nongovernmental organizations* (NGOs), and their structure, mission, and relationship with government.

An intrinsic element of republican government is the expectation that decision makers behave ethically and in concert with the core values of a republic: honestly, openly, without favoritism, effectively, and efficiently. Getting beyond platitudes to the hard choices required of ethical decision making is the focus of Chapter 4. These expectations of behavior, like the

1

laws and structures defined by constitutions and statutes, constitute the
fundamental environment of today's public administrator.

Finally, one rationale for federalism was to enable citizens to participate in government, which is the focus of Chapter 5. Advances in
technology and demands for self-determination have led to a plethora
of opportunities for citizens to be informed and involved in government
policies, programs, and decisions. The participation of citizens is the
hallmark of our Republic and remains among its greatest challenges.

# 1

# Understanding the Context for Public Administration

Outside Independence Hall when the Constitutional Convention of 1787 ended, Mrs. Powel asked Benjamin Franklin, "Well, Doctor, what have we got—a republic or a monarchy?" Franklin responded, "A republic, if you can keep it."

Twelve years before the drafting of the Constitution, Patrick Henry declared, "Give me liberty or give me death." Liberty is a core value of *self-government*. Liberty is a community effort. Citizens enjoy liberty because they willingly obey laws which they participated in making. Those who disobey these laws are operating outside of the community's wishes and rob the community and its citizens of their liberty.

## WHAT KIND OF GOVERNMENT DO WE HAVE?

The U.S. Constitution speaks of liberty and a republic but not of democracy. Democracy at the time of the nation's founding was called "popular government" and was seen by Federalists as unstable, violent, and unjust. The demands of individuals for freedom needed to be balanced against the community's interest and long-term welfare. The Founders envisioned a national republic that spanned a continent and provided stability while state and local governments provided the means for citizens to engage directly in government and community action.

The United States has a unique governing system. Other nations forge their national identities around a common ethnicity, language, land, and/or religion. The United States built its national identity around a concept of self-government called a constitutional federated democratic republic.

3

## Constitutional Government

The nation has 50 state constitutions and a national constitution. The federal Constitution is a relatively short contractual document with seven articles that define the structure of the government (legislature, executive, judiciary, and states) and 27 amendments. The first 10 amendments define a person's rights and protections, and the last 17 expand participation in the United States to former slaves, women, residents of the District of Columbia, and 18-year-olds, and define more specifically governing mechanisms (judicial power, election of senators, income tax, presidential succession, and term limits).

In the United States the Constitution specifies the powers of the federal government and denies specific powers (raising military, printing money, and declaring war) to state governments. However, the states and the people of the United States retain any power not granted to the federal government or denied to the states (10th Amendment).

## Federal System

The American system is federal. All states have constitutions and are required (under the U.S. Constitution) to have a mechanism (election process) by which the people select those who hold political power and control the machinery of government. The requirement that those who hold power get approval directly or indirectly from citizens is what makes the United States a republic. While all governments are under the authority of the Constitution, state governments operate within their own geographical areas independently of the central government in the District of Columbia. State constitutions can organize state governments in any number of ways. A legislature can have two chambers (bicameral) or one (unicameral, such as Nebraska's), a single independently elected executive (such as Alaska's) or 12 independent executives (such as California's governor, lieutenant governor, secretary of state, four members of the Board of Equalization, treasurer, superintendent of public schools, insurance commissioner, controller, and attorney general). Court systems vary from state to state. Some states elect judges; others have judicial commissions or rely on legislative confirmations of nominees.

While the U.S. Constitution establishes a federal system, state constitutions are *unitary*, or state-dominated, systems. The powers exercised by counties, cities, districts, or any political jurisdiction are those authorized by states' constitutions and/or legislatures. Some states afford great latitude to local jurisdictions while others do not. Jurisdictional levels that exist in one state may not exist in another. County governments exist widely throughout the United States but may be called by different names. Louisiana calls its county-like jurisdictions parish governments, and Alaska calls them boroughs. However, neither

Connecticut nor Rhode Island has county government by any name. Instead, the local instruments of state authority are exercised by towns, townships, and/or municipalities.

This diversity in structure and process is a key element of having a federal system. The Federalists argued that when a governing practice needs to be uniform, standardized, and singular, it belongs with the central government (such as coining money, regulating patents, Indian affairs, and declaring war). However, most government processes need to be customized to the populace, and therefore extensive powers remain with the states: family law, marriage, adoption, licensing professionals, protecting resources, educating youth, policing, and so forth.

The Founders of the American political system were more attached to their state governments than to a central government. Historically, state and local governments have provided the day-to-day public services and protections citizens required, hired citizens to execute public policies, and operated their own tax systems. State and local governments were designed to dominate in times of peace. Only in times of war or crisis would the public's natural attachment to its own local/state government shift to national issues and concerns. The framers of the Constitution established a system of checks and balances between state and federal governments so that neither would have a monopoly of power.

There are consequences to a federal system:

- Federalism, with its emphasis on state and local government, encourages citizen participation in government. It is easier for citizens to be involved in a school district or township than in policies regarding national defense or world peace.

- Public participation in the governing process teaches patience, prudence, obligation, and self-reliance. These skills and disciplines are necessary if a people are to govern themselves.

- Public participation teaches citizens about cause-and-effect relationships and reasoning. The public can critically assess proposals and propositions of politicians.

- Diversity in weather conditions, natural resources, demographics, and culture naturally leads to diversity in laws, policies, and programs. Whereas central governments tend to encourage uniformity, federated systems foster experimentation and variety.

- Although centralizing government policies and practices can sometimes be less costly when economies of scale are used effectively, policies and programs that are customized and varied to meet local needs avoid wasteful and time-consuming bureaucracies inherent in centralized government.

- Accountability to the public is a key element of federalism. Local school boards, airport or port authorities, and others spending local, state, and federal money must account to national agencies, state legislators, authorized administrators, and fellow citizens for both policy and funding actions.

- Federalism promotes friction between national and state governments, which has resulted in federal encroachment into state policy areas by such means as unfunded mandates, crossover regulations, and federal preemption of a range of issues from abortion to water quality.

- Federalism confounds any decisive response to a national crisis when state authority is dominant. For example, since World War II there have been 13 U.S. presidential administrations, while in Italy there has been 69, roughly a new government every 13 months. However, Italy acted decisively in February 2020 when COVID cases soared to 5,883, and the death toll for a single day rose to 793. The Italian government sent in the army and enforced a lockdown from February 27 to March 22, 2020. The U.S. national response was decidedly different. In February, the FDA allowed for non-approved tests for COVID, Congress approved $8.6 billion for the development of a vaccine, and the Executive Office extended travel bans to foreign nationals who had been to Iran. By March 13th, the federal government declared a national emergency, pushed for more COVID testing, improved the availability of medical supplies, encouraged Americans to alter their behaviour, and extended travel bans to Europe, the United Kingdom, and Ireland. COVID-19 cases in the U.S. in March had risen from 100 (March 4), to 10,000 (March 18) to 100,000 by March 27th. Lockdowns were left to the States.

Federal laws and regulations provide protection to the public. Historically states could enact laws and regulations that exceeded federal standards but could not reduce them unless they received a specific waiver from a federal agency. The Obama era standards reaffirmed the *Corporate Average Fuel Economy* (known as CAFE) standards to raise auto company fleet averages to 54.5 miles per gallon. In 2019 the Trump administration authorized the *Safer Affordable Fuel-Efficient Vehicles Rule* (known as SAFE) which lowered standards for fuel efficiency to 40.5 miles per gallon and sought to rein in state authority to deviate from national standards. By May 2020, California with 23 other states, the District of Columbia, and four cities joined in a civil suit against the SAFE rules in federal court. Meanwhile, the California Air Resources Board forged its own accord with major car manufactures to lower emissions and improve mileage to 50 miles per gallon by 2026. Implementation of federal standards without state cooperation is problematic, at best. By December of 2020, president-elect Biden selected Michael Regan to be the director of the Environmental Protection

Agency. Regan has committed to zero greenhouse gas emissions by 2035, which will also depend on cooperation from the states.

## HOW BIG IS THE GOVERNMENT?

While the U.S. Constitution accounts for 51 governments, the U.S. Department of Commerce's Bureau of the Census (2017 survey) indicates the total number of government entities at all levels is 90,073, of which 38,778 are general-purpose governments and 51,295 are special districts. The United States added 606 governments between 2011 and 2017.

Are 90,073 governments too many or not nearly enough? In 1942 the United States had 150.6 million persons and 155,116 governments. There was roughly one government for every 971 persons. Today there are an estimated 330.22 million Americans and 90,073 governments, or a government for every 3,666 people. Those who champion direct public participation or democracy prefer systems wherein relatively small numbers of people constitute a government, while those who favor representative systems prefer more persons per government.

It is estimated that 22.59 million people, or roughly 14% of a workforce of 162.79 million, work for some level of government (see Table 1.1). This estimate of 22.59 million employees is based on the official count of employees published by the U.S. Department of Labor and does not include the shadow employment of millions of Americans who are paid through grants, contracts, or other agreements. A discussion of America's shadow government at the state and local levels is presented in Chapter 15, "Contracts and Procurement." At the federal level alone, there are an estimated 10 million "shadow" employees. Currently there is no accounting of the number of shadow employees paid by grants and contracts of state, county, and subcounty governments or special districts.

The distribution of public employment reflects the importance of local government. Eighty-seven percent of all public employees work at the state and local level. This includes 35% who are employed in education and 28% who are employed in all other local governments. State governments comprise 23% of all public employment, and the federal system employs 14%. The trend has been to see an increase in state, local, and regional government jobs and a decline in federal jobs.

There is not a single accounting of what all this government costs. The official federal budget was $6.55 trillion in 2020, but this figure reflects only budgeted items and does not include Social Security payments or other entitlement programs that are "off budget." Also absent from this accounting are expenditures for clandestine operations by national security and intelligence agencies. In addition to expenditures of tax revenues are expenditures that are funded from government borrowing: the federal debt. In 2020 the national government debt was about $26.9 trillion, which is four times the size of the national budget.

**Table 1.1    Size of Government by Jurisdiction and Employees in 2020**

| Jurisdiction | Number | Employees |
|---|---|---|
| Federal Government (District of Columbia) | 1 | 2,897,000 |
| States | 50 | 5,039,000 |
| Local and Regional (General Government) | 38,778 | 6,128,200 |
| Special Districts (not education) | 51,295 | n.a. |
| School Districts | 13,800 | 7,492,300 |
| Subtotal: | — | 21,556,500 |
| Nonprofit Organizations | 1,500,000 | 12,300,000 |

Source: U.S. Bureau of Labor Statistics B-1. (2020). *Employees on non-farm payrolls by industry sector and selected industry detail.* https://www.bls.gov/news.release/empsit.t17.htm

Nonprofit organizations are discussed more thoroughly in Chapter 3. Some nonprofits perform functions that augment governmental programs or functions, such as mental health services or disaster relief, or they provide civic services that the government cannot. For this reason, they are sometimes called nongovernmental organizations (or NGOs), although this term is most frequently used outside of the United States. Nonprofit organizations are defined by federal tax policies, specifically those in section 501(c) of the Internal Revenue Code. Although most people are familiar with 501(c)(3) organizations such as churches, 501(c)(3) is not the only designation. The IRS today has 29 designations including 501(c)(6) for nonprofits involved in political campaigns, 501(c)(4) for civic leagues, 501(c)(5) for labor and agricultural organizations, and so forth.

State and local finances are available for 2017, the most recent U.S. Census Bureau survey year. The survey is conducted every five years. The status of state and local finances in 2018 was as follows:

**Table 1.2    Finances of State and Local Governments in 2017 and 2018**

| Category | 2017 (in trillions) | 2018 (in trillions) |
|---|---|---|
| Revenues raised | $3.92 | $4.08 |
| General Revenues | $3.12 | $3.29 |
| Expenditures | $3.67 | $3.81 |
| Debt* | — | $3.10 |

* Debt, across a jurisdiction, is best understood when seen as the debt burden per citizen rather than as the aggregated government debt. Debt is the accumulation of deficits governments amass when the dollars raised in revenue are insufficient to meet the expenditures made. The difference between revenue and expenditure is filled by borrowing money from the private sector. These borrowed monies are the debt.

Source: U.S. Census Bureau. (2020, Oct). *Release CB20 TPS 66.*

State and local governments are in debt with some rare exceptions (Wyoming, Alaska). In 2018 state and local debt on average was $13,248 per person. This would be the per person cost for reducing the government debt to $0. The disparity is significant across states. The highest burden is found in New Jersey ($67,200) and the lightest burden found in Oregon ($300).

Congress sets the debt ceiling for the federal government. State constitutions and legislatures set the state debt limit and in some cases limit what local debt may be.

# WHAT IS THE STRUCTURE OF LOCAL GOVERNMENT?

The structures within states vary, and what is true in many jurisdictions may not be true in a particular state or community.

## County Governments

The United States has 3,143 counties. One of the most densely populated counties is Los Angeles, with 10.5 million residents, and the least populated is Kalawao, Hawaii, with 86. The typical county serves 104,500. County governments are the nation's oldest subdivision and were adopted from the British system. Counties are controlled by the state and administer its laws and programs. County governments function often as the branch offices of state government. County governments have historically assessed property, maintained roads, and administered elections and the courts. More recently counties have been tasked with consumer protection, economic development, welfare, and homeland security. Consequently, county government may cover a broader range of services, or far fewer services than it once did, depending on the competition for functional autonomy from other subgovernments in a state. In California, for example, counties provide services from police, fire, recreation, streets, and lighting to community development, public health, and welfare. Persons in "unincorporated" areas (areas not part of a city or municipality) receive a range of public services directly from the county which include services that are typically provided by cities.

Counties are generally governed by councils of representatives selected by geographical districts. These elected representatives constitute the county legislature and, in this capacity, determine policies, raise taxes, authorize expenditures, and oversee public agencies and programs. In California elected county representatives are called county *supervisors*, while in New Jersey they are called *freeholders*.

Typically, cities and counties are separate jurisdictions, but there are some notable exceptions: Baltimore, St. Louis, New York, Philadelphia, Nashville, Miami, and San Francisco, to name a few. In these cases, the city and county geographical borders are the same, and the scope of services provided by government reflects the broader county agenda.

## Municipal Level of Governance

*Municipality* is a general category for local government that includes towns, villages, and general-law cities that are located within a county and normally have fewer powers and responsibilities than the larger counties that surround them. However, the powers they have and how they are administered varies from jurisdiction to jurisdiction. Except for those cities that are consolidated and/or coterminous with their counties, subcounty governments have smaller populations.

Cities that have their own charters have more powers than general-law cities. Cities with charters enacted by the voters have a greater degree of "home rule," meaning that they can adopt laws independent of their counties and states. In California, for example, Los Angeles, San Francisco, and San Diego are all charter cities and are considerably larger entities than many counties in the state.

While there are no rules for determining what is a city, town, or municipality, they are all government entities. A definition of a government is an entity which has discretion in the management of its own affairs and is legally separate from any other government structures. Representatives of local governments have several titles including councilmember, alderman, selectman, freeholder, or commissioner.

Specifically, a governing entity

- is incorporated by law, which enables it to sue in court and be sued, acquire property, and dispose of property;
- relies directly or indirectly on public elections to select persons to represent the jurisdiction and use its authority;
- has the expressed power to levy taxes, expend funds, and issue debt; and
- is accountable to the public for its decisions, programs, and policies.

Most jurisdictions operate in a specific geographical area, providing services to a specified sector of the population. Often what distinguishes one subcounty government from another is how it elects to govern itself.

## Local Government Models

There are four types of local government models: town meeting, mayor and council, council-manager, and commission.

The oldest and most democratic form is the *town meeting* system wherein adults meet periodically to pass a budget, elect officers, discuss community needs, and set policy. In this system the citizen is his or her own representative, and communities are small enough for residents to meet at a single location (gymnasium, community hall).

As communities become larger, direct democracy and participation are replaced with representative systems comprising an elected executive or *mayor and council*. Councilmembers may be elected from specific geographical areas as they are in larger cities such as Philadelphia, Pennsylvania, and Pomona, California, or relatively small communities such as Colton, California. Councilpersons may be elected *at-large*, representing no specific geographic area, or they may be elected by district or ward, representing a specific geographic area. The executives or mayors may be strong both functionally and politically in their cities. A strong mayor or county executive has budgetary responsibilities, has administrative authority over departments and programs, and is directly elected by the public for a specified term, which may or may not be concurrent with the terms of the legislature. Town or city councils may comprise representatives of districts, at-large representatives, or both district and at-large members.

Limited executives (sometimes called "weak mayors") may be selected by the public or by their fellow councilmembers and perform largely ceremonial functions in the name of the jurisdiction. These mayors may not hold independent authority over administrative and budget matters. In systems with limited-authority mayors, the management of the jurisdiction may be executed by a city/town manager who serves *at the pleasure of the council*. A system with a ceremonial mayor, a manager, and a council is called a *council-manager* government. The difference between strong- and limited-executive functions is not rigid, and executives in many communities would fall somewhere between these two extremes.

Finally, in some systems the public elects *commissioners* or *councilmembers* and these representatives serve in both a legislative and an administrative capacity.

If counties provide all or most of the services permitted by the state, why have subcounty governments? Subgovernments are a function of historical factors, local traditions, and community self-determination. Americans seek government that is responsive to their wishes and needs. Consequently, when citizens perceive their interests and agendas are not being adequately addressed by larger jurisdictions there is an impetus to establish a more responsive jurisdiction of their own.

Not all subcounty governments are geographic; some governmental entities are functional and are called *special districts*.

## Special Districts

Special districts are the newest form of government. In some cases, a special district is contained within a county or municipality, but in other cases a special district may cover more than one county or municipality. Special districts tend to provide a specific service. For example, municipal governments operate the school systems in 13 states. However, the most common approach is to establish a separate school district. Some school districts come under the authority of the county or subcounty government, which appoints the school board members (Alaska, Hawaii). However, 31 states provide for public education solely through independent school districts. These independent boards select the district's superintendent and augment state policies and practices with those of local interest. While school boards are typically inside county lines, they may serve more than one city, town, or subcounty area or population. As noted earlier, most government employees are in the business of educating the nation's youth from kindergarten through 12th grade. A fundamental requirement of citizens in a republic is to be educated. With the importance of education to the Republic, it is not surprising that schools are governed by persons closest to those who use and rely on these institutions. The number of school districts has been in significant decline largely due to district consolidations and reorganizations.

School districts are not the only special districts. There are special districts for hospitals, air quality management, transit, fire protection, libraries, mosquito abatement, flood control, water/sewage, and cemeteries, to name but a few. Special districts are organized by law and/or policy as specific entities, are governmental in character, and have substantial autonomy. Special districts, such as school districts, often represent special interests and citizen concerns that are deemed too important to be subsumed under county or subcounty governments and finances or to overlap other government entities (e.g., air quality agencies—because smog does not respect geographic boundaries of political jurisdictions). In such cases the governing body of the special district may include elected representatives of the cities or counties within its geographic jurisdiction.

A special district allows a greater degree of administrative and political concentration on a functional area. While general purpose governments (counties, municipalities, townships) tend to be constant over time, special districts have higher turnover. Between 2012 and 2017, the U.S. Census of Governments survey added 1,500 new special districts while 1,260 had ceased to operate.

The governmental sector accounts for 14% of employment in the country, and approximately 1.5 million nonprofit organizations account for another 7% of the workforce. These organizations and associations often partner with government agencies to provide or supplement public programs. When serving in this capacity the agencies are sometimes referred to as *community-based organizations* (CBOs). The balance of the nation's employment (75% to 78%) is in the private, for-profit sector.

## PRIVATE VERSUS PUBLIC

What determines whether a good or service belongs in the public or private sector? In part it is determined by whether it is feasible to exclude consumption of the good or service once it is produced. It is also determined by whether many users can benefit from a good/service without reducing the benefits to others.

Apples, socks, personal computers, and so forth are *private goods*, which are distributed in the marketplace. If I buy and eat an apple, my ownership excludes others, and my use, in theory, consumes the apple's value.

The clearest example of a *public good* is national defense. A defense system is produced for and benefits all citizens, even those who have not paid for it. The same is true for roads, street lighting, and municipal courts. Although not everyone may use these resources, no one is excluded, and no one person's use diminishes use by others.

Because public goods are not exclusive, there is the problem of the "free rider." A free rider benefits from a product but does not pay for it. Thousands of visitors to a community benefit from street lighting but do not pay for it because they reside outside the jurisdiction. However, governments pay for these services by taxing a broad base of residents through property taxes or property-related assessments.

Public goods sometimes suffer under what is called the *tragedy of the commons*. When a person does not pay for the goods he or she consumes, the person tends to consume these goods as though they were private goods but maintain them as though they belonged to somebody else. An example is the use of public parks. Park goers use facilities (tables, cooking areas, equipment, etc.) as though they owned it but clean up and maintain the grounds as though the park were someone else's responsibility.

Public ownership is more complex than private ownership. It may be feasible to exclude someone from a toll bridge even though one consumer does not diminish the service for another. The government manages public roads and bridges through tolls to ensure that they are widely available and accessible to all travelers. In the case of roads and bridges, the government elects to sustain authority over a common good/service to ensure that costs are spread widely to generate the greatest benefit for the greatest number.

In the 18th century the city of Philadelphia did not have a fire department. A resident who wanted fire protection bought insurance from a private company, and the company provided a plaque to be placed high on the front of the building. If the building caught fire, independent fire brigades arrived on the scene and could see which properties had insurance coverage and which did not. Insurance companies would pay the brigades for putting out the fire. There was no guarantee of fire protection for properties that were not insured. Consequently, fire brigades would respond quickly to fires but only extinguish fires affecting their insured properties. The priorities of the brigades were not to save lives, extinguish fires quickly, or limit property loss in general, but to limit the insurance company's financial loss. Today this approach seems unrealistic, as fire protection has come to be considered one of the most basic government services. Citizens recognize that containing fires benefits the entire community by minimizing its spread to all properties.

Also, the government is involved in regulating goods and services created by the private sector and distributed in markets because these goods create a consequence that cannot be corrected through markets alone. Governments regulate automobile emissions because auto pollution adversely affects third parties (neither the buyer nor the seller), and the true costs to health and welfare of car usage are not adequately accounted for in the market transaction. In addition, governments regulate markets to ensure consumers have adequate and accurate information, whether they are buying stocks and bonds in sophisticated financial markets or an aspirin at the neighborhood drugstore.

Finally, individuals yield sovereignty to the government but not to organizations in the private sector. The government may compel the filing of income tax or deny a person's life and liberty having first met the obligation of due process. No similar power is held by the private sector. Consequently, demands on public managers to be equitable as well as efficient, to provide information to citizens and the media, and to be responsive to the legislature are not equivalent to any responsibility held by private or nongovernmental managers. These distinctions prompted Graham Allison (originally published in 1979) to note that the public and private sectors are "fundamentally alike in all unimportant respects" (Allison, 2007).

## PUBLIC POLICY AND PUBLIC ADMINISTRATION

According to the website *PoliEngine*, there are 519,682 politicians in the U.S. We have estimated there are some 21 million government employees executing the will of these elected officials. How does a federated republic mobilize 21 million people to serve the interests of 330.2 million? The policy process begins with agenda setting, or the expression of the public's will, either directly through petitions, elections, and ballot initiatives or indirectly through the proposals of their representatives, advocates, or lobbyists. Getting an issue on the public agenda can take minutes or years. America's entry into World War II after the attack on Pearl Harbor was authorized in less than an hour. Passage of the Medicare health program in 1963 under Lyndon Johnson was a policy agenda item initiated under the Truman administration in the 1940s.

Administrative agencies play a critical role in policy formation. For example, California's Inland Empire Resource Conservation District met in July 2009 to update its long-range plan, set the organization's policy direction, predict achievements over the next five years, and identify and discuss trends in the areas of technology, open space, population growth, and economic development. Members of every level of the organization participated. Based on the discussion, participants prioritized resources, outlined measures for success, and formulated an action plan for accomplishing goals. These steps are essential for the agency to contribute to the policy formulation agenda in the coming years and to prepare itself for questions and concerns from legislators and/or the public (R. Ledgerwood, personal communication, July 15, 2009).

At some point a legislature needs to decide, and *no decision* is a decision. In a republic there are multiple entry points for getting the government to act: appeals to the executive branch and its administrators, the legislative process, use of the courts, and use of the media. Once authorized decision makers approve a program or policy, then the means for implementation need to be authorized. In 1966, with great fanfare, President Lyndon Johnson was granted authorization for the Teacher Corps. The innovative program provided new teachers and resources for inner-city schools. However, Congress failed to fund the Corps in 1966 and barely funded the program in 1967. Once the authorized program was funded it became the responsibility of the Department of Health, Education, and Welfare to work with local communities to identify candidates for the Teacher Corps, fund positions, locate and place faculty in targeted area schools, and report to Congress on program operations, spending, and consequences. These Department of Health, Education, and Welfare tasks and those undertaken by public and private colleges and universities, school boards, principals, and faculty are called *program implementation*. This phase of the policy process requires the participation and expertise of persons employed in the public sector as administrators. Administrators are responsible for not only implementing the program but monitoring program efforts and reporting to the executive and legislature. Policy and program reporting, along with input from citizens, the media, clients, and providers, becomes part of the policy feedback loop that influences perceptions of the policy agenda and reinvigorates the policy process (see Figure 1.1).

**Figure 1.1 The Policy Process**

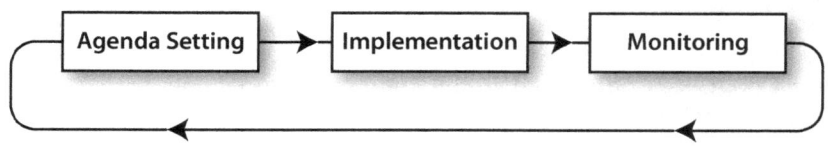

In the model above, public administration is defined as the implementation and monitoring phases of the policy process. However, scholars have defined public administration as the enactment of the public interest, the utilization of the instruments of government to achieve collectively what is not feasible individually, the regulating or policing of behavior, and the management of public resources. In addition to its role in the broader social and political context, public administration is an academic discipline (primarily at the college or university level), an occupational category, and a professional career in public service.

While some see government service as a noble enterprise and profession, the view is not universal. Some conservatives seek to limit governments to pure public goods such as national defense and policing. Other tasks (health, education, welfare, transportation), they argue, are best managed by free markets and/or the nonprofit/charity sector.

In the 1980s President Ronald Reagan asserted that government did not solve problems, but that government was the problem. There was a plethora of programs (especially federal programs) that reached into areas that had previously been left to states, localities, and/or nonprofits. Federal funding took tax dollars out of areas and funneled it through the national government in the District of Columbia and then into federal regional offices, states, counties, and localities. This process, critics suggest, spent more resources on the administration than on the programs themselves. A more effective and efficient approach would be to lower taxes and let markets, state governments, and local governments manage their own programs.

Cutting federal funding to programs is politically difficult, as the Reagan administration quickly learned. Congressional representatives campaign on their ability to bring programs and funding back to their districts. Congressional offices spend considerable time and energy identifying federal programs that are needed in their districts and working with businesses, local governments, and interest groups to see that resources reach the voters. In addition, many big-ticket expenditures in the federal system are entitlement programs (e.g., Social Security) that are off-budget items. The costs for these programs are not limited by budget allocations passed by Congress but by the definition and scope of coverage in the entitlement legislation. Medicare costs, for example, are driven by the number of persons who are retired, how often the retired persons need medical services, and the severity of illnesses during the year while Medicare revenues are driven by the number of persons who are working. To cut Medicare costs Congress would need to cut the coverage provided (e.g., allow three medical visits per year rather than six); attempts to make these changes mobilize the elderly, the medical community, pharmacies, and health care providers. In the final analysis the Reagan administration was unable to substantively change federal expenditures. Office of Management and Budget Director David Stockman, who had been a member of Congress prior to being Reagan's budget administrator, lamented that the congressional budget appropriations accounted for only 14% of all federal expenditures.

While the Reagan revolution had relatively little impact during Reagan's administration, it had a profound influence on the public's desire to cut public spending and operate public services in more effective and efficient ways. Governments had begun experimenting with contracting services to the private sector rather than providing services using public employees. In 1978, the city of Phoenix, Arizona, decided to contract with the private sector for garbage collection and opened a competitive bid process for that and other public works projects. By 1988 costs for public services in Phoenix had been significantly reduced, and public sanitation efforts had successfully competed and won back all but five district contracts.

The competitive entrepreneurial approach fostered reforms in budgeting by categories (personnel, office supplies, rent) resulting in budgeting by outcomes or objectives (lower crime rates, faster response times, fewer potholes). In addition, governments became more customer friendly and employed techniques widely used by business: focus groups, customer councils, user surveys, and electronic transactions or e-government. By the 1990s Osborne and Gaebler (1993) called this new direction in implementation "reinventing government."

Today there are several public services that are implemented by hiring private firms, partnering with private or nonprofit organizations, or co-sourcing or co-producing services that are provided in part by public employees and in part by hired contractors.

From a management perspective public administration is similar to business administration. There is a continuous effort to get the greatest output and results at the lowest cost. Ideally operations will be efficient. Public administration and business administration, however, are significantly different.

Private firms can limit their costs by customizing their product and marketing to the most profitable segment of the market; public service providers cannot. In the area of health care, private insurers and health maintenance organizations set fees that work best for working adults with subsidized coverage from employers rather than for adults who are elderly, on fixed incomes, or at or below the poverty level. If one can limit one's health care business to relatively well-paid, healthy clients; it is reasonable to earn adequate net income while providing low-cost care and meeting client expectations. Public health providers do not have the same latitude, and if they priced out the poor and elderly there would not be services for those citizens. The demand to be market efficient without the capacity to limit users and/or demand via pricing, or any other mechanism, places requirements on public services that are substantively different from those of for-profit businesses.

Exclusivity or the lack of it is not the only difference between the public and private sectors. The other key difference is politics.

## Politics

The popular notion of politics is campaign politics: making speeches, attending rallies, kissing babies, raising funds, and shaking hands. Politics is a broader process that includes convincing, cajoling, influencing, persuading, intimidating, and reasoning in an attempt to get something at some time for some purpose. In 1936, Harold Lasswell expanded the definition of politics to be a person's ability to produce an intended effect on other people. Richard Neustadt (1960) later suggested that politics is most pervasive in the executive or administrative branch of government. Presidents rely on a combination of personal persuasion, professional reputation, and public prestige to get things done. Neustadt retells the story of Harry Truman's assessment of the new president-elect: "He'll sit here and say, Do this! Do that! . . . and nothing will happen, Poor Ike [nickname for Dwight Eisenhower], it won't be like the Army, and he'll find it frustrating."

Ike indeed found presidential politics frustrating. In the span of less than 75 years the image of the executive/administrative branch of government had gone from the least to the most political arena in government. The same is often felt by representatives and administrators at the local level who aspire to serve the public interest and operate above the political fray but quickly find that politics triumphs here as well.

## Political/Administrative Dichotomy

In *Federalist* No. 70, Alexander Hamilton argues for unity in the executive branch: one person to be held responsible for the actions of government. He suggests that the appropriate place for contention, disputes, and discord (partisan politics) is in the legislature with its broad representation of various interests. However, once the legislature has authorized a policy, then a republic requires an energetic, single, responsible, and accountable executive to carry out the will of Congress. In part Hamilton assumes a dichotomy between the political fervor of Congress and the less partisan decisions of the executive.

At the end of the 19th century Woodrow Wilson wrote that administration "is removed from the strife of politics" and that administrative questions are not political questions (Shafritz and Hyde, 2007, 22). This theme—that politics is legislative and that planning, organizing, management, and so forth are matters of efficiency and effectiveness—was echoed in the writings of scholars and practitioners such as Wilson, Goodnow, White, Willoughby, Gulick, and Urwick during the early part of the 20th century (Shafritz and Hyde, 2007).

By the Kennedy/Johnson era, executive power was a far cry from that described in Hamilton's *Federalist* No. 70 and the apolitical management framework that dominated at the turn of the 20th century as espoused by Woodrow Wilson. The change in perspective was a response to Supreme

Court decisions under the leadership of Earl Warren. The Court took on controversial issues such as civil liberties, interracial marriages, and defendants' rights. Also, during this period, the federal government took on policy initiatives in education, welfare, and housing. This proactive, ambitious agenda influenced scholars and practitioners. At the Minnowbrook Conference in 1968 young public administration scholars sought to redefine the discipline as one promoting democracy, social equity, decentralization, and problem solving rather than primarily institution building. This new perspective argued that public administration was not apolitical but had a responsibility for eradicating injustice, expanding opportunities for the disadvantaged, and promoting the equitable distribution of resources. This more proactive and engaged definition of the discipline dominated future Minnowbrooks in 1988 and 2008. The next scheduled meeting is 2028 and the anticipated issues are social equity, justice, transparency, accountability, in the American Republic and around the world.

## Public Trust and Public Employment

Congress has persistently sought to depoliticize the administrative branch, even as early as 1939, when it adopted the Hatch Act, which defined permissible political activities by government employees. Although the law was declared unconstitutional in 1972, it was reaffirmed on appeal in 1973 and reauthorized as the Federal Employees Political Activities Act of 1993. The 1993 law relaxed many constraints of the original legislation by allowing federal employees to run for office, participate in voter registration drives, and campaign for candidates in partisan elections, but it continued to restrict public employees using their positions as public servants or their proprietary knowledge to engage in political activities. It sought to balance the public employee's rights as a citizen with their responsibility as a public servant. As a citizen, an employee is entitled to vote, register, make private donations, and support candidates; but as a public servant they are discouraged from campaigning or using public authority or resources to advance one political party interest over another.

State and local laws have tended to parallel federal legislation with regard to limiting public employees using or exploiting their positions in government to advance partisan political interests. The meaning of *political activities* is narrowly defined. It addresses political endorsements of candidates by the employee in their official role in government and/or the collection of campaign contributions at a government site but does not recognize the actions of public officials carrying out their normal functions, which may also have political implications (e.g., releasing information about employment or unemployment statistics after an election rather than before the election). A discussion of the implications of administrators engaged in political activities is discussed in more detail in Chapter 4, Ethics.

Elected officials are expected to engage in partisan and emotive speech since they represent constituents who may feel passionate about a particular issue. Administrators, on the other hand, are expected to act and speak rationally, logically, and without bias or emotion. Despite this veil of neutrality and objectivity, their underlying political views may not be entirely submerged as they make decisions about efficiency, effectiveness, and use of public resources. This "political" activity is more subtle than that addressed by the Hatch Act and the related legislation described above.

Any administrator with discretionary authority makes judgments that are influenced by political views: whether more or less government is needed, whether policies are environmentally feasible, or whether constituents are well served by a practice.

If the federal executives are highly political, then is this also the case for governors, mayors, city managers, administrators, or bureaucrats? As scholars and practitioners critically examine administrative discretionary decision making, they become increasingly convinced that administrators and bureaucrats are fundamentally engaged in politics. Efficiency and effectiveness are not value-neutral perspectives and do affect who gets what public resources, when, and how. The debate over the proper role of public servants is as old as the Republic. The following fictional response to Jefferson's *Declaration of Independence*, which appeared in a 1974 article in *Social Policy* (Schwartz, 1974), humorously demonstrated how bureaucrat values may influence a response to policy and decision making.

Mr. Thomas Jefferson
Continental Congress
Independence Hall
Philadelphia, PA.

Dear Mr. Jefferson:

We have read your "Declaration of Independence" with great interest. Certainly, it represents a considerable undertaking, and many of your statements do merit serious consideration. Unfortunately, the Declaration as a whole fails to meet recently adopted specifications for proposals to the Crown, so we must return the document to you for further refinement. The questions which follow might assist you in your process of revision.

1. In your opening paragraph you use the phrase "the Laws of Nature and Nature's God." What are these laws? In what way are they the criteria on which you base your central arguments? Please document with citations from the recent literature.

2. In the same paragraph you refer to the "opinions of mankind." Whose polling data are you using? Without specific evidence, it seems to us, the "opinions of mankind" are a matter of opinion.

3. You hold certain truths to be "self-evident." Could you please elaborate? If they are as evident as you claim, then it should not be difficult for you to locate the appropriate supporting statistics.

4. "Life, liberty, and the pursuit of happiness" seem to be the goals of your proposal. These are not measurable goals. If you were to say that "among these is the ability to sustain an average life expectancy in six of the 13 colonies of at least 55 years, and to enable all newspapers in the colonies to print news without outside interference, and to raise the average income of the colonists by 10% in the next 10 years," these would be measurable goals. Please clarify.

5. You state that "whenever any Form of Government becomes destructive of these ends, it is the Right of the People to alter or to abolish it, and to institute a new Government. . . ." Have you weighed this assertion against all the alternatives? Or is it predicated solely on the baser instincts?

6. Your description of the existing situation is quite extensive. Such a long list of grievances should precede the statement of goals, not follow it.

7. Your strategy for achieving your goal is not developed at all. You state that the colonies "ought to be Free and Independent States," and that they are "Absolved from All Allegiance to the British Crown." Who or what must change to achieve this objective? In what way must they change? What resistance must you overcome to achieve the change? What specific steps will you take to overcome the resistance? How long will it take? We have found that a little foresight in these areas helps to prevent careless errors later on.

8. Who among the list of signatories will be responsible for implementing your strategy? Who conceived it? Who provided the theoretical research? Who will constitute the advisory committee? Please submit an organization chart.

9. You must include an evaluation design. We have been requiring this since Queen Anne's War.

10. What impact will your program have? Your failure to include any assessment of this inspires little confidence in the long-range prospects of your undertaking.

11. Please submit a PERT diagram, an activity chart, and an itemized budget.

We hope that these comments prove useful in revising your "Declaration of Independence."

Best Wishes,

Lord North

Source: Schwartz, Edward. (1974). Dear Mr. Jefferson. *Social Policy* 5:2. Reprinted with permission of *Social Policy*.

## CONCLUSION

> If men were angels no government would be necessary. If angels were
> to govern men, neither external nor internal controls on government
> would be necessary. In framing a government which is to be adminis-
> tered by men over men, you must first enable the government to con-
> trol the governed and in the next place oblige it to control itself.
>
> —James Madison, *Federalist* No. 51

This is the challenge of public administration: to wield resources and authority—sparingly. In 1789, with the ratification of the U.S. Constitution, the nation developed a complex republic of federal and state governments. In 2010 the population of the United States was 281.4 million and in 2020 it was 331.4 million, an increase of 17.76%. We have seen a modest decline in the number of political jurisdictions, but an explosion in the number of special districts throughout the United States. The nation has over 90,000 governments and special districts. These public agencies need managers, administrators, analysts, and specialists of all kinds. Fifteen percent or more of all employment in the nation is in the public sector.

Public administrators, like their counterparts in business, seek to get the greatest productivity from the fewest resources, but unlike the private sector, the public sector is required to provide goods and services to all citizens. This places unique demands on the public sector.

This text discusses administrators' decision-making environment, and the tools administrators use in carrying out their responsibilities. The focus here is on government operations at the local and regional levels. Section 1 defines the context of public administration, which includes the functions of government (Chapter 2), the role of nongovernmental nonprofit organizations (Chapter 3), ethical challenges to decision making (Chapter 4), and the obligation of a modern republic to inform and involve citizens (Chapter 5). Given this environment, public administrators need skills in community relations, planning, coordination, communication, and designing and directing complex systems. Section 2 discusses the challenges of envisioning and mobilizing resources into a coherent, comprehensive, and interconnected whole. This section begins with a discussion of the planning process (Chapter 6) and examines how diverse and multiple stakeholders may be mobilized to develop policy and program options (Chapter 7). Stakeholder participation is critical but may be supplemented by other means to enable fuller understanding of the opinions and expectations of the public (Chapter 8). While articulating a vision is the first challenge for the administrator, making optimal and informed choices is his or her next challenge (Chapter 9). Finally, the administrator needs to pull together into a coherent whole the tasks, timeline, and resources that enable objectives to be realized as a policy practice, public good, and/or public service (Chapter 10).

Section 3 discusses mobilizing people to implement public policies. Chapter 11 explores the personnel system developed in the public sector, and the following chapter (Chapter 12) addresses how benefits and risks define unique aspects of public employment. Section 4 discusses financial resources. How revenue is raised (Chapter 13) and how money is spent to fund daily operations (Chapter 14) and large construction projects and improvements (Chapter 15). Revenue and expense budgets are plans authorized by legislatures. Implementing these plans is realized through funding to public departments and/or through contracts with outside agencies and organizations (Chapter 16). Sometimes contracts are defined by external funding sources (state or federal governments) in the form of grants (Chapter 17) that provide additional resources and challenges for administrators. Section 5 discusses how the government is accountable for and measures its performance. Meeting the public's expectations and leading staff, employees and volunteers is the overarching role and responsibility of the public administrator. Whatever the source of public revenue and whatever the amount of money authorized, administrators are asked to assess, measure, and demonstrate the value added (Chapter 18). This is just one of many new challenges that have come to define public service.

Section 5 concludes by discussing performance management. Whatever the source of public revenue and whatever the amount of money authorized, administrators are asked to assess, measure, and demonstrate the value added (Chapter 18). This is just one of many new challenges that have come to define public service. The final chapter discusses leadership in a government that is a complex, federated, republic that relies primarily on public participation and support, rather than force (Chapter 19).

In conclusion, the appendices provide practical information about writing and oral presentations that enable administrators to be effective and persuasive, preparing and making presentations, as well as interviewing from both the perspective of the interviewer and the interviewee.

## PRACTICING PUBLIC ADMINISTRATION

1. How many persons in executive and legislative positions represent you? Starting with the president of the United States, make a list of your representatives at all levels of government. How many can you name? Access Project Vote Smart at www. votesmart.org. Enter your zip code on the upper left of the screen and compare your list with those at Project Vote Smart.

2. Identify the political jurisdictions that govern (provide goods and services to) the residents and businesses in your community. Which general purpose governments, county governments, and special districts operate in this area, and how are these governments structured?

3. Should health care be a public or a private good? Which criteria might be applied to determine which sector should be the provider?

4. In the past few years, many public services have been contracted out to the private sector. Should the work of the IRS (tax collecting) be privatized? What would be the advantages and disadvantages?

5. In this chapter we have discussed consequences of a federated system. Which advantages and disadvantages do you observe in the delivery of services and/or public goods in your community that arise due to federalism?

6. Visit the U.S. Senate Webpage on the Constitution at www. senate.gov/civics/constitution_item/constitution.htm, and click or scroll to the discussion of specific powers granted to the central government under Article 1, Section 8. Since this is a list of federal powers/authority, why are there federal education policies, Medicare drug policies, housing programs, and so forth?

## BIBLIOGRAPHY

Allison, G. T. (2007). Public and private management: Are they fundamentally alike in all unimportant respects? https://www.cide.edu/wp-content/uploads/2020/10/5.-Graham-Allison.pdf

American Counts Staff. (2019). *From municipalities to special districts, official count of every type of local government in 2017 census of governments.* https://www.census.gov/content/dam/Census/library/visualizations/2019/econ/from_municipalities_to_special_districts_america_counts_october_2019.pdf

Bowornwathana, B. (2010). Minnowbrook IV in 2028: From american minnowbrook to global minnowbrook. *Public Administration Review, 70*, S64–S68. http://www.jstor.org/stable/40984099

Gorden, G., & Milakovich, M. (1998). *Public administration in America.* (6th ed.). New York, NY: St. Martin's.

Hale, Z. (2020). California, green groups sue Trump administration over auto rules rollback. *SNL Energy Power Daily.*

Hatch, J. (2004). Employment in the public sector: Two recessions' impact on jobs. *Monthly Labor Review, 127*(10), 38–48.

Lasswell, H. (1936). *Politics of who gets what, when and how.* New York, NY: McGraw-Hill.

Light, P. (2008). *Fact sheet on the new true size of government.* Washington, D.C.: Center for Public Service, Brookings Institute.

Mikesell, J. (2003). *Fiscal administration.* (6th ed.). Belmont, CA: Wadsworth.

Neustadt, R. (1960). *Presidential power: Politics of leadership.* New York, NY: Wiley.

Osborne, D, & Gaebler, T. (1993). *Reinventing government: How the entrepreneurial spirit is transforming the public sector.* New York, NY: Plume.

PoliEngine. (2013). *How many politicians are there in the USA?* https://poliengine.com/blog/how-many-politicians-are-there-in-the-us

Rosenbloom, D. H., & Ravchuk, R. (2002). *Public administration: Understanding management, politics, and law in the public sector.* (5th ed.). Boston, MA: McGraw-Hill.

Salamon, L. M., Sokolowski, S. W, & Associates. (2004). *Global civil society: Dimensions of the non-profit sector.* (Vol. 2.) Bloomfield, CT: Kumarian Press, Inc.

Schmidt, B. S. (2007). *American government and politics today.* (7th ed.). Belmont, CA: Thomson Wadsworth.

Schwartz, E. (1974). Dear Mr. Jefferson. *Social Policy, 5*, 2.

Shafritz, J. M., & Hyde, A. C. (2007). *Classics of public administration.* Boston, MA: Thomson/Wadsworth.

Torri, E., Sbrogiò, L. G., Di Rosa, E., Cinquetti S., Francia, F., & Ferro, A. (2020). Italian public health response to the COVID-19 pandemic: Case report from the field, insights and challenges for the department of prevention. *International Journal of Environmental Research and Public Health, 17*(10), (2020 May), 3666. https://www.mdpi.com/1660-4601/17/10/3666. DOI: 10.3390/ijerph17103666 PMCID: PMC7277676

U.S. Bureau of Labor Statistics. (2020). Employment projections. https://www.bls.gov/emp/tables/employment-by-major-industry-sector.htm

U.S. Census Bureau. (2002). *2002 census of governments*. Vol. 1, No. 1. Government Organization GC02 (1)-1. Washington, D.C.: Government Printing Office.

————. (2004). *Compendium of public employment: 2002*. Vol. 3, No. 2. Government Organization GC02 (3)-2. Washington, D.C.: Government Printing Office.

————. (2020). Census bureau releases state and local government finances summary report. https://www.census.gov/newsroom/press-releases/2020/state-and-local-government-finances.html

# 2 ◆—◇—◇—◆—◆

# Government Functions
# and Organization

In May 2020, the U.S. Supreme Court found that the Wagoner County Oklahoma District Court could not prosecute Jimcy McGirt, because the county lacked jurisdiction. Crimes committed on land that was set aside by the federal government for the Creek Nation were under the federal government's Indian Major Crime Act jurisdiction and not the State of Oklahoma. This sent Oklahoma into a tailspin. Could the county enforce civil judgments; could they collect property taxes? Rarely has the question of what level of government could perform what tasks been brought into question in such a dramatic manner. If the state did not have authority over the land, were tax collection and services under the jurisdiction of the Creek Nation?

Many citizens cannot define what is specifically the responsibility of the local, state, or national government. Many are unaware that government responsibilities overlap and, in some cases—particularly in policing, health, and education—they are duplicated within a geographic area.

Wagoner County Oklahoma provides a variety of services. These include promoting economic development, assuring fair elections, promoting healthy communities, managing land use, and providing emergency management, fire protection, roads, bridges, and courts. Seventy-two percent of property tax is spent on health and education programs, while the 1% sales tax is spent primarily on sheriff services, economic development, storm water and flood plain management, the courts, senior centers, and fire protection equipment.

The concepts of federalism and various forms of government were discussed in Chapter 1. This chapter examines in more detail the functions of different levels of local government. It also explores some organizational concepts that help make government work—concepts such as management and position control.

State governments provide functions not prohibited to them by the U.S. Constitution and are responsible for the general welfare of their citizens. States determine which functions should be provided at the state, county, special district, or municipal level. States enact civil and penal codes to regulate conduct; enforce laws; build and maintain prisons, roads, parks, and facilities on state lands; and establish educational systems from elementary to higher education. States may also establish and manage welfare programs for unemployed, injured, and disabled persons as well as children and senior citizens. States have National Guard militias allowed by the Second Amendment to the Constitution, which may be nationalized by the federal government during time of war, as was done during the Iraq War. However, the primary function of militias today is to respond to state and national disasters. Local government is responsible for those state functions that a state elects to delegate from the broad authority granted under the state's Constitution.

The U.S. Constitution does not mention local governments. Beginning in the 1860s the courts started to define the relationships between state and local governments with the adoption of Dillon's Rule by the Iowa Supreme Court (*Clinton v. Cedar Rapids and Mo. River RR*). This opinion, which is used in 39 states, essentially says that local governments have only the powers granted by the state. However, to counter this legal principle 43 states have adopted constitutional or other legal provisions acknowledging the right of citizens, through their municipal governments, to exercise local decision-making power with the weight of law. This principle is known as "home rule." Home-rule powers vary from state to state. In some, authority is extended only to certain classes of cities, counties, and towns. In others that have adopted Dillon's Rule, which subordinates municipalities to state legislatures, there may still be some form of municipal chartering. Home-rule states have the fewest local constraints. While state legislatures have tended to limit home-rule prerogative, people have asserted more local democracy.

States delegate many functions to counties, which are essentially branches of the state government, and others to special districts and cities. Cities have a greater level of independence, particularly if operating under their own charters under the principle of home rule. Local control is logical if (1) government wants to customize services to meet the demands of citizens with different circumstances and expectations, (2) it is less costly and more effective to operate at a local level, and (3) it fosters community involvement and participation. Consequently, it makes sense for local government to have control over community development, policing, and education but not over prisons or navigation of waterways. The taxing authority and structure at various levels of government also conform to the type of services provided by various levels of government. For example, local government provides property-related services such as maintenance of public streets, building safety, and law enforcement. It is therefore logical that these services are funded to a large extent by property taxes collected at either the county or the city level. In contrast, sales taxes collected at the state level fund more diverse government services at both the state and the local levels. However, there are often overlapping functions and jurisdictions. Law enforcement is an example: states enforce traffic laws on state and federal highways, county sheriffs often operate local jails and enforce laws in unincorporated areas, and municipal police departments enforce traffic laws on city streets and enforce state penal and civil codes within their jurisdictions.

There is no ideal organization, and the types of organizations vary from locality to locality. There are many factors that influence the functions performed, from historical growth of population centers to climate or geographic considerations. Depending on whether towns and cities or areas of unincorporated county grew first, functions may be divided up differently between them. In geographic areas with large counties and many small municipalities within the county, more services may be provided by county government. In areas where there are large cities surrounded by smaller ones, there may be more sharing of functions.

Some functions are unique to municipalities with specific geographic features. Those near harbors may operate ports, those near rivers may operate bridges, those near oceans may manage beaches, and those in cold climates may have responsibility for snow removal. Some local governments may operate airports or convention centers.

Expenditures for various functions vary depending on the type or level of local government. On a nationwide basis, kindergarten through grade 12 (K–12) education is the largest state and local government expenditure, followed by public welfare, health, and hospitals. These latter functions are often carried out by special districts or counties. Cities and towns that do not have responsibility for education, health, and welfare usually have their largest expenditures for police and fire protection (see Figure 2.1).

Within governments are organizations that carry out their functions. They may have different names such as departments, divisions, or sections. Sometimes the functions listed below will be found in a single department; sometimes multiple functions will be found in a department; and functions may be contracted to the private sector.

**Figure 2.1   State versus Local Expenditures.**

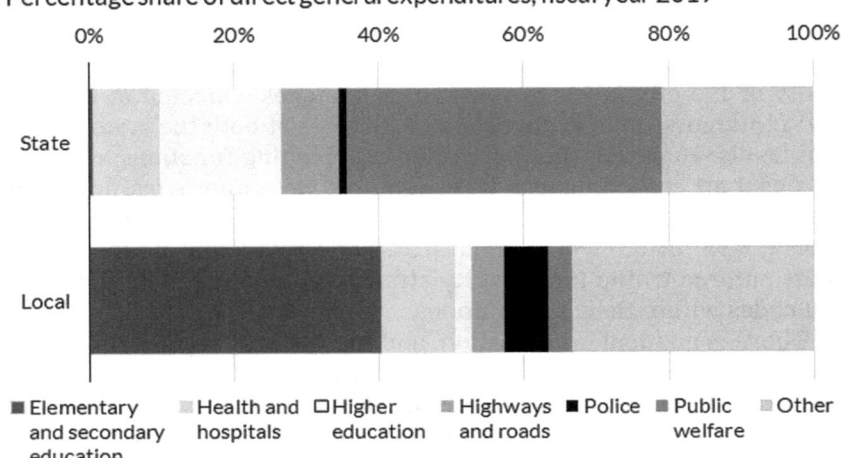

## State versus Local Expenditures

Percentage share of direct general expenditures, fiscal year 2019

- ■ Elementary and secondary education
- ▒ Health and hospitals
- □ Higher education
- ▒ Highways and roads
- ■ Police
- ■ Public welfare
- ▒ Other

Source:  US Census Bureau Annual Survey of State and Local Government Finances, 1977–2019 (compiled by the Urban Institute via State and Local Finance Data: Exploring the Census of Governments; 09 Aug 2022: https://www.urban.org/policy-centers/cross-center-initiatives/ state-and-local-finance-initiative/state-and-local-backgrounders/state-and-local-expenditures Note:  Excludes spending on government-run liquor stores, utilities, and insurance trusts. Medicaid spending is divided between the public welfare and health and hospitals functional categories, with the majority allocated to the former.

Departments are sub organizational units that carry out various types of work. These organizations may be characterized as centralized or decentralized, and they may have a hierarchy with many layers of supervision or with very few. They may deal directly with the public or provide support functions. These concepts are discussed in this chapter.

## FUNCTIONS OF LOCAL GOVERNMENT

### Public Safety

Among the most basic functions of government are public safety and law enforcement. Protecting lives and property requires a three-pronged approach: prevention, response, and adjudication. The key departments responsible for these functions are police, fire, and emergency medical services. However, as discussed below, there are other programs and services tied to public safety.

## Police Protection

Police and fire protection is the most significant responsibility of local government, at least in terms of the amount of funding and resources devoted to these activities. Keeping citizens safe is the key role of government, whether at the national level or local level. All jurisdictions provide these functions, although not necessarily with their own departments. Towns with small populations may still use volunteer departments because their public demand for services does not warrant full-time departments, and small- and medium-population cities may contract for fire and/or police services with the county or other larger-population jurisdictions in the area.

The most visible police function is patrol, in which officers respond to emergency and other calls for service to enforce laws and protect against crime. Police departments also investigate crimes, operate crime laboratories, and operate emergency dispatch centers to support their efforts. In recent years the concept of community policing has gained acceptance. Police departments that use this approach are proactive in developing ongoing relationships with citizens to engage them in helping to fight crime in their communities. For example, officers organize and attend neighborhood watch committees, attend community meetings, and generally have a presence even when there are no reported crimes or arrests to be made. Another popular citizen outreach program is Drug Awareness Resistance Education, in which police officers visit schools to discourage children from taking illegal drugs.

Police departments have their critics and state legislatures are imposing new limitations on police practices such as no-knock warrants, use of informants, use of chokeholds, and so forth. The restrictions in Minnesota were a consequence of the trial and conviction of Officer Chauvin for the death of George Floyd in May 2020. Many jurisdictions are reconsidering their budget allocations to police and have elected to reallocate some funds to social services and mental health programs as part of a new definition of public safety.

Internal investigations are an important function in police departments. They have been around for years to prevent and investigate corruption. Today they also have a major role in handling citizen complaints alleging improper use of force and/or racial profiling.

According to an analysis by the Urban Institute, the largest single state expense is public welfare (40%) followed by police (20%). At the local level the largest expenses are education and policing (40% each).

## Fire Protection

Fire departments are responsible for fire suppression, that is, responding to fires and putting them out. Increasingly, in many jurisdictions, fire departments are also responsible for emergency medical response, although this function may be assigned to a health department and in some instances to police departments. Emergency medical response is the predominant part of the workload in agencies that have that function.

Fire inspection is the primary activity to prevent fires. Fire inspectors develop and enforce fire safety building codes such as sprinkler and fire extinguisher requirements, evacuation procedures, maximum occupancy limits, structural requirements such as fire doors, and brush clearance requirements. Large departments also have functions such as specialized units to inspect high-rise buildings.

Arson investigation is another activity that may be performed by fire departments but also may be performed by police departments. Fire departments focus on the causation element, while police departments (or law enforcement personnel within fire departments) focus on the criminal investigation.

Other specialized fire functions include air support (helicopters and fixed-wing aircraft) to fight brush fires in some areas, swift water rescue units, hazardous materials squads, and specially trained disaster teams. Some fire departments may also regulate and inspect underground storage tanks used for gasoline and other flammable liquids. These specialized functions are typically found in large city and county departments. Smaller surrounding local governments, even those with their own departments, often rely on these larger agencies to provide necessary services through "mutual aid" or contractual arrangements.

## Emergency Preparedness

Emergency preparedness is a function that involves coordination across agency lines at the local level and with state and federal agencies. It may be administered by a city manager/administrator, a fire or police department, or a separate agency. The function involves development of plans to respond to and recover from natural and manmade disasters such as hurricanes, floods, fires, earthquakes, or terrorist attacks. It includes activities such as training and preparing the community, liaising with government and private agencies for disaster response, and obtaining and monitoring grants or other funds for disaster relief. In many cases the local agency must formally request assistance from the other agencies such as FEMA (Federal Emergency Management Agency) after declaring a state of emergency; the other agencies cannot simply jump in and start providing disaster relief.

Fires have become a major concern in the western states. In 2020 there were 10,431 fires in California which burned 4,092,150 acres. Oregon lost 1,141,612 acres in 2,215 fires while Arizona lost 978,567 acres in 2,525 fires. Natural disasters continue to rise throughout the United States. The National Center for Environmental Information reports that between 2010 and 2019 the U.S. had 119 billion-dollar natural disasters or about seven per year. In 2020 alone there were 22 billion-dollar disasters. The hardest hit by this trend in natural disasters has been Texas with 124 billion-dollar events since 1980 when NOAA first began tracking billion-dollar disasters.

## Criminal Prosecution and Jails

Prosecution of the offenders arrested by sheriff and police departments is part of the public safety function. District attorneys at the county level and city attorneys at the city level carry out the activities as well as file civil complaints. Prosecutorial functions may be included in the same office with representing and advising agencies on civil matters, or the functions may be in separate agencies. Counties also provide public defenders for criminal defendants who are unable to afford private counsel. Convicted offenders are incarcerated in county jails (or are sent to state penal facilities for longer sentences). Cities may also operate jails, although these more often are for holding arrestees pending charges and transfer to the county jail system. District and/or city attorneys may be elected offices or departments under executive authority.

## Probation and Parole

Providing oversight for convicted offenders and transition from prison back into society are the responsibilities of probation departments. These functions are often provided by counties in conjunction with their responsibilities for prosecuting and incarcerating criminal offenders.

## Emergency Medical Services

A very significant public safety function is response to accidents and life-threatening illnesses, whether provided by a fire, police, or health department. How communities organize this function depends on population density, availability of private or nongovernmental resources (hospitals), cost, and historical expectations about providing the service. The public sector also may use private emergency companies to address medical crises. In some cases, one agency provides emergency response while another has the ambulance transport function, which may be privately contracted. A consortium of smaller agencies may also get together to provide the function. Because of the structure of the nation's health insurance system, emergency response has become a lifeline in large urban areas. Many citizens who cannot afford medical care now rely on emergency response for conditions that are not emergencies and not urgent. In other cases, they may neglect less serious problems until they become emergencies. While government requires emergency medical service, it does not necessarily cover all costs, and citizens pay for services either out of pocket or through health insurance. However, if citizens are not insured and unable to pay, the government agency absorbs the cost. This is one of the health system challenges facing the nation today.

## Building and Safety

Ensuring buildings are safe is another important public safety function. Building departments help keep buildings safe to occupy by ensuring that building codes are established and enforced, by inspecting new construction and alterations of existing buildings, and by issuing building permits. They deal with many codes such as building, electrical, plumbing, mechanical, engineering, and zoning codes. In addition, they may inspect equipment such as elevators and boilers or enforce fire sprinkler codes if this is not done by fire departments. In addition to safety, these departments protect against blight and over-crowding by enforcing maximum occupancy limits and ensuring that abandoned buildings are cleaned up or demolished.

## Animal Regulation

Animal control is often included in the public safety function. The dogcatcher has long been identified as a local government fixture. The function may be provided directly by a local agency but is sometimes contracted to a local Society for the Prevention of Cruelty to Animals or another nonprofit entity. Animal control departments typically provide shelter to animals they pick up on the streets or to unwanted animals that are left by their owners and attempt to provide new homes for them. The departments enforce leash laws, issue licenses, and may provide spay and neuter services as a means of controlling the population of stray animals in the community. An area of controversy today is the policy of euthanizing animals in overcrowded shelters. Since many municipal shelters do not have the capacity to shelter all the animals left on their doorsteps, many animals are euthanized each year. Animal rights activists seek to eliminate this practice. Advocacy of mandatory spay/neuter laws is one way of addressing this issue, and the laws are increasingly being enacted.

Public safety functions break down into the categories of prevention, response, and adjudication. Specific agencies tend to have a primary focus. Police and fire departments are often called "first responders" because they are first on the scene in emergency situations. However, these departments are committed to prevention activities through community policing and fire inspections. Building departments focus on prevention through code development and enforcement but also have an emergency response function after major disasters such as earth-quakes. Prosecutors are known for their adjudication function but may also become involved with police departments in crime prevention programs, and many public safety departments become involved in adjudicating complaints from the public through their internal affairs functions. Consequently, elements of all these categories can be found in public safety agencies.

# PLANNING

Planning is how communities define their vision for how to utilize their land and develop their infrastructure. It is an important part of social policy and a function that sets jurisdictions apart from one another. Control over land use is often the issue that prompts incorporation of cities so that they may exercise this important element of self-determination. Whereas some communities do welcome growth and high-density development, others seek to limit access and prevent urban sprawl. Planning encompasses land use, urban planning and design, transportation, and environmental planning. States usually dictate a minimum number of focus areas for planning.

Planning departments develop standards through general and specific plans, zoning codes, and ordinances to guide those who build and change communities. These standards designate areas for industrial, commercial, and residential development and cover building density or height limits as well as park or open space requirements.

Transportation planning concentrates on moving people through their communities and developing strategies to manage traffic flow and control congestion. It helps policy makers with decisions about public transportation facilities and expansion of roads and highways as well as sidewalks, bike paths, etc.

Environmental planning may be incorporated into land use or into transportation planning or identified as a unique function. Wherever it is located within an organization, the focus is on reducing pollution, protecting habitats, and promoting energy efficiency.

Ideally, planning is a first step in developing a livable and sustainable community. In practice, many jurisdictions do not have a strictly enforced formal planning function and may grow in a haphazard manner for many years. Sometimes, after a period of uncontrolled growth, urban sprawl, or deterioration, the public and community leaders recognize the need for a planning function to improve their quality of life. When planning does exist, it provides the framework for the next major function to be discussed—public works and infrastructure.

## Public Works/Infrastructure

Public works activities, like public safety, are core local government responsibilities and may be found in different types and combinations of organizations that are responsible for construction, renovation, and operation of facilities and infrastructure. The following are some of the key functions.

## Engineering

Most local agencies have an individual designated as a chief engineer who has responsibility for all engineering functions but may also head a public works department with the additional functions listed below. This engineering function is responsible for design and construction of municipal facilities such as streets, bridges, sewers, storm drains, police and fire stations, libraries, parks, constituent centers, and other public buildings. The function might also include contract administration of major facilities constructed by outside firms, providing quality assurance to ensure that the work and materials for public works projects meet all applicable laws and standards.

## Refuse Collection and Sewage Disposal

Although refuse collection is a basic local government function, it is also an activity that is often contracted or provided by the private sector. Sewage disposal and treatment is often handled by special districts because it overlaps municipal jurisdictions, but it may also be a city function for larger agencies.

The function is divided into solid waste and wastewater (sewage) disposal. Wastewater disposal involves the construction and operation of sewers, storm drains and open water storm channels, storm water pumping plants, and wastewater treatment plants. It may also include water reclamation and some production of electrical energy (from very large plants).

Solid waste activities include household and commercial refuse collection (trash trucks), disposal in landfills, and waste recycling. As governments and citizens become more sensitive to environmental concerns, recycling has become a more significant activity. Today, household refuse may be divided into green waste, recyclables, and other trash to reduce the amount of trash sent to landfills. Agencies also may sponsor recycling centers to collect glass, cans, hazardous chemicals (paints and automobile fluids), and electronic waste (computer parts, batteries).

## Street Services

The street services function is responsible for the maintenance of streets, bridges, tunnels, pedestrian subways, and related structures, including repairing, resurfacing, cleaning streets, and removing hazards. It may also include maintaining trees, landscaped medians, and embankments as well as modifying streets and providing ramps to comply with disabled access requirements under the Americans with Disabilities Act.

## Street Lighting

The construction, maintenance, and design of street lighting systems are other local functions. The street lighting function may be financed either by local governments or by property assessments of areas where lights are installed. It may be provided by a public works agency or an electrical utility.

## Transportation

Local governments are responsible for the streets and highways in their jurisdictions, although some roads within local government boundaries may be the responsibility of a county, state, or federal government (e.g., freeways and interstate highways). The transportation function includes design and operation of transportation control devices and measures such as traffic signals and signs, street lane striping and pavement markings, street name signs, and parking meters. Local governments may also develop and operate bus, train, and subway transit and toll bridges; regulate taxicabs; design bikeways; and provide school crossing guard and intersection control services.

## Environmental Protection

There are two local environmental protection functions: regulation and compliance. Local agencies, often special districts such as air pollution control districts, are responsible for issuing rules regarding air pollution emissions from stationary sources such as refineries, factories, and other businesses. Emissions from mobile sources such as automobiles are regulated at the federal and state levels. The local agencies issue permits to construct and operate air pollution control equipment, inspect facilities, and provide design assistance. They carry out regulatory mandates from both the federal and the state levels.

On the compliance side, each county or municipality must ensure its own operations comply with regulatory standards. Counties and municipalities may also adopt policies that expand on those required by regulatory agencies. This compliance function may be included in a separate organization that coordinates activities in all departments or dispersed throughout an agency in various departments. The function has responsibility for understanding environmental laws applicable to the agency, such as the National Environmental Protection Act, and recommending policies and programs within a government agency to further environmental goals. Programs may include water conservation, trash recycling, purchase of environmentally friendly materials, promoting energy-efficient and sustainable building practices, and ensuring that solid waste facilities are operated in a manner that protects public health, safety, and the environment.

## Utilities

Some agencies supply their own water and/or power utilities; others rely on the private sector. Power utilities construct, generate, and distribute power from various sources, including hydroelectric, biomass, wind, solar, coal, or gas-fired plants. Water departments focus on providing clean water (although this function may be combined with the operation of sewage plants), which may include the operation of wells or bringing in water from local or distant sources by aqueduct or pipeline.

Telecommunications is one of the newer utility services provided by government. It includes providing fiber-optic cable to facilitate data transmission for telephone and computer networks, although these are also commonly provided by franchise agreements with the private sector.

Public works and utility agencies focus on infrastructure as well as services. As with public safety agencies, we usually find a combination of both types of activities. Street, lighting, and transportation departments usually have responsibility for the designing and building of streets, lighting, and traffic control measures, but they also provide services, such as street cleaning, or traffic enforcement, such as intersection control. Water and sanitation departments invest heavily in infrastructure such as sewage plants, pipes, and catch basins but also deliver their product (or take it away in the case of refuse) directly to the public.

# RECREATION AND LEISURE

As with safety and infrastructure above, recreation, leisure, and cultural functions are typically provided by the level of government closest to citizens. These functions reflect local interests, tastes, and demographics. The range of activities is discussed below.

## Recreation

Most localities operate and maintain parks and recreation facilities, which may include swimming pools, sports fields, golf courses, tennis courts, hockey or ice rinks, beaches, and child care and/or senior centers. Larger parks include maintenance of hiking trails. Operating zoos may also be included in this function.

## Libraries and Cultural Activities

Libraries, museums, historical sites, gardens, or observatories are often operated and maintained by local government. This may include providing educational and cultural programs associated with these facilities. Designation of cultural and historical sites and provision of grants for public arts and entertainment are other ways government supports the arts.

## Sports Venues and Convention Facilities

Local agencies may own hockey rinks, baseball or football stadiums, and/or arenas used for a variety of sports activities, concerts, and other events. They may also own convention centers. These venues have the purpose of providing opportunities for both recreation and economic development. Large sports or convention facilities help improve the economic base of a community by attracting both citizens and visitors to spend money and patronize the businesses that support and surround the facility, such as restaurants and hotels.

Recreation, leisure, and cultural activities range from educational and artistic exhibitions to sports and events. In the context of government activities, these are often considered secondary in importance to public safety and public works. They may lose out in the competition for scarce budgetary resources; however, they have been traditionally and remain important functions of local government.

# COMMUNITY AND ECONOMIC DEVELOPMENT

The development and redevelopment of America's neighborhoods became part of the federal agenda in 1965 when Congress authorized the Department of Housing and Urban Development under the Johnson administration. Although community and economic development was not a function of the federal government initially envisioned in the Constitution, the federal government intervened because of unwillingness by the banking industry to invest in deteriorating, older, inner cities. Therefore, the Department of Housing and Urban Development was authorized to grant federal funds to local governments to remove blight and redesign and revitalize community housing and businesses to entice long-term capital investments by banks and investors. Since the mid-1960s, federal, state, and local governments have sought to use federal funding to spur local economic investment. The specifics of who uses the funds for which projects are left to local governments. The functions that have arisen out of this intergovernmental partnership are noted below.

## Housing and Redevelopment

Local agencies construct and operate public housing for eligible low-income citizens and may provide rent assistance as part of their affordable housing programs. They also operate programs to eliminate slums and blight and reverse deterioration of urban neighborhoods. Redevelopment agencies may receive federal grant funds or receive funds through a form of financing known as "tax increment" in which property taxes from new redevelopment projects are redirected into other projects in a designated area instead of into the general revenues of the city/county.

Administering rent control regulations is another housing-related function, as is enforcing housing nondiscrimination laws.

## Community Services

Community services encompass a variety of programs, often funded by federal block funds (discussed further in Chapter 17, "Grants"), to create economic, social, and employment opportunities for disadvantaged individuals, families, and neighborhoods. Some typical services include job/retraining programs for youth or seniors, childcare, services for the disabled and persons with AIDS, programs to fight gang activity, mortgage assistance, and services for the homeless.

## Ports and Airports

Cities and counties may provide services to shipping firms and airlines engaged in transporting passengers and cargo. These enterprises contribute to a jurisdiction's economic growth. State, regional, and local governments establish *authorities* (special districts) typically governed by a board of commissioners which may include elected members of the local jurisdiction. The ports/airports are referred to as *enterprise agencies* because they spend the funds they raise from operating a service, e.g., landing fees for runways, parking fees for boats and land vehicles, rental fees for use of retail space, and so forth. It is often the case that when the authorities are established, there is a provision that all funds raised by the enterprise are spent on operating, maintaining, and improving that enterprise and no funds can be used by other agencies or governments. Since enterprise agencies do not use tax revenue, they may exercise more autonomy over their budgets and policies than agencies that rely on taxes.

## Public Health and Health Services

While there is a consensus that public health programs and resources are the responsibility of local government, the scope and delivery of these services vary widely. In some cases, these services are provided by special districts or county governments. Elsewhere they are assumed by cities or municipalities. Public health and health services may be provided in the same or separate departments, depending on the size of the agency.

Public health activities include the control of infectious diseases, for example, programs to educate the public about the need for immunizations and the prevention of AIDS and other sexually transmitted diseases. Related activities include the maintenance of vital data on births, deaths, and reportable illnesses. Restaurant inspection is another public health function.

Operation of health services through public hospitals and clinics is a significant responsibility that can be handled at the county or city level. Some of the issues mentioned under Emergency Medical Services apply to hospital operations as well. Lack of affordable medical care has placed tremendous burdens on public health facilities, particularly emergency rooms. As private hospitals close their emergency rooms, the pressure increases on public facilities

Public health agencies faced new challenges due to pandemics such as COVID-19. Under normal circumstances hospitals, clinics, medical centers encourage health care providers to bring customers to their facilities so they may keep the number of empty beds to a minimum. The private sector was not prepared to provide medical services lasting two or more weeks to 10% to 12% of a population while their own staff was also becoming ill. The situation was further confounded by a lack of information on who was ill, where, with what symptoms, what treatments were available, and for how long treatment would be needed. The public health agencies lacked information on the pandemic and lacked authority over private providers to alter their practices. The private sector had no authority to enforce restrictions on the public to contain the spread of the pandemic. It was left to state governors, public health directors, emergency staff, and first responders to manage the crisis. The pandemic amplified every shortcoming of the public health delivery system: lack of data, lack of coordination, lack of authority, lack of money, dubious supply lines for medical equipment/materials, and access to limited medical personnel.

Agencies that do not have hospitals may still provide health services for their employees and for detainees in jails operated by the jurisdiction. These agencies had even fewer options to respond to the pandemic.

## Water Treatment

In California, water treatment is governed by the State Water Resources Control Board (SWRCB) but ultimate responsibility for safe and reliable water is left to city, counties, and special districts. In Los Angeles responsibility for water quality falls to the Los Angeles Regional Quality Control Boards which are organized geographically around water resources e.g., Los Angeles River Watershed. Water supplies are pooled and distributed by government agencies and/or private firms under contract with local jurisdictions.

Mosquito abatement and agricultural pest control are specialized public health functions that are provided at the local level, although often by special districts. Eradication of mosquitoes prevents several serious diseases, most importantly malaria. Agricultural pest control helps protect crops from the spread of destructive insects such as the Mediterranean fruit fly.

## Education

As mentioned earlier, education is among the largest public expenditures below the federal level. Although funding sources and educational standards may be established directly by states, K-12 and community college education is a local government function provided by school districts that correspond to municipal boundaries or that serve several municipalities. Public university education is more often provided at the state level, although there are examples of cities with such educational institutions.

A new and growing area for local municipal governments is after-school programs. Prior to No Child Left Behind federal legislation, after-school programs were run by school districts rather than other government agencies and/or nonprofits. After-school programs may be provided by schools, recreation/community centers owned and operated by municipalities, or nonprofit groups funded by government grants.

## Public Welfare and Social Services

States typically provide unemployment assistance (based on taxing companies throughout the state), while counties are often responsible for administering welfare programs for the chronically unemployed and disadvantaged, which are funded by the state or federal government from general tax dollars. Counties also administer social services for children and older citizens. Activities may include investigating alleged child or elder abuse, protecting children in detention facilities, and operating foster care programs.

# ADMINISTRATIVE AND SUPPORT FUNCTIONS

Finally, all government functions require staff in human resources, finance, and record keeping, which are needed to support the government services the public expects. These support tasks are described below.

## Finance and Budgeting

All governments have departments responsible for preparing budgets; analyzing and controlling how public dollars are spent; recommending how they should be spent; and monitoring their use. The function may be housed in the office of a mayor, a city/county manager, or an administrative officer. More details about the various financial aspects of government are provided in Section 4 of this text.

## Tax Assessment and Collection

Government has some form of tax collection. The primary sources of taxes at the state level are typically income and sales taxes. Counties, which collect property taxes, have the largest role at the local level. Property value assessment can be a complicated activity when property tax values fluctuate wildly from year to year. While there is significant incentive by governments to reassess property when values are rising, there is little incentive to lower assessments when values fall because that reduces revenues. Reassessments may be done on a regular cycle or based on property owner appeals. These appeals may be delayed thereby mitigating the revenue loss. Sales taxes, also called sales and use tax, are collected by each business on each sale or services provided in a jurisdiction and the tax is then sent to the state on a monthly or quarterly basis. If there is a city sales tax, it is typically collected at the time of the sale and sent to the state with the other sales tax remittance; the state then send the city its portion.

A less common form of tax is a city income tax. Tax collectors set up the process and seek out tax evaders. They may require registration for business licenses and payment of fees.

## Records and Election Services

The records and election services function, often provided by an official known as a city or county "clerk," includes providing support to elected officials such as city councils and boards of supervisors by preparing and maintaining agendas, report files, and council files. It also typically includes storage, archiving, and reference services for agency records such as ordinances, contracts, leases, deeds, historical documents, and land and tax records for all properties in the jurisdiction. Clerks also conduct national and local elections.

## Control of Money

Local government controllers can have responsibility for accounting and auditing functions, or a separate auditor may provide the auditing function. Controllers supervise all funds and accounts, prescribing the methods and installation of accounting systems. They prepare payrolls; maintain all payroll/benefit records; approve, record, and audit all receipts and payments to employees, contractors, and vendors; and ensure that all money is used for authorized purposes. Auditors review completed transactions to determine if money has been spent properly (financial auditing) and may audit programs for efficiency (performance auditing).

Treasurers are the custodians and disbursement agents of public funds, including cash, securities, and bonds. As the agency banker, the treasurer makes payments, invests principal and interest earnings, administers purchasing or credit cards, and negotiates agreements for financial services such as banking services.

Controllers, auditors, and treasurers are often elected offices, particularly in large jurisdictions, recognizing the need for checks, balances, and accountability to the electorate for the custodianship and proper use of public funds. When these offices are elected, their functions may be influenced by political motives, particularly in the area of auditing. For example, an elected auditor may focus on subjects that generate more public interest or controversy, such as performance auditing.

## Human Resources

The human resource function includes recruitment, testing, hiring (including background checking), classification, training, employment opportunities, insurance benefits, and worker's compensation. Safety programs including monitoring, training, and industrial hygiene may be included in this function. In civil service agencies it also includes appeal processes for employees who are disciplined or terminated. Labor relations activities, such as negotiating contracts with labor unions and handling grievances in agencies governed by state and/or labor laws, is also a human resources function.

Operating retirement systems, although related to the human resources function, is typically administered in a separate organization under the authority of a board with fiduciary responsibility for investing significant amounts of money to pay the benefits.

Section 3 of this manual provides more information on managing human resources and the benefits.

## Information Technology

The information technology function includes responsibility for developing and maintaining communications and computer systems, networks, hardware, software, and databases. It also often includes oversight of large systems programs designed and implemented by private contractors or third parties. Examples of large systems include 911 emergency dispatch systems, payroll systems, and centralized purchasing/warehousing systems.

## Facilities and General Services

All agencies have one or more departments with responsibility for the purchasing of supplies and equipment, materials management, and warehousing. Facilities departments may also be responsible for the purchase (or lease) and repair of vehicle fleets and other heavy equipment. General services departments typically are responsible for construction and maintenance of agency-owned buildings, property leasing and management, parking, custodial, recycling, mail, messenger, telephone, moving, and printing services are related functions.

## Risk Management

The risk management function minimizes liability for governments by purchasing insurance, reviewing contracts, and administering safety and workers compensation programs. This may be done by the human resources department or in a large organization it may be its own department.

## Legal

All government agencies have legal staff to advise policy makers, prepare legislation (ordinances), and defend against civil liability. For example, localities are often sued by private citizens who incur property damage or injury resulting from potholes in city streets, broken sidewalks, or fallen trees. Legal staff also defend in lawsuits alleging discrimination against employees, police misconduct, or violation of environmental regulations by sewage treatment plants or other government-run utilities. Larger agencies employ, or elect, their own district or city attorneys; smaller ones typically contract with law firms.

Administrative and support functions are many and varied. They are often criticized as being responsible for the increasing size and bloat of government. Although they always existed in some form, they have grown during the past 50 years in response to new laws and the greater complexity of government. For example, civil service systems and civil rights legislation have placed many demands on human resources and legal professionals to develop and enforce regulations. In the financial field, accounting and investment have become more complex and placed new demands on controllers and treasurers, and information technology as we know it today certainly did not exist during prior generations. These services are natural outgrowths of a developed, postmodern, urban society.

# ORGANIZATION AND MANAGEMENT

How does all this government get organized into a coherent whole? Communities address this issue with some basic management principles. Local governments, like most organizations, have organization charts that illustrate the reporting relationship through the organization, starting at the top with the mayor/council and working down to the department level and then to organizations within departments. In looking at these organizations several concepts should be kept in mind.

The functions tend to fall into two categories: (1) line or operating functions and (2) staff functions. Operating functions typically refers to those functions that provide a direct service to the public. All citizens are familiar with the police and fire departments, trash department, and recreation department. Citizens do not normally think about the functions that provide necessary support, such as the departments that handle hiring, prepare the payroll, design computer systems, and handle the jurisdiction's bank accounts. But these staff activities are important to the workings of any organization. They were described in the above section about the functions of government.

The organization chart of a typical large city (see Figure 2.2) illustrates the departments that have line and staff functions. It summarizes many of the functions and organization concepts described in this chapter. As a city example it is not inclusive of functions that are more commonly performed at the state, county, or special district level, such as education, some social services, and public health. Similarly, from the preceding discussion we know that not all of these functions will be found in all municipalities but are more commonly found in larger ones.

**Figure 2.2    Generalized City Organization Chart**

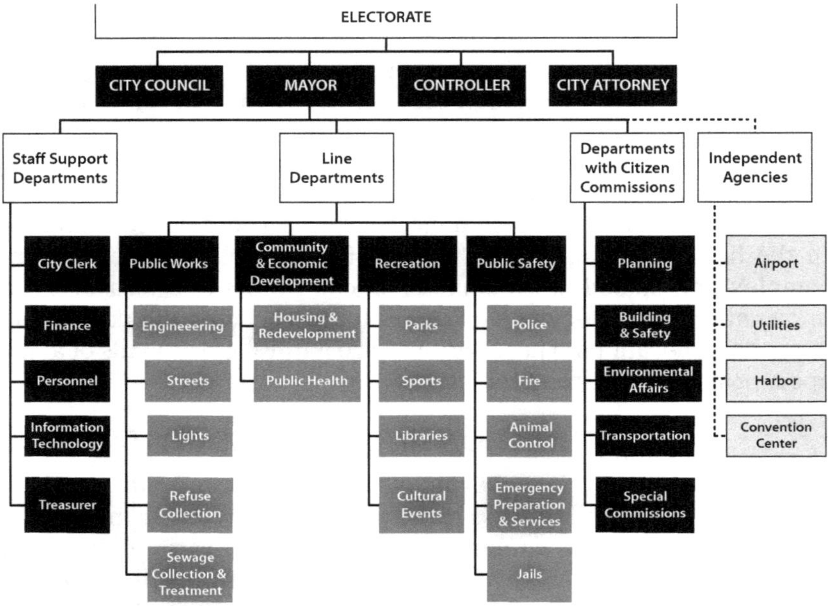

## Authority and Responsibility

Classical management theory discusses concepts relating to authority in organizations, which include the following:

1. Responsibility should come with adequate authority.
2. Subordinates should have one supervisor.
3. Supervisors should have a limited number of subordinates to adequately monitor and guide activities.
4. Line personnel should have primary authority, with staff personnel in an advisory role.

While these principles are still valued in many organizations, they have evolved to meet the needs of modern organizations. In local government we often see them violated, particularly at the highest levels, in part because of the checks and balances inherent in our federal system. For example, local governments have both an executive and a legislative branch, which means that department heads may have reporting relationships to both a mayor/city manager and a city council. While the mayor/manager may have hiring and firing authority, the council or county supervisors may have concurring or veto authority. This often means split loyalties and confusion when the two branches have conflicting goals or agendas. Department heads normally submit budgets and other requests to the executive branch, but the legislature (City Council) has final approval, which presents challenges in trying to anticipate and satisfy multiple bosses.

There are also checks and balances for organizations that control funds. There is usually one organization that handles budgeting decisions about how to spend the money, another to authorize already approved expenditures (i.e., accounting department or controller), and a third that acts as the custodian of the money (i.e., treasurer). While this may not always be efficient, it is designed to provide oversight and to minimize fraud and misuse of funds. It is a model used in the private sector for the same reasons.

Within departments, the same issues may arise. The organization chart may show the department head as the highest authority figure over the staff; however, separate commissions, city councilmembers, or citizen oversight committees may have direct or indirect authority over department heads and overrule their decisions.

The organization chart example (Figure 2.2) shows a few departments with advisory citizen commissions, notably Building and Safety as well as Transportation. Citizen commissions (sometimes called "boards of commissioners") present interesting challenges for department managers who must deal with their oversight while having authority and responsibility for their departments. These commissions may have unique responsibilities in addition to oversight of a department's primary function. For example, planning commissions rule on zoning and land use issues; civil service commissions act on disciplinary appeals; pension commissions have fiduciary responsibility for departments that handle large amounts of pension funds; and police commissions provide oversight of paramilitary organizations. Citizen boards may also be associated with proprietary functions such as airports or utilities operated by municipalities. A more detailed discussion of these types of board can be found in the chapter about citizen participation (Chapter 5, "Informing and Involving the Public").

## Centralization and Decentralization

As mentioned earlier, sometimes a function is performed by a separate department, and at other times it is dispersed throughout an organization. A core concern for local government is centralization and decentralization of functions and services. Decentralization refers to the delegating of decisions to the lower levels in an organization. Educational institutions, particularly large K–12 districts, are well known for debating this topic. Local schools are always seeking control over funding and curriculum, whereas the boards of education (and sometimes mayors) seek to retain centralized control, each alleging that its model will improve accountability and student performance. Districts have engaged in many experiments, ranging from creating smaller districts within a district to establishing charter schools that operate independently from others in the district. A few (notably New York City and Los Angeles) have centralized control even further by moving all or part of the authority to mayors. There does not appear to be a right or wrong answer as the debate continues throughout the country.

All organizations have internal supply needs: the purchasing and warehousing functions. In decentralized organizations, individual departments, or sections of departments order most of their own equipment and supplies as needed and are responsible for warehousing. In a centralized purchasing organization, these activities are housed in a separate department that handles purchasing and warehousing for the entire agency, including the establishment of specifications or standards and utilization of volume discounts. In some organizations there is a combination: centralized purchase of high-cost items or services and decentralized purchase of lower cost operating supplies or services.

We also see examples of centralization and decentralization in the human resources function. Larger agencies may have a centralized human resources department with responsibility for conducting civil service recruiting, conducting testing and classification activities, administering benefits, and establishing disciplinary guidelines and hearing appeals. However, at the department level there may be human resources directors with responsibility for all or portions of the hiring process (interviews and recruiting) and for establishing departmental procedures for handling discipline or safety. Carrying decentralization one step further, individual supervisors may make the final decisions about whom to hire or discipline.

There may be any combination of centralized and decentralized decision making within an organization related to its primary line operations functions. All important decisions may be reserved for the department head or the level immediately below the department head. Often in law enforcement organizations, which are based on a military model, policy and many significant operational decisions are reserved for top executives because of the need for accountability to elected officials and the community. However, even in police departments, individual officers or first-level supervisors are delegated authority to take necessary actions to protect citizens and make sure arrests are handled properly. Below are some of the pros and cons of each organizational style. The advantages of a centralized organization are the disadvantages of a decentralized one, and vice versa.

The advantages of centralization include the following:
- better coordination and conformity when decisions come from one point—avoidance of contradictory decisions from different parts of an organization;
- more expertise and specialization by staff;
- broader supervisor and manager knowledge and perspective;
- minimizes duplication of resources, staff, and equipment and provision of opportunities for volume discounts when dealing with commodities; and
- reward of strong managers.

The disadvantages of centralization include the following:
- more distance from customers or users of service;
- time delays as decisions are relayed through multiple levels of the organization;
- stifling of creativity and enterprise at the operating level—it is less democratic;
- inflexibility of policies and procedures, which are less easily adapted to user needs;
- less opportunity for lower-level individuals to learn by doing; and
- more difficult to measure performance.

There are various factors to be considered when setting up centralized/decentralized organizations. These include the following: size of the organization in terms of both number of staff and facilities and the geographic area served; knowledge and skill of the managers and the staff; time frame and significance of the decisions; information system technologies used; need for coordination and conformity; and goals of the organization. Because there is no one organization in which all the advantages or disadvantages apply, one tends to see a mix of each style.

## Chain of Command

Whether an organization is described as centralized or decentralized, it normally has an organization chart showing the levels of authority, starting with the highest levels and working downward to lower levels. The chain of command concept assumes that each level will give direction to the next lower one (although there may be "dotted line" relationships that show some overlapping or concurrent authority, as discussed in an earlier section).

Most of the time, the standard is maintaining the chain of command. In practice, bypassing links in the chain of command occurs frequently; it is a common complaint among supervisors and can also be a problem for subordinate employees. Why does this occur? In some instances, it is an issue of expediency when it is quicker for a manager to bypass an intermediate supervisor and deal with that supervisor's direct reports. While time pressure is a common reason for bypassing the chain of command, a supervisor may be bypassed when they are a weak link in the organization because they either lack the skill or knowledge expected of the position or is known to be a bottleneck because of disorganization or indecision. If a higher level manager is the one bypassing, it can place the subordinate employees in an awkward situation, particularly if the supervisor insists on all communications going through them and being kept informed of the employees' activities. It requires judgment and tact on the part of employees to satisfy an immediate supervisor as well as a higher level manager and avoid a negative evaluation. The situation wherein employees bypass weak supervisors may be less difficult if the supervisor is not engaged and does not care about being bypassed. It is more challenging when the supervisor insists on being included in the chain but is not performing their job. In this case the employees may need to take the initiative to bypass the supervisor to protect their own performance and reputation, recognizing they are not receiving appropriate direction. Sometimes seeking out other supervisors at the same level for guidance works in a staff organization, but it is less practical in line operations. While none of these situations is ideal, they all are common in the workplace and need to be anticipated.

### Functional Authority or Supervision

A concept related to the above discussion is that of functional authority. It refers to the right to direct those outside of a department on a particular function or subject. This occurs most often in staff functions, which have tended to proliferate in modern organizations as they have increased in complexity. The budget officer of a department often has authority to direct an entire organization on issues pertaining to the budget such as procedures, formats, and deadlines for submission of budget requests. Similarly human resources directors may have the authority to instruct supervisors and employees on employment policies and procedures. However, neither can exert direct authority over the line functions of the organization. They cannot tell an engineer how to design a building or a firefighter how to fight a fire.

The use of committees, increasingly popular in the public sector, creates a form of functional authority. When committees are vested with decision-making authority, they may supersede traditional organizational authority. For example, oversight committees may need to approve all major decisions related to implementation of a systems or capital program.

## CONCLUSION

This chapter has identified the primary functions performed by all levels of government and provided a description of key organizational elements as well as some of the issues and challenges of bureaucracies and the workplace. While the organizational issues are not unique to the public sector, they certainly take on the culture of the government organization. Those who choose public-sector careers will observe and experience well-functioning and dysfunctional organizations. This discussion should help one become aware of the characteristics of those organizations.

## PRACTICING PUBLIC ADMINISTRATION

1. Visit the website of a municipality or local government in your area. From its discussion of offices, programs, and services, locate the following:

   a. chief executive officer;

   b. public safety officer(s);

   c. public works and/or agencies responsible for community infrastructure;

   d. recreation, leisure, and cultural departments and their managers; and

   e. commissions for specialized populations: elderly persons, children, disabled persons.

2. Based on a review of the local municipal website:

   a. Determine if the organization is highly centralized or decentralized.

   b. Identify the opportunities available for citizens to participate on commissions, boards, or advisory councils.

3. Assume you work for a small city of 25,000 residents. Identify some of the issues in providing emergency medical services to your community such as who should provide services and how they might be delivered. Consider whether the population density of the community will have an impact.

4. Your agency has decided to establish an environmental program, and you are responsible for recommending the appropriate organization chart. Identify the critical questions to ask when coming up with your options and recommendations and identify which department(s) will be affected.

5. What would be the advantages and disadvantages of a decentralized public safety program in your community? Identify the specific aspects that might be centralized or decentralized.

6. Under what circumstances should employees bypass the chain of command?

## BIBLIOGRAPHY

Ammons, D. (2001). *Municipal Benchmarks: Assessing local performance and establishing community standards.* Thousand Oaks, CA: Sage Publications, Inc.

Carlisle, H. M. (1976). *Management: Concepts and situations.* Chicago, IL: Science Research Associates.

Chaudhuri, J. (2020). Reflection on *McGirt v. Oklahoma. Harvard Law Review, 134*(1), 82–85.

Fox, J. (2020). "The politics of Defunding the police". Granada Hills: Newstex. https://www.foxandhoundsdaily.com/2020/06/the-politics-of-defunding-the-police/

Giventer, L. L. (2003). *Governing California.* Irvine, CA McGraw-Hill.

Gowen, A., & Barnes, R. (2021, July 24). "Complete, dysfunctional chaos": Oklahoma reels after Supreme Court ruling on Indian tribes. *Washington Post.* https://www.washingtonpost.com/national/complete-dysfunctional-chaos-oklahoma-reels-after-supreme-court-ruling-on-indian-tribes/2021/07/23/99ba0b80-ea75-11eb-8950-d73b3e93ff7f_story.html

Janiskee, B. P., and Masugi, K. (2008). *Democracy in California: Politics and governing in the Golden State.* New York, NY: Rowman & Littlefield.

Karnowski, S. (2021, June 30). Minnesota lawmakers pass modest police accountability bill. *AP NEWS.* https://apnews.com/article/minnesota-bills-police-police-reform-death-of-george-floyd-4408e2d14a9c6cd282f379d-810ed9ebe

Kemp, R. L., Ed. (1999). *Forms of local government: A handbook on city, county and regional options.* Jefferson, NC: McFarland & Company, Inc.

Lewis, M. (2021). *The premonition.* New York, NY: W.W. Norton & Company.

Martinez, F. (2006). *Your government at a glance, facts about the city of Los Angeles.* Los Angeles: City Clerk Office.

National League of Cities and Local Solutions Support Center. (n.d.). Principles of home rule for the 21st century. NLC Center for City Solutions. https://www.nlc.org/wp-content/uploads/2020/02/Home-Rule-Principles-Report-WEB-2-1.pdf

NOAA National Centers for Environmental Information (NCEI). U.S. billion-dollar weather and climate disasters. (2021). https://www.ncdc.noaa.gov/billions

Rudd, H., Ed. (2007). *The development of Los Angeles city government: An institutional history from 1850–2000.* Los Angeles, CA: City of Los Angeles Historical Society.

Sonenshein, R. (2006). *Los Angeles: Structure of a city government.* Los Angeles, CA: League of Women Voters.

State and Local Finance Initiative (2011–2020). State and local backgrounders: State and local expenditures. Urban Institute. https://www.urban.org/policy-centers/cross-center-initiatives/state-and-local-finance-initiative/state-and-local-backgrounders/state-and-local-expenditures

Statista (2020). Number of fires and acres burned due to wildfires in the United States in 2020, by state. https://www.statista.com/statistics/217072/number-of-fires-and-acres-burned-due-to-us-wildfires/

# 3 ◆ ◇ ◆

# Nonprofit Organizations

> ... I have often admired the extreme skill with which the inhabitants of
> the United States succeed in proposing a common object to the exertions
> of a great many men, and in inducing them voluntarily to pursue it.
>
> —Alexis de Tocqueville, 1864, p. 130

During the American Revolution, after a brief trip to America, a British statesman, Edmund Burke, told the House of Commons that Americans were different culturally from their British counterparts. They were not simply transplanted Englishmen. In the 1700s, these new Americans wanted freedom, but knew they could not survive on their own. If a person needed to build a barn, he was unable to complete the task alone. The unwritten social contract in these early days was that neighbors would offer to help each other, with the unspoken understanding that he would, in turn, help them. From the time of the Revolution onward, Americans have used the concept of assistance and reciprocity to build communities and the country. People would voluntarily give of their time, talents, and resources to those help others in their communities.

In 1831, Alexis de Tocqueville noted that new undertakings in England and France were headed by the government, but in the United States associations were involved. With a desire by state legislators and the founders to limit the role of the government, civic and charitable organizations were used to create homes for orphans, provide health care to the needy, create libraries, universities and scientific research centers, as well as building parks, concert halls, and churches. Reliance on civic and charitable groups had been a conscious decision by states. In the mid-1800s, James Smithson, who had never been to the United States, bequeathed money to the United States government which was used to establish the Smithsonian Institution. Early in the 1900s, charitable giving entered the phase of *scientific giving* when philanthropists such as Andrew Carnegie and W. K. Kellogg began formalizing the idea of philanthropic giving. Carnegie was said to have identified with the poor and encouraged the rich to provide the "ladders on which the aspiring can rise."

As the role of the federal government rose it was able to collect income tax from individuals and businesses throughout the United States. This new capacity enabled the federal government to expand its role by funding programs at the state and local levels. Many European countries chose to operate social programs as basically a governmental responsibility while in the United States exceptions were made for charitable organizations to be exempt from paying federal income tax when these organizations contributed to civic and social efforts. In the wake of the Great Depression of the 1930s, legislation was passed to provide tax deductions for corporations that give money to charities. Arguably the greatest gift the government can give any corporation is to make it exempt from paying federal income tax. Tax leniency promoted corporate and philanthropic activities to continue in tandem with a rise in federal government social programs such as Social Security.

By the 21st century, the American charitable sector was thriving, with 1.54 million nonprofit organizations registered in the country, employing 12.3 million people, and holding nearly six trillion dollars in assets. Conversely, European nations, such as France, with high tax rates going to the government, have a barely visible private charitable sector, but proportionally five times more government employees than the United States. Economists believe that as the state takes over more responsibility for the provision of public goods and services, altruism, and voluntary cooperation atrophy.

This sector of voluntary associations often works in concert with the public sector to provide a wide range of goods and services that make civic life possible. Functionally, nonprofits are active in the arts, education, environmental protection and services, animal care and rights, health, human services, international relations, religion, and mutual memberships focused on hobbies, interests, professions, and so forth. How nonprofits implement their programs varies considerably. Nonprofits may be advocacy groups, provide management or technical services, serve as a community for like-minded professionals, and provide monetary and/or non-monetary support. In the United States the definition of a nonprofit organization is specified by the Internal Revenue Service (IRS) codes of the federal government, primarily Section 501(c). For the purpose of this discussion, we will focus on the meaning of nonprofit primarily as defined by federal tax policy.

## DEFINITION OF NONPROFIT

When most people hear the term "nonprofit" they think of charitable organizations. However, the term is much broader than that. Nonprofit is a term used in the United States referring to the IRS tax code.

Similar organizations around the world are generally referred to as Nongovernmental Organizations (NGOs). The functions may be similar, however, there are financial and legal ramifications surrounding a nonprofit organization based in the United States.

In the United States, there are several types of organizations that may request to be exempt from paying federal income taxes. The most common nonprofit classification exempt from paying federal income tax is under section 501(c)(3) of the IRS tax code. These organizations include (1) religious organizations such as churches, mosques, temples, synagogues, etc.; (2) charitable organizations such as the American Red Cross, Habitat for Humanity, American Cancer Society, Boys & Girls Club, etc.; (3) educational institutions such as K–12, colleges, and universities; and (4) others including literary organizations, amateur sports organizations, prevention of cruelty to children and animals, etc. The distinct feature of these organizations is that they are exempt under section 501(c)(3) from paying federal income tax and donations given to them are tax deductible for those to give. No other exempt status has that "gift" of a tax deduction.

Other types of organizations that may be exempt from paying federal income tax, but where donor contributions are not tax deductible, include:

- Internal Revenue Code section 501(c)(4) provides for the exemption of two very different types of organizations with their own distinct qualification requirements. They are:
  - » social welfare organizations: civic leagues or organizations not organized for profit but operated exclusively for the promotion of social welfare, and
  - » local associations of employees, the membership of which is limited to the employees of a designated person(s) in a particular municipality, and the net earnings of which are devoted exclusively to charitable, educational or recreational purposes.
- Homeowners' associations and volunteer fire companies may be recognized as exempt as social welfare organizations if they meet the requirements for exemption. Organizations that engage in substantial lobbying activities sometimes also are classified as social welfare organizations.
- Community welfare, in section 501(c)(4), includes organizations such as the Sierra Club and National Association for the Advancement of Colored People (NAACP). These organizations are (c)(4) because of their political advocacy activity.
- Common business interest groups, in section 501(c)(6), includes the Chamber of Commerce and professional sports leagues. In 2019, the National Football League lost its tax-exempt status.

- Social clubs, fraternities, and country clubs are a few examples of exempt organizations under 501(c)(7) of the federal income tax code.

- Credit unions are examples of exempt organizations under 501(c)(14) of the federal income tax code.

- Employee funded pension organizations are examples of those with an exempt status under the federal income tax code 501(c)(18).

These are but a few of the categories provided for by the federal income tax code and is not an exhaustive list of all provisions. In these circumstances, contributions to these organizations may be for a public purpose of community members. An example of this arrangement is when a person lives in a community and pays homeowners association dues. The association doesn't pay income tax on that money. Rather, it is a holding organization to redistribute the money for the betterment of the community, such as maintaining a community pool, landscaping, and other common-area issues. All these organizations are considered "tax exempt" but only those organizations exempt under section 501(c)(3) also have the benefit of donations being tax deductible to the donor.

Nonprofits are categorized by their intent and how they are organized. Basically, those on the board of directors and those who manage organizations exempt under section 501(c)(3) do not own the property or resources they manage and cannot benefit when the organization ceases to exist. Consequently, when a nonprofit ceases to exist, its assets are transferred to another nonprofit organization.

Nonprofits are a formal organization legally incorporated under state law as a charitable or nonprofit organization and are designed to serve a public purpose which may entitle them to be exempt from federal income tax, according to the IRS. If a state has an income tax, it may extend a tax-exempt status to the organization as well, but this varies state by state. When the organization is incorporated under state law it identifies its mission, the public benefit for which it is incorporated, and the self-governing mechanism (typically a board of directors) that will have oversight regarding the organization's policies and practices.

## STARTING A NONPROFIT

To start a nonprofit, the organization begins by creating a legal entity, usually a corporation, in one of the states. All legal documents are similar to those needed by a for-profit entity complete with bylaws and articles of incorporation. Articles of incorporation are formal legal documents required by the government that basically identifies who is creating the corporation or entity for what purpose; when, where, and how. Included in articles of incorporation are the organization's bylaws or the statement of the rules that govern members activities and entity's operations. Once the legal entity is established, they may petition the

IRS to exempt them under section 501(c)(3) or other appropriate section of the IRS tax code. Once approved, income received by and for their "exempt" purpose will be exempt from income taxes.

Nonprofit organizations are required to file annual financial and operational reports to the federal and state governments even though they do not have to pay income taxes. Nonprofits are not exempt from paying other taxes, such as sales tax or property tax, although some states do provide such exemptions.

Contrary to popular mythology, nonprofit organizations may make a "profit" every year. They should bring in more donations, grants, and sponsorships than they spend. They should keep a reserve in savings for years when donations are low. Unlike their for-profit counterparts, profits cannot be distributed to shareholders, or anyone associated with the organization, but must be put back into the organization. Also, being a nonprofit charitable organization does not require that everyone be a volunteer. Nonprofit organizations can have a mix of paid and volunteer staff. In 2021, the average salary for a nonprofit employee was $58,114, although large, multinational nonprofit CEOs can make salaries over one million dollars per year. Although salaries vary widely throughout nonprofit organizations, donors are critical of organizations with high "overhead" costs, i.e., expenditures not directly related to its purpose. Charity Navigator evaluates thousands of charitable organizations in the United States and rates them based on the percentage of donations used for the organization's purpose verses overhead. For example, if a nonprofit provides counseling and support to cancer patients, donors expect to see most of the funding going towards counselors and other direct services. However, they also understand that someone needs to process payroll, develop strategic plans, pay utilities, insurance, etc. However, if most of the funding is going to top-level management, and minimal funding to the direct support of the cancer patients, donors may find other organizations to support in the future.

## RELATIONSHIP BETWEEN NONPROFIT ORGANIZATIONS AND GOVERNMENT AGENCIES

Throughout the history of nonprofit organizations in the United States, there has always been a relationship between charities and government. Early in the country's history, cities and states faced the challenge of striking a balance between services provided by the government and services provided by charitable organizations. For example, in the 1700s, the Commonwealth of Massachusetts originally embraced the concept of the government providing for the poor, whereas the City of Philadelphia favored services that were provided by charitable organizations. All agreed that widows and orphans needed assistance, but should the community voluntarily provide funding to charities and churches for the services, or should the government take the money, through taxation, to provide the services? These ideas are still being discussed as the relationship between government and non-profits continues to evolve. In 2000, Dennis Young, Visiting Professor at the School of Applied Social Science at Case Western Reserve University developed three models that encompass differing views of the role of charitable organizations:

- Supplementary Model regards charitable organizations as fulfilling the demand for public goods that are left unsatisfied by government. For example, the government may provide resources to care for a foster child such as food, housing, health care, and education. But the government may not be able to allocate funding for music lessons, sports camps, prom dresses, or electronic devices. However, some communities have established nonprofit organizations to supplement the government funding for additional quality of life items and experiences.

- Complementary Model regards charitable organizations as partners to government, helping to carry out the delivery of public goods and services which are largely financed by the government. Lester Salamon (1995) discussed that nonprofit organizations and government agencies can be engaged partnerships (contractual) in which the government agency finances the public service, and the nonprofit organization deliver the service. This outsourcing has benefits to the government agency because the contract is only active for the duration of a program, and then can be discontinued. This allows for the government to reduce costs as soon as the program or service is complete. Additionally, many nonprofit organizations have strong community ties to the people and may be a more effective service delivery vehicle. For example, if a city fire department wants to distribute smoke detectors to members of the community to prevent fatalities in residential fires, some members of minority communities may be reluctant to engage with a uniformed firefighter from a government agency. However, if the Fire Department contracted with a local nonprofit that has already built trust within the community, education and distribution of the smoke alarms may be more effective.

- Adversarial Model regards charities as entities which are responsible for prodding the government to make changes in public policy and maintain accountability to the public. For example, a nonprofit that provides services to individuals with physical disabilities may attend city council meetings to advocate for improved ramps and building access throughout the city on behalf of their clients.

These three common models are by no means mutually exclusive. Nonprofit organizations may engage in all the models simultaneously. But these models provide a starting place for the role of the nonprofit organizations in modern American society.

## Pros and Cons of Government Contracting With Nonprofits for Services

Above are three of the models describing the relationship between government and nonprofits: to supplement, to complement, and to challenge. Below are some of the advantages and challenges associated with contracting with nonprofits.

The pros:

- They may provide a voice for ethnic and marginalized communities who typically are not well served by the public or private sectors.
- They may be innovative and nontraditional in how they serve community interests, e.g., Planned Parenthood is able to provide birth control information and pills when local governments are not permitted to do so. However, nonprofit services must comply with all regulations regarding health, safety, professionalism, etc., when engaged in services to public.
- They may mobilize persons and serve as source of information and advocacy, e.g., for HIV-infected children, households with food insecurity, etc. Nonprofits may use multiple methods to serve client needs.
- They may preserve and maintain resources for the public, e.g., historic societies, museums, libraries, special collections, etc.
- They may be more cost effective on a case-by-case basis because many positions are filled by volunteers versus paid personnel.
- They may provide a symbiotic relationship between public and private organizations, for example, a public library and a used books store operated by Friends of the Library who spend used book donations from customers to buy books or special resources needed by the library.

The cons:

- They may become too focused on securing revenue, which interferes with the avowed mission and service model of the nonprofit.
- They may blur the lines between what the government is accountable for and what the nonprofit is responsible for. This may be especially problematic when the nonprofit relies on government contracts for most of its revenue.

- They may place new and extensive record-keeping requirements on the nonprofit which are consistent with governmental accountability but exceed the requirements typically placed on a nonprofit.
- They may find concerns and obstacles to maintaining a respectful separation between the nonprofit's religious freedoms, sensitivities, etc., and the government while avoiding religious discrimination. Successful implementation depends heavily on government contract stipulations and oversight.

## NONPROFIT OPERATIONS

Nonprofit organizations are usually governed by a Board of Directors (usually volunteers) and run by an Executive Director, typically a paid position. Small nonprofits may only have a few (or no) paid positions, whereas the large nonprofits will have structured hierarchies similar to large for-profit corporations. The role of the Board of Directors is to ensure the organization is being run in accordance with applicable laws/regulations as well as to provide oversight and accountability. If laws are breeched by the organization, the board members can be held personally liable. Most boards have a variety of officers including:

- Board President: supervises all business and affairs of the board.
- Board Secretary: responsible for meeting minutes and ensuring the actions taken comply with the bylaws and articles of incorporation.
- Board Treasurer: keeps accurate accounting records and files the required annual state and federal reports.

Board members are often selected for their passion for the work done by the nonprofit. However, board recruitment should strive for a mix of talents including accounting, legal, personnel, strategic planning, and organization-specific topics. Board members are often also expected to be significant financial supporters of the nonprofit.

While the board is responsible for governance, the Executive Director is responsible for day-to-day management. The Executive Director, therefore, oversees personnel matters, maintains records and compliance activities, provides direction to the staff, oversees fundraising and sound financial practices.

In nonprofit organizations, the board of directors has a legal fiduciary responsibility to the donors, while in a for-profit organization the board of directors has a legal fiduciary responsibility to the shareholders.

### Fundraising

Nonprofits have a variety of ways to obtain funding for the exempt purpose activities. In smaller organizations, the Executive Director may conduct all fundraising activities. In larger organizations, several staff may lead different fundraising areas. Most Board members are also expected to participate in fundraising.

*Private Donations.* These are money or merchandise that may be solicited from individuals or businesses to help the operations of a nonprofit. This can be as simple as accepting cash donations outside a grocery store, finding donors through mail or social media outreach, or asking a local store for donations of products to help with the organization's mission.

*Major Donations.* These are similar to other donations but may be for assets, such as land for a new building. The term "major" is relative. For a new, start-up nonprofit, a gift of $500 may be classified as a major donation, whereas for larger nonprofits, major contributions may be upwards of $10,000 or more. These "asks" are usually well researched and planned to identify possible donors that match the donor's giving focus with the organization's mission. Board members may be required to identify potential donors and participate in, or host, events to promote donor involvement. The Board of Directors' president may be responsible for enforcing these requirements.

*Grants.* These come from two sources: (1) government agencies (federal, state, or local), and (2) foundations. Unlike private donations, grant applications are much more formal and often require substantial documentation. They usually require nonprofits to have a successful track record (e.g., operating for five years or more), and may require audited financial statements, copies of articles of incorporation and bylaws, along with insurance policies and other related documentation. Grants are competitive and are awarded to the best nonprofits that can provide outstanding performance in meeting the specific objectives of the granting organization. Grants are generally not awarded to organizations without a track record or strong financial stability. Additionally, grants (especially federal funding) can require annual audits and reporting on the success of the process.

*Special Events.* These may be multifaceted. They may be to raise money, such as a walk-a-thon where participants raise money for each mile they walk. They may be to raise awareness of an issue, such as breast cancer risks. They may also be known as "friendraising" events where people who were not aware of the good work being done by the nonprofit become engaged with the organization and develop into potential future donors or volunteers.

*Corporate Sponsorships.* These are funds set aside by businesses to foster goodwill in communities by sponsoring events or programs of a nonprofit. Although they may have altruistic motives, they are often swayed by events that get their name in front of their target market. For example, a local car dealership may want to sponsor a charity golf tournament. The sponsorship may get their company logo on all mailings and banners, so that attendees relate the dealership with a positive image of philanthropy.

*Capital Campaigns.* Large expenditures, such as a new building, will take time to fund for most nonprofit organizations. Donors are asked for funding that is earmarked only for the construction of the building. This can result in "naming" opportunities, meaning that for a sizable donation, the donor may be able to get the building (or a wing of the building or a special room) named after them.

*Selling Merchandise.* Some organizations think that revenue from selling items, such as t-shirts or bags with the organization's logo, is a great way to make money for the nonprofit. However, there needs to be caution taken regarding the tax implications. Although the nonprofit is allowed to sell items, the income received from the venture may result in corporate income tax, particularly if the sales volume becomes a major part of the nonprofit's activities. It still may be a good choice for revenue but knowing the rules up front will help to avoid an unexpected tax bill at the end. Also, the tax-deductibility of a donation is reduced by the value of the items sold; thus, if a donor receives a T-shirt worth $10 when they make a $100 donation, only $90 of the donation is tax deductible to the donor.

## Tax Returns: IRS Form 990

Nonprofits must file an annual report to the IRS to maintain their nonprofit status. A nonprofit organization that normally has $50,000 or more in gross receipts is required to file a federal IRS Form 990 (or Form 990-EZ) annually. Small organizations with less than $50,000 in gross receipts may be required to submit an Annual Electronic Notice (Form 990N). The Form 990 can be viewed on websites such as guidestar.org and are a way not only for the IRS to determine tax liability, but also for potential donors to review the solvency of an organization and where it receives and spends its money.

## Annual Reports

Many mid- to large-size nonprofits also produce an annual report of challenges, activities, and accomplishments each year, separate or as part of the financial report. These reports are ways to communicate with potential donors and clients. They can be used to highlight a nonprofit's mission and impact by including compelling stories and photos. They can take the opportunity to thank volunteers, supporters, and donors, and make a case for future donations to the organization.

## COMPLIANCE AND SAFEGUARDING
## THE TAX-EXEMPT STATUS

### Scandals Within the Nonprofit Sector

When we think of nonprofits, we tend to think about the cancer patients being served at St. Jude's Hospital, children's spirits being lifted by the Make-A-Wish Foundation, and disaster victims helped by the American Red Cross. But despite the altruism and efforts on the part of many, the sector is not without its problems. Scandals have rocked the nonprofit sector for decades that highlight ethical breaches and illegal practices. For example, in 2004 the former CEO of United Ways' National Capital Area plead guilty to charges of fraud and admitted to defrauding the United Way of $500,000. The scandal had a direct impact on his chapter of the United Way, and their fundraising plummeted. The former CEO was convicted and sentenced to serve a two-year jail sentence. In 2008, the CEO of United Way in North Carolina made $1.2 million in a single year. Although the CEO did nothing illegal, the Board of Directors was held up to scrutiny for approving such an extravagant salary.

In 2002, Congress passed the Sarbanes-Oxley Act, one of the most sweeping anti-fraud legislations in American history, to strengthen the government's role in enforcing and monitoring for-profit corporate practices. Although most provisions of Sarbanes-Oxley apply only to for-profit companies, at least two criminal provisions apply to nonprofit organizations:

- provisions prohibiting retaliation against whistleblowers; and
- prohibiting the destruction, alteration, or concealment of certain documents for impeding investigations.

In 2004, on the heels of the passage of Sarbanes-Oxley, the IRS testified before Congress that they were losing an estimated $15 billion a year in revenue due to abuses in the nonprofit sector. During the latter half of the 1900s, the IRS was not actively auditing or regulating nonprofit organizations. But after the passage of Sarbanes-Oxley, Congress began a closer investigation of corporate accountability, including nonprofit corporations. By 2004, the IRS began investigating nonprofits, with warnings and sanctions increasing annually.

Although little research has been done to determine the cause of the "abuse," the problem may lie in misunderstandings of the legal parameters required of nonprofits on the part of their Boards of Directors rather than malice or ill intent. One main difference between the Board of Directors for a for-profit and a nonprofit is the level of commitment and expertise. Nonprofit board members are recruited to volunteer because of their ability to raise funds and/or their commitment to the cause. It is not uncommon for Boards of Directors to have members recruited from the populations they serve. For example, nonprofits that assist cancer patients may recruit board members who have the disease, or who have recovered from the illness. There are no certifications, education, or training requirements to be a board member other than a willingness to serve. So, if abuses to the tax code occur, it raises the question: are the abuses done out of greed or malice, or out of ignorance of the tax code?

## Commonly Misunderstood Aspects of Nonprofit Organizations

*Taxation.* One area of confusion for board members is the concept that being exempt from federal income tax means any and every activity is tax free. However, that is not true. See the earlier discussion about selling merchandise. Business activities not related to the organization's exempt purpose are subject to the Unrelated Business Income Tax (UBIT). The major function of UBIT is to regulate competition between nonprofits and for-profit firms. Profit-making activities that a tax-exempt nonprofit organization undertakes primarily to raise revenue but is unrelated to the nonprofit's purpose, is taxed as income. For example, if a charitable organization that saves stray dogs has an extra office space in their building and decide to rent it out—the rental income received will be taxed at the standard corporate rate. To help nonprofits distinguish between what is taxable and what is not, there are reference materials such as Bruce Hopkins's book, *The Law of Tax-Exempt Organizations.* These sources are helpful for board members to understand the rules and limitations surrounding nonprofit organizations.

*Political Activity.* Restrictions on political activity by nonprofits also provide confusion for board members. This is restricted in two ways:

- nonprofits may only conduct an insubstantial amount of political lobbying; and
- nonprofits may not participate in, nor intervene in (including the publishing or distributing of statements) political campaigns on behalf of, or in opposition to, a candidate for public office.

For example, if a nonprofit organization hosts a fundraising gala and invites the incumbent mayor to speak at the event, this may be considered a violation of "intervening in political campaigns" if the event is held during an election cycle and the other candidates running for mayor are not provided the same opportunity to speak.

Organizations that violate either restriction may lose their tax-exempt status and the eligibility to receive deductible contributions. If a nonprofit organization loses its ability to fundraise, most organizations will go out of business immediately.

There are some nonprofits, such as political action committees and political campaign committees, which are created specifically to enable political activity. These nonprofits have their own specific reporting requirements which we will not pursue.

*Illegal Activities.* Although it should go without saying that nonprofit organizations cannot engage in illegal activities or violate fundamental public policy, seemingly simple actions can quickly put an organization's tax-exempt status at risk. For example, if representatives from an environmental group decide to handcuff themselves to trees to protest clearing land for another purpose, once the trespassing is deemed illegal and the protesters are arrested, the nonprofit can lose its tax-exempt status.

## WORKING RELATIONSHIP WITH NONPROFIT PROVIDING SERVICES TO PUBLIC SECTOR

A major challenge for the public sector is determining what is a public service that requires public authority and money and what is not a public responsibility. An intruder entering a business after hours requires public authority because the government polices what is a person's property and what is not. However, what sector is responsible for the homeless person asleep at the entrance to the business? The owner calls 911. The police are authorized to issue a citation and perhaps move the vagrant from the business's doorway. Where should the police relocate the vagrant to? Which business, doorstep, park bench would suffice? What about the following day when the vagrant returns? Do the police repeat the process? Does this repeated effort represent an efficient use of police resources?

While a public agency may be called to address a concern, it does not mean that the public sector has the means, personnel, or expertise to resolve the concern. It is said that *nature abhors a vacuum.* This means that no amount of citizen neglect and indifference will result in the issue fading away. It also means the public sector will remain the arena for the concern even though it is ill-equipped to address the problem.

What should be done with concerns that fall between private markets and public agencies that provide goods and services? This category includes homelessness, mental health incidents, drug addiction, and food insecurity to name a few. The public administrator has had to identify new ways to attend to these problems while avoiding taking time and resources away from services the public agency was designed to deliver.

In some cases, the public administrator has joined forces with nonprofits. The discussion below is how one city on the eastern area of San Bernadino County, Rialto, CA, took on the challenge of homelessness. This is not a typical practice in policing but is one example of how institutional capacity is built with NPOs.

## The Process of Working With a Nonprofit Organization

*Step 1: Recognize There Is a Problem.* The police initially identified 160 homeless in a city of approximately 108,000 (or 0.15% of the population). This was not considered an extraordinary level for a city of Rialto's size. However, the Chief of Police recognized that the level of homelessness drained police services as officers were called repeatedly to address panhandling, health concerns, defecating in a public area, etc. The police arrested the homeless, took them to jail, and in time, let them go. The next day they began again with no end in sight.

In 2019 the city got a grant from the state of California for homeless outreach. The program was assigned to Rialto's Community Services Department, which includes Parks and Recreation. The funds were used to provide pamphlets to the homeless on a myriad of services available from many sources, including the Social Security Administration, Veterans' Administration, Department of Social Services, health care, and mental health care providers. In addition, the funds provided a voucher for temporary housing, outside of Rialto. Access to the out-of-town housing and agencies assumed that the homeless knew where to go, had transportation and/or had a cell phone/internet connection that enabled them to secure the help they needed. None of the assumptions were workable. Parks and Recreation staff didn't have transportation resources, expertise, or personnel to address the issue of homelessness either. The pamphlets and vouchers offered little in terms of immediate relief and no long-term solutions. What the city had was $600,000 in state funds which it could spend on tasks related to homelessness, but it didn't know how to address the problem.

An officer working in the homeless outreach section in the Rialto Police Department advocated for the homeless and attended a convention concerning issues regarding the homelessness in California. At this convention the advocate learned about the Social Work Action Group (SWAG), a nonprofit with an impressive track record. In a three-year period, SWAG served 2,669 people and permanently established 1,132 persons in homes. These 1,132 were called *street exits*. It was the street exits that attracted the attention of Rialto's administrators.

*Step 2: Proceed With Caution.* Rialto had found an option but was unsure it had found the solution. Rialto sought out information from neighboring jurisdictions currently using SWAG, observed SWAG operations firsthand, and got to know the staff and their capabilities. SWAG was able to provide the following:

- staff with practical experience in social services and with social service agencies such as the Department of Motor Vehicles for ID cards, Veteran Affairs for medical services, housing, and related services;

- staff knowledgeable and experienced in case management;
- staff experienced with housing programs such as rental assistance, emergency solution grants, rapid rehousing, and permanent support for housing;
- staff trained as mental health first responders and on substance abuse cases;
- staff with vehicles to transport the homeless to appropriate agencies;
- staff skilled at conducting follow-up visits with the homeless—these ongoing client contacts (eight to 10 meetings per client) served to build relationships and trust between the social worker and the client;
- staff that was knowledgeable about mental health services, medical care, dental care, and counseling;
- managers and staff with access to data on who was assisted, how, when, where, and the long-term outcome.

This latter capacity to maintain data that reflected the long-term efforts, rather than episodic police contacts, was the most important feature of the collaboration with the nonprofit. Any solution to serving the homeless would be based on building relationships with these clients that led to permanent housing.

*Step 3, Part A: Implementation: The NPO Working Relationship.* Implementation involves developing a working relationship with the nonprofit and determining what services will be used and paid for by the political jurisdiction. While these two criteria are developed simultaneously, this discussion will encompass how the working relationship was developed and the approaches taken to fund these efforts.

The social work/social service conference presentations, which the Rialto police staff attended, did not provide a plethora of organizations or programs to choose from, nor did it provide the criteria that jurisdictions needed to make an informed decision. Instead, it provided a platform for local organizations to discuss their programs, approaches, and resources for addressing the housing crisis.

After the preliminary exploration regarding who SWAG was and what they did, the Rialto Police Department considered what a working partnership would require. The city had state funding for a homeless outreach effort. It would be necessary to transfer these resources from Parks and Recreation to the Rialto Police Department (RPD). The demand for "homeless" services did not come from the homeless but from businesses, voters, taxpayers, etc., who wanted the homeless removed. The RPD service is to assess the level of threat to public safety and link the homeless person with someone who can assist with needed services.

The RPD established the Community Services Bureau within the police department to identify who and where support was located. The bureau was staffed with five officers and two civilians. The bureau had two teams and each team had two sworn officers and one civilian, identified as a community specialist who was the social worker from SWAG.

The city's sworn officers were trained in diagnosing cases concerning the homeless, substance abuse, mental health, and so forth. The community specialist provided case management and follow-up services. From this model the RPD established the Quality-of-Life Team, which included the two teams and a community compliance officer, and is housed in the Rialto Police Department. It is a multi-jurisdictional team comprised of Rialto police officers, SWAG, San Bernardino County behavioral health specialists, public works, and code enforcement.

When a call comes into the police department for homeless-related issues, an officer is dispatched to ensure the scene is safe. Once the scene is secured, it will be turned over to SWAG for additional homeless service support, and if needed a behavioral health specialist, public works staff, and/or code enforcement. Since all members of the Quality-of-Life Team are housed in the Rialto Police Department, all necessary members are immediately dispatched to the call simultaneously to ensure a comprehensive and timely delivery of services. Once a team member is no longer needed, they leave the scene to continue with other duties.

RPD services are in response to RPD calls for service. SWAG and police officers utilize police radios to assure they can communicate about the clients' needs (mental health, housing, etc.) and to enable the officer and SWAG specialist to begin to build the trust and links needed for the immediate and long-term solutions to homelessness.

*Step 3, Part B: Financing.* The initial funding for the RPD's bureau and two teams was drawn from a combination of the state's initial homeless outreach program (services) and from a federal Community Oriented Policing Services (COPS) grant for three of the bureau's officers (personnel).

Since California's initial funding, the state has continued its support for the homeless under a half-billion-dollar program called HEAP (Homeless Emergency Aid Program). From this state allocation Rialto received a grant of $600,000. The city's primary approach to funding homeless services has been to closely follow the state's budget allocations and continually apply for state funding. In addition, the RPD seeks federal funds (e.g., COVID-19 Emergency Solution Grants) whenever possible. The ongoing cost, primarily for personnel, is $20,000 per month or $240,000 annually. Transportation and related operating expenses for officers are provided out of the city's general fund for policing. SWAG specialists have their own transportation and operating expenses provided by the nonprofit organization.

The close working relationship between SWAG and city police enable the city to efficiently and effectively utilize other city services to address citizen concerns. For example, RPD was concerned with homeless encampments in flood zones such as storm channels and riverbeds. With the assistance of SWAG, the RPD Quality-of-Life Team undertook an effort to remove a homeless encampment from these high-risk areas and have the public works department remove approximately 50 tons of trash. The coordination of city departments does not require additional funding but effectively utilizes the funding already available from the city's general revenues. The expertise of SWAG enables the city to make more effective use of County mental health services.

Finally, the city understands that federal and state funding may not last in the long run. To ensure the Community Outreach Team continues addressing quality of life issues in the City, Rialto has enacted an annual $300 Community Facilities District (CFD) fee on new housing construction. These are dedicated funds that are attached to property but are not a property tax. The CFD fee enables the city to fund the RPD's Community Services Bureau in the absence of federal and state grants, should that need arise in the future.

***Step 4: Data and Thinking Strategically.*** One of the major benefits of SWAG for Rialto is its case management relationship with the homeless, which provides data about the homeless population and the services needed. When homelessness is addressed as strictly a policing activity, the homeless avoid contact with police for fear of being jailed. Interacting and serving the homeless means that getting them the services they need that are available will take on average five to seven follow-up contacts by a social worker before trust is established between the city and homeless client.

In the short run a rise in homelessness among parolees and/or veterans may cause the city to use its influence and SWAG's expertise to leverage funds and resources from programs earmarked to provide services for these populations. The homeless problem for Rialto will not disappear in the long run. The factors that contribute to its persistence is the lure of the pleasant weather in Southern California. A contributing factor for the persistence of homelessness is the ongoing expansion of mass transit stations to suburban communities. The introduction of each new station along the expanding rail line introduces a pipeline for homeless from inner cities to the suburbs. The impact of transitory homelessness results in an impact on the quality of life in communities along the way.

Rialto is aware that each neighboring city has its own program and there is little coordination among cities. There is no regional approach to getting the homeless services, and the need for county and state policies to strategically address the problem are not forthcoming. It is as if the state, county, and local municipalities address homelessness in silos.

Data and what the data mean is critical. Meaningful data are what the NPO provides. When the homeless effort was initiated, the city guessed it had about 160 homeless. Today it has 233. Rialto appears to be losing ground in its effort to reduce homelessness. Rialto has determined the increase is consistent with the growing homelessness population in the Southern California region. However, the value of the program is not the per night snapshot of the number of homeless, but the number of *street exits* (those permanently housed). In this regard the city has made progress. In the most recent report from SWAG 46 persons are off the streets temporarily and 25 persons have exited permanently. This represents substantial improvement for approximately 44% of the original 160 homeless or roughly 30% of the city's current homeless population. Information is provided to the city council semiannually on both program successes and challenges. During these semiannual reports RPD updates the council on program improvements and additional resource requests.

## ETHICS

There is an extensive discussion of ethics in Chapter 4, which views ethical issues from the perspective of the public administrator. The objective in this chapter is to explore the role and nature of ethics in the nonprofit sector.

The objectives of a code of ethics, or what is sometimes called a *statement of values*, are threefold:

- to attract talent (employees, board members, donors);
- to foster transparency in how the nonprofit relates to stakeholders; and
- to foster trust with all parties that have an association or relationship with the organization.

The nonprofit may have two distinct codes of ethics: one for employees/volunteers and another for its board of directors. Nonprofits typically have a three-step process with regards to their code of ethics.

1. Establish, revise and/or renew the code to assure that it is a strong reflection of its values.
2. Share the code. This task may take many forms: employees may have training sessions; the code may be posted in a public area, and/or be summarized on the organization's documents, such as advertising.
3. Periodically audit compliance with the standards by employees and board members.

Public and private audits typically focus only on the accounting system. While an accounting audit is appropriate for a nonprofit, the relationship between stakeholders is more critical to its long run viability as an organization. Consequently, ethics audits examine practices and processes that support the ethical standards and use qualitative and quantitative methodologies to collect evidence that decisions and actions were supportive of ethical standards.

## Code of Ethics Design

A code of ethics is derived from the organization's mission statement (see Chapter 6, "Strategic and Other Types of Planning"). It is an opportunity to take the mission statement and develop the organization's standards of behavior in more detail. For example, the mission statement may identify core intentions such as providing professional and quality care. The code of ethics may identify the organizations' tasks (provide a service, assist, influence) and the specific behavior that is subsumed (timeliness, kindness, consistency). These statements serve as a basis for conducting an ethics audit of the organization. Are services provided, how frequently, are the intended behaviors found and is the behavior consistent?

When government contracts with a nonprofit, the government agency may request the codes of ethics and recent audits or audit reports. Like other documentation, it is a means for understanding the organization's culture, practices, and adherence to standards.

As mentioned earlier, Boards of Directors may have their own code of ethics. The overarching values of boards are to exercise care in carrying out board functions, be supportive of the organization's mission, and use any information and resources in a manner that promotes the organization's best interests. Finally, it is typically left to the board to assure that policies and practices of the organization comply with external laws as well as internal rules and regulations. As with the code that governs employees and volunteers, compliance audits of the board are a critical task of the nonprofit.

The duties of board members can be encapsulated in the three Ds:

- Duty of Care: Board members must be reasonably informed about the organization's activities and participate in the making of decisions in good faith. This is achieved by regularly preparing for and attending board meetings, obtaining information before a vote, and reviewing and providing oversight on legal and financial matters.
- Duty of Loyalty: Board members must exercise their power in the interest of the organization, and not in their own interest or the interest of another entity. They must put the organization's interest ahead of their own by disclosing any conflicts of interest and avoiding the use of corporate opportunities for individual benefit.

- Duty of Obedience: Board members must comply with applicable federal, state, and local law, adhere to the entity's article of incorporation and bylaws, and remain guardians of the mission. They must examine and understand all documents governing the organization and its operations, as well as make decisions that fall within the scope of the organization's mission and governing documents.

The National Council of Nonprofits has compiled standards for the nonprofit sector and have resources to help organizations develop their own ethical standards.

## CONCLUSION

Nonprofit collaboration and independent support for community efforts has been a time-honored practice in America since its founding. This sector has grown steadily in the 21st century. The definition of what is and what is not a nonprofit is defined by the federal tax code Section 501(c). What distinguishes nonprofits from other sectors of the economy is its reliance on fundraising as means for securing revenue. Similar to the for-profit sector, nonprofits also rely on a Board of Directors for governing the organization, and reporting requirements set by the IRS and others.

As the demands for public services evolve while the willingness of the public to pay for services declines, government agencies and civic groups are exploring new ways to work collaboratively to meet public expectations. The example provided in this chapter is the partnership between the city of Rialto's police department and SWAG to assist the homeless. These collaborations open new avenues to government agencies in their efforts to serve the public interest and address community demands.

## PRACTICING PUBLIC ADMINISTRATION

1. Visit the Ronald McDonald House Charities and review their IRS Form 990 for the 2019 tax year at https://rmhc.org/-/media/Feature/RMHC-Production-Images/About-Us/Files/Media-Resources-and-Financials/2019-990.pdf. Based on the documentation provided by the NPO, identify the following:
   a. mission
   b. staffing:
      i. number of employees
      ii. number of volunteers
   c. funding
   d. total revenue from all sources
   e. net assets
   f. activities in 2018-2019
   g. number of families that stayed at the Ronald McDonald houses in 2018
   h. what illness children have been diagnosed with to make them eligible for RMHC
   i. what private or public organizations would partner with RMHC
   j. pay-to-top executive of NPO
   k. how much Vincent Bryson, CEO of RMHC, receives in income
   l. how much he earns per hour
2. Review the Form 990 for the Los Angeles Philharmonic Association in 2019 at https://www.causeiq.com/organizations/view_990/951696734/7da96476189720bb42b9e10e5a0f7d96
   a. What is the mission of this NPO?
   b. What is the IRS designation or category for this NPO?
   c. How much is Alison Sowden, VP and CEO of Phil and Productions, paid?
   d. What was the NPO's total revenue from all sources?
   e. What is its IRS code status?
3. How charitable are Americans? Use https://wallethub.com/edu/most-and-least-charitable-states/8555 as a reference.
   a. What state has the highest overall charitable ranking (#1) in the United States?
   b. What state has the lowest (50th) overall charitable ranking in the United States?
   c. In what state is volunteering and service highest? Where is volunteering and service lowest?

4. Review IRS Resources. The IRS has developed a series of
   training videos on the Stay Exempt website: https://www.
   stayexempt.irs.gov/
   IRS Introductory Course: Applying for Section 501(c)(3) Status

   a. Visit the website and click on the Starting Out tab near the
      top of the page. Complete the course titled "Applying for
      Section 501(c)(3) Status." This is an overview course related
      to nonprofits. Students should print out the certificate of
      completion at the end of the 40-minute course.
      IRS Advanced Courses [optional]

   b. Visit the website noted above and click on the Existing
      Organizations tab near the top of the page. Watch the videos
      listed below. Each course ranges from approximately 20–35
      minutes. Print out the certificate at the end of each course.
      Courses include:

      » Maintaining 501(c)(3) Tax-Exempt Status

      » Form 990 Overview Course

      » Employment Issue

      » Required Disclosures

      » Unrelated Business Income

      » Political Campaigns & Charities: The Ban on Political
        Campaign Intervention

      » Charitable Gaming for exempt Organizations

      » Can I Deduct My Charitable Contributions?

## BIBLIOGRAPHY

Ahmed, S. (2013). *Effective non-profit management: Context, concepts, and competencies.* New York, NY: Routledge.

Board Source. (2018). Nonprofit Board Member Codes of Conduct and Ethics. https://boardsource.org/wp-content/uploads/2018/05/Code-of-Conduct-Ethics.pdf?hsCtaTracking=508c16c3-f23d-48cb-87e3-e72111881869%7Ce9e66529-f81f-4def-81c1-8973c53d66bc

Bureau of Democracy, Human Rights and Labor. (2021). Non-Governmental Organizations (NGOs) in the United States. U.S. Department of State. https://www.state.gov/non-governmental-organizations-ngos-in-the-united-states/

Congress, E. P., Luks, A., & Petit, F., Eds. (2016). *Nonprofit management: A social justice approach.* New York, NY: Springer Publishing Company.

Cornforth, C., Hayes, J. P., & Vangen, S. (2015). Nonprofit–Public Collaborations: Understanding Governance Dynamics. *Nonprofit and Voluntary Sector Quarterly, 44*(4), 775–795. https://doi.org/10.1177/0899764014532836

de Tocqueville, A. (1864). *Democracy in America.* Sever and Francis.

Hopkins, B. R. (2019). *The law of tax-exempt organizations* (12th ed.). Hoboken, NJ: John Wiley & Sons, Inc.

Johnson, A. F., Rauhaus, B. M., & Webb-Farley, K. (2020). The COVID-19 pandemic: A challenge for US nonprofits' financial stability. *Journal of Public Budgeting, Accounting & Financial Management, 33*(1), 33–46. https://doi.org/10.1108/JPBAFM-06-2020-0076

McCann, A. (2021, Nov 9). Most Charitable States for 2022. *WalletHub* at https://wallethub.com/edu/most-and-least-charitable-states/8555

National Council of Nonprofits. (2019). Nonprofit impact matters: How america's charitable nonprofits strengthen communities and improve lives. Washington, D.C.: National Council of Nonprofits. https://www.nonprofitimpactmatters.org/site/assets/files/1/nonprofit-impact-matters-sept-2019-1.pdf

Poister, T. H., Aristigueta, M. P., & Hall, J. L. (2014). *Managing and measuring performance in public and nonprofit organizations: An integrated approach* (2nd ed.). San Francisco, CA: Jossey-Bass.

Pynes, J. E. (2011). *Effective nonprofit management: Context and environment.* New York, NY: Routledge. https://doi.org/10.4324/9781315704920

Salamon, L. M. (1995). *Partners in public service.* Baltimore, MD: Johns Hopkins University Press.

Smith, S. R. (2008). The challenge of strengthening nonprofits and civil society. *Public Administration Review, 68*(s1), S132–S145. https://doi.org/10.1111/j.1540-6210.2008.00984.x

Urban Institute. (2019). The nonprofit sector in brief 2019. National Center for Charitable Statistics. https://nccs.urban.org/publication/nonprofit-sector-brief-2019#the-nonprofit-sector-in-brief-2019

U. S. Bureau of Labor Statistics, U.S. Department of Labor. (2018). Nonprofits account for 12.3 million jobs, 10.2 percent of private sector employment, in 2016. *The Economics Daily.* https://www.bls.gov/opub/ted/2018/nonprofits-account-for-12-3-million-jobs-10-2-percent-of-private-sector-employment-in-2016.htm, accessed August 23, 2022.

Young, D. R. (2000). Alternative models of government-nonprofit sector rela-
    tions: Theoretical and international perspectives. *Nonprofit and Voluntary
    Sector Quarterly, 29*(1), 149–172.

# Ethics

Consider the following examples from recent events in the news:

## I'VE GOT THE POWER, YOU'VE GOT THE MONEY

A Southern Californian councilmember was sentenced to 14 months in federal prison for his acceptance of gifts—including $15,000 in cash—from a businessman during trips to Las Vegas and Palm Springs. The judge noted that the councilmember's "elaborate and clandestine scheme" to cover up his conduct has "undermined the public trust."

During the trip to Las Vegas, the councilmember accepted from his business associate an envelope with $10,000 in cash, a hotel room, $1,000 in casino gambling chips, $34,000 in bottle service at a nightclub, and a $2,481 group dinner. The business associate also paid for two female escorts to arrive at their hotel and meet the councilmember. Later, at a golf tournament in Palm Springs, the councilmember accepted an envelope containing $5,000 in cash from the business associate. Shortly thereafter, the councilmember arranged for his business associate to pitch his business to a friend of the councilmember's who was a developer.

## SAFETY EXCHANGED FOR CASH BY SENIOR CRANE INSPECTOR

Within weeks of a construction tower crane accident that killed a local resident, a second crane collapsed in the city, killing a passerby. As investigators began to delve into the questionable coincidence, they discovered that the chief crane inspector was taking bribes to allow cranes to pass inspection without being approved for operation. In addition, the crane inspector was found to be taking bribes from a crane company to help ensure that its employees would pass the required licensing exam by altering their public exam records. The inspector was arrested for bribery and record tampering.

BOOSTING BILLBOARDS FOR FAMILY FUN AND CAMPAIGN FUNDS

A county supervisor and his family members accepted free vacations from a billboard owner who was lobbying to lease parcels owned by the county flood control district. In addition, the billboard owner contributed over $33,000 to the supervisor's campaign committee.

The county supervisor later voted in favor of leasing property to erect the billboards, deferring lease payments to the county, and extending building permits. The county supervisor issued several support letters to city and state agencies requesting that they grant special permits necessary to build the billboards. Lastly, the supervisor voted to allow the billboard owner to sell five billboards to another business for $4.4 million.

Later, the county supervisor pleaded no contest to one felony count of conspiracy to violate the state's conflict-of-interest law. He served three years on probation, paid $20,000 in fines, and was barred from running for future office.

These are but a few examples of ethical challenges at the local level. The daily news often brings us yet another government scandal. Sometimes it is about politicians, but more and more frequently it is about government agencies and employees. This chapter examines the challenge to build, maintain, and embody ethical behavior and decisions in all aspects of public administration. It discusses policies to promote objectivity, transparency, and the responsible use of public resources. Such policies and programs generally constitute ethics programs. However, as we can see from the examples above, ethical foundations for good public practices are not always a top priority. Public administrators need support from top management and elected officials to be aware of ethical pitfalls and to engage in ethical behavior. Public administrators may need to recognize that simply working for government does not make one inherently ethical, despite the existing checks and balances in government work and the absence of profit-only work.

But why do we care so much about the institutionalization of ethics? It is the foundation of the public trust.

Beginning with the Watergate scandal in 1974, the public became aware of many government and corporate ethical deficiencies. In response, there was a rise in the number of laws and regulations addressing ethical behavior as well as an expansion of ethics commissions at the local and state level. Currently, 42 states have ethics commissions as do a number of municipalities and counties. The increase in ethical oversight also includes the Federal Office of Government Ethics, which was established in 1978.

Sarbanes-Oxley legislation of 2002 was created to counter the public loss of confidence in private corporations following the accounting scandals of Arthur Anderson, WorldCom, and Enron. Under Sarbanes-Oxley, the federal government required that CEOs assume personal responsibility for corporate financial statements. This legislation required that a publicly held corporation have a code of ethics, ethics training, reasonable checks to deter wrongdoing, means to promote accountability, compliance with law, accurate reporting, honesty, ethical conduct, and protections for those persons reporting misconduct.

This rise of formal ethics institutions and commissions at the state level has often been stronger than at the federal level, where elected officials have not been held to the same standards as administrative employees. Public scandals during the Trump administration (e.g., Ryan Zinke) and state scandals (New York Governor Cuomo) dominated the news from 2016 to 2021. (D'Angelo, C., 2018; Judicial Watch, 2021). Some Trump cabinet officials engaged in conflicts of interest. In addition, the president was unwilling to separate himself from his real estate and hotel businesses, thereby creating an image of a presidency for sale. Loopholes in federal ethics laws that allowed such conflicts were being addressed by Congress, with the proposed bill, Protecting Our Democracy Act, which sought to provide consistent ethics rules for the office of the president along with other federal office holders and employees, as well as to limit executive power. Earlier congressional efforts, Stop Trading on Congressional Knowledge Act of 2012, or the STOCK Act, focused on clarifying that a member of Congress or an employee of Congress may not use nonpublic information derived from their government position or from the performance of their responsibilities as a means for making private profit.

The purpose of ethical guidelines and legislation was to ensure public trust in government by making government accountable to the highest standards of conduct. How is this done? Achieving the highest standards of conduct can occur with three steps. The first is by establishing ethics laws applicable to all public officials; the second is through training and education about these ethics laws and policies; and the third is through the cultivation of understanding about what constitutes an ethical dilemma and how to make ethical decisions in challenging situations. These steps encompass both formal and informal ethical awareness. This chapter discusses these methods and begins with the concept of ethics in the public sector.

## EVOLUTION OF ETHICAL CONCEPTS

When we speak of ethics, we refer to standards of behavior that are acceptable in a society or can be tested against accepted community standards. When we speak about ethics in government, however, we refer not only to the actions of employees but to the broader concept of public trust. Without public trust, no society can advance or sustain itself in any meaningful way.

Lord Moulton, the British parliamentarian, once said, "Ethics is adherence to the unenforceable." Laws and rules are enforceable, but ethics resides in a different domain. No one is arrested for being untrustworthy, being dishonest, being disrespectful, lacking integrity, or being an overall lout. Yet a world in which the kinds of people mentioned above are encouraged to thrive would not be conducive to a healthy society. Adherence to the unenforceable is adherence to a set of values that promote excellence, integrity, responsibility, honesty, courage, respect, and kindness among individuals, organizations, or communities. It is the strength and application of ethical values that builds public trust.

## THE IMPORTANCE OF ETHICAL BEHAVIOR IN PUBLIC ADMINISTRATION

In the recent 2020 Global Business Ethics Survey that included government organizations, two times as many U.S. employees felt pressured to compromise standards and had observed misconduct than was reported in earlier GBE surveys. Reported unethical behavior has steadily risen in survey findings over prior years. Actions qualifying as misconduct include conflicts of interest, abusive or intimidating behavior, and lying. In addition, 79% of all U.S. employees reported experiencing retaliation. Clearly, even though many organizations have formal standards, such as codes of ethics, there is a continuing need to train, retrain, and educate decision makers and administrators on employing ethical behavior to build and maintain trust.

In the public sector, unethical behavior may lead to cynicism and alienation. Alienated citizens may view government employees as adversaries instead of as supporters of the community and the citizens may choose to withdraw their participation. Without public support, a republic cannot survive.

## BUILDING AN ETHICAL ORGANIZATION

Acting ethically means engaging in open and transparent decision making and ensuring employees are not placing their personal interests ahead of the welfare of the organization or public. Government should serve the greater good and discourage decisions or actions that provide undue advantage to one individual or group over others. Acting ethically builds trust in government, its processes, and its decisions. Of course, processes themselves, while seemingly neutral, can be flawed. Methods and consequences of processes are viewed differently over time, creating perceived and/or real inequities in public policy. These changing conditions, too, must be honestly addressed when creating an ethical organization.

The first and most important step in ensuring there is an ethical environment in government is to ensure or develop strong, ethically minded leadership. This requires the organization's highest officials to lead by example and support ethical decision making. This entails ascribing values that the organization lives by and that guide decision making. Such organizational leaders stress the importance of actualizing ethical values in daily work. Operational concerns, such as budget cuts, policy changes, and other unanticipated challenges, are met with a holistic view to ensure efficaciousness within the parameters of the organization's values. Ethical leaders show consistency in words and actions. Without ethical leadership, trust in management is weakened and irresponsible behavior may flourish. Not talking about values or the importance of ethical behavior at the top leaves a communication vacuum and inadequate decision making by managers and employees. Such conditions may be demoralizing and lead to poor behavior, dissension, and unsatisfactory performance.

With strong leadership in place, policies, procedures, and guidelines for meeting the goals and objectives of an organization and establishing the standard of expected behavior become easier to implement. Organizations cannot rely solely on the executives to model ethical behavior to ensure employees will do the right thing. While everyone has some standard of individual morality with which he or she has grown up, it can be expressed very differently from one person to the next. Most professional organizations (accountants, public administrators) have codes of ethics. An agency's code of ethics provides guidance regarding what is expected from all employees and ideally is closely aligned with the organization's mission statement. A state's ethics commission promotes the state's code. Depending on the locality, cities or towns may create their own codes or adapt their respective state codes. Codes can vary from legal-based principles to value-based principles. Many codes draw on one's responsibility as a government employee to the public.

While codes of ethics establish the general principles for how employees are expected to behave, the successful implementation of codes of ethics require organizations to actively use the codes and update them as necessary to stay consistent with an organization's purpose and leadership. Having a code of ethics but not using it will create its own ethical dilemma, as it provides a false sense of security to management.

In addition, code of ethics which are either aspirational or compliance-centric do not provide instructions about how to behave in specific situations, which is necessary to affect the culture of the organization. For that, governments must ensure adequate ethics policies, procedures, and training are in place that allow employees to carry out their work in an orderly, professional, and ethically aware environment. These policies can take the form of laws/ordinances adopted by the legislature, guidelines issued by the executive, and labor contracts. Ideally, these policies are disseminated in a consistent manner, in written form, throughout the organization, and compliance to these policies is understood to be a condition for continued employment.

In addition to having comprehensive policies, government organizations must provide the opportunity for all employees, including commissioners and executive managers, to be trained in these policies. Training on the most salient issues, such as conflicts of interest and disclosure of financial interests, should occur on a regular basis. Such training should also foster the review and re-envisioning of the values of the organization and how these values are to be demonstrated.

Finally, ethical organizations should have in place a process by which employees can solicit guidance and assistance in addressing ethical issues beyond the creation of a code of ethics and ethics training. This includes establishing instruments such as a helpline and providing a referral resource for employees on ethics-related matters.

A review of standard ethics policies is below. These policies and procedures fall into two categories:

1. encouraging objectivity and transparency, and
2. protecting public resources and preventing their misuse.

---

### CASE STUDY: THE NEW PARKS DIRECTOR

The city parks department received a grant to build a new sports complex and three adjacent ball fields at a neighborhood park that had not had any capital improvements in nearly 20 years. Before a request for proposal was issued, the parks director, newly arrived from a similar job in a nearby county, gave instructions to change the usual evaluation criteria by reducing the percentage weight given to the cost of the project so it had equal weight with technical specifications and experience.

When the proposals came in, ABC Development Company, a nationally known construction company, had the highest total ranking, scoring very strongly on the technical and experience components. The other companies, while scoring well on the cost criterion (low-cost bidders), did not score well overall on the other criteria. ABC Development was awarded the contract.

A month later, one of the local companies that had competed for the bid protested the award decision because it had discovered ABC Development had recently conducted a similar project for the park's director at his prior job. The claim was that the parks director influenced the evaluation process so his favored contractor would win the construction bid.

The parks director countered that he was not on the evaluation committee and that all bidders knew the evaluation criteria before the
proposal submission was due. In addition, he said, the neighborhood
deserved a state-of-the-art complex and not just a 'government building" that met only the lowest-bidder criterion. Internally though,
employees felt uncomfortable because the director had asked more
than once if ABC Development had submitted a proposal but never
mentioned that he had worked with the company previously.

---

The city employee appears to be earnest in his efforts to get the new
sports complex and ball fields done in a manner befitting the neighborhood. Yet the process he engages in creates questions about his intentions and casts doubt on whether he meets the ethical standards that
are expected. Changing an evaluation criteria rating at the beginning
of a bidding process is not in itself a problem. Nor is knowledge of contractors problematic since it is assumed certain companies will bid for
similar projects over time. However, by not disclosing his association
to the winning company early in the process, his efforts to alter the
evaluation criteria and inquiries about this company's standing in the
bidding process to his employees created at the very least the perception that he had influenced the contracting process to a chosen end.
His actions lacked transparency and introduced doubt into the minds
of others involved in the process as to whether the director was doing
what was best for the department or best for friends and associates
close to him. (For further discussion of contracting issues, see Chapter
16, "Contracts and Procurement.")

## ETHICS AND COMPLIANCE POLICIES: ENCOURAGING OBJECTIVITY AND TRANSPARENCY

### Conflicts of Interest

Conflict of interest is at the heart of many ethical dilemmas because
it is a common situation that may take many forms  The conflict occurs
when the employee allows their personal interest (financial, personal,
and/or job related) to take priority or to influence their actions while
discharging the responsibilities of a government position. For example, a procurement manager secures a contract with a supply company
owned by his brother. The procurement manager may benefit from
this arrangement at the expense of the agency, and this opportunity is
largely due to the public employee's position rather than to a systematic comparison of suppliers. A conflict of interest may be either positive or negative. For example, a real estate development might either
increase or decrease nearby property values. A planning commissioner

who owns one of those properties has a conflict of interest in the decision to allow the development. Conflicts may be real or perceived. A range of possibilities is summarized below.

## Perceived Conflicts of Interest

A perceived conflict of interest occurs when there may not be factual evidence of a conflict of interest but there is the appearance of a conflict—or a future conflict. The perceived conflict arises when the relationship between two or more parties appears to be influenced by outside or personal interests rather than considerations of benefits to the agency. For example, a pension manager recommends her municipality invest a sizable percentage of its assets in a mutual fund where her husband serves as a member of the board. This is certainly a perceived conflict of interest since there is a question as to whether the pension manager or her husband might benefit from the investment of municipal funds now or in the future.

Ensuring all appropriate parties understand conflicts and how to avoid the perception of a conflict is critical to building and maintaining trust in the agency. The more transparent public decisions are, and the greater diligence paid to preventing conflicts of interest, the more trust stakeholders will have in public officials.

## Pay to Play

An issue related to the above is sometimes referred to as "pay to play." This is a more subtle form of favoritism than quid pro quo situations wherein favors are directly given in exchange for money or other benefits. In pay-to-play situations the benefit is access to the inner circle of public decision makers. It occurs, for example, when officials or candidates for public office solicit campaign contributions/donations for public projects (including charitable causes) with the understanding that the contributions will lead to access to the decision makers, even if it does not guarantee the award of business or other favorable actions. Even when a donor does not directly benefit financially, the criticism is that access gives those donors or sponsors an advantage over others (bidders or members of the public) seeking legislative or administrative actions. Consequently, there is a perception of favoritism even when there is no direct evidence.

## Financial Disclosure for Business, Investments, Gifts, and Travel

Public organizations often require elected officials, higher ranking officers, and employees with key decision-making authority to disclose assets and financial interests. The disclosure form requires that the official/employee identify and report income, real property, and investments.

Public disclosure helps to ensure that official/employee decisions are not based on financial self-interest. For example, an official who owns property within a jurisdiction might benefit from zoning, land use, or building permit decisions by his or her agency.

These same decision makers are often required to disclose gifts, meals, travel, or entertainment tickets received from anyone who does business with his or her agency to avoid the perception of undue influence. There is typically a threshold above which disclosure is required, recognizing that insignificant amounts are unlikely to bias a decision maker.

## Procurement and Contracting

Issuing contracts and procuring goods and materials are significant government activities with a potential for favoritism and conflict of interest. Since the dollar value of many contracts is significant, government agencies establish procedures that ensure that the selection process is competitive and that bidders do not have a favored relationship with those involved in the decision. The goal of requests for proposal, requests for qualifications, and so forth is to establish a fair and objective standard for evaluating bidders and to avoid awarding sole-source contracts, particularly to relatives, friends, or business associates of government officials.

## Outside Employment

Public organizations often limit, or require disclosure about, second jobs or outside activities to ensure the interests of an external employer do not conflict with those of the public agency. Such restrictions or prohibitions also seek to minimize potential time conflicts wherein an employee might be unable to devote sufficient time or energy to his or her public position. Public employees may be restricted, or prohibited, from accepting honoraria for speaking engagements or for work as consultants in areas related to their government positions if the subject matter or materials are proprietary to the government agency (e.g., intellectual property, discussed below). In addition, it may be questionable for a public employee to accept added pay (private funds) for work already compensated for with public money. In theory, everyone (the public) has contributed to the public employee's compensation, and the additional funds are not for the work performed but for benefits that may arise in the future.

## Future Employment

A government agency may prohibit its former employees from doing business with the agency for a specified period (one or two years) following termination of employment. This is sometimes called a revolving door policy. This policy is designed to discourage promises of employment in exchange for favorable treatment by the government official toward his or her future employer. In addition, the policy seeks to discourage a former agency employee from exercising undue influence.

## ACTIONS TO ADDRESS CONFLICTS OF INTEREST

### Recusal

Recusal is the removal of a person from participating in or influencing a decision because they have, or may be perceived to have, a conflict of interest in the decision. The recusal often includes not participating in or even being present during discussions leading up to a decision since the conflicted person's participation or even their presence may influence the decision.

Decision makers may also be required to recuse themselves from decisions in which family members or business associates have financial interests. When several decision makers are disqualified, a quorum may not be feasible. In this case the recusal policy should provide for action by an alternative legislative or administrative body.

### Lobbyist Disclosure

Persons or businesses that lobby government officials on behalf of clients who do business with the government or who advocate legislative action may be required to disclose their activities, finances, and the names of their clients. This assists the public in identifying who is attempting to influence government decisions and fosters greater transparency in the decision-making process.

## ETHICS AND COMPLIANCE POLICIES: PROTECTING PUBLIC RESOURCES AND PREVENTING MISUSE

### Fraud and Misuse of City Funds, Equipment, and Supplies

Common areas for ethical abuse include misrepresenting or improperly accounting for employees' time and use of funds. Timekeeping, travel expenses, mileage, employment applications, and financial records are areas wherein fraudulent activity may occur. Misuse of equipment and supplies also jeopardizes public resources.

While there are often rules requiring accurate timekeeping and prohibiting the use of agency copy machines, computers, or phones for personal use, there is often flexibility in enforcement when financial losses or risks to the public are minimal. The occasional long lunch or use of computers or fax machines for personal use is often tolerated. However, when the frequency and extent of violations become standard operating behavior, small or inconsequential instances can result in greater costs and concerns over time.

Misuses of resources are unacceptable and unethical when they rise to intolerable levels and place public resources at risk. An office employee who repeatedly uses the copy machine to make flyers for her softball team, the plumber who takes equipment without authorization for moonlighting jobs in the neighborhood, and the inspector who repeatedly borrows the agency car for personal errands during the workday are misusing government property. Similarly, falsified timesheets, mileage reports, and/or travel expense reports jeopardize an agency's internal controls and create financial and legal liability. Because these are clearly actions that violate the public trust, they will likely result in disciplinary action for the offending employee.

## Information Technology and Government Records

A growing area of ethical concern is unauthorized use or misuse of information technology: cell phones and smartphones, internet access, email accounts, and computer hardware, software, and data. In addition to the concerns raised above related to overuse or misuse of these resources for personal business, there are concerns that include exposure or loss of confidential information (personnel, investigative, legal, patent research), the downloading of pornography, the manipulation or theft of technology or security systems, and/or the exposure of an agency's computer network to viruses through malware or phishing activities.

Government agencies collect and maintain vast databases of sensitive information about citizens. A prime example is health care data collected by hospitals and public agencies. Safeguards to prevent the inappropriate viewing and release of patient information are critically important. The Health Insurance Portability and Accountability Act (HIPAA) is a major piece of federal legislation concerning the use and disclosure of "protected health information." Hospitals and health care facilities have worked for years to implement procedures to comply with this act. (For more details about the Health Insurance Portability and Accountability Act, see www.hhs.gov/ocr/hipaa/) Computerized and digital records present a particular challenge in today's world because of the potential for access by so many people in an organization. The disclosure to the media of medical records of prominent citizens by employees of a public university hospital is the type of scandal that highlights today's challenges in this area.

Ethics also concerns how public administrators handle the growing volume of electronic data. Safeguarding data to prevent access by outsiders and intentional or inadvertent release is more difficult now than at any time in the past.

## Intellectual Property

Federal agencies have a significant responsibility for the oversight of publicly held companies, the approval of food and drugs, the safety of and access to drinking water, information on individuals, proprietary information related to granting patents, to name a few. Individuals and firms that receive approval from federal agencies for their innovations may earn billions of dollars from these efforts. Therefore, it is critical that the information be secure to prevent misuse of information or corporate espionage.

There is also an interest by government agencies to protect resources it initiates and develops. Computer applications and databases, patents, and blueprints are examples of intellectual property that government agencies need to secure for their own use or to provide on a limited basis to authorized users. Employees who work for these agencies may be faced with making judgments about appropriate and inappropriate disclosure of the agency's proprietary information.

Finally, there are appropriate times and often legal responsibilities to provide information to the public about many of these issues. However, information is considered confidential during the process of gathering, researching, reporting, developing formulas, or preparing legal briefs is under consideration.

The discussion above has outlined various types of ethical and compliance-related concerns.

Rules and regulations assist in addressing issues, but often persons do not perceive there is an ethical issue. Consequently, it is important to understand how to identify and consider ethical issues as well as how to comply with rules and regulations.

## STEP-BY-STEP APPROACH TO APPLYING ORGANIZATIONAL STANDARDS

While policies and regulations are necessary to provide direction in meeting the organization's goals and preventing ethical problems from arising, simply following the rules may not always be enough. The policies need staff to implement them. This requires employees to be proficient at decision making, implementation, and discerning ethically challenging situations, especially where two policies may contradict each other. The following is a snapshot of steps employees should take when they encounter ethical dilemmas.

### Step 1: Identify the Ethical Issue

Having a code of ethics and providing frequent training on confronting ethical issues sensitizes officials and employees to the potential ethical concerns of their decisions. In the New Parks Director case study that appeared earlier in this chapter, the first issue is that the park director did not recognize that the process may be as important as the results. Therefore, he did not identify the ethical issue implied by his actions.

## Step 2: Investigate Facts and History

When an ethical issue arises, consultation should occur with an individual (an ethics officer or legal counsel) with expertise. Concurrently the decision maker should gather the facts and history on the issue. For example, how did the community address contract roles and responsibilities in the past, and are there policies and procedures that guide decisions and actions now? Are there extenuating circumstances?

## Step 3: Apply the Rules or Regulations

In the case of the park director discussion above, what needs to be done to rebuild public trust? The rules were followed for bidding on the new sports complex, but there was a change in the process. Communication about the change should be provided. In this situation the director may need to rebid the construction contract to ensure integrity of the process. A rebid may result in the same decision; however, the effort to be transparent and fulfill the mandate of a fair bidding process may provide for greater public support and trust.

## Step 4: Document the Action Taken

The process and actions taken should be documented to demonstrate transparency and record that the appropriate policies and procedures were followed, or not. Documentation also provides a reference point for future actions and decisions. If other options were considered and rejected, document the rationale for these as well. Complex decisions should be made in partnership with others: colleagues, mentors, the agency's in-house counsel, ethics officer, and/or ombudsman. Collaboration and open dialogue with others may help reduce confirmation bias as well as flush out ethical principles and consequences for a final decision. Finally, indicate why a particular alternative was taken and the perceived consequences of those actions.

## Step 5: Explore the Broader Perspective

What lessons were learned from the situation that may suggest structural or substantive changes in policy, law, or procedures to avoid similar concerns in the future? A review may include using the case's circumstances as a teaching tool, referring to how similar behavior is addressed by professional organizations, and/or exploring what the consequences of unethical practices may have had on third parties. Also, it may include reviewing decision-making models or introducing review mechanisms to ensure concerns about conflicts of interests are always addressed and resolved. Precedent and past practices are powerful influences in developing an ethical organization. Organizations need to evaluate whether the process and outcomes realized from a case are those the organization wants to see repeated.

In addressing ethical concerns such as conflicts of interest, misuse of funds, and misuse of equipment, many issues can be resolved by applying ethical standards and guidelines. More complicated issues arise when there are conflicting priorities or values, when discretion over process is extensive, or when guidelines/regulations do not exist. It is when we address more complex situations that adherence to ethical values becomes significant and has the greatest long-term impact on the organization.

## ETHICAL DECISION-MAKING MODELS

The more complicated a situation, the more likely it is there will be different values competing against one another for priority. Here a person needs to draw on their best ethical decision-making skills.

Listed below are a few core decision-making models and the historical/traditional labels associated with them. The three models used most often are the utilitarian approach, the duty approach, and the virtue ethics approach.

### The Utilitarian Approach

Utilitarianism, developed by British philosophers Jeremy Bentham and John Stuart Mill in the 19th century, suggests that ethical decision makers strive for the greatest overall good for the greatest number while committing the least amount of harm. Determining the overall public good is not a popularity contest. If a majority community supported the building of a new park but would have to tear down existing low-income housing, this would not meet the utilitarian standard. While the low-income families could use the park, they would have lost their homes. Utilitarian decisions do not reflect simply what the majority may want regardless of the cost to the less fortunate.

To analyze an issue using the utilitarian approach:

1. identify the various courses of action available,
2. ask who will be affected by each action and what benefit and harm will most likely result from each, and
3. choose the action that will produce the greatest benefits (aggregate good) and the least harm—the ethical action is the one that provides the greatest good for the greatest number.

### Duty or Principles Approach

Another classical philosopher is Immanuel Kant, who is known for his *ethics of duty*. Writing in the 18th century, his belief was that humans shared an innate ability to reason and could frame moral questions similarly regardless of education because of this innate trait. As opposed to the utilitarian approach, which looks at the consequences of an action, duty ethics focuses on the principle or duty underlying the action to be taken. The most important step in making an ethical decision is to question, "Can I ask everyone else to act in the way I wish to act?" The answer would be yes only if it met everyone's rational sense of morality. The action must be based on a principle to be adopted by rational beings. Such a principle might be "Do not lie" or "Be kind to strangers."

In the housing situation described above, a community agrees to a public project (new park), and the development of that project displaces some residents. Kant's duty principle would suggest that displaced residents receive just consideration (monetary or alternative housing). Compensation to the low-income residents may result in the new park's being more costly than originally anticipated. However, duty requires that full consideration be met regardless of the consequences of the consideration.

Kant believed that since everyone can conceive of moral actions, all people have inherent dignity as rational and autonomous human beings. Human dignity means having respect for one another, not using a person merely for one's own personal gain and treating each person as someone with unconditional worth.

The person using the duty approach would consider the following:

1. What is the underlying duty or principle by which I am making this decision (honesty, duty, loyalty, etc.)?

2. Could my decision be replicated by others as an action that is morally worthy?

## Virtue Ethics Approach

The virtue approach to ethics assumes that there are certain ideals toward which all persons should strive, which provide for the full expression of our personhood and our values in the specific acts we undertake. These ideals are discovered through a deliberative exercise that weighs three alternative actions to the same condition. At one extreme is excessive behavior, and at the other extreme is a minimal response. The third and best action is the mean (called the "golden mean") or the middle of the former two expressions. This third option is what Greek philosophers, in particular Aristotle, called "virtue," which means excellence.

To continue with our park and housing example, the excessive behavior would be to build both the park and housing, which would be extravagant and beyond the capability of the residents or citizens to adequately maintain over time. The minimalist behavior would be to build the park but provide temporary rent waivers or inadequate housing units for the persons displaced. The virtue-based solution would be to build the park and build new housing for the residents that would improve their living situation within fiscal limitations.

Virtues are attitudes or character traits that enable us to act in ways that develop our highest potential. Honesty, courage, compassion, generosity, fidelity, integrity, fairness, self-control, and prudence are all examples of virtues. Aristotle believed that virtues are developed by practicing them. If you want to become more compassionate, you must practice acts of compassion.

The following are questions one might ask when using this approach:

1. What virtue or character trait would be most appropriate in the situation?
2. How would that trait be demonstrated?
3. What are the ways the trait might be over- or undercompensated?

## Ethical Dilemmas Arising from Competing Values: The Case of Flint, Michigan, Water

In the following case, the ethical dilemma involves several competing values. One critical issue in being ethical is to assure one has not assumed a *false dilemma*. A false dilemma occurs when a limited number of choices, outcomes, or views are presented as the only possibilities when, in fact, more possibilities exist. As such, it unjustifiably puts issues into black-or-white terms. There are few cases where the decision maker has only one or two options. If the choices are too limited and/or no choice seems to support core community values, the probability is that the actual ethical issue has not been identified and decision makers are chasing solutions to false dilemmas. The Flint, Michigan, water crisis is such a case.

This case is described in five sections: (1) service prior to April 2014, (2) the decision in April 2014 to switch the water supply to the Flint River, (3) the period after the switch in service, (4) the decision to reject Detroit Water and Sewerage Department's (DWSD's) offer followed closely by the decision to accept DWSD's offer, and (5) efforts to adjudicate the outcomes in criminal and civil courts.

*Prior to April 2014.* In the mid-20th century, Flint, Michigan, had a population of 200,000 and a growing economy. In the 1970s and 1980s, rising gas prices and imported cars resulted in significant layoffs by Flint's major employer, General Motors. By 2014, the city had dropped to 100,000 residents. Fifty-seven percent of the city's population was African American. Forty-two percent lived below the poverty line. Flint's health outcomes (e.g., life expectancy) were among the lowest in Michigan. The Flint River had not been a source for drinking water. The site was "an industrial legacy river" having served as the "unofficial waste disposal" for Flint's many industrial plants during the boom economy of early 20th century.

*Decision in April 2014 to Switch Water Services.* In April 2014, the City of Flint switched from getting their water from the DWSD service, which drew water from Lake Huron, to getting their water from the Flint River. The decision to change the water source was made by Emergency Manager, Darnell Early, who had been appointed by the Governor to manage the city's government. The appointment of an Emergency Manager was the latest response to the city's many financial challenges. The city's reliance on Flint River water lasted from April 2014 until October 2015. Flint residents were exposed to toxic levels of lead poisoning during this period.

When the decision to switch Flint's water source was made, testing of the water for bacteria and lead had not occurred and corrosion control treatment, which was necessary because of the presence of lead pipes in Flint, had not been established. Flint city engineers relied on Michigan Department of Environmental Quality (MDEQ) officials who certified the water was safe to use, and therefore did no new testing regarding the quality of water and operation of the water delivery system to provide EPA standard drinking water to Flint households.

*After the Switch to Flint River Water.* The shift in water supply was immediately evident since the water was brownish and had an odor. Residents were advised to boil the tap water since dangerous levels of bacteria may have been present. City officials acknowledged there were elevated levels of carcinogenic trihalomethanes in the river water but that the water remained safe to drink. The change to the Flint River water coincided with an outbreak of Legionnaire's disease that killed 12 and sickened 87 people.

The Legionnaire's outbreak prompted the Flint River water to be retested and it was determined that there was insufficient chlorine in the water. Additional chlorine was added to Flint's water at its treatment plant, which inadvertently served to accelerate the corrosion of the lead pipes and the leaching of lead into the drinking water.

The Flint River water was never treated for lead, which was required by EPA regulations, given the size of the population it was serving. Corrosion control treatment to keep lead out of the water was a standard treatment for the DWSD system, but it was not added to the Flint River water, due to state staff misinterpreting what the federal policy on lead treatment prescribed. Rather, the Michigan Department of Environmental Quality (MDEQ) planned to test the water in two, six-month intervals and evaluate the water before possibly adjusting for corrosion control. The consequences of lead exposure were greatest for Flint's children, and the effects were long-term cognitive and behavioral problems.

Frustrated with the city's lack of response to protests and faced with growing concerns for her child's health, a Flint resident sent samples of the water to EPA in Washington, DC. The EPA forwarded the samples on to Virginia Tech which found high lead content in the water and reported its finding to EPA. In turn, EPA forwarded the finding to MDEQ, but the agency took no action.

When the testing of the water was finally completed by MDEQ, outliers in the data were omitted which resulted in MDEQ's analysis significantly underestimating the lead in the water. Based on its interpretation of its data, MDEQ reported the water was safe. Public protests continued and a local pediatrician did a study of her patients' blood, which revealed high lead content. Michigan's Department of Health and Human Services finally confirmed the pediatrician's findings at the end of September 2014. The next month, General Motors stopped using the Flint River water at its machinery plants due to concerns about the water's corrosiveness.

*The Decision to Reject and Later Accept DWSD's Offer.* DWSD offered to reconnect Flint to its system but the city's new Emergency Manager, Ambrose, declined the DWSD's offer after consulting with state officials. In March of 2015, EPA reported concentrations of lead in Flint water that was 25 times greater than the limit set by EPA for water that was classified as a hazardous waste. In April of 2015, the EPA regional manager, Miguel Del Toral, expressed concerns about the absence of corrosion controls in Flint's water treatment process, but the Michigan Department of Environmental Quality insisted that additional steps were not needed to mitigate the levels of lead and copper in the water. By October 1, 2015, Genesee County recommended residents use a water filter or bottled water. A week later, the Governor provided $9 million to fund switching the Flint water supply back to DWSD and on October 16th the water supply was reconnected to DWSD.

*Efforts to Adjudicate the Outcomes in Criminal and Civil Courts.* After the DWSD system was reconnected, experts recommended residents not drink the water due to nearly 18 months of exposure to corrosive water. At the end of October 2016, the Governor created an independent task force to review the events leading to the water crisis. (Davis, Kolb, Reynolds, Rothstein & Sikkema, 2016)

The taskforce released a report and placed the blame for the crisis on the MDEQ among a host of others including Michigan's Department of Health and Human Services, the Governor's Office, the Emergency Managers, City of Flint Public Works Department, and the U.S. Environmental Protection Agency. In January of 2016 another state of emergency was declared for Genesee County (which included Flint) and the state's National Guard assisted with water distribution. The ongoing crisis in Flint drew the attention of the Obama Administration, and the U.S. House of Representative's Oversight and Government Reform Committee.

Michigan's Attorney General brought criminal charges against two MDEQ employees and the city's utilities administrator, in April of 2016. In the long run, more than a dozen state and local officials were indicted on charges and prosecutors secured misdemeanor convictions against seven defendants through plea bargaining but the most serious charges were dropped by 2019. In 2021 a new round of indictments was issued for seven officials from the former governor (Snyder), two former Emergency Managers (Early and Ambrose) along with six administrators from the state agencies. It should be noted that none of the earlier criminal indictments resulted in convictions, prison time, or fines.

Meanwhile, in November of 2021, federal judge Judith Levy gave approval to a $626.25 million settlement of civil claims against the state of Michigan and a handful of other parties for the lead poisoning of city residents. (Egan, 2021). The settlement assigned nearly 80% to children (those under the age of 18 in 2014 and 2015 residing in Flint) affected by the lead toxins. The judgment left about $1,000 per adult for some 50,000 people.

Flint's water has been deemed to be safe to drink and 10,000 pipes have been replaced. The residents of Flint still won't drink the water (Robertson 2020); instead, they rely on bottled water. The fallout from the Flint, Michigan, crisis is best summed up by State Senator Ananich,

> I can't tell someone they should trust [the claim that the water is safe], because I don't trust them—and I have more information than most people. Science and logic would tell me that is should be OK, but people have lied to me. (Robertson, D., 2020)

What remains in Flint, Michigan, is the shattering of trust due to the unethical behavior of political officials and administrators.

This case is complex and demonstrates a key component of ethical dilemmas in the public sector, which is the diffusion of decision making spread across multiple agencies over long periods of time. While any number of issues and unethical practices populate this case, this analysis will focus on the decision to deny the external evidence and its impact on the decision by the Emergency Manager to reject DWSD's offer.

## Application of Decision-Making Models

*Using Ethical Models.* Using the three ethical models described earlier, let's review the decisions and activities of the emergency manager who oversaw all government decisions in Flint in April 2015. When reviewing a case study years later, it is important to recognize that the information you have in the present day is not the information held when officials made their decisions.

The information basis will be what was known as of April of 2015: Flint's water is coming from the Flint River; the EPA has reported lead levels 25 times the allowable limit and has concerns about the lack of corrosion controls; and MDEQ insisted that additional steps were not needed to mitigate the levels of lead and copper in the water.

Assume you are the emergency manager: what decisions would you make moving forward at this point? Would you reconnect back to DSWD water or treat the existing Flint River water? What are some areas or stakeholders that have been overlooked? Here is how one might address these considerations:

1. **Break the Issue Down.** What are the known facts? A decision was made a year earlier by the former Emergency Manager to switch the city's water supply source from the DWSD to the Flint River primarily to save money. Community complaints on the water quality, color, and smell have been ongoing. Excessive lead levels have been found in a few homes, but state officials claim the water was safe, but the EPA had questions and concerns.

What was the main question or issue? The 2015 core question was, do we continue using the Flint River or do we go back to using the Detroit system? If the water is safe, as the state officials claim, why are so many residents protesting?

2. *Are There Existing Policies Regarding This Issue?* A federal law, the Lead and Copper Rule, states that municipalities with populations over 50,000 people must treat drinking water for lead contamination. The state of Michigan has an Emergency Management Act that required responsible agents protect the health and safety of residents.

3. *What Is the Agency's History in Dealing With This Situation?* Prior to 1967 the city used the Flint River as its water source. In 1967 the city switched to the DWSD system due to concerns that the Flint's system could not meet the area's water needs. In April 2014 former Emergency Manager, Darnell Earley, made the initial decision to switch Flint water source from DWSD back to the Flint River to save money. MDEQ officials were not familiar with the federal Lead and Copper Rule.

4. *Does the Agency Have a Code of Ethics? What Does It Say About the Proposed Action?* Often codes of ethics or codes of conduct will lay out policies and the reasons for adhering to certain standards of behavior. The State of Michigan Ethics Act was passed in 1973 and included in Michigan's Civil Service Commission. The state's ethics code follows a compliance structure listing prohibited and unethical behaviors for public officers and employees such as soliciting gifts, engaging in business transactions for one's benefit, accepting employment which might conflict with public duties, and so forth. In addition, the law created a State Board of Ethics specifying penalties for violations and the process for hearing and resolving ethical cases.

5. *What Course or Courses of Action Are Available?* In April of 2015, the goal of the Emergency Manager was to ensure the water was safe, and that the water source and delivery complied with federal and

state law. The emergency manager could: (a) cont_nue using Flint River water and continue taking information from the state environmental officials without question, or (b) continue using the Flint River water but with a more diligent review of the safety of the water standards and the testing being conducted, or (c) accept Detroi:'s offer to switch the water source back to DWSD.

**6. *What Are the Consequences of These Actions?*** Residents did not complain about the quality of the water from DWSD. However, going back to that source would be more costly than continuing to use the Flint River. Conducting a more thorough review of water safety would allow the Emergency Manager to have more information to consider other options and address the safety issues.

**7. *On What Basis Could Decisions Be Justified?*** The approaches to arriving at this decision are discussed below.

***Utilitarian Approach.*** From the utilitarian viewpoint, the basis for a decision is to provide the greatest aggregate good with the least amount of harm.

What constituted the aggregate population to be considered? Was the population the residents of Flint, of Genesee County, or the state of Michigan? For the people of Flint, the greatest good was the safest drinking water, which was not what they were receiving. For the state of Michigan, the greatest good was reducing costs, but not at the expense of poisoning the population. Considerations would look first to confirming if the current water source (the Flint River) could be treated to meet the standards of care. Otherwise, the known water source from DWSD would be the next option, even with the increased cost. Continued use of the Flint River water would be the least favored option because as more complaints came in, the safety of the water appeared to be a growing concern.

Limitations of utilitarianism are its assumptions about who constitutes the population to absorb the costs and benefits of public action. Unaddressed in this approach is what protections and rights are held by the minority who may disproportionally bear more of the costs and share in less of the benefits. As a theoretical framework, utilitarianism is appealing in part because it appears nonjudgmental and objective. In practice, utilitarianism may be fraught with the same subjectivity as other models.

***Duty Approach.*** From the duty perspective, the basis for acting would be recognizing one's inherent obligation. But should the action be based on duty to the job and the ways to be technically compliant, or to the state's executive management, or to the citizens? Again, duty to safety of human life was more important than financial savings or to technical compliance, which in this case were different. Could the existing path of using the Flint River be considered safe? While prior responses from state officials said "yes," demonstrable evidence suggested otherwise. The next question would be whether using the Flint River water and treating it correctly would produce safe, clean drinking water at the same level or better than the Detroit water. If that was not or could not be discerned, then the decision to switch back to DWSD would be the best choice.

**Virtue Ethics Approach.** From the virtue point of view, the basis for taking a particular action would be centered on what the right action was.

In virtue ethics, the goal is to understand what the *golden mean* would be that would neither be too aggressive nor insufficient. Essentially, three options would be considered to discern the best course of action.

a. The *minimalist* approach would be to do nothing and continue with the current water source of the Flint River, and not question any of the information provided by the state officials at MDEQ or Health and Human Services or by the people who continued to protest the quality of the water. This, however, conveys a lack of courage and integrity. To have citizens in dire circumstances and to do nothing, is callous and inhumane.

b. The *aggressive or rash* approach would be change course without consideration of the reasons the water supply was problematic. This could either mean starting to treat the Flint River water for corrosion control or switching back to the Detroit water system without understanding the costs and benefits of doing so. Either choice may be right, but without sufficient understanding, it may add to more delays to obtaining safe water.

c. The *golden mean* would be to find the optimum ground where the manager is taking the right steps at the right time for the right reason. Determining if the water was actually safe would be a first step. Included in this step is understanding why the state officials keep saying the water was safe when residents along with other stakeholders (area pediatricians, the VA Tech researcher) said the opposite. The final step is to determine what could be done faster and more efficiently: treat the existing water source; switch to the Detroit system; or something else (e.g., replace all of the existing lead pipes). Using this approach, one is able to address the safety of the issue and the efficaciousness as well.

## CONCLUSION

Ethical behavior is essential to a democratic republic because it fosters trust between the government and the public. Without trust the public's willingness to cooperate with and participate in its own governance is compromised, and self-government (liberty) is lost. Consequently, over the more than 200 years of the Republic ethical standards have been developed at the federal, state, and local levels. As a rule, ethics codes, guidelines, and legislation focus on two issues: the objectivity/transparency of decision makers and protecting public funds and resources. Organizations need to develop ethical standards and implement these standards through the wide distribution of information, training, discussions, hotlines, and other means. Such imbedded ethical standards and systems for implementation promote an environment that enables issues to be addressed internally by managers and staff.

Ethical issues arise out of conflicts in values, priorities, and personal relationships. In these cases, standards alone may not provide sufficient guidance to someone facing an ethical dilemma. While there are many approaches to reaching an ethical decision, this chapter has focused on utilitarianism, virtue, and duty. Each approach suggests questions to be raised rather than specific answers to be drawn. This is the challenge and opportunity for all public administrators.

## PRACTICING PUBLIC ADMINISTRATION

Read the following case studies and respond to the questions below.

### CASE 1: PROGRAM AUDITOR'S DILEMMA

Joe works in the Program Audit Department monitoring service delivery options for all transportation programs in the city. He has been working long hours because the city is under considerable pressure to bring costs down. For months he has been working on one report that indicates there has been some improvement in one area where services have been contracted out. However, no improvement has been noted in other areas, and costs rose significantly for one department. He released the report to the city council but not to the media. Last evening, he attended the city council's open meeting where a councilmember quoted sections of his report as evidence the city was getting costs in line with projected revenues. The information provided was accurate, but the overall representation of the data and report led to significant misrepresentation of the facts. Joe is the senior auditor for the Program Audit Department. He is mystified by the councilmember's actions and concerned about the long-term consequences of this misinformation. You are Joe's supervisor and among one of the highest civil servants in the city.

1. What is Joe's ethical responsibility?

2. What should he do?

3. Now that you (his supervisor) are aware of the situation, do you have an ethical responsibility?

4. What, if anything, should you do?

### CASE 2: ALCOHOL BOARD INSPECTOR

An inspector named Maria at the state's regional Alcohol and Beverage Control Board is a volunteer at a local animal rescue league that holds a gala, among other events, to raise money for animal protection, adoption, and medical care. The annual gala is a widely recognized and well-attended community event.

Maria decides to consolidate her efforts by personally dropping off invitations to the gala to the businesses in her district and asking them to make contributions by placing ads in the event program. She is enthusiastic and upbeat about the upcoming gala but is also very knowledgeable about the businesses she covers since she has been the primary inspector for the past five years. You accompany her on a couple of last-minute calls to area businesses. While business owners are cordial, you are uneasy about her being both the area inspector and the event planner at the same time.

1. Is there an ethical concern here? If so, what is it?

2. Under what circumstances should she be an advocate for the rescue league, and under what circumstances is it not appropriate?

3. As a business owner in the district, what might be some of your concerns regarding a donation to the rescue league collected by the area's inspector?

---

## CASE 3: INTERIOR DEPARTMENT

You work for a small division at the Department of the Interior that leases public land for the extraction of natural gas and oil drilling for public and private uses. As the contract evaluator, you have uncovered documentation of improper contract awards and negotiation procedures with two companies whose 15-year lease agreements with the department are now up for renewal. At the same time, you inadvertently receive an email indicating that both these companies have been providing lavish gifts, all-expenses-paid weekend getaways, recreational drugs, and occasional sexual services to officials in your department. While chatting with an area supervisor, your concerns are validated when you are told that several employees have taken advantage of these "extra services." Indeed, such activities appear to be part of the organization's culture. At a department debriefing later that day, you discover the department has just won an ethics award for its employee ethics guide and is to be honored at a congressional function in the coming week. The lease agreements for the two companies are now on your desk and are scheduled to be finalized in two days.

1. What are your options?

2. What do you do, and whom do you involve?

3. If you decide to act, when do you take action?

4. How do different ethical perspectives inform your decision?

# BIBLIOGRAPHY

Adams, G. (2004). *Unmasking administrative evil.* Armonk, NY: M. E. Sharpe.

Appleby, P. (1952). *Morality and administration in democratic government.* Baton Rouge, LA: Louisiana State University Press.

Ban, C. (1995). *How do public managers manage? Bureaucratic constraints, organizational culture and potential for reform.* San Francisco, CA: Jossey-Bass.

Blake, R., Grob, J., Potenski, D., Reed, P., & Walsh, P. (1998). Nature and scope of state government ethics codes. *Public Productivity and Management Review, 21*(4), 453–459.

Bowman, J. S., & West, J. P. (2015). *Public Service Ethics: Individual and Institutional Responsibilities.* (1st ed.). Northridge, CA: CQ Press an imprint of SAGE Publications.

Bruce, W. (1992). Rejoinder to Terry Cooper's responses to the review of the responsible administrator: An approach to ethics for the administrative role. *Public Administrative Review, 52*(3), 313–314.

Circle of Blue. (n.d.). Flint Water Crisis. Circle of Blue web site at https://www.circleofblue.org/flint/?gclid=EAIaIQobChMIvKz7z-Xw9AIVYhpMCh3AZ-gyNEAAYAiAAEgIQ9PD_BwE, accessed 12/22/21.

Cooper, T. (1998). *The responsible administrator: An approach to ethics for the administrative role.* San Francisco, CA: Jossey-Bass.

Cooper, T., & Wright, D., Eds. (1992). *Exemplary public administrators: Character and leadership in government.* San Francisco, CA: Jossey-Bass.

D'Angelo, C. (2018, July 23). Scandal Pile Up for Interior Chief Ryan Zinke. *The Huffington Post* at https://www.huffpost.com/entry/ryan-zinke-growing-scandals_n_5b5496f2e4b0fd5c73c65990 accessed December 2021.

Davis, M. D., Kolb, C., Reynolds, L., Rothstein, E., & Sikkema, K. (2016). Flint Water Advisory Task Force Report, Flint Water Advisory Task Force (FWATF). http://flintwaterstudy.org/wp-content/uploads/2016/03/Flint-task-force-report_2438442_ver1.0.pdf, accessed December 2021.

Egan, P. (2021, Nov 10) Federal judge gives final approval to $626.25M settlement in Flint water crisis. *Detroit Free Press.* https://www.freep.com/story/news/local/michigan/flint-water-crisis/2021/11/10/federal-judge-approves-settlement-flint-lead-poisoning-case/5556131001/, accessed 12/22/21.

Frederickson, H., Ed. (1993). *Ethics and public administration.* Armonk, NY: M. E. Sharpe.

Garofalo, C. (1999). *Ethics in the public service: The moral mind at work.* Washington, DC: Georgetown University Press.

———. (2006). *Common ground, common future: Moral agency in public administration, professions and citizenship.* Boca Raton, FL: Taylor and Francis.

Garofalo, C., & Geuras, D. (1994). Ethics education and training in the public sector. *American Review of Public Administration, 24*(3), 283–297.

Global Business Ethics Survey. (2021). *The state of ethics and compliance in the workplace: A look at global trends.* Vienna, VA: Ethics and Compliance Initiative.

Harmon, M. (1995). *Responsibility as paradox: A critique of rational discourse on governance.* Thousand Oaks, CA: Sage.

Huddleson, M., & Sands, J. C. (1995). Enforcing administrative ethics. *Annals of the American Academy of Political and Social Science, 537*, 139–149.

Kidder, R. M. (1995). *How good people make tough choices.* New York, NY: Fireside.

———. (2006). *Moral courage.* New York, NY: HarperCollins.

Lewis, C. (1991). *The ethics challenge in public service: A problem-solving guide.* San Francisco, CA: Jossey-Bass.

Martin, H. (2004). Supervisor's achievements a counterweight to plea deal. *Los Angeles Times,* January 2, 2004. https://www.latimes.com/archives/la-xpm-2004-jan-02-me-eaves2-story.html

Menzel, D. (1997). Teaching ethics and values in public administration: Are we making a difference? *Public Administration Review, 57*(3), 224–230.

Plant, J. (1983). Debate on ethics. *Public Administrative Review, 43*(6), 576.

Robertson, D. (2020, Dec 23). Flint has clean water now. Why won't people drink it? *Politico.* https://www.politico.com/news/magazine/2020/12/23/flint-water-crisis-2020-post-coronavirus-america-445459), accessed 12/22/21.

Sampford, C., Ed. (1998). *Public sector ethics: Finding and implementing values.* Alexandria, New South Wales, Australia: Federation Press.

State of Michigan Ethics Act (1973). Standards of Conduct for Public Officers and Employees. Michigan Civil Service Commission at https://www.michigan.gov/mdcs/0,4614,7-147-6881_13592-26139--,00.html, accessed December 2021.

Thompson, D. (1992). Paradoxes of government ethics. *Public Administrative Review, 52*(3), 254–259.

Zajac, G., & Comfort, L. (1997). The spirit of watchfulness: Public ethics as organizational learning. *Journal of Public Administration Research and Theory 7*(4), 541–569.

# 5

# Informing and
# Involving the Public

In tough times the Jacksonville, Florida, Sheriff's Office is seeking to connect with residents and potential police recruits using MySpace, Facebook, and Craigslist. As of the writing of this book, the city has not reached out using Twitter. Throughout the nation, local governments are trying to connect with residents, suppliers, and potential employees with a full menu of social media—Facebook, Twitter, Instagram, TikTok, etc.

Public participation is a cornerstone of democracy and representative government. At the local government level, this has meant many things—conducting meetings in public, distributing reports, and appointing citizens to advisory or policy boards, to name just a few. This chapter looks at the variety of methods for involving and informing the public.

Governments use many of the same mechanisms for informing the public that are used by for-profit companies and other sectors of the economy. They may organize campaigns that use printed and electronic media to inform citizens about their organizations and programs. They may develop sophisticated public relations programs to help ensure that citizens see their organizations and programs in a positive light. They attempt to influence behaviors, beliefs, and values through educational campaigns encouraging citizens to stop smoking, get flu shots, recycle, and so forth.

Involving the public has many meanings in governments. Citizens own the government and act as shareholders. They pay government employees' salaries and use government services. As customers and shareholders, they expect to participate in government decisions. They vote for candidates for elected office; they approve or disapprove issuance of new bonds to finance capital programs or initiatives and referenda that may add new programs or change policies or programs. They may serve on boards or commissions. Citizens may have high levels of interest in government in general or be interested in particular issues and may come regularly to meetings of a legislative body to talk about the issues. They may have websites that examine government policies and actions and advocate for particular points of view. Regardless of citizens' participation in government, government owes them information about how it is managing the citizens' money and affecting their lives.

Traditionally public participation has focused on petitioning the legislature, running for public office, and being informed of public policies and programs on a regular basis by reading budget messages, executive statements about the state of the city, city clerks' minutes of council meetings, and so forth. These are one-way communications from the agency or government to the citizen. Public participation in the current context means a broader incorporation of citizens in policy and program development, implementation, and assessment wherein some citizens are interacting with decision makers and staff in a systematic manner over many months and/or years.

Like private companies and other sectors, governments have used a variety of media to inform and involve the public; and for all organizations, media have changed significantly over the past few decades. Governments have traditionally used newspapers, radio, and television to publicize meetings and events, explain policies and procedures, and get out the vote or otherwise seek support and provide information. In the 1970s and 1980s, governments started using cable television to broadcast public meetings and other original programming to explain issues and new initiatives. More recently, governments have developed and used their own websites to distribute budgets and other documents and broadcast meetings. The internet is used to allow citizens to do business with government agencies to pay taxes, request services, and so forth. The successful presidential campaign of Barack Obama marked a turning point in the use of new media such as websites, Facebook, and other social media to get both financial and campaigning support.

The key advantages of public participation are the following:

- Public participation is critical to a democratic society and has long been a cornerstone of civil society in America. Alexis de Tocqueville applauded the ability of Americans to form associations of all sorts to promote public safety, commerce, industry, and so forth, and to serve as a guarantee against the tyranny of the majority.

- It recognizes that public administrators are not apolitical or disinterested participants in the policy process but are an interest group that needs the understanding and cooperation of the public.

- Public participation can bring a more balanced approach to policy and program efforts. It can improve programs by providing input from the target customers of a particular program about how the program is achieving its goals. In this way, it can influence public decisions.
- Public participation can build support for public services and programs in difficult fiscal periods.

Participation, however, has some distinct disadvantages as well, including the following:

- Participation is not representative of a cross section of the public but tends to be populated with persons who are better educated and command higher incomes. The poor, disadvantaged, or ill-educated may not be well represented in this effort.
- Attempts by governments to reward participation of underrepresented groups have sometimes led to the advancement by some of their own self-interests rather than those of the larger community.
- Pluralism, or the inclusion of various interest group concerns, is not necessarily the equivalent of the public interest. While it is important to solicit and encourage public comment, it is one of many resources for understanding the public's perceptions and the public interest. Opinion alone might not be very useful to administrators attempting to design or revamp a program.
- Participation efforts are time consuming for managers and can be emotionally draining.
- There are costs to public involvement; the more extensive the involvement, the greater are the costs.
- Initiatives and procedures recommended by experts may not be understood and consequently may be opposed through citizen participation efforts, thus delaying or derailing innovations and/or needed changes.

One hears calls for increased transparency in government. What is transparency? In practical terms, it means making the inner workings of an organization visible to the public: making staff reports, forms, and instructions clear and easy to read and available; explaining the basis for decisions; holding community meetings at convenient times and places; listening to citizens who speak before the governing board; appointing commissioners who represent different segments of the community; and helping the public navigate the bureaucracy by making forms and instructions clear.

Public information officers help managers work toward transparency by ensuring that the government's policies and actions are explained. They often have the responsibility of securing citizen involvement by going to meetings, writing and analyzing surveys, running government websites, keeping lines of communication open to ensure transparency, and so forth.

This chapter looks at citizen education and involvement at two levels: (1) informing the public and (2) involving the public.

## INFORMING THE PUBLIC

Governments have long used methods such as distributing reports to the public, working with the media, and designing and producing educational campaigns to inform the public.

### Reports to the Public

Governments regularly prepare and distribute a variety of reports to the public. These include:

- budgets and budget summaries,
- annual financial and performance reports, and
- reports about special projects and programs.

In the past, and even today, governments distributed these directly to the public on request or make them available in public libraries. Shorter reports, such as budget summaries, might be included as supplements in local newspapers.

A new community reports initiative is part of the long history of good-government movements. The Association of Government Accountants' Citizen-Centric Government Reporting initiative advocates issuing standardized reports by governments and public organizations to allow citizens to easily compare performance and financial status. Many governmental units have begun to issue "public budgets," condensed summaries for easy access by the public.

### Media Relations

Governments at all levels deal constantly with the media, including television, radio, newspapers, and the internet. Media help make government transparent and accountable to citizens by asking questions and acting as citizens' representatives. Media also help governments send messages to citizens about new policies and laws, emergencies, and other matters.

Senior managers and elected officials deal most frequently with the media, but government employees at all levels need to know some basics:

- Know the employer's policies and procedures for dealing with the media. Usually one point of contact—often the public relations or public information director or the highest ranking official, such as the city manager—is designated. No other employee answers questions or provides information to a media representative unless directed to by this point of contact.

- If the employer has a public relations or public information manager, ask for training if one is likely to come into contact with the media.
- If the office has no public relations or public information manager, ask others in the government how the local media work. Which reporters handle the political jurisdiction's beat, what are the deadlines, how are press releases and media advisories distributed?
- In interviews or press conferences, know the facts, prepare a statement, practice answering questions, be truthful, and offer to provide additional information later if necessary.
- In responding to telephone inquiries from the media, stick to the information requested. Be cautious of tenacious reporters who attempt to confirm rumors or get an opinion on an issue. When in any doubt, refer the inquiry to the appropriate spokesperson.

Professional associations, both national and their local chapters, often have workshops and conference sessions regarding dealing with the media.

## Community Education Campaigns

Governments use marketing techniques to "sell" policies and ideas to the public. A big success in community education is recycling. With relatively little use of monetary penalties, many local governments have sold their residents on the need to recycle items to reduce using landfills.

Here are some typical steps in developing a community education campaign:

- Understand the product, service, or regulation. What are its features? Why is it important?
- Understand the customers. Different residents and businesses may have different perspectives. There may be different ways to reach them. They may also use different terms to refer to the same products or services; it is important to use language that the customers will understand.
- Develop a message, and test it with a sample of customers. Do they understand?
- Use the message consistently in a variety of media. This might include ads on television, radio, and the internet; posters at government and other facilities; brochures; and so forth.
- Track responses to the marketing effort. Is it working? Does it meet goals set for the project?

**Box 5.1  Freedom of Information Requests**

When members of the public are not satisfied that they are receiving adequate information, they may make demands under Freedom of Information Act (FOIA) statutes. The federal government as well as each state has its own FOIA laws that generally provide that any person has a right, which is enforceable in court, to have access to government records. Such requests can be made by private individuals, the press, labor organizations, and attorneys seeking to supplement information they have received from government. For example, freedom of information requests are made for some payroll information regarding individual employees (previously considered confidential as private personnel data), for information on citizen complaints against an agency, and for surveys or reports that governments may not have made public. There are some categories of information that are exempt from public exposure, such as classified information for national security or trade secrets; each state's statute and the federal statute lists the specific exemptions.

## Technology and E-government

Since the late 1990s, having websites has been essential for governments as a way to provide information to residents and others. At first, governments used the internet as an adjunct to posting agendas and minutes on public bulletin boards. Later, governments posted budgets, reports, and other types of information. Now government sites advertise recreation classes and take enrollments; allow residents and businesses to pay parking tickets, utility bills, and other fees; allow tracking of the status of building and other permits; and, for businesses, show the status of invoices submitted for payment for services rendered to the government. Some government officials have even created their own websites and applications (apps) or use Twitter to communicate semi-official information. Use of Twitter and other technology by individuals within government raises issues about whether the content supports overall goals or represents the official position of the governmental unit.

The advantages of existing and emerging technology offer special opportunities to government. Technology has made communication faster and more convenient, affordable, customized, and interactive than ever before. For example, a hard copy of tax codes once was available only by securing pounds of books that took days to reach a user by mail. Today, codes are published on the internet, available at any time, and have search functions and/or designated portals to guide users to needed information. New software tools enable even those with limited technical skills to post videos, photos, and blogs. Citizens may not only follow the public agenda via the internet but can also participate by providing testimony, documentation, and visual evidence to decision makers and neighbors about a policy or program. Internet participation is facilitated by cell phone and smartphone technology and software that enables users to access resources anywhere.

The drive for open and unfettered access has prompted cities such as Riverside, California, to offer free wireless access to citizens throughout the city. This public policy removes a major obstacle to e-government: the cost of access. Sleeker, lighter, and less costly personal computers have reduced citizens' capital costs as well. The computer is almost as pervasive in American households as the television. Websites provide users with access to a broad range of information sources and now even reach out and contact users with specialized information at the user's request. For example, government job banks not only allow job seekers to post resumes but also alert them to new job postings by employers and enable them to customize a resume to respond to the specific needs of interested employers.

Open data initiatives in many cities attempt to make relevant city and other data available to the general public and researchers. The data can be raw data available for analysis and data visualization. Many local governments are also providing dashboards (visual presentations of data that focus on key indicators, much like a car's dashboard) using their own and regional data to explain budgets, demographic changes, and other issues.

Governments at all levels will need to find new ways to reach the public to both disseminate information as well as foster public input and participation through blogs and other interactive means.

## INVOLVING THE PUBLIC

Traditionally citizens have participated in government in a number of ways, as civic-minded residents and as residents especially concerned about specific actions of a governmental body. They have run for office and voted for candidates, initiatives, charter changes, and bond measures. They have attended meetings of city councils, boards, commissions, and other bodies. They have served on boards and commissions themselves. As the baby boomers age, it is likely that the growing ranks of retirees will be even more interested in participating in government than their parents were. As technology facilitates interaction with government, it is also likely that non-retirees will participate more in government.

An organization can effectively ascertain community input through a robust community relations program that helps identify key community issues that may affect the organization as well as key community leaders who can help open up a two-way dialogue between the community and the organization. It is important to have an ongoing relationship with the community to help build a reservoir of goodwill and trust. Government agencies cannot tap into that reservoir only when they need something from the community; it has to be an ongoing relationship and presence in the community regardless of what benefits the agencies may reap at a particular time. While the organization will not have agreement with the community 100% of the time, the relationship and dialogue will allow information to be shared and policy makers to make informed decisions.

It is important to see community relations as something that can be built over time. Ongoing programs, such as those outlined in the case study later in the chapter, advertise the organization's name in the community and develop relationships with community members and groups.

## Holding Office and Sponsoring Initiatives

One of the oldest forms of citizen participation is running for elective office. Candidates begin the process by completing a candidacy form, seeking signatures from other registered voters to qualify for the ballot, and then campaigning for office.

Citizens also participate by sponsoring initiatives for such things as new taxes, repeal of existing taxes, changes in policies, etc. Initiatives typically are the result of the efforts of interested groups that collect signatures of registered voters.

Although term limits for executive positions have their roots in the beginning of the Republic, the 1990s brought significant increases in term limit legislation at the state and local levels. While the initial focus was on shaking up entrenched politicians, proponents argued that it brought fresh faces needed to provide more accountability and keep government free from corruption. Opponents have argued that term limits result in a more powerful non-elected bureaucracy and discourage elected officials from thinking about the long-term implications of their actions. In the context of this chapter, they result in greater influence by special interest groups.

## Serving on Boards and Commissions

Why appoint citizens to commissions, task forces, and other public boards? Citizen commissions, as permanent bodies, help city councils and county boards oversee departments or functional areas, set general policies and priorities, monitor implementation, and hold managers accountable. Members of these commissions may also have special expertise that is valuable in overseeing particular departments or public interests.

The policy maker should address core issues and ask the following questions when thinking about how to involve citizens:

- Developing a context and rationale for the citizen group: Why does the group exist? What value is added by input—public participation, policy discussion, recommendations, advice?

Is there an arena for participation that makes a substantive difference? How is participation related to value added? What can be shared with the public in terms of responsibility and how?

- Recruiting participants: Are there organized groups or citizens who have expressed an interest? How can less organized members of the public be included? Can current members of groups or boards assist in recruiting others?

- Identifying roles: Should the participants serve as sources of information (key contacts, citizen-initiated efforts, new technologies) about government efforts? Should they take part in surveys, fill out customer response cards, or participate in open meetings or advisory committees?

There are a number of ways for managers to work with citizen boards or commissions:

- Encourage recruitment of citizens who will take active roles on the board and who represent the department's constituents. Board appointments may be used as rewards for campaign contributors or more ideally as a way to expand citizen participation. One way to expand participation is to educate citizens about the activities of government and its boards. Long Beach, California, for example, has sponsored a citizens' academy with the local chamber of commerce. In a number of sessions, participants meet elected officials and department heads and find out how the government works and what challenges it faces. Another way is simply to open up the appointment process by advertising openings on boards on the internet and in local newspapers and creating a screening and appointment process. Skilled community relations staffers employed by the government or organization can monitor community groups and their leaders to keep track of who the effective community opinion leaders are.

- Educate new and current board members. To give members a common footing for evaluating items that may come before the board, citizen participants will need an initial orientation or briefing and written reference materials explaining how the department and/or board operates. Likewise, reports with sufficient background information provide a context for future items and decisions. Board members also are typically advised of conflict-of-interest laws.

- Have a clear charter for the board. Most boards are organized to provide policy direction, general oversight, and community input to departments. Some boards go beyond this to attempt to micromanage departments. One reason this happens is that it is easier to focus on how much is spent on travel or furniture, for example, than on tackling abstract issues. Besides making clear the board's role in a charter or an ordinance, providing background information about the task at hand—policy direction—can help the board.

- Encourage the board to form committees. Large boards, like any large organizations, sometimes suffer from inertia. It is usually easier to work with smaller groups. Committees focusing on topics such as finance, audit, and operations can help the board fulfill its mission.

- Encourage participation by all board members. Sometimes boards are dominated by the board chairperson or just by the most vocal or politically connected member. Some ways to handle this are to encourage all members to participate on committees, as described above, and to encourage everyone to request that items of special interest be placed on the board's agenda.

- Make sure everyone understands the applicable open meetings acts. Many states have laws that require public meetings to be open. This usually means posting agendas publicly 72 hours or so before the meeting, not considering items that are not listed on the agenda (except for emergencies that arise after the agenda is posted), and allowing the public the right to speak on any matter before the governing body or within its jurisdiction at every meeting. It is important that managers and legal counsel understand these rules and ensure that all citizens participating on boards and commissions understand them.

### Box 5.2 Open Meetings

Several states in the United States mandate that government meetings be open to the public, one of the most basic methods of informing and involving the public. Open meetings acts have objectives such as the following:

- "Public bodies exist to aid in the conduct of the public's business and . . . the people have a right to be informed as to the conduct of their business" (Illinois).
- Open meetings serve "to encourage and facilitate an informed citizenry's understanding of the governmental process and governmental problems" (Oklahoma).
- "The people of this state do not yield their sovereignty to the agencies which serve them. The people in delegating authority do not give their public servants the right to decide what is good for the people to know and what is not good for them to know. The people insist on remaining informed so that they may retain control over the instruments they have created" (California).

Most open meetings acts require that governments take a variety of steps to inform the public of their meetings. These include posting agendas for specific minimum periods of time (e.g., 72 hours) in advance of meetings and in public places.

Traditionally agendas were posted on paper outside of city halls or other meeting places, and that practice continues. Agendas are also posted on websites and may be mailed to interested parties. A council or commission cannot take action on any item that is not on the posted agenda unless an emergency comes up after the posting of the agenda. Attorneys may need to approve criteria for emergencies. Members of the public must be allowed to speak on each agenda item before the body can take any action, such as a vote. Members of the public are also generally allowed to speak to the council or commission on any topic that comes under the purview of that body; although the council or commission usually cannot take any immediate action if that topic is not on the agenda.

There are several exceptions to open meetings laws. For example, personnel matters, negotiations of labor contracts, real estate negotiations, and pending litigation are discussed in closed sessions with the actions reported in general terms in the open meeting. The general subjects of possible closed-session agenda items are announced on the published agenda and at the meeting.

Open meetings laws also place limits on what can be discussed by the council or commission members outside of regular meetings. They prohibit nonpublic meetings that include a quorum of an elected legislative body or commission. They also prohibit "serial meetings" among elected officials sequentially to poll them or discuss a topic. Serial meetings can involve any type of communication among the officials that are not during the publicly noticed meeting, including email, phone calls, letters, or face-to-face discussions.

Other types of committees are advisory in nature. They may be established by councils and commissions as temporary (ad hoc) committees to advise the larger body on specific issues. Advisory committees usually do not have the same powers as councils; they do not, for example, approve budgets or award contracts.

## Volunteering

Governments have successfully used volunteers to supplement government services for many years in particular functions—in schools, parks, zoos, animal shelters, hospitals, libraries, and police and fire departments. In some cases they fill gaps in services when there are cutbacks, but in all cases they provide a network of communication and support that keeps the community involved. Programs such as neighborhood watch work closely with police departments and act as additional eyes and ears in crime prevention. Homeowner/business groups that plant trees to beautify neighborhoods are other examples of volunteers working closely with government agencies.

## Serving on Oversight Committees

Increasingly, members of the public are being included in the workings of government as members of either oversight committees convened on an ad hoc basis or institutionalized committees. These committees may be seen in a variety of fields from oversight of major bond-funded construction programs to education. The following example illustrates how one of these oversight committees was implemented.

### Box 5.3  Masters in Public Administration Advisory Council

To comply with the National Association of Schools of Public Affairs and Administration accreditation requirements, the Masters in Public Administration (MPA) program at California State Polytechnic University, Pomona, formed an oversight council, the Masters in Public Administration Advisory Council (or MiPAAC).

MiPAAC met for the first time in October 2005. It has several functions. It reviews final papers from students and determines if their work meets professional standards. It assesses the program requirements and provides expertise about public and nonprofit training needs, including classes for the curriculum and skills to be developed. Its members also help present classes, such as budgeting, technology, and strategic planning, to MPA students. The members can communicate information about the program to members of the community and provide referrals for internships and career positions.

There are currently about 10 active members. The members represent state, regional, federal, and local governments; nonprofits; academia (regular and adjunct faculty who teach in the program); and MPA program alumni. There are no set terms for the MiPAAC members but it is assumed that most will serve for four to five years. The council has a brief charter that outlines its purpose, membership policy, contributions, organization, committees, and meetings. Besides attending the twice-yearly meetings, members make presentations to classes, work with students and alumni, and occasionally speak on behalf of the MPA program to colleagues and other professionals.

MiPAAC is rated as generally very useful by the MPA program manager. It may be underutilized due to time and funding. The biggest problem is finding a time and location that is convenient for everyone to meet. The MPA program manager would like the students to have more contact with the members through informal communication and formal mentoring programs.

## Serving on Neighborhood Councils in Los Angeles

The next step in involving the public is to institutionalize citizen participation by giving citizens meaningful roles in government beyond those discussed above. The City of Los Angeles's neighborhood councils provides a good example.

For years, citizens of Los Angeles debated ways of enhancing citizen participation in a city with a growing population and expansive geographic boundaries. Even as a charter city with a total of 15 elected councilmembers, there were perceived issues dealing with representativeness and responsiveness. By 1999 momentum had grown to actually do something, in large part to counteract several secession movements. The alternatives included increasing the number of elected councilmembers, creating a borough system (similar to that of New York City), and splitting the city into several smaller municipalities.

Ultimately, the issue of representation was addressed when the charter of the city was amended to create neighborhood councils in 1999. Voters rejected the secession proposal that was on the same ballot and approved the creation of a new city department specifically to develop the details of the neighborhood council program. The goal was to create neighborhood councils throughout the city that would give citizens increased opportunities to participate and encourage government responsiveness to local needs. The vision was to have small neighborhood councils composed of representatives of the diverse interests in communities who would have an advisory role on issues of concern to the neighborhoods. As of 2021, a total of 99 neighborhood councils serve the city population.

Regulations establish the procedure and criteria for recognition and certification of neighborhood councils. At a minimum the bylaws of a neighborhood council must include the method by which its officers are chosen, a representation that it will reflect the diverse interests within its area, assurance that it will communicate with stakeholders on a regular basis, assurance that there will be a system for financial accountability of its funds, and guarantees that all meetings will be open and public. Stakeholders generally include residents, business owners and employees, and representatives of churches and nonprofit organizations. So, unlike city councils and most types of commissions, nonresidents can serve on these neighborhood councils, as stipulated by the charter of each neighborhood council.

The neighborhood councils may only advise the city council; they have no direct authority to make decisions. They have discretion over the kinds of issues they want to address. They may advise the city about broad policy issues, providing input about such things as budget priorities, planning, and land use matters, or they may tackle smaller issues in their neighborhoods such as crime activity or traffic congestion and mitigation measures.

The charter also allows the city council to delegate its authority to neighborhood councils to hold public hearings prior to the city council's making a decision on a matter of local concern, although the city council has so far been reluctant to actually delegate this authority. In addition, each neighborhood council may present to the mayor and council an annual list of priorities for the city budget. The charter makes neighborhood councils responsible for monitoring the delivery of city services in their respective areas and for periodically meeting with responsible officials of city departments.

By charter, the city has a responsibility to provide early notification to neighborhood councils about matters of interest. This process has not been fully defined, but to date it includes sending minutes, agendas, and committee referrals regarding city council business to the neighborhood councils and providing early notice about matters of city department interest such as a proposed change in a land use or zoning law.

The charter also requires that procedures be established for receiving input from neighborhood councils prior to decisions by the city council, city council committees, and boards and commissions. City agendas now routinely note when a neighborhood council has submitted comments about an item. Neighborhood councilmembers can also submit community impact statements for items of concern on the city council's agenda, and those statements are formally included in the deliberative process.

Because of new requirements to allow neighborhood councils' input into decision making, neighborhood councils have the potential of adding another layer of bureaucracy without making government more effective. On the other hand, if notified early enough in the policy-making/decision-making process, neighborhood councils can expedite decision making by providing necessary community support for new programs or policy changes.

Approximately a year into the program the councils gained additional resources when the city council agreed to provide funding to each certified neighborhood council on an annual basis (initially $50,000 in total, the figure as of 2021 is about $32,000 per neighborhood council). The purposes of these funds were to (1) facilitate outreach (newsletters, blogs, etc.); (2) provide administrative support for neighborhood council meetings (mailings, clerical support, meeting space costs, computers, meeting refreshments, etc.); and (3) fund community improvements such as fixing curbs or purchasing radar guns for the local police.

A 2007 review of neighborhood councils by the city had some key findings and recommendations. Almost half of all households surveyed had either participated in or were aware of neighborhood councils, giving them a strong base. Neighborhood councils had already played a significant role in rolling back an increase of water rates and in building a coalition for a proposed development in one suburb. However, the relationship between city hall and the neighborhood councils needed to be redefined with clear missions and divisions of work. Neighborhood councils needed more help from the city on outreach and on running elections for members.

Although not part of the formal assessment, an underlying lesson is that the city council and departments are not necessarily comfortable sharing decision making with the public and providing necessary resources.

The neighborhood councils provide input on a variety of programs and policies that may influence efforts in numerous city departments over time. The case study below explores how a proprietary agency uses many means to inform and include the public about issues, programs, and policies unique to its operations.

## A COMPREHENSIVE CASE STUDY—INFORMING AND INVOLVING THE PUBLIC AT AIRPORTS

Airports are typically run by cities, counties, or public authorities. They serve several major publics or stakeholders, all of whom have different interests. A major stakeholder is travelers. They want to know how to use the airport—which airlines are located in which terminals, which amenities are available in the terminals (food, gifts, ATMs, spas, special lounges, etc.), which means of transportation to use to get to the airport, and where to park. To meet these needs, airports provide brochures and websites and applications describing services, interactive information about airline schedules and parking, and signage for airport users as they approach and enter the airport.

Airlines and other companies that use airports represent another stakeholder. Companies in this category include concessionaires in terminals, catering and service companies that work with airlines, cargo carriers and similar companies. Airlines in particular need good facilities, either built directly by the airport operator or built by the airlines with assistance of the operator. They want facilities that are modern and convenient places to serve their passengers. Airport operators solicit the opinions of airlines and their service companies by organizing advisory groups and working with the airline officials directly or through representatives.

Travel professionals—agents and tourist boards that serve leisure and business travelers—want much of the same information as travelers do about airport services. Travel professionals also want airport participation in tourist and business promotions and signage and amenities for special events such as conventions. To serve this public, airports provide websites and printed materials, and airport staff may organize exhibits at conferences and conventions to promote use of the airport. Airports usually attempt to learn about the needs of these groups by conducting surveys of passengers and travel professionals and participating in conferences.

Another group of stakeholders is the airport's neighbors, both residents and businesses. Residents' main concern is often the noise produced by an airport. To meet residents' needs, airports often provide noise complaint hotlines and websites with information about flights so residents can report which planes are loud, off course, or otherwise noisy. Airports also often organize local groups to discuss noise issues and propose solutions to regulatory bodies such as the Federal Aviation Administration; working with groups of this type also helps airport managers know what local opinions are. Airports also provide speakers to local groups to explain how the airport operates and how it is attempting to control noise. Many airports also manage programs to insulate heavily noise-impacted homes and businesses or purchase them outright and demolish them.

Neighboring businesses, both those adjoining the airport and those in the region, are another stakeholder. These businesses are often very interested in working with the airport on construction projects and selling the airport goods and services. To reach these stakeholders, airports might conduct periodic meetings to explain the airport's contracting policies and procedures, publicize business opportunities in local media, and provide expert speakers.

Another key stakeholder group is local policy makers. Policy makers from the city, county, or airport authority sponsor individuals to serve on boards charged with governing or advising the airport management. The individuals on the board may represent local interest groups such as unions and businesspeople, and some may be local residents in areas affected by the airport. Governing boards are usually responsible for awarding contracts, approving budgets, and hiring and reviewing the airport manager. Advisory boards review management actions and provide more general advice to both management and the sponsor. Airport management obviously works closely with these boards, providing information, documents, tours, and so forth.

Local policy makers who are not part of the sponsoring organization as well as legislative and administrative officials at the state and federal levels are also key stakeholders. Airports work closely with these stakeholders to ensure they understand the airport's needs for funding and regulations.

Airports, like other complex government agencies, serve a number of publics, all with their own perspectives and needs. Airport public relations staff and senior managers use a number of methods to determine the needs and interests of each group and design different types of programs to reach all of them.

## CONCLUSION

Public and community relations functions in a government are charged with helping the government present itself accurately and positively to various publics and to receive input from the public. All employees of government organizations, however, need to be aware of how to work with the public.

Traditional methods of providing information and involving the public are giving way to newer means. Methods of involving the public such as running for office, serving on commissions, and attending meetings will always exist. Large cities, such as Los Angeles, are wrestling with more meaningful involvement for a larger number of citizens using neighborhood councils that are intended to allow more direct participation in decision making. While the message has not necessarily changed, the methods for informing the public certainly have. Besides printing and distributing reports and working with the news media, governments—like nonprofit and for-profit organizations—are using cable television and the internet to speed interaction.

## PRACTICING PUBLIC ADMINISTRATION

1. How have new media such as the internet changed the ways that governments reach the public? How do political campaigns use new media?
2. Suppose you had to inform the public of a new policy regarding park usage. How would you do it?
3. What are the benefits of appointing a vocal opponent of your organization to the advisory board? What are the drawbacks?
4. Review a local government's website and applications.
   a. How do they encourage participation?
   b. What kind of information is available?
   c. Can citizens pay bills online?
   d. Are meeting agendas posted?
   e. Are meetings televised online?
5. The city council approved issuing bonds to raise money for park improvements, and citizens must vote on the bonds that will increase their property taxes by $50 per year for the next 20 years on average. In a group, have individuals assume the roles of community members, businesses, and representatives of an anti-tax group.
   a. How might each group view these bonds?
   b. What means should the city use to reach each group?

## BIBLIOGRAPHY

Buss, T., Guo, K., & Redburn, F. (2015). *Modernizing democracy: Innovations in citizen participation.* New York, NY: Routledge.

Eggers, W. D. (2005). *Government 2.0: Using technology to improve education, cut red tape, reduce gridlock and enhance democracy.* Lanham, MD: Rowman and Littlefield.

Faga, B. (2006). *Designing public consensus: The civic theatre of community participation for architects, landscape architects, planners and urban designers.* New York, NY: Wiley.

Frantzich, S. (2008). *Citizen democracy* (3rd ed.). Lanham, MD: Rowman and Littlefield.

Herbert, S. (2006). *Citizens, cops, and power: Recognizing the limits of community.* Chicago, IL: University of Chicago Press.

Kotler, P. (2007). *Marketing in the public sector: A roadmap for improved performance.* Upper Saddle River, NJ: Wharton School.

Lee, M., Neeley, G., & Stewart, K., Eds. (2021). The practice of government public relations. *American society of public administration series in public administration and public policy* (2nd ed.). New York, NY: Routledge.

Levenda, A. M., Keough, N., Rock, M., & Miller, B. (2020). Rethinking public participation in the smart city. *The Canadian Geographer, 64*(3), 344–358.

Melitski, J. (2003). Capacity and e-government: An analysis based on early adopters of internet technologies is New Jersey. *Public Performance and Management Review, 26*(4), 376–390.

Neighborhood Council Review Commission, City of Los Angeles. (2007). *The neighborhood council system: Past, present, and future.* Final Report, September 25, City of Los Angeles.

Stoll, M. (2001). Race, neighborhood poverty, and participation in voluntary associations. *Sociological Forum, 16*(3), 529–557.

Sweeney, J. (2019). *Public sector marketing: The definitive guide to digital marketing and social media for government and public sector.* Chambersburg, PA: JS Press/Bookshop.

Tocqueville, A. *Democracy in America.* (2004). New York, NY: Penguin Putnam.

Wiland, H., Bell, D., & D'Agnere, J. (2006). *Edens lost and found: How ordinary citizens are restoring our great cities.* White River Junction, VT: Chelsea Green.

Yavuz, N., & Welch, E. W. (2014). Factors affecting openness of local government websites: Examining the differences across planning, finance, and police departments. *Government Information Quarterly, 31*(4), 574–583.

# Section

# 2

# Planning and Analysis

Prior to about 2010 a discussion about planning would not have appeared in a text about public administration. As we discuss in Chapter 6, planning had once been the sole domain of planning departments, planning commissions, and public employees with the word *planning* in their titles. Public law and local governments saw planning as primarily a process for developing community infrastructure and transportation networks. No more. Today, public administrators are planners, and this Section 2 discusses the planning roles they have and the resources they need.

Strategic planning focuses on goals that communities hope to achieve over a long period, typically five to 10 years or even longer. It is built around a community's mission and goals and requires data gathering and analysis, research, and community participation. While there are many planning methods, Chapter 7 focuses on the SWOT (strengths, weaknesses, opportunities, and threats) technique and provides the reader with examples of the process and step-by-step guidelines. Another concern in meeting needs is understanding community sentiment. Chapter 8 discusses two approaches to determining a community's needs and expectations: surveys and focus groups.

Long-term strategies become the guideposts for developing policies, programs, and operational plans. To identify and select the best option available in the short term, decision makers may employ the multi-attribute utility technique (MAUT), which is discussed in Chapter 9.

Chapter 10 discusses how staff and frontline supervisors address program management efforts. This chapter describes the program evaluation and review technique (PERT), which enables administrators to see the scope and progress of a project and plan for immediate and long-term deadlines. Through periodic updates of flowcharts, administrators may assess their progress and make strategic and tactical adjustments to ensure that objectives are reached in an efficient and timely manner. While some methods are commonly used for the long term rather than the short term, they may be adapted for any time frame.

# 6

## Strategic and Other Types of Planning

Failing to plan is planning to fail.

—Old Proverb

You can always amend a big plan, but you can never expand a little one. I don't believe in little plans. I believe in plans big enough to meet a situation which we can't possibly foresee now.

—Harry S. Truman, 33rd president of the United States, 1945–1953

This chapter looks at planning, a common function of governments and almost all other organizations. Many people view planning as what the city planning department does, but planning is more general than this. We will look at types of planning and then discuss planning in general, focusing on strategic planning.

### WHAT IS PLANNING AND WHY DO GOVERNMENTS PLAN?

Planning is the art and science of imagining the future. It envisions a future state, either minutes or years distant, and develops a way to achieve that future state. The important point is that planning is done not just by people who have *planning* in their job titles; it is done by everyone—managers, teachers, parents, and students. Planning is a process. Some might view it as an end, the goal being a written plan. But plans are living documents that change as circumstances change.

There are several major types of planning. Cities and counties engage in general land use and facilities planning to decide where certain activities (residential, commercial, agricultural, etc.) should be

129

located, how goods and people will flow between the uses (roadways, mass transit, airports, harbors, etc.), and what the end uses should look like (street design, art in public places, etc.). For a discussion of planning functions see Chapter 2.

To achieve their goals, governments are increasingly doing formal financial planning. They have always done financial planning in the sense of developing operating and capital budgets that link strategic and program priorities to funding sources. The new emphasis is on developing multiyear projections of revenues and expenditures to determine if priorities are achievable with or without making changes.

More and more, governments are borrowing the practice of strategic planning from the private sector. This type of planning looks at how decision makers want the government and community to be perceived by residents and nonresidents. Should the community be perceived as a great place for recreation, as family oriented, or as business friendly? *Strategic* is substantively different from *operational*. Strategic plans look at what the ends should be and ways to achieve those ends; operational management looks at how to do the work to achieve the ends. Some communities undertake strategic planning to guide all government functions, which can be very time consuming. Perhaps more common, governments use strategic-planning techniques in departments and programs rather than government-wide.

Strategic plans are also different from tactical and short-term plans. Strategic plans are usually for longer periods of time, often over 10 years. Governments may develop shorter term plans, one to two years, to break a longer-term plan into smaller segments. Tactical plans are generally more concrete and smaller in scope than strategic plans.

## LAND USE PLANNING

When most people think of planning, they think of what planning departments do. This is undoubtedly the most developed and regulated form of planning in the public sector. State laws may require cities/counties to adopt a general plan, which is a document that prescribes land use, transportation/traffic flow, housing, conservation, open space, safety, noise, and the general needs of a jurisdiction. A general plan may be described as the plan for future physical and economic development and preservation of community, environmental resources, and cultural resources. Environmental plans for capital projects are detailed analyses of how a project affects the environment, positively or negatively. The plan defines a community's vision for quality of life and serves as a foundation for the jurisdiction's decision makers.

General plans consist of broad goals, policies, and programs. Zoning codes, zoning maps, redevelopment plans, subdivision regulations, capital improvement programs, specific plans, development agreements, building and housing codes, and budgets are much more specific implementation tools and must all be consistent with the general plan. An important consideration in planning is sustainability, or, generally, whether the plan can be implemented successfully throughout the period the plan covers. Does the plan and other government functions require resources that will not be available in the future? State law may require that the general plan cover the local jurisdiction's entire geographic planning area and address the broad range of issues associated with the jurisdiction's development. A city's planning area typically encompasses the city limits and potentially annexable land within its sphere of influence.

The most important parts of a general plan are its policies, which help direct decision making and adoption of implementation measures through the years. The plans are organized with goals, objectives, policies, and suggested ways to implement the policies. A general plan is long range, comprehensive, and internally consistent. A general plan is not intended to be a fixed document. As a community grows or as technology changes, the community's needs and vision may change. Therefore, state law may recommend that a general plan be updated regularly, typically about every five years. Additionally, periodic interim amendments to the general plan may occur to address timely matters.

## Implementing a General Plan

A government's zoning ordinance, design guidelines, and specific plans set forth the development and design standards for communities that implement the jurisdiction's vision as identified in the general plan. The zoning ordinance is the primary tool to implement the general plan. It provides detailed standards for development or the use of land. Cities/counties are divided into zones, and each zone has specific requirements for using and improving or developing the property. Zoning codes are established to maintain the character and design of neighborhoods. They regulate which types of uses are permitted in a particular zone, minimum lot size, building height restrictions and setbacks from property lines, parking requirements, wall heights, sign criteria, and other standards. Typically, areas have design guidelines, which address the aesthetic image of the jurisdiction. These guidelines will describe the mass or scale of the building, compatibility with adjacent developments, and landscaping. On occasions a community or developer may desire a special plan that addresses design/development standards for a specific area of land. This special (or "specific") plan either replaces the standards of the jurisdiction's zoning ordinance and design guidelines or provides standards that enhance existing regulations. Some states do not rely on zoning to implement plans; they focus on deeds and other means.

Planning departments are typically headed by community development directors, with support from other professional and technical staff. The planning staff approves signs, home occupation permits, and minor site/façade improvements. In all other cases, the planning staff is responsible for guiding development activities through the city's review and approval process.

## The Planning Process

Developing a general plan involves several bodies, all of which are appointed by the governing body to advise it regarding planning issues:

- Planning commission—The members review the general plan, specific plan amendments, and zoning changes and either approve or recommend them to the city council for approval.

- Zoning adjustment board—The members review and approve changes in zoning such as variances and conditional use permits.

- Architectural review or design review board—The members review projects for adherence to community aesthetic standards.

Some states' laws require public hearings before most planning actions are approved. During the hearings the local official or one of the above advisory boards explains the proposal and listens to public comments before voting. Usually decisions of any of the above boards may be appealed.

Following are some typical steps for developing a general plan, taken from the City of Los Angeles:

1. Research—Planners determine the need for a plan (such as a specific plan or general plan update); review existing plans, maps, and relevant data; conduct field and land use surveys; identify issues and opportunities; and develop clear project goals and objectives.

2. Focus groups—Planners meet with stakeholders to discuss the project, identify the community's goals, set priorities, determine objectives, and receive greater insight and direction regarding the community's expectations.

3. Public workshops—Here the planners showcase the ideas from focus groups and get additional opinions and ideas. The workshops usually include presentations of background information, ideas from the focus groups, and facilitated discussions with workshop attendees.

4. Preliminary plan and environmental clearance—Planners compile and review information from focus groups and workshops. They analyze this information along with previous research to draft a preliminary plan. In many cases, the plan needs environmental review and clearance. For this step, planners prepare needed documents and allow time for public review and comment.

5. Open house—Planners present and distribute the preliminary plan to the public and answer questions. Participants are invited to future hearings if they have comments or seek changes.

6. Public hearing—The planners take formal testimony, both verbal and written, about the preliminary plan.

7. Proposed plan—The planners take the testimony into consideration and write the plan.

8. Decision makers' review—The proposed plan is sent to planning advisory bodies and other government agencies for review. In Los Angeles, it goes then to the planning commission for a hearing, approval, and recommendation to council. The plan then goes to a council committee devoted to planning issues for another hearing, approval, and recommendation to full council, which also holds a hearing.

9. Adopted plan—The proposed plan with any changes is final and effective when it is adopted by the local governing body and signed by the jurisdiction's highest elected official.

This lengthy process ensures several points at which the public can make its comments and wishes known. See Chapter 8 for more information on understanding community sentiment and conducting surveys and focus groups.

Technology, lifestyles, resources, and community interests change over time. Consequently, elected officials, citizens, businesses, residents, and investors may seek to appeal the regulations and standards established in the current strategic or long-range plans. In land use planning, these appeals to ease restrictions are called "variances." Variances, like changes in other types of plans, are not an indication that the community has an inappropriate or unworkable strategic plan but that plans need to be reexamined and updated on a continuous basis to accommodate the evolving needs of the community. Consequently, communities have relatively standardized procedures for evaluating and agreeing on variances.

Larger counties, cities, and municipalities use geographic information systems to plan and manage land use within their jurisdictions. Geographic information systems include layers such as aerial photos, mapping, zoning, the general plan, assessor parcel information, and so forth that can be readily available to provide to the public. However, map-based systems are still used within smaller populated and/or geographical jurisdictions.

The internet provides valuable tools for planning agencies as well. Some sites provide current aerial photos for agencies that cannot afford to pay for aerial images every few years. In addition, agencies can readily access past aerial images by using websites such as www.historicalaerials.com to view images from the 1930s through the present and access topographical information through the U.S. Geological Survey website.

## FINANCIAL PLANNING

Less well known than land use planning, financial planning is an essential type of planning. Financial planning's format and process are not mandated by higher levels of government, although organizations such as the Government Finance Officers Association have promoted financial planning for years.

As later chapters regarding budgeting show, it is customary to consider several years' worth of information in formulating a budget. Budgets for routine operations such as policing, garbage pickup, and fire protection usually consider at least a one- to two-year period. This period includes actual dollars expended one or two years before the budget year, the budget year (which is one year in the future), and the current year's budget for which there may be actual projected expenditures. (See Chapter 14, "Operating Budgets: Funding Programs and Policies," for a discussion of budget periods.) Capital planning for construction of large projects, like community centers and roads, looks at a longer time horizon, usually at least three to five years, and often include bonds which are paid off over 20 years or more.

Major structural changes in the national economy, like the rise of internet purchasing and changes in revenue sources, may make using a longer planning horizon as a best practice. Some jurisdictions develop biennial (two-year) budgets to help expand the planning time frame. These budgets often present a detailed first-year budget and a less detailed second-year budget which is modified and adopted later. A better practice is to project both revenues and expenditures five or more years into the future to determine how shifts in either will affect the budget.

Financial planning requires assumptions about the economy, regulations, and other factors. This type of planning may be incorporated into other forms of planning.

There are no specific programs that all local agencies use in financial planning. Each local agency is unique in nature due to population and geographical size, types of services provided, revenue sources, and so forth. Local agencies formulate budgets and projections by using the previous year's budget and then evaluate baseline incremental impacts, such as the cost of doing business and caseload changes, by inputting the information into spreadsheets to determine their ongoing liability.

Agencies use sources from specialized programs such as property information management systems to track and project sales and property taxes. In addition, agencies use information provided by their state's department of finance to forecast funds from the state. For example, the state of California uses realignment funds—a portion of sales taxes and vehicle license fees—to reimburse counties for health and human services as well as mental health programs. In addition, jurisdictions may use local university and financial institution data and/or reports to augment their economic forecast information.

## STRATEGIC PLANNING

Strategic planning is actually a general form of planning that looks at an effort along an extended timeline rather than the short term. For example, a captain of a supertanker cannot make course adjustments within a few feet but must adapt to obstructions miles away. Approaching a goal with a long-term perspective is essential for persons in executive and senior management positions and for those aspiring to those positions.

Managers and other officials in all sectors, whether they plan social programs or construction projects, use strategic planning. The process and content of strategic plans are not mandated by law and tend to vary significantly from organization to organization. Strategic planning is commonly closely linked to budgeting. An organization develops its goals and ways to attain them, and then these are translated into budgets for salaries, equipment, and so forth, as well as human resources plans. The goals should have a means to determine if they are achieved, as we will discuss in later chapters.

One advantage of strategic planning is that it helps focus efforts on key goals and "the big picture." Organizations, especially governments, often have a large number of departments managing a variety of functions directed to many goals. These functions usually grow over time as citizens request new services or other levels of government demand new services and/or provide funding for specific types of services. When operations must be cut back due to financial setbacks or other reasons, it helps to know where to focus. Strategic planning has its drawbacks: it is expensive, is time consuming, and may divert management attention from daily operational concerns.

## A GENERAL MODEL OF PLANNING

Regardless of what is being planned, the general approach is the same. This section outlines a traditional, rational model of planning and expands on it later:

1. Understand the environment.
2. Determine where you want to go.
3. Identify and evaluate options.
4. Select an option or options.
5. Determine the actions necessary to implement the selected option(s).
6. Implement.
7. Evaluate the end result.
8. Modify the plan or process based on the evaluation.

As originally practiced, this model tended to rely heavily on the work of professional planners to handle almost all steps. Before the 1960s, planners employed by the government would develop plans, present them to elected officials, hold a few hearings to get community comments, and hope to get approval. Often plans were adopted but never implemented because of resistance from communities. Civil rights, community organizing, and other movements of the 1960s changed this model. Ordinary citizens began to demand more say in the process. As a result, this model was modified to include more involvement of stakeholders in all steps (see Chapter 5, "Informing and Involving the Public"). In some cases, the stakeholders have driven the planning process by developing their own community and policy plans independent of planners employed by government and getting them approved and implemented by governments.

## 1. Understand the Environment

To begin planning, it is important to understand exactly where you are now. Planners and analysts typically do this by "scanning" the environment, looking at a broad range of issues, trends, conditions, and so forth to get a comprehensive picture. This information is typically collected, assembled, and presented to a committee or governing body. Some governing bodies participate in all of these steps, and others delegate some steps to task forces of staff and/or citizens and then discuss, modify, and approve the output of the step or the entire plan. Others hold public meetings to generate ideas for mission and vision statements and to review analyses produced by planners.

In doing strategic and other types of planning, planners and analysts may ask questions such as the following:

- Who are our residents? What are their ages? Which ethnic and income groups are represented? How have characteristics of our population changed over time, and how are they expected to change in the future? Population figures and socioeconomic information are available from U.S. Census reports every 10 years. Local universities, banks, and other organizations often update these reports. County assessors can provide information about local housing values.

- What is our community's economic situation? Where do our revenues come from? What companies are the major employers? How has this changed over time? State and local government tax collectors often have this information. States can provide statistics about retail sales.

- What services do we provide and to whom? Governments can survey the users of their services to find out exactly who is being served. (See Chapter 8 for discussion of surveys and focus groups.)

- Are our residents and businesses satisfied with the services? Surveys can be used to determine levels of satisfaction.

- How are the services funded? Government finance departments have this information.

- What are the trends in demand, actual use, revenues, and expenditures? Most governments do their own trend forecasting, which they often compare to forecasting done by local economic development consultants and agencies, banks, and universities.

- What is our competition? Do other governments, organizations, or companies provide the same services? Can our residents or businesses easily use these other services, or do they have to use our services? How do we stack up? Governments often select comparable agencies to use as benchmarks, or points of comparison.

- Which regulations govern what we do? How might these change? Governments conduct legislative and regulatory analysis themselves and in cooperation with associations of cities, counties, and other units of government.

- What are our values? What is important to us? Governments may use surveys and focus groups, which are discussed in Chapter 8, to determine these.

In planning land use, some of the same questions would be asked, in addition to questions about the natural and built environment, transportation, public works, and so forth. Planners would also look at the composition of the community (age, race, household type, education, income) and the economy (trends in tax revenue, major employers, and so forth). Financial planning would look at issues such as revenue growth patterns and trends and projected changes.

Besides looking at the current environment, answering these questions often requires forecasts of what a community will look like in the future. Planners should look at likely changes in regulations, for instance. They should also forecast demand for services.

There are several methods for forecasting and analyzing trends. Most of these are covered in basic and intermediate statistical texts. As shown in Figures 6.1 and 6.2, the unit of time is indicated on the horizontal axis, and the measure of interest is on the vertical axis, using whichever unit of measure is appropriate. The measure might be population, tax revenues, housing starts, demands for service, or, as in our example, population trends in an area.

**Figure 6.1    Forecasting and Analyzing Trends**

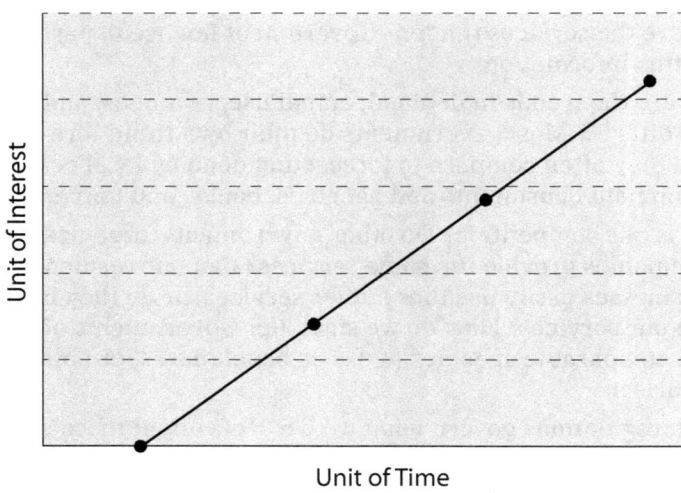

**Figure 6.2    Population Forecast and Trend**

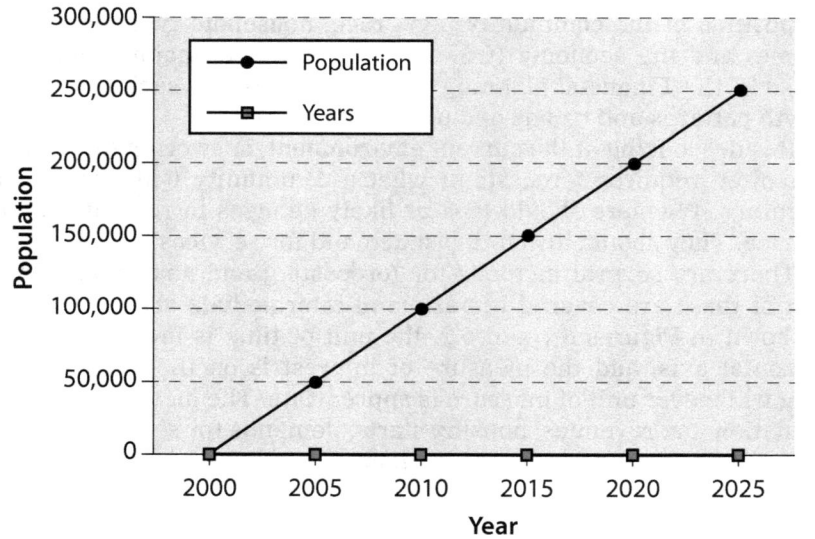

A way to improve on simple trend analysis is to develop a model using a number of statistics (or variables) that might be related to the measure in question. For example, we may be interested in crime rates and how these respond to increased city spending. But other factors affect crime rates, such as unemployment rates and income levels. Our model can include measures of these other factors. Spreadsheet programs such as Excel have functions to support this type of analysis.

## 2. Determine Where You Want to Go

Strategic planning emphasizes the need for good vision and mission statements to provide a focal point for planning efforts. Given the assessment of the environment, what should a community do? The next step is to translate vision and mission statements into goals and objectives. Vision statements often put into words the beliefs, values, and philosophy of an organization and go hand in hand with codes of ethics and codes of conduct, which are discussed in Chapter 4.

*Vision Statements.* Vision statements give a picture of what the end result should be. A vision of a better future is important for determining the best way to achieve this desired outcome. It focuses on several items, such as how an agency implements programs and services to best fit the needs of its customers while improving the quality of life in the community. This can be accomplished by such means as environmental stewardship, economic development, and preserving the culture of the community.

Vision statements are usually written in the present tense. They can be written for the county, the city, the organization as a whole, or individual departments or programs.

*Values Statements.* Many cities and organizations have supplemented vision statements with statements of values. These core priorities represent the jurisdictions' traditions and include items such as transparency and ethics in operating the government, defining its customers (e.g., youth, adults, employees), being fiscally responsible, using teamwork, and so forth.

*Mission Statements.* Mission statements indicate why the city or organization exists and what it provides. This incorporates items such as providing quality services, safeguarding the community, promoting community involvement, and creating a healthy community. The mission statement may be incorporated into the agency's charter and/or the jurisdiction's laws and statutes.

*Goals and Objectives.* Goals and objectives translate mission statements into concrete actions. The terms goals and objectives are often used interchangeably. They can, for academics and some jurisdictions or organizations, have specific meanings. Goals typically are more general statements of direction, while objectives may be measurable results with a time frame. Ideally, objectives should be SMART: specific, measurable, achievable, relevant, and time specific.

The 2005 strategic plan for the city of Albany, Oregon, illustrates the relationship between goals, objectives, and actions.

The goal of the city was to provide a safe community for its residents. The goal focused on protecting the citizens and their property as well as providing a clean and sufficient supply of drinking water and sewage disposal.

The objectives used to achieve the goal of the city council were to identify measurable outcomes by setting benchmarks regarding increasing police, fire, and emergency response services by 2010; exceeding national standards for drinking water; and reducing the loss of water within the system. Additional benchmarks included increasing the capacity to treat wastewater and controlling floodwaters to reduce property damage.

After setting objectives, the city outlined actions that would help achieve the objectives listed above. This could be achieved through accessing the current services, developing plans and strategies, and/ or creating new codes or policies. A 2017 plan for Albany follows the same pattern.

How do cities/counties and organizations develop vision, value, and mission statements and goals and objectives? The best practice is to involve as many types of stakeholders as possible. Obviously, a good  starting point for the discussions is the environmental scanning material gathered in the first step. Eventually, the governing body should formally adopt the vision and mission statements as well as goals and objectives.

### 3. Identify and Evaluate Options

The process of identifying and evaluating options translates the goals and objectives into more tangible activities. In some cases, the options are obvious, and there might be only one. But often there are many options from which to choose.

Stakeholders, who can be citizens, public officials, and internal managers, along with the assistance of analysts and planners can list all options and evaluate them in a number of ways. Brainstorming is a good way to begin listing options. This involves listing all possible options without censorship or analysis. The list is then pared down by answering questions such as the following:

- Would implementation require a major change in operations?
- Are any needed regulations in place currently?
- What are the costs? How can we pay for it?
- Are behavioral changes needed?

## 4. Select an Option or Options

Chapter 9, "Making Complex Decisions," presents techniques for evaluating options.

Something to consider when selecting an option or options are the advantages of creating a pilot program. It is often possible to launch a program in one neighborhood or for one group of people. The pilot program is then used to evaluate the planning, management, and probable success of the program. For example, is the program reaching those intended? Is it more expensive than originally envisioned? Reviewing the pilot program gives valuable insight into what should be changed before full-scale implementation—or abandoning the program.

## 5. Determine the Actions Necessary to Implement the Selected Option(s)

In this step, planners, managers, and others charged with implementing the program develop a detailed action plan listing the steps that need to be accomplished. The steps might include changing laws at other levels of government, securing funding, hiring staff, opening facilities, and publicizing the program.

The selected options and ways to implement them are often presented to the governing body as budget initiatives and for final approval to proceed.

## 6. Implement

This step puts the action plan into effect. The best practice is to establish a plan from the beginning to monitor the program financially and programmatically. The specifics of implementation are usually the responsibility of a public agency authorized to execute a policy by the legislature.

## 7. Evaluate the End Result

At the end of a specific time period (such as a year or the natural conclusion of a pilot project), it is very useful to evaluate the end results. Did the program accomplish what it was designed to accomplish? For details about analyzing results see Chapter 18, "Performance Measures."

## 8. Modify the Plan or Process Based on the Evaluation

Implementation efforts will be met with both successes and failures. In part these will be a consequence of unexpected external factors. Other challenges will be unintended factors and/or internal organizational dynamics. Consequently, course corrections and adaptations to the plan need to be addressed systematically and regularly. Short-term, low-cost, incremental variations from the plan may be left to the discretion of middle and upper managers; however, significant deviations need to be addressed more broadly by an updated strategic-planning effort. Consider the following questions:

- What accounts for successful implementation efforts?
- Why were efforts slow or successful?
- Is the approach under way the most feasible, efficient, and effective?
- Has the goal or objective changed?
- How should the strategic plan and its implementation be reinforced and/or amended?

An organization in flux needs to be mindful that changes are a means to an end and need not change its mission or objectives. For example, the Department of Labor's (DOL's) objective is to broker information about available jobs and candidates. The agency was created during the Franklin D. Roosevelt administration at the height of the Great Depression when hundreds of candidates would reply to a single job notice. Employers were overwhelmed, and local Employment Services (state agencies funded by DOL) screened the most appropriate candidates to employers. The practice was to encourage employers to publicly post jobs to a broader cadre of applicants than in the past. In the 1960s, DOL was tasked with promoting nontraditional applicants for consideration for positions: women, minorities, and disabled persons. An unintended consequence of this new agenda was that employers and labor unions were not adequately prepared for the changes and withdrew job announcements, thereby making Employment Services less effective in breaking down barriers for those subject to discrimination. The DOL experience reflects the need for agencies to clearly communicate how new efforts are integrated and consistent with their core missions.

The shift in operations need not be dramatic. In the early 1990s a small community projected significant growth in the long run but in the short run faced declining revenues. As a means for addressing the dilemma, the city charged developers and real estate investors a fee for reviewing and approving building plans and plan amendments. The new fee-for-service approach became a lucrative revenue stream for the beleaguered city. However, residents saw the new developments as degrading the community's natural habitat, generating congestion, and shifting the commercial life of the community away from its historic center. Many residents saw the planning department as a partner in developing urban sprawl and in opposition to the public interest.

## PLANNING ANEW

The need for an organization to revisit the plan and calibrate it anew is critical. At a minimum this examination should occur annually and more frequently when possible. As in the cases above it is important to monitor that the tactics employed are not derailing the mission and core values for which the organization was designed.

The utility of planning is not in the drafting of the plan, but rather in the assessment of the operational consequences. In practice all plans are in need of being revised and reconsidered. In some instances, the plans have been altered in practice through variances. In other instances, the plan has been revised through new public bonds or reallocations of funding by the legislature. Plans are expanded or pared down based on the government's ability to meet public needs in a systematic manner or in moments of crisis. For more details see Chapter 18, "Performance Measures," regarding monitoring and assessment.

## ETHICS, EQUITY, AND PLANNING

Some types of planning were once the exclusive domains of the experts with little or no involvement by citizens. While expertise in a technical area is desirable, the shrouding of public decisions in jargon, formulas, and abstract theories does not instill trust, confidence, or cooperation from citizens. Public involvement and education have become the cornerstones of planning in the public sector; early and frequent input by citizens is becoming the norm. In this regard, planning and the planning process are becoming more inclusive and ethical. Public involvement in planning also fosters transparency and accountability in government. Acknowledging that all stakeholders have a voice in the community demonstrates an intrinsic respect for all members of the community.

Equity is an important consideration in making plans of all types. How are different types of communities and individuals affected by plans? Are public services available to all communities and individuals? Questions like these can be answered by looking at who participates in making plans and who receives services.

A good example is planning for parks. Planners can use ratios like park acreage, population, and hours of recreation activities available in different communities. Historical studies and standards set by professional organizations can help determine whether, for instance, 100 hours per month of recreation activities is high or low. Surveys, like those described in Chapter 8, can help determine the types and how many hours of activities are desired by different communities. One community may want several soccer and baseball fields along with children's playgrounds, while another community may want a quiet place where they can walk and sit. Other data, such as the distance from population centers to current and proposed parks and the capacity of the parks, may be considered in the planning process.

## CONCLUSION

The discussion above addresses long-range and strategic planning for land use, finances, and risk management. Many state governments require that localities have land use plans or master plans for their communities. Many citizens perceive planning as exclusively concerned with land use questions. The plans typically try to direct the development of housing, businesses, and transportation systems over a five- to 10-year period. These master plans are then supported by local ordinances (laws) and governing boards to ensure the plans are implemented. However, localities recognize that plans do not necessarily treat everyone equitably, and there are policies and procedures for deviating from plans, which are called variances.

In addition to long-range planning regarding land there is a need for long-range planning to meet financial obligations and to develop infrastructures and systems that can meet emergency situations. More and more in the wake of September 11 and Hurricane Katrina, communities are engaged in systematic long-range planning for their communities. The steps and processes of addressing these needs are discussed above.

## PRACTICING PUBLIC ADMINISTRATION

1. Visit your city/town's website. Does the jurisdiction post its master plan for the use of land, and if so, what does the master plan suggest the city/town/county is doing to ensure the community is livable and economically viable?

2. Does your city have a strategic plan? Look at your city's website; the plan may be posted separately or included in the budget. What process was used to develop it? Do departments in the city have their own strategic plans? Do they align with the city's strategic plan?

3. Visit your locality's website. Is there a published process for variances? If so, how does it compare with the process noted in this chapter? Is it more or less stringent in its review of requests?

4. Does your locality have a financial plan for developing infrastructure needs? If so, what is the locality's approach?

5. In a group, develop a plan for a library department's strategic plan. Who should be involved? How? What steps should be taken?

## BIBLIOGRAPHY

Allison, M. & Kay, J. (2005). *Strategic planning for nonprofit organizations.* Hoboken, NJ: Wiley.

Andrews, R., Boyne, G. & Walker, R. (2006). Strategy content and organizational performance: An empirical analysis. *Public Administration Review 66*(1), 52–63.

Bryson, J. M. (2011). *Implementing and sustaining your strategic plan: A workbook for public and nonprofit organizations.* Hoboken, NJ: Jossey-Bass.

Bryson, J. M. (2018). *Strategic planning for public and nonprofit organizations: A guide to strengthening and sustaining organizational achievement.* (5th ed.). Hoboken, NJ: Wiley.

Chapman, J. (1987). *Long term financial planning: Creative strategies for local government.* Washington, D.C.: ICMA.

Chaven, A., Peralta, C. & Steins, C., Eds. (2007). *Planetizen's contemporary debates in urban planning.* New York, NY: Island Press.

Gearhart, J. (1999). Activity based management and performance measurement systems. *Government Finance Review 15*(1), 13–16.

Halegoua. G. (2020). *Smart cities.* Cambridge, MA: MIT Press.

Hoch, C. J., Dalton,L. C. & So, F. S., Eds. (2000). *The practice of local government planning.* (3rd ed.). Washington, D.C.: International City/County Management Association.

Kavanagh, S. C. (2007). *Financing the future: Long-term financial planning for local government.* Chicago, IL: Government Finance Officers Association.

Keebler, D. (2007). Process analysis and standardization: The road to strategic-planning success. *Indiana Libraries 26*(4), 37–42.

Kemp, R. L., Ed. (2008). *Strategic planning for local government: A handbook for officials and citizens.* Jefferson, N.C.: McFarland.

Levy, J. M. (2016). *Contemporary urban planning.* (11th ed.). Oxfordshire, UK: Routledge.

Lukensmeyer, C. & Boyd, A. (2004). Putting the "public" back in management: Seven principles for planning meaningful citizen engagement. *Public Management 86*(7), 10–15.

Plant, T. (2008). Holistic strategic planning: Achieving sustainable results. *Public Management 90*(10), 17–20.

Poister, T. & Streib, G. (2005). Elements of strategic planning and management in municipal government: Status after two decades. *Public Administration Review 65*(1), 45–56.

Steiner, G. A. (1979). *Strategic planning: What every manager must know.* New York, NY: Free Press.

Weber, R., & Crane, R., Eds. (2015). *The Oxford handbook of urban planning.* Oxford, UK: Oxford University Press.

## PERSONAL INTERVIEWS

Arabatzis, D., San Bernardino County assistant county administrative officer, July 15, 2009.

Burnett, C., City of Rancho Cucamonga senior planner, July 14, 2009.

Gillison, J., City of Rancho Cucamonga deputy city manager of administrative services, July 21, 2009.

# 7 ◆──◇──◇──◆

# Shaping and Supporting
# a Strategic Process
# (SWOT)

One seminal difference between politicians and administrators is that administrators are position seekers; they want a job for the purpose of providing goods, services, meeting the public's needs, and so forth. Some politicians seek to secure the greatest number of votes but are not interested, nor able, to do the job. These politicians seek affirmation (popular support) from voters. The essence of a republic is that voters choose a candidate to do a job and that the best candidate for the job is then elected. However, elections do not preclude voters from selecting a candidate they like, have an empathy for, share their values or biases, or is popular and yet who has no experience in political office or public service and does not serve the needs of the voters. Clint Eastwood won the nonpartisan office of mayor of Carmel-by-the-Sea, California, but had no political nor administrative expertise at the time. In Eastwood's case, he was able to rise to the occasion and do the job, but this is not always the case.

Politicians that seek public affirmation have no strategic outlook regarding actual governing. Instead, they have preferences, they are confrontational, polarizing, and connect with others around shared emotions rather than shared practices or objectives. These politicians have been a part of American politics since Andrew Jackson in 1829.

Public administrators shun many of these attributes. They value consensus, cooperation, and reason. Consequently, they are drawn to and engage in strategic practices rather than passioned appeals or rhetoric. Strategic thinking requires developing a vision and plan and taking into consideration one's strengths and weaknesses as well as the opportunities and challenges that may affect success. Strategic thinking typically requires mapping an approach to a goal that is five to 10 years, or more, in the future.

Public officials and administrators need to think and act both strategically and tactically. If there is a flash flood or wildfire in the community, the tactical response is to move residents to safe areas, mobilize public safety personnel into special shifts, move injured persons to whichever medical facilities are available, and call for backup resources from neighboring communities and the state. The long-term strategic response includes amending zoning regulations, building and retrofitting water and sewer systems, training public safety personnel and citizens in prevention and rescue procedures, building accords with neighboring communities regarding mutual support, assessing water supplies, and inventorying blood bank capabilities and medical supplies to be used at emergency facilities. Citizens expect government public services and resources to be available when a crisis arises.

Risk management concerns are not the only area for strategic planning and action. Economic recessions, demographic shifts in the population, technological advances, public opinion, and organizational successes and failures present administrators and officials with challenges and opportunities to serve the public interest and to mitigate harm. Reacting to circumstances only when a crisis is evident is neither efficient nor effective. The dire consequences to life and property by using tactics only were evident during Hurricane Katrina and the western wildfires in California, Oregon, and Washington.

## STRATEGY: PUBLIC VERSUS PRIVATE CONSIDERATIONS

Strategic thinking in the private sector is predicated on the premise that an organization has clear objectives, can develop innovations, and rationally devises means for realizing specified goals in the future. This approach was popularized by business in the mid-1960s and sought to provide decision makers with a competitive market advantage by carving out a niche and mobilizing resources (or divesting functions) to ensure a firm's future. The success or influence of strategic planning in business is controversial, with some authors suggesting that market success is more a consequence of trial and error, opportunism, accident, and/or luck. Despite the absence of empirical evidence that strategic planning influences high-ranking decision makers or produces market success, the idea of strategic planning continues to thrive in both the public and private sectors.

One of the challenges of taking a strategic approach in the public sector is that some assumptions are not applicable. Public organizations have few clear, specific objectives but multiple and competing (often inconsistent) goals that arise out of a pluralistic society of taxpayers and beneficiaries, debtors and creditors, and friends of business versus friends of the environment. Vision and mission statements, and goals are broad, inclusive, and sweeping statements of values. See Chapter 6 for a discussion of visions, missions, goals, objectives, and actions.

In the public sector, strategic planning is used to address concerns that are different from those of the private sector. Public sector concerns are managerial control over public employees and contractors, funding uncertainty, and public demands for transparency.

## MANAGERIAL CONTROL, FUNDING UNCERTAINTY, AND TRANSPARENCY

Since the era of Progressives in the 20th century, public-sector employment has encouraged merit and professional expertise over nepotism and political connections. An unintended consequence of Progressive reforms was that the resolution of problems was controlled by professionals: teachers determined how best to educate, police how best to track and restrain suspects. Less emphasis was paid to accountability for outcomes, resource capabilities, and costs. Strategic planning in the public sector strives to impose this managerial perspective on decisions about program objectives and the resources to be used to meet objectives as defined broadly by vision, mission, and goals.

A parallel issue for public-sector managers is how best to manage resource constraints, specifically funding. When participants in strategic-planning sessions are asked to think creatively and innovatively, it is primarily about how outcomes and/or outputs might be sustained or expanded using less tax money. The basic standard for a private-sector manager is to generate revenue from goods/services that provides a distinct advantage over competitors. The emphasis in the public sector is to effectively use and/or to leverage available resources by working cooperatively with others to meet demand while containing costs.

Consequently, innovative businesses offer goods and services that are readily accessible, user friendly, and popular; while public-sector services seem to remain unchanged, cumbersome, and inconvenient. Legislators and voters have questioned whether the public services provided are what voters want and if agencies are accountable for outcomes and consequences. Do police patrols reduce crime? Do educational programs improve academic performance? How do voters/taxpayers assess benefits or justify public costs?

The strategic approach may or may not produce an effective plan in either the public or the private sector. Its value is in providing an ongoing sounding board for trying new approaches and educating participants about the merits of public programs and the related costs. In brief, it is a mechanism for discussing public goods and services as a managerial effort that holds providers accountable and demonstrates value to voters and taxpayers. Meaningful participation requires extensive efforts to collect, organize, interpret, analyze, and share information so that the emerging process represents a fundamental commitment by both administrators and citizens to achieve a shared vision.

## Methods and Tools

There are a variety of analytical planning tools: benchmarking; environmental scanning; and strengths, weaknesses, opportunities, and threats (SWOT) analysis. SWOT was developed nearly 70 years ago to help businesses identify market opportunities. The process was adapted and used by local government as part of its planning and social-economic development efforts.

## Pros and Cons of SWOT

The pros:

- The process is conceptually simple and flexible. It may be used in diverse situations and enables participation by persons at multiple levels of an organization and from a variety of organizations.
- It is an easy process to learn and adapt.
- It draws on the personal experiences and insights of those participating in the process. Specialized technical knowledge is not required.
- SWOT analysis, when treated as a dynamic, ongoing process, may serve to keep an organization well prepared to serve the public and cope with change.
- Since public programs serve a multitude of people and are by nature complex, the collaborative approach benefits from a diversity of interests and the willingness of participants to work together to promote change.

The cons:

- SWOT may be attempted without sufficient objective data about internal operations and/or external trends. Such efforts are generally futile.
- Collecting the quantitative data and related facts needed for discussion can be time consuming and costly.
- There may be a lack of precision regarding the definition of terms and how these terms are understood and measured. For example, how might technological advances be identified, and their magnitude expressed?
- This tool is not a substitute for leadership, a clear mission statement, or action.

- There are no specific means for limiting the number of factors for consideration or resolving differences of opinion about the relative merits of various factors. SWOT analysis may be highly subjective.

- Ignoring and underestimating one's weakness and the threats in the environment can limit the process's utility. Overvaluing one's importance or influence also may weaken the utility of SWOT.

## An Example of Using SWOT

When do we use SWOT? At the height of Italy's COVID-19 pandemic, the Department of Prevention of the Italian National Health Services conducted a SWOT analysis to develop a managed response to the crisis, with input from medical experts and frontline professionals. Italy was a COVID hotspot. Two rounds of discussions were held using the online technology of the extended college for *Prevention, Public Health and Medical Directories*. They focused on three themes:

- coordination of medical services among regions;

- internal reorganization of services, for example, what nonurgent activities of the national public health service could be postponed; and

- blocking and tackling or determining how and when quarantine protocols were to be in force, defining swabbing and testing for COVID, and defining practices of surveillance for those in quarantine.

These were less than ideal circumstances. However, Italy's use of SWOT demonstrated the importance of strategic planning and thinking when government must act. The example provided in this discussion is what a SWOT analysis would look like for a large urban county in the United States facing an ever-growing number of cases of COVID after the introduction of widespread vaccinations.

## Los Angeles County

Los Angeles County's Department of Public Health has a service area of 4,753 square miles with a population of over 10 million. Among its responsibilities are communicable disease control, substance abuse prevention, emergency preparedness, injury/violence prevention, maternal/child/adolescent health programs, sexually transmitted disease programs, tuberculosis prevention, etc. It has approximately 5,200 employees and a budget of $1.126 billion. The department's director since 2017 has been Dr. Barbara Ferrer.

The Department of Public Health is comprised of three bureaus: staff support, health services (disease control), and health promotion. The Bureau of Health Promotion accounts for 39% of the department's budget and 50% of its personnel.

The Department of Health has experience developing strategic plans. For example, in 2015 it developed a countywide program called the Community Health Improvement Program (CHIP) to guide service delivery for the next five years. The plan included input from 400 stakeholders. The objective was to increase access to medical care including clinical preventive service, mental health, dental, and medical services. In 2015, two million residents of the county reported having difficulty accessing medical care. At that time the barriers to care were a shortage of providers, lack of culturally competent care, and transportation for those who did not have a car. Long-term strategic planning in 2015 was led by two interim directors, Cynthia Harding, and Dr. Jeffrey Gunzenhauser.

The caseload reflected in Table 7.1. represents the increasing demand on health services while the budget reflects the ability and willingness of voters to be taxed. The trend is that there is a persistent gap between the demand for services and the capacity of the county to meet demand. Not all responsibilities of Health Services are reflected in budget reports. For example, the demand for and use of health promotion programs is not reflected in annual budgets.

**Table 7.1    History of County of Los Angeles Bureau of Health Services: Workload and Budget**

|  | 2019 | 2020 | 2021 | Change |
|---|---|---|---|---|
| Percent of total budget for Bureau of Health Services | 33% of $35,461 billion | 33% of $35,461 billion | 33% of $36,184 billion | +2% |
| Inpatient, daily workload | 1,081,000 | 1,137,000 | 1,145,000 | +5% |
| Outpatient Visits** | 2,661,000 | 2,567,000 | 2,862,000 | +7% |

** Services provided by DHS and Community Partner Operated Clinics.

Source: County of Los Angeles Budget and Operations. (2019, 2020, and 2021). https://ceo.lacounty.gov/budget/

More recently, the primary challenge of the Los Angeles County Health Department has been monitoring and responding to the demands of COVID-19. There was a lack of ambulances, ventilators, hospital beds, masks, and health care personnel. There was an abundance of both patients and misinformation. The County Public Health Department, Health Promotion, dealt quickly and professionally with the crisis and Dr. Ferrer won one of three local hero awards from the media.

Specifically, she was cited for:

Dr. Barbara Ferrer was deemed uniquely qualified to lead and serve the community's diverse populations with over 40 years of professional experience as a philanthropic strategist, public health director, educational leader, researcher, and community advocate. At the outbreak of the COVID-19 pandemic, Dr. Ferrer became the voice and face of calm to millions of residents throughout California, dispensing consistent, knowledgeable, and useful information; sharing the facts as she knew them and encouraging Southern California residents to follow evolving guidelines. (Shields, 2020)

**Table 7.2    COVID in Los Angeles County in 2020**

| Date | Cases | % change | Deaths | % change |
|---|---|---|---|---|
| March 31 | 3,011 | — | 54 | — |
| April 30 | 23,183 | 669% | 1,111 | 1,957% |
| May 31 | 54,996 | 137% | 2,363 | 113% |
| June 30 | 103,529 | 88% | 3,363 | 43% |
| July 31 | 188,481 | 82% | 4,621 | 37% |
| August 31 | 241,768 | 28% | 5,784 | 25% |
| September 30 | 270,229 | 12% | 6,551 | 13% |
| October 31 | 307,618 | 14% | 7,071 | 8% |
| November 30 | 400,919 | 30% | 7,700 | 9% |
| December 28 | 733,325 | 83% | 9,555 | 24% |

Source: *Los Angeles Magazine*. (2020, December).

Confirmation of a viable COVID vaccine was announced in December 2020 and distribution of the vaccines began in California in February 2021. After nearly a year, the state and county potentially had a tool to combat the pandemic.

The County Department of Public Health continued to closely monitor COVID testing, positive results, hospitalizations, and deaths. Their findings were published on the web.

Figures 7.1 through 7.3 are the results reported by the County's Department of Public Health.

By mid-July of 2021 the cumulative total death toll for Los Angeles County was 24,905 or net of 14,223 over the first seven months of 2021, which is 2,031 per month. While 2021 did not have the dramatic spikes of 2020, there was a steady upward trend in deaths.

**Figure 7.1    Number of Persons Tested for COVID, with Moving 7-day Trendline —May to August 2021**

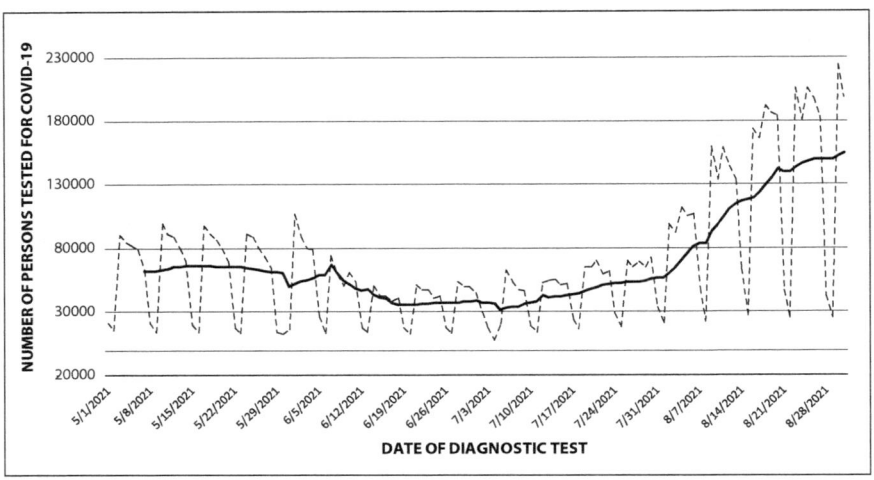

**Figure 7.2    Percent of Positive COVID Tests ,with Moving 7-day Trendline— May to August 2021**

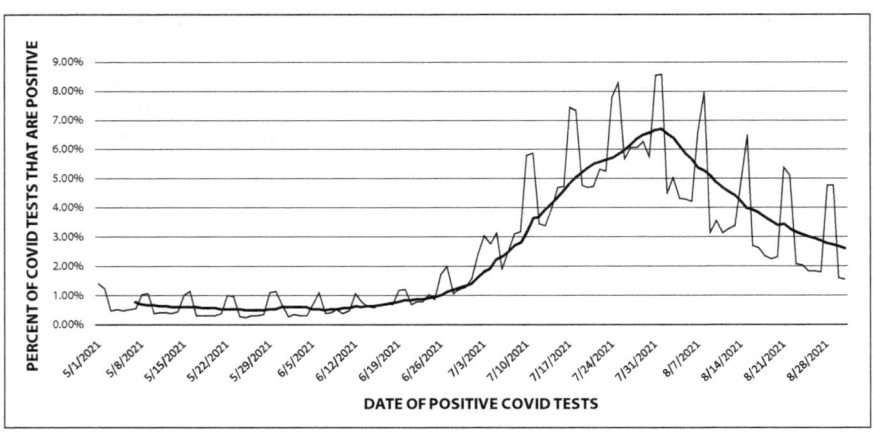

**Figure 7.3    Number of Hospitalized COVID Patients—May to August 2021**

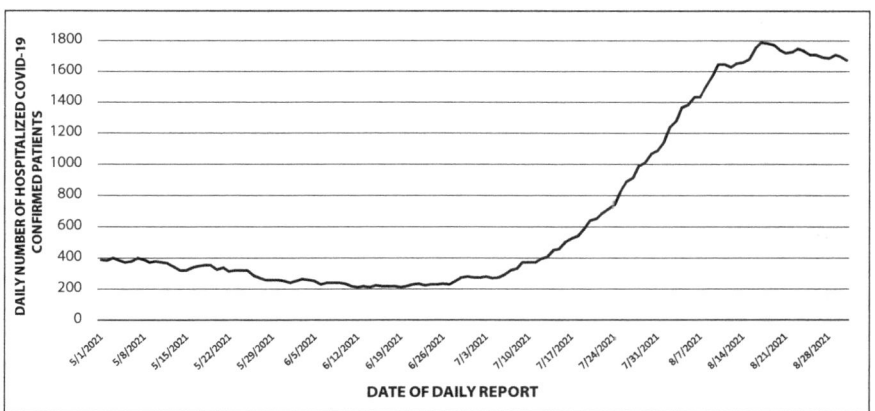

By mid-July of 2021 the cumulative total death toll for Los Angeles County was 24,905 or net of 14,223 over the first seven months of 2021, which is 2,031 per month. While 2021 did not have the dramatic spikes of 2020, there was a steady upward trend in deaths.

Several factors contribute to who dies of COVID. Based on the LA County's data of deaths by race, ethnicity and poverty, a summary of who is most likely to die may be constructed. Assuming a monthly total of 877 deaths, the distribution of deaths has been as follows:

**Table 7.3    Mortality Rates in Los Angeles County—May to August 2021, by Race, Ethnicity, and Rates of Poverty**

| Race/Ethnicity | County Population Percent | Mortality Rate |
|---|---|---|
| Asian / Pacific Islander | 12.6% | 15% |
| Black | 9.7% | 20% |
| Hispanic | 44.6% | 34% |
| White | 31.1% | 11% |
| Other (estimate) | 2.0% | 20% |
| **Rate of Poverty** | | |
| < 10% | | 12% |
| 10–20% | | 21% |
| > 20–30% | | 28% |
| > 30% | | 30% |

As noted in Table 7.1 on page 154, total spending by the county has increased and spending by the Bureau of Health Services has risen by 2%. The county needs a strategic response to the continuing crisis. To address these challenges the county would confront unique challenges.

## Practical and Ideal SWOT Conditions

In terms of management practices, it is always a good idea to have a current strategic plan and approach for the long-term development of a viable, effective, and productive organization. As a practical matter, public agencies and organizations tend to institutionalize their practices and processes quickly with little overall review. This behavior is expected by the public as routine operations can be both effective and efficient.

The disadvantage of institution building is that public organizations get into the habit of operating in the current year based on the previous year, looking neither at emerging trends nor at changing potential opportunities and risks. Organizations are generally unprepared to address crisis rapidly. Consequently, SWOT analysis tends to be done at pivotal moments in an organization's development, such as a period of significant unexpected growth or a period of crisis or reduced revenues. Ideally strategic plans should be developed when there is time for extensive data gathering, analysis, and reflection. In practice, SWOT analysis is done when there are limited data and relatively little time for analyses or reflection. However, despite the gap between the ideal and the actual, it may serve as a useful methodology for strategic thinking and action.

Any number of people can participate in a strategic planning and analysis effort. In its simplest form, SWOT may be undertaken by a single manager or staff member as a method to analyze a program or issue and to suggest options. It is usually best to include a diverse group of people to get a wider perspective on issues or programs. Managers and staff most familiar with the operations of the program should certainly be included. Customers, regulators, elected officials, and others can help evaluate the operations as well as the environment of the organization.

# A STEP-BY-STEP GUIDE TO SWOT

## Step 1: Preparation

An extensive amount of preparation needs to be completed before one engages in a SWOT exercise. Some of the topics are discussed in detail in Chapter 6, "Strategic and Other Types of Planning."

The objective of SWOT is to examine factors and issues in an organization's structure, operations, environment, etc., that will enable it to operate effectively and efficiently in the future. If an agency is seeking to plan five years ahead, then the analysis of trends should look at least five years in the past. The number of years in the future that the design is intended to serve should be supported by the analysis of data for an equivalent period in the immediate past.

In the discussion of Los Angeles County's COVID response above, we see a steady upward trend in the demand for health services but not an equally upward trend in revenue and resources to meet demand (see Table 7.1). In addition, there is an increase in positive COVID tests and hospitalizations six months after the introduction of COVID vaccines (see Figures 7.2 and 7.3). Table 7.3 indicates that different populations with different socioeconomic status's experience different levels of risk. If the trend continues, there will be a disproportionate number of preventable deaths in areas of the county with minority and low-income households. A graphic of these emerging demographic trends is provided in Figures 7.2 and 7.3. Other trend data of interest about the external environment that should be compiled and analyzed might include:

- changes in the socioeconomic status of the population by geographic area (where are the concentrations of at-risk populations, and what level of medical assistance is needed to mitigate the risk of death or long-term hospitalizations?);
- funding levels from various sources, for example, taxes, fees, grants, and foundations;
- number of persons entering health science disciplines which could be mobilized to meet future staffing needs and mobilized as interns in the short term;
- operational changes in goods or services delivered to citizens, (e.g., can public goods and services be provided by private pharmacies, hospitals, and clinics?);
- technology changes in production, distribution, and/or use of goods/services; and
- capital programs for facilities, renovations, and expansion to meet current and estimated growth.

*The Rate of Change Analysis.* Understanding past and emerging trends is critical in strategic planning. The rate of change is a simple algebraic formula and is discussed in Box 7.1, Rate of Change Analysis for Planning. Note that when comparing changes in money over time, a dollar today is not equal to a dollar three years ago the analyst needs to translate the value of money into its present value for each time period.

---

**Box 7.1   Rate of Change Analysis for Planning**

The rate of change is derived by dividing the most recently measured level by the past number and subtracting 1: (current number ÷ prior number) – 1.

If a health department's service planning area has 400 hospitalizations on June 30 and 470 hospitalizations by July 15, then the rate of increase is

$$(470 \div 400) - 1 \quad \text{or} \quad 1.175 - 1 = 17.5\%$$

*(continued)*

Money is different from other tangible factors. Five thousand dollars in 2019 is not equal to $5,000 in 2021. The buying power of money varies from year to year due to inflation. For example, to have the buying power of $5,000 dollars spent in 2019, one would need to spend $5,370 in 2021. Therefore, if the budget was $5,000 in 2019 and is $5,307 in 2021, the effective change is $0. ($5,307 in 2021 is the present value of $5,000 in 2019. [$5,000 ÷ $5,000] – 1, or 1 – 1, = 0.)

Analyze the change in LA County's health services budget between 2019 ($11,702.13B) and the budget in 2021 ($11,940.72B). The value of 2019's $11,702.13 budget in 2021 is $12,420.54. While it appears as though the county consistently allocates 33% of its budget to health with a modest increase of 2%, the actual change is between $12,420.54B (the 2021 value of the 2019 $11,702.13B budget) and the 2021 budget of $11,940.72B is ($11,940.72 ÷ 12,420.54) – 1 = – 4%. If the demand for services increases by 5% and 7% respectively for hospitalization and outpatient services, then the revenues available to spend on services declined by four percent, rather than remain constant.

To make adjustments regarding the value of a dollar, visit the Federal Reserve Bank of Minneapolis at https://www.minneapolisfed.org/about-us/monetary-policy/inflation-calculator . To determine what $1 (in 2019) is worth in terms of 2021 dollars, complete the online entry fields with $1 in 2019 is worth _____ in 2021. Select the calculate button; the answer will be $1.06.

*Other Data Needed for SWOT.* In addition to external factors that influence programs, outputs, and outcomes, the documentation of internal successes and challenges needs to be compiled and presented in simple terms using graphs and charts to reflect trends. Examples of these data follow:

- personnel changes among professional, technical, and support staff (average number of years' experience, permanent versus temporary positions, etc.);
- turnover rates (for the different categories of employees: professional, managerial, technical, support, and other);
- personnel costs, including benefits;
- operating costs;
- level of effort (e.g., number of patients served, number of calls, etc.);
- outputs (e.g., number of vaccines provided, days of inpatient care, percent of patients returning in 30 days);
- outcomes (e.g., days missing from work due to illness, days missed at school, lost pay, changes in employment rates, crime rates);
- overhead costs and ratios of overhead to direct services;

- innovations in program delivery; and
- challenges: application of new drugs, storage of materials, supply line delays, etc.

Sixteen bulleted items are noted in the above sections. These are not complete lists but are intended to give the reader a general idea of the scope of the inquiry attempted in SWOT. The first six items are external factors, and the last 10 are internal factors. While some participants will be comfortable with raw data and/or statistical analysis, many will not. Therefore, it is recommended that the data be displayed in terms of net changes and statistical analysis with graphs and charts to aid SWOT participants in understanding what the data indicate (see Tables 7.1–7.3 on pages 154–157).

## Step 2: Recruiting a Facilitator to Guide the SWOT Process

The facilitator needs to be someone who:

- is comfortable in a collaborative environment;
- has a positive, can-do attitude;
- is sensitive to participants (can coax persons to contribute ideas and insight);
- is comfortable with ambiguity and indecisiveness;
- is not judgmental;
- is an active listener;
- does not micromanage the process; and
- can identify and clarify similarities and differences among views in a conversation.

The process is only as good as its ability to incorporate many perspectives, diverse experiences, and data into a coherent whole. The facilitator should be an expert in group dynamics and facilitation rather than in any aspect of the organization's operations, environment, area of expertise, or mission.

## Step 3: Recruiting Participants to the Process

A strategic-planning process may be undertaken by persons who are the stakeholders in the organizational mission. SWOT is probably best at an agency, district, or jurisdictional level rather than at the micro level of a unit or section of an organization. The target group of participants should include:

- all levels of management: executive/appointed, managers, middle managers, supervisors, and employees;
- representatives from functional areas from initial input to termination, such as recruiters or intake personnel, direct

providers of goods/services, and positions that determine when the process is completed and/or should be terminated;

- support personnel in the areas of budgeting, personnel, administration, and labor union representation, when applicable; and

- external stakeholders, including current clients or participants, former clients, suppliers, and providers of related services to the organization and its mission.

The number of persons who can work together effectively as a coherent whole is limited to somewhere between 15 and 35, depending on the scope of the project. While diversity among participants is vital, all participants need to share some attributes:

- agreement on the organization's mission and vision;
- willingness to promote positive change;
- tolerance of the views of others; and
- willingness to learn and adapt.

The group of potential participants should be as broad and inclusive as possible. When placing each name on the list, indicate which attributes that person brings to the process: new ideas, institutional history, expertise, a track record of success, experience managing organizational challenges, and so forth. For each person on the initial list, identify a possible backup or alternate.

Participation may be required for those inside the organization, but for those outside some inducement might be necessary. Each member of the SWOT team should be invited to participate and should be informed of the anticipated commitment in terms of time and effort. How long the process lasts depends on the development of the premeeting package, the experience of the SWOT participants, the number of persons in the group, the level of detail needed, how quickly collaborative working relationships can be established, and other factors. It is generally the case that the process requires several meetings over weeks or months and is not likely to be completed in one or two sessions. In a crisis situation, this adjustment time may get significantly truncated.

Since the Los Angeles County Department of Health had engaged in an extensive countywide study (CHIP) in 2015, those stakeholders could be a rich source of information and support for the organization's continued efforts. Examples of stakeholders might include by sector the following:

**Table 7.4   Los Angeles County High-Risk COVID Area, Examples of Stakeholders for SWOT Analysis**

| Private | NPOs |
|---------|------|
| Sol Cal. Electric Co.<br>University of Southern CA<br>Kaiser Permanente | Alma Family Services<br>Building Health Communities<br>Salvation Army Red Shield Youth<br>South Central LAMP (Los Angeles<br>   Ministry Project)<br>Concerned Citizens of<br>South Central Los Angeles |
| **Political Jurisdictions** | **County Services** |
| Los Angeles Supervisorial District 2, Holly<br>  Mitchell<br>City of LA, Mid City Neighborhood<br>  Council<br>City of Los Angeles West Adams,<br>  Neighborhood Council<br>City of Carson<br>City of Compton, etc. | Los Angeles County Department of<br>  Children and Family Services<br>Los Angeles County Department of<br>  Public Social Services<br>Los Angeles County Public Health<br>  Services<br>Health office for SPA 5 and 6, health<br>  educators |
|  | **Special Districts** |
|  | Los Angeles Unified School District |

## Step 4: Introduction to the Process

The first meeting of the team needs to focus on the following:

- meeting and building relationships with members;
- reviewing the planning process and projected timetable, which should include meeting times, dates, means, places, and anticipated agenda items. (Specific agendas will be developed on a meeting-by-meeting basis as the process develops. These projected agendas indicate a broad outline of the process and how it may be addressed by a particular organization.) For example, the Italian administration determined early in their process to focus on three themes (see discussion An Example of Using SWOT);
- distributing and reviewing information about external trends and internal operations and performance;
- identifying other data needs or concerns; and
- planning team operating principles regarding
  - » mutual respect,
  - » full participation,
  - » willingness to challenge the conventional wisdom,
  - » listening to and considering all ideas,

» seeking out root causes for success and weaknesses, and

» supporting the team process.

Feedback sheets should be completed at the end of each session. The evaluation need not be elaborate or extensive. There are three basic questions:

1. What worked or is working well in meeting team objectives?
2. What is not working well?
3. What immediate change should be made to improve the process?

The comments should be reviewed, summarized, and forwarded to the facilitator as part of the agenda for the following meeting.

## Step 5: External Factors—Opportunities and Challenges

Before a public organization can initiate change it needs to understand the context in which it operates and the changes occurring in that environment. The context includes political, economic, technological, and social/lifestyle changes and trends. These trends either may present the organization with opportunities and means of support or they may be challenges or threats.

The exploration of the political, economic, social, and technological environment is sometimes referred to as "PEST analysis" in the literature or as an "environmental scan."

This general template (see Table 7.5) identifies core categories and provides participants with an initial framework for listing factors as challenges or opportunities. The initial listing is not intended to be comprehensive but a launching point for discussion. In Figure 7.3 on page 157, one can see the demographic changes in terms of race and income on potential hospitalizations and deaths. This combination of poverty and racial groups suggests that the organization may need to focus some attention on service planning areas with concentrations of poor and minority residents.

The next task is to share the different lists and compile a composite that best reflects the team's view of the organization's external environment. The team may begin to prioritize the strengths and threats from the most important to the least important. Also, team members may need additional trend data. Economic trend data are available from the U.S. Department of Labor and Department of Commerce. Additional information may be available from the local chamber of commerce, the state finance office, and/or the local jurisdiction's budget office. Social/lifestyle data are available from the Census Bureau and from planning and budget offices at the state, regional, and local levels. Political trend information may be available from scholars, from political journalists, and as polling data reported by the media. However, planning teams should not underestimate the importance of the issues of local elected officials and their constituents, which may not be quantified in any database. Similarly, technological changes may be topics of professional journals and online blogs but not be systematically tracked or reported by a public agency. The discussion and analysis may require that materials be added to the initial team database as discussions develop.

Once the available data are seen as reasonably complete and items are listed and prioritized, the team may discuss how opportunities and threats might be measured or categorized. Some users refer to this as "POWER SWOT," where POWER stands for personal experience, order, weight, emphasis, and rank or priority. When there is a general agreement on a working list of opportunities and threats, the team moves to Step 6. The agreement need not be determined by a vote but should represent a consensus among members of the group.

**Table 7.5   External Environmental Factors Outline with Sample Data**

| Categories | Opportunities | Threats/Challenges |
|---|---|---|
| Political (campaign issues, public opinion, court decisions, mandates [CDC, FDA], intragovernmental relations) | Authorizing vaccines for general use | Disparity in monitoring and reporting on diseases by CDC and WHO |
| Economic (employment, changes in private investments, sales) | Working remotely, rise in tech jobs | Loss in hospitality jobs and service jobs available to low-income populations |
| Social/lifestyle (demographic changes, leisure, work, generation issues) | Disruption to households that have lost loved ones, care takers, etc. | Increased family time, use of entertainment services e.g., Netflix |
| Technological (mechanization, applications) | Meetings via Zoom, virtual offices, classrooms, etc. | Loss of personal contact, fellowship and social connections |
| Other | TBD | TBD |

# Step 6: Weaknesses and Strengths

After identifying the external environment, the next step is examining the internal workings of the organization and categorizing the factors as either weaknesses or strengths. Here it is best to be specific. If the categories are too broad the strengths and weaknesses may not be clearly delineated. For example, personnel may be seen as both strengths and weaknesses. Personnel may have good working relationships with clients and strong technical skills but be disgruntled about pay and working conditions. A template for internal factors is included below in Table 7.6.

**Table 7.6    Internal Environmental Factors Outline**

| Categories | Strengths | Weaknesses |
|---|---|---|
| Personnel (knowledge, skills, licenses, abilities, training attitudes, languages, motivation) | Staff bilingual, working relationships with community partners | Lost personnel and expertise due to 2020 funding cutbacks |
| Facilities (size, age, capacity, location) | Well maintained | Aging |
| Standard operating processes/practices (inputs, throughputs, and outputs) | Understood and followed | May be cumbersome in emergency situations |
| Operating resources (supplies, tools, phones, volunteers) | Operational | Dated |
| Clientele/patrons (users, clients, demands, expectations) | Grateful for resources | Reluctant to use resources until crisis situation arises |
| Performance (services provided, goods produced, outputs, reports, feedback) | Quality services | Time on reporting but little on review and application |
| Technology (vehicles, equipment, computers) | Operational | Dated |
| Long-term financing (bonds, debt) | Debt issue not directly related to providing health services | Has grown to $1.8 billion primarily due to demand of criminal justice system |
| Reputation/profile in community (media coverage, participation, visibility in area) | Support and acknowledgment of health services value, better understood, and more favorably reported | Episodic and erratic related to crises rather than covering prevention and wellness |

This template is not a complete list and will vary from organization to organization. Much of the success of this aspect of the process depends on the consistent monitoring and assessment of inputs, throughputs, outputs, and outcomes of the organization's own processes.

These internal factors need to be prioritized, measured, and/or categorized. The SWOT team needs to come to a general consensus that what is listed represents its best effort for a complete picture and that the assessment of each factor is as concise and accurate as possible.

## Step 7: Matrix Opportunities

For each weakness and/or threat, look across the matrix (see Table 7.7) for an opportunity and/or strength.

**Table 7.7   Combined Matrix of Strengths, Weaknesses, Opportunities, and Threats**

|  | Positive | Negative |
|---|---|---|
| **Internal** | **STRENGTH**<br><br>Skilled staff | **WEAKNESS**<br><br>Vacant and defunded positions<br>Dated equipmen |
| **External** | **OPPORTUNITY**<br><br>Positive profile in community<br>Working relationships with<br>community partners in CHIP | **THREAT**<br><br>Declining revenue to county<br>Rising unmet client needs |

Combine the work of the external and internal analyses into a single chart. Indicate the importance or ranking of each factor and note how each factor is observed and/or measured, when feasible. Have team members think outside the box, and for the purpose of the exercise assume that any option is possible. Discuss each negative attribute and weakness, and scan across the matrix to the noted strengths and opportunities. Are there untapped resources and means that can address the immediate or long-term concerns? In Table 7.7 one weakness is vacant positions, but on the plus side the organization had a positive image in the community, support from interest groups, and a rise in the number of community partners willing to volunteer. How can these factors serve to buttress the weaknesses in vacant positions? An option is redesigning positions to be filled by volunteers, interns, or temporary personnel. The use of the organization's goodwill with the public and interest groups may be mobilized to help manage and/or organize nonpaid staff. If some full-time paid positions were reduced, more resources could be available to fill professional, technical, and staff positions that are more critical to operations.

Similarly, a rising client population may increase the demand for services but may also enable the organization to encourage private and university programs to train health professional by serving the department's clients. The objective of Step 7 is to place on a to-do list every conceivable option that is—or may be—available to the organization. Some options may be immediately available, such as reorganizing processes and procedures, while others may require a long-term investment of labor and resources. For example, if the organization has outgrown its facilities and needs more space, then building or locating resources will require a long-term capital plan that may take five or more years to implement. A long-term time frame indicates that to realize a goal, immediate steps and follow-up will be required.

It takes time and patience before a range of options emerges. The team is together for several meetings, and all are encouraged to participate and contribute ideas. While not every concern may be addressed, the process should be nurtured until most major concerns have been addressed with plans/tasks for resolution.

## Step 8: Generating Options From Analysis

Options emerge from the analysis of strengths, weaknesses, opportunities, and threats. One potential proposal from the discussion above might be a new approach to internships and volunteer programs with area colleges, universities, medical centers, and high schools to enable those entering the health care fields to gain relevant administrative and/or nonacademic experience.

Implementation of the option would require that human resources (HR) identify the tasks that interns/volunteers could do and prepare training materials or sessions that would enable this potential labor pool to be utilized quickly, efficiently, and effectively. The HR administrator would need to establish procedures to ensure that volunteer/ internship candidates are expedited quickly.

Based on a preliminary analysis, the HR specialist would develop a draft job description, ad, or flyer about the position. As with other SWOT materials, this material would be reviewed and expanded by the appropriate planning team or subcommittee. Once the position has been identified, the planning team/subcommittee would develop a proposal for distributing announcements, encouraging participation, mobilizing existing community volunteer programs, screening, and selecting applicants, and acknowledging the volunteer/intern efforts.

Proposals that change practices are typically reviewed by the jurisdiction's top administrator (city manager) and/or by its legislature (council). Communities may have templates that outline how decision makers expect materials to be organized (see Appendix A, "Writing Reports and Speaking Effectively"). A legislature typically must prepare a resolution that defines what the new procedure/approach will be. Supporting this resolution is a statement of the issue to be addressed, the relationship between the means employed, and the consequences of, the costs of, and a timeline for implementation.

More complex proposals for capital improvement or large-scale funding will need to be incorporated within the jurisdiction's existing practices with the added feature of collaborating and sharing information with the strategic planning committees. These efforts, like the planning process itself, require commitment by participants to shape proposals and to serve in the community as advocates for and educators about the strategic-planning process.

## ETHICS AND EQUITY

What ethical and equity issues are associated with a tool? A tool, like SWOT, appears value neutral. This is only partially true. The tool is value free, but the use of any tool is fraught with ethical challenges. This is most evident when identifying and recruiting who will be part of the SWOT discussion group. The most effective use of SWOT requires the broadest and most inclusive recruitment of participants who represent the diversity of interests related to the issue at hand. Consequently, it may be necessary to actively recruit for SWOT discussions, those who have not participated in the past and use websites, social media, public events to encourage new participants to the process. In addition, it is often the case that the data we have is not the data we need. We may know a good deal about the lack of ventilators, personal protective equipment, number of hospital beds but have no information on number of households close to a clinic or hospital facing food insecurity, the number of first responders caring for high-risk family members, or the resources for health care providers when they are caring for others. The asymmetry between what data we have and what data we need presents numerous challenges for using SWOT. It suggests that those using this tool need to collect and organize a wide range of data to inform participants initially and need to develop ongoing means for collecting data to plug the information gaps that arise as the discussions of strengths, weakness, opportunities, and threats evolve over the course of process.

## CONCLUSION

Elected officials and high-level appointees often articulate the community's vision, mission, goals, and objectives. In both shaping and supporting this public agenda, public decision makers need to engage in strategic decision-making processes. Public and private organizations use many such processes. This chapter has explored the use of SWOT as a semi-structured approach to strategic planning. It may incorporate the best of quantitative analysis along with qualitative methods and intuition. It suggests an approach to building solutions but does not prescribe specific solutions, criteria, or problem-solving practices. SWOT depends on the goodwill and reasoning of participants and the process facilitator. This is both the process's greatest weakness and its greatest strength.

## PRACTICING PUBLIC ADMINISTRATION

1. If you were developing a strengths, weaknesses, opportunities, and threats (SWOT) team for your organization, which types of participants would you include on the team?
2. Download and review the Network of Schools of Public Policy, Affairs, and Administration's self-study accreditation outline from https://www.naspaa.org/sites/default/files/docs/2019-11/2019%20 Self-Study%20Instructions%20FINAL.pdf. Identify the internal and external factors that are quantified.
3. What would be the advantages and disadvantages of using the data from an accreditation report for SWOT analysis? What is provided and what is missing?
4. Using the data in Figure 7.3 on hospitalizations, determine the rate of change in hospitalizations between July 1 (at 398) and July 31 (at 1,100).
5. Examine the cost of health care expenditures reported by USAFacts of as a percent of GDP. The link is at https://usafacts. org/data/topics/people-society/health/healthcare-expenditures/ healthcare-expenditures-as-of-gdp/. The chart graphs costs from 1960 to 2019. Place your cursor over the line and it will identify for each year the percent of GDP which is spent on health care. For example, in 2019 the percentage was 17.71%.
   a. How much of an increase has occurred since the Affordable Care Act (ACA) was passed in 2010?
   b. What is the relative rate of increase in the decade prior to ACA, between 2000 and 2010?
   c. Explain why the rate of change is different between 2000 to 2010 than for 2010 to 2019.
6. Based on the information on Figure 7.1:
   a. Describe what factors influence a rise or decline in the number of persons being tested for COVID.
   b. Compute the rate of change in the number of tests on June 6th (7,000) with the number of tests on July 4th (3,000).
   c. How might one interpret this change in behavior between June and July, among county residents?
7. Prioritize the relevance of the external data provided on Figures 7.1, 7.2, 7.3 and Table 7.3. Which data on the county's environment is most critical to managing the crisis at hand? Why?

8. Open the video on masks at Iowa State University (ISU) at https://
www.kcci.com/article/iowa-state-covid-19-guidlines/37377781#.

   a. What needs to be the response of the ISU administration if
   Iowa state COVID-19 hospitalization rises. Why?

   b. What needs to be the response of the ISU administration if
   Iowa state COVID cases plateau and/or decline. Why?

# BIBLIOGRAPHY

Awe, S. C. (2006). *The entrepreneur's information sourcebook: Charting the path to small business success*. Westport, CT: Libraries Unlimited.

Balamuralikrishna, R. & Dugger, J. C. (1995). SWOT analysis: A management tool for initiating new programs in vocational schools. *Journal of Vocational and Technical Education*, 12(1). https://doi.org/10.21061/jcte.v12i1.498

County of Los Angeles, Chief Executive Office. (2021–2022, 2020–2021, 2019–2020). Recommended budget charts at https://ceo.lacounty.gov/budget/

Crosby, B. C., & Bryson, J. M. (2005). *Leadership for the common good*. (2nd ed.). San Francisco, CA: Jossey-Bass.

Dyson, R. G., & O'Brian, F. A. Eds. (1998). *Strategic development: Methods and models*. Chichester, UK: Wiley.

Garner, R. (2005). "SWOT" tactics basics for strategic planning [strengths, weaknesses, opportunities and threats]. *FBI Law Enforcement Bulletin* 74(11), 17–19.

Gayle, G. (2007). *Teacher teams that get results: 61 strategies for sustaining and renewing professional learning communities*. Thousand Oaks, CA: Corwin Press.

Gorski, S. E. (1991). The SWOT team—Focusing on minorities. *Community, Technical and Junior College Journal* 6(3), 30–33.

Grandy, G., & Mills, A. J. (2004). Strategy as simulacra? A radical reflexive look at the discipline and practice of strategy. *Journal of Management Studies* 41(7), 1153–1170.

Hamai, S. A. Chief Executive Officer. (2020, April). County of Los Angeles (2020–2021) Recommended budget, volume one, at https://ceo.lacounty.gov/wp-content/uploads/2020/04/2.-2020-21-Recommended-Budget-Volume-One-Online.pdf

Han, W., & Guangrui, T. (2018). The SWOT-PEST analysis of the construction of incentive system for state-owned enterprises' scientific researchers. IOP Conference Series. *Materials Science and Engineering* 439(3), 320–329. https://doi.org/10.1088/1757-899X/439/3/032032

Hill, T., & Westbrook, R. (1997). SWOT analysis: It's time for a product recall. *Long Range Planning 30*(1), 46–52.

Jackson, S. E. (2003). Recent research on team and organizational diversity: SWOT analysis and implications. *Journal of Management* 29(6): 801–830.

Llewellyn, S., & Tappin, E. (2003). Strategy in the public sector: Management in the wilderness. *Journal of Management Studies* 40(4), 955–982.

Mintzberg, H. (1994). *The rise and fall of strategic planning*. London, UK: Prentice Hall International.

Money, L. & Lin II, R-G. (2020). Ambulance scarcity, long 911 response times: COVID pushes L.A. County to "brink of catastrophe." *Los Angeles Times*. https://www.latimes.com/california/story/2020-12-31/back-to-back-records-push-californias-covid-deaths-past-25000

Regardie, J. (2020, December 30). A month-by-month look at how LA wrestled with its greatest crisis ever. *Los Angeles Magazine*. https://www.lamag.com/citythinkblog/covid-19-2020/

Rueda, D. (2021). Is populism a political strategy? A critique of an enduring approach. *Political Studies 69*(2), 167–184.    https://doi.org/10.1177/0032321720962355

Shear, M. (2008). Will Thompson roll the closing credits? *Washington Post*, (January 22), A8.

Shields, J. P. (2020, December). Local heroes Dr. Barbara Ferrer, Ben Caldwell and Tam Nguyen recognized by KCET and PBS SoCal for continued leadership, innovation and community support during Covid 19. *KCET PRESS ROOM* at https://www.kcet.org/press-room/2020-local-heroes-dr-barbara-ferrer-ben-caldwell-and-tam-nguyen-recognized-by-kcet-and-pbs-socal-for-continued-leadership-innovation-and-community-support-during-covid-19

Torri, E., Sbrogiò, L. G., Di Rosa, E., Cinquetti, S., Francia, F., & Ferro, A. (2020). Italian Public Health response to the COVID-19 pandemic: Case report from the field, insights and challenges for the Department of Prevention. *International Journal of Environmental Research and Public Health 17*(10), 3666. https://doi.org/10.3390/ijerph17103666

Weyland, K. (2021). Populism as a political strategy: An approach's enduring—and increasing—advantages. *Political Studies 69*(2), 185–189.

# 8 ⬥—◇—◇—◆—◆

# Understanding
# Community Sentiment

# Surveys and Focus Groups

Modern public administration assumes that the solutions of professionals, experts, or public servants are the solutions sought or valued by the public. However, the public does not always agree. Disaffected and excluded citizens may become angry. Citizen disfavor takes many forms including demands for cuts in funding, media scrutiny, legislative oversight, special audits, public demonstrations, and court challenges. In the case of nongovernmental organizations (hospitals, private schools), the public may demand that organizations either demonstrate that their efforts meet a community need or surrender their tax-exempt status.

In response to public dissatisfaction, elected officials enact legislation that calls for public participation in setting department or agency agendas, policies, and in some cases programs such as the Government Performance Results Act. The issue for this act is not efficiency but results or effectiveness. Legislating public participation in setting values, needs, and objectives is easy. Getting public participation that can substantively inform decision making is complicated. See the discussion in Chapter 5, "Informing and Involving the Public."

The challenges for scholars and administrators include:

- ensuring participation and input reflect the public as a whole and not fractious special interests,
- ensuring the input is meaningful and not a pro forma exercise,
- balancing public sentiment with agency expertise, and
- employing participation methods that are effective and efficient.

175

## Ensuring Public Participation

Public administration is both a scholarly discipline and a practicing profession. There are differences between administrators' and scholars' perspectives regarding what is *the public*. Scholars prefer sampling community members based on rigorous methods that ensure the sample is representative of the population from which it was drawn. Mathematically such sampling enables one to estimate the true population's response, plus or minus random sampling error. Scholars prefer large samples (e.g., 1,500 respondents) with data collected periodically in a consistent manner so that they may be compared and contrasted over time. A robust sampling system for scholars is the General Social Survey or the American National Elections Survey. The objectives for scholars are to describe, explore inferences, and model relationships among variables to determine the utility of theories or assumptions in the discipline. For example, do participation efforts, such as formal organized group discussions (focus groups), surveys, and open meetings, increase public interest in agency efforts or do they increase the public's frustration?

The practicing administrator's public is defined as program/policy users and/or advocates, program detractors, community spokespersons, and stakeholders and/or interest groups. The population is framed in terms of the administrator's understanding of *community*. The challenge is to balance the interests and perspectives of less educated, disadvantaged, ill, and/or marginalized citizens with that of better educated, articulate, taxpaying, wealthier members. Consequently, administrators may be comfortable with sampling agency directors, staff, users, and community associations or advocacy groups. This sample represents the population already engaged with the agency rather than a broad demographic group. The likelihood is that this engaged group will be more responsive to participation efforts and better informed about programs and issues. However, the findings drawn from this sample are not representative of the population as a demographically defined whole.

### Methods for Determining Results and Unmet Needs

If crime rates decline by 10% per 100,000 or graduation rates rise by 5%, aren't these the agency's results? Isn't *need* the difference between these rates and the benchmarks or objectives established for the programs? Isn't this information already captured by agency records and monitoring?

Public records have limitations: time and geography. This year's data will be compiled into next year's report, which may be distributed in the following year. Public records often lag by one or more years. When the data are available, they may not be for the agency's geographical area. This is especially problematic for nongovernmental organizations with service areas that cover a variety of political jurisdictions or only part of one jurisdiction or a geographic area that contains parts of several political jurisdictions. The same is true for public administrators who operate a school or health clinic in an area that is not a discrete reporting area.

Needs assessment is not only about objective, measurable outcomes but also about community perceptions of the situation and the governance process in which the agency is engaged. Do citizens get and use agency information? Are requests addressed promptly and to citizens' satisfaction? Does the public trust the agency? Public sentiment and process issues are not routine but are periodically monitored primarily using focus groups and surveys. While focus groups and surveys are not the only means for assessing community needs, over the past quarter century they have been the most consistently used and documented mechanisms.

## The Needs Assessment Instrument

The needs assessment data gathering techniques, including sampling methodology, and survey questions, differ depending on whether one's perspective is primarily as a scholar or as a practitioner. For example, a scholar may be interested in whether efforts to include citizens are effective. The scholar seeks a universal definition of effectiveness by identifying and itemizing what *effective* means and how it is measured. Is a program or policy deemed effective because the efforts are perceived as fair to diverse groups, provide easy access to decision makers, or produce new solutions? The scholar seeks to dissect *effective* into component parts so that effective as measured today in this location is roughly equivalent to effective measured tomorrow and/or somewhere else. The practitioner's concern is usually specific to a program, location, and time. Do stakeholders perceive this agency's efforts as effective? Does the needs assessment instrument enable stakeholders to identify their perspectives on the level of effectiveness? Collectively does the aggregation of responses reflect how well the agency is meeting community expectations?

Since needs assessments are specific to a jurisdiction or agency and typically are in response to public dissatisfaction or dissent, the literature is populated primarily with case studies using a variety of terms and definitions rather than with studies that promote rigorous, uniform terminology.

## Reliability and Validity

The problem with defining terms and conducting sporadic studies is that they give rise to other contentious issues: reliability and validity. *Reliability* refers to an instrument's (e.g., a question's, a record's) producing roughly the same results over time. If a researcher uses a measuring tape to delineate the distance from a patron to the receptionist, that distance will be the same this year and next and the same if measured by an experienced researcher or a novice. The instrument has reliability. However, if the researcher asks respondents if they "feel close" to the agency receptionist over time, the same question may produce divergent responses because it may be interpreted differently by respondents depending on the interviewer's tone of voice, a change in the agency's receptionist, or the physical restructuring of the reception area. The same question over time lacks reliability.

However, measuring the number of feet between the client and receptionist may be reliable but not valid. A valid measurement is one that measures what it asserts it measures. If the researcher uses the respondent's physical distance from the receptionist as an indication of the agency's openness or inclusiveness, he or she may be challenged as to whether the instrument is valid. Validity may be addressed in several ways:

- experts or scholars have tested the question or measuring instrument and find it to be robust (consistently works in the same way with different respondents);
- a pretest of the questionnaire indicates that respondents appear to understand the question;
- the question correlates appropriately to other questions in the instrument; and/or
- the question enables researchers to predict.

Scholars tend to prefer multiple and rigorous tests of validity, which is consistent with the desire for the universal and specific definition of terms noted above. Practitioners tend to rely more extensively on "face validity" (how a typical or responsible person might interpret a question) and/or the validation of questions based on pretest results. Instruments need to be both valid and reliable to substantively contribute to an understanding of public sentiment and contribute to the agency's decision-making process. However, there is often a trade-off between validity of instruments and their reliability.

## Interpreting and Serving the Public Interest

The primary objective of seeking to understand community sentiment is to use it as a basis for making changes in practice and/or programs. Consequently, for the administrator the data need to be interpreted, distributed, and utilized. The scholar can find that there is a significant correlation between citizen assessment of agency operations and their assessment of outcomes, for example, safe neighborhoods and the incidence of crime. The scholar can determine which factors may be causes and which may be results, but implementation is left to administrators and representatives.

Applying research findings has special challenges. A study of the Inland Empire in Southern California demonstrates that there is a high correlation between citizens' evaluation of police operations and their assessment of crime and street safety in the community. However, the direction of responses indicates that views on street safety and crime influence the opinions of police operations but not vice versa. Police agency approval benefits from the community's broader quality-of-life image; police must be doing a good job if the community's circumstances are favorable.

What should be done if the police are improving call response rates, arrests, and convictions but the public's assessment of performance remains low? The options might be to persevere with existing policies and programs despite the public's assessment, direct resources to advertising service and outcome improvements, and/or direct resources to participating in more community-based events, thereby making a closer connection between community life and police operations. All options raise concerns for the administrator. Not responding to the information may give citizens the impression of business as usual and negatively affect agency's standing in the community, while self-promotion might be seen as self-serving rather than as responsive to community needs. Getting the agency's word out by being more involved in community events and activities may require stretching already limited resources. No option is without costs and using research findings can be particularly problematic.

In a study of a Connecticut county, the public was asked which public health issues were of greatest concern and which programs should be emphasized. The response indicated that AIDS/HIV and drug abuse were core issues, and the emphasis and funding should be focused in these areas. The study also indicated that there was a significant relationship between the publicity of state and national programs and support for local public health efforts. However, analysis of the county study data indicates that local AIDS/HIV cases and drug abuse are well below national and state levels. Lyme disease, however, is more prevalent in this county than anywhere else in the state or nation but was on no one's list of issues or programs. Why consult the public if their knowledge of issues is ill-informed?

Public participation and input are not substitutes for professional and administrative responsibility. Public participation defines the context within which agency staff must operate to serve the public interest. The public's perception is not without value. While Lyme disease is widely prevalent, it is addressed with antibiotics, which the public may feel adequately meet the need. Drug abuse and AIDS/HIV, while less prevalent, pose significant life-and-death issues. The severity of consequences may be more important to the public than the incidence of a disease and should shape public health efforts for utilizing scarce resources.

## Ethical Issues

The scholar finds value in expanding knowledge, which is why systematic, empirical research is an intricate tool. However, the scholar understands that those who participate in surveys, focus groups, and so forth are to be valued as persons and not seen as a means to an end. Scholars seek to ensure that participant responses are kept confidential, and that respondents' participation is anonymous. Practitioners understand and support ethical practices for their own sake and because citizens, stakeholders, and so forth will not participate in future studies if these principles are violated.

Practitioners have additional ethical considerations. How might information be used to serve the public interest and foster public participation and self-governance? Does the utilization of information improve understanding or the quality of life? To ensure ethical application of needs assessment efforts, administrators need to understand what makes data collection methods robust, efficient, and effective. While needs assessments may be conducted using any number of methodologies, the most pervasive examples are surveys and focus groups. Consequently, the focus of this chapter will be in these areas.

## SURVEYS: AN EXAMPLE

A large city in California was interested in citizen views of police services in an area with relatively high crime rates. See Table 8.1 for examples of the city's questions. To gauge use of services, the survey included the questions noted in Table 8.2 and demographic questions listed in Table 8.3. Since the target community was predominately Hispanic/Latino, the survey was available in both Spanish and English.

## A STEP-BY-STEP GUIDE TO CONDUCTING A SURVEY

The discussion below introduces basic principles that are used for a variety of survey practices: in person, by phone, online, mail, etc. Today, interviewers may also use Zoom or other electronic meetings.

### Step 1: Identify the Objective of the Survey

Typically, surveys seek to understand user satisfaction with a public good or service, but related issues may evolve. Examples of questions are: "How does the public prioritize public services?" and "What funding levels are seen as adequate?"

### Step 2: Identify the Population to Be Surveyed

If the objective is to survey geographic areas, census tract information is useful. If the survey is of service users, then enrollment records or payment sheets might serve to estimate the total population in the survey.

**Table 8.1  Safe Streets and Related Police Outcomes**

| | |
|---|---|
| Today, how safe do you feel out **alone** in your neighborhood during the day? | a. Very safe<br>b. Somewhat safe<br>c. Somewhat unsafe<br>d. Very unsafe<br>e. Don't know |
| Today, how safe do you feel out **alone** in your neighborhood *after dark?* | a. Very safe<br>b. Somewhat safe<br>c. Somewhat unsafe<br>d. Very unsafe<br>e. Don't know |
| Have you found any signs that someone tried to break into your home, your garage, or another building on your property to steal something? | a. Yes<br>b. No<br>c. Don't know |
| In the past two years, has **anyone stolen something** from you or a member of your family by force or by threatening you with harm in your neighborhood? | a. Yes<br>b. No<br>c. Don't know |

**Table 8.2  Use of Police Services**

| | |
|---|---|
| In the past two years, have you called the police to report a crime that happened to **you or a member of your family?**<br><br>If response is YES, go to Question 2;<br>if NO or Don't Know, skip to Question 3. | a. Yes<br>b. No<br>c. Don't know |
| How satisfied were you with the police response? | a. Very satisfied<br>b. Somewhat satisfied<br>c. Somewhat dissatisfied<br>d. Very dissatisfied<br>e. Don't know |
| Today, how responsive are the police in your neighborhood to community concerns? Are they . . . | a. Very responsive<br>b. Somewhat responsive<br>c. Somewhat unresponsive<br>d. Very unresponsive<br>e. Don't know |

**Table 8.3  Demographic Information about Respondents**

| | |
|---|---|
| In which age range do you fall? | a. 18–25<br>b. 26–35<br>c. 36–45<br>d. 46–55<br>e. 56–65<br>f. Over 65<br>g. Refused to answer |
| Are you a homeowner or renter? | a. Homeowner<br>b. Renter<br>c. Don't know or refused to answer |

## Step 3: Determine the Sample Size

To determine an adequate sample size for a given population size visit www.surveysystem.com/sscalc.htm. A survey should be representative of the population at a confidence level of 95% to 99%. This means that there is a 95% to 99% likelihood that a statistical finding (e.g., the median) from the survey data would also be found for the entire population from which the sample was drawn. The fewer the errors in estimating the population's views from the information gleaned from a sample, the higher is the confidence level and the larger is the required sample size. In addition, the researcher will want the error rate in responses to be small, perhaps 3%. In such a case the *confidence interval* would be 3%. If a response rate norm for a sample question is yes = 54%, then a 3% confidence interval would suggest that the population response rate would be from 51% to 57% (54 – 3 = 51 and 54 + 3 = 57). The smaller the confidence interval desired, the larger is the sample size required. In national polls a confidence interval of 3% is considered sufficient. Using the website identified above, enter the sample size required for a confidence level of 95% and confidence interval of 3% for the following populations: 2,500, 25,000, 250,000, 2,500,000, and 25,000,000. The first sample size is 748. What are the sample sizes as the total number increases?

## Step 4: Select a Sample

A systematic sample is used when there is a list of everyone in the population, such as voter registration roll, or matriculated college students enrolled for the term. With a complete list of the population and a sample size, the researcher may divide the population size by the sample size to select the random samples. For example, with a population of 2,500, a 95% confidence level with a 3% confidence interval would suggest a sample size of 748 (see the sample size discussion above). Calculate 2,500 ÷ 748 = 3.3, which is rounded to 3. Pick any data point to be the first for the sample; then skip the next three data points and select the fourth, which will be the second item in the sample. Proceed in this manner (skip three and select, skip three and select) until 748 have been chosen. Since some elements on the list may be incorrect, missing, and so forth, researchers select more than the minimum of 748 by 3% to 5% (22 to 38 for this example), for a sum of 770 to 786. This standardized method for selecting a sample at random assures that the sample is unbiased.

When there is no complete listing of items to be sampled, then the systematic sampling approach described above is not possible. For example, there is no listing of all residents in a census tract. However, every geographic area has at least one telephone area code and designated prefixes. (The prefix is the second 3-digit number in the 10-digit phone number.) If the population to be surveyed has phones, then the researcher can pull the area codes and prefixes from the local phone directory. Let's assume that our community of 2,500 is in a single area code with 10 prefixes. Then the survey would seek to get about 75 responses from each prefix to spread the survey evenly among the 10 prefixes. To generate the last 4 digits of the sample phone numbers, visit www.random.org/integers. At this site enter the number of random numbers you want generated, the number of subcategories desired, and the range of numbers the system should use to generate sufficient options. In the case of the last 4 digits of phone numbers the range would go from 0000 to 9999. As in the situation above, one would want the system to generate more numbers than the minimum of 748. Some numbers will be disconnected, not in service, not yet issued to residents, or connected to businesses rather than residences.

If the study is using a definitive list of stakeholders, then perhaps all stakeholders will be surveyed.

## Step 5: Develop the Survey Questions

There are numerous resources to use in developing survey questions. The largest and most widely used are the American National Elections Survey, conducted during biannual congressional elections, and the General Social Survey, done annually. In addition, there are numerous instruments on the web that can be accessed depending on the topic area, for example, policing or health care. Using questions from other established surveys may ensure the questions are valid and reliable.

In some cases, the researcher may need to adapt and/or develop specific questions. There are some guidelines to apply when developing closed-ended questions:

* Be sure the respondent can answer the question. *"At what age did you begin to talk in full sentences?"* is not a question a person could answer. It may be a question only for a parent or caregiver.

* The response options should be mutually exclusive and collectively exhaustive.
  Sample question: *How old are you?*
  *Circle the appropriate age group: younger than 20, 20–35, 35–55, 56–65, 66 or older*
  This question is collectively exhaustive since there is no age that lies beyond "younger than 20" through "66 or older." However, the question is not mutually exclusive since a 35-year-old would not know if he or she should choose "20–35" or "35–55." If more than one response is applicable, then the options are not mutually exclusive.
  The following question was recently placed on the web:
  *Have you stopped smoking? ___ Yes ___ No*

This question is neither mutually exclusive nor collectively exhaustive. It does not have an option for the individual who has never smoked.

- The tone of questions and response options should not bias the respondent by suggesting an appropriate answer.
  *Sample question: Don't you agree that X policy is the best option?*
  ___Yes ___ No ___ No opinion
  This question suggests to respondents that the proper answer is "Yes." It is human nature to want to agree, rather than disagree, so biased questions will yield little to no variation in responses and are useless in a survey. A better question would be the following:
  *Policy X is the best option.*
  ___ Strongly agree ___ Agree ___Disagree ___ Strongly disagree
  ___ Don't know
  The responses above are based on a scale in which gradations from one extreme to the other are provided for the respondent. This ensures that no clue has been provided to suggest a particular response option.

- Avoid negatively worded questions such as
  *Is it true you don't like peas? ___ Yes ___ No*
  The "No" response means, "No, it is not true that I don't like peas," which means, "I like peas!"

## Step 6: Develop an Introduction for the Survey

Be sure to include in the introduction to the survey: who is conducting the survey and why, the importance of the respondent's participation, how the respondent's participation will be kept anonymous, and how responses will be kept confidential. The respondent should be given the name and phone number of a person to contact if there are any problems or complaints. Each respondent should be thanked for participating and given a means for getting the survey findings if he or she is interested.

## Step 7: Pretest the Instrument

To ensure that the questions are workable, try out the survey on a group of people who have similar attributes to the target population but who are not members of the target population. A sample of 25 to 50 participants using test questionnaires will determine if there are a range of responses to the questions, if questions regarding the same attribute overlap with similar questions about that attribute, and if respondents have problems reading or understanding the question or answer options. Feedback from the pretest surveys should be reviewed and analyzed before one settles on the final survey.

## Step 8: Train the Interview Staff

Have all interviewers react to respondents' questions and concerns in the same manner. It is important that the interviewers treat each situation in the same way so that variations are due to respondents' views and not differences in interviewers' behavior or comments to participants. The uniformity of behavior is essential regardless of how data is collected (focus groups, online surveys, in person, or by phone). Surveys and focus groups are primarily tools for collecting information about public sentiment. Other means for communicating with the public and getting input, such as town hall meetings and ad hoc surveys, are less rigorous and are not part of this discussion on formal surveys and focus groups methodology.

## Step 9: Transfer the Data from the Survey to a Spreadsheet

Once the entry of data into a spreadsheet has been verified, shred the respondents' instruments to ensure confidentiality. In some cases, interviewers may enter survey data directly onto a spreadsheet electronically while in the field. Regardless of when the data is aggregated, do not place any identifying information (e.g., address, name, Social Security number) about the respondents on the spreadsheet. In this way anonymity and confidentiality may be protected.

## Step 10: Analyze the Data and Present the Findings

The simplest summaries are indications of the most frequent response (mode) or middle response (median) to each question and whether there were significant differences among categories of respondents, for example, men versus women or young versus older persons. More sophisticated statistical analysis and identification of trends may be appropriate to understand the data.

Present the findings in ways that helps inform the decisions of the responsible appointed and elected officials. Specifically, what does the survey indicate are unmet and/or insufficient services? Are the public's concerns general or specific to one geographical area or subgroup, for example, youth? How do the data and analysis inform administrators and elected officials about current and future program efforts? Be modest and conservative in drawing conclusions from the data and analysis. A survey is a snapshot in time and not the ultimate guide for action.

## SURVEY TECHNOLOGY

The internet has introduced new surveying technologies, e.g., Survey Monkey and Qualtrics. These online applications provide a template for questions and access to persons who are willing to respond to online-computer-generated surveys. The process for developing an adequate instrument and a sample size is the same regardless of whether respondents are contacted in person, by phone, or via the internet. What is unique about internet services is that they are populated with persons who are most comfortable with technology: young, well-educated, and wealthy. For those scholars and practitioners needing a more diverse sample, online surveys may need to be augmented with other technologies. Using more than one technology means testing responses to assure that there is no bias introduced by the technology. For example, one question that was added to the American National Elections Survey was, "Do you own a dog? Yes, No." Differences in technology would be unrelated to owning a dog, so researcher expected that the response from phone and internet surveys would be insignificant. When this proved to be the case, they were satisfied that the medium had not affected respondent's answers.

Many online services are free, but this often means that the online company retains the raw data and provides only a question-by-question summary of responses. Typically, scholars and practitioners want the raw data so that they may conduct their own analysis. However, if the raw data is needed, surveying services may charge users. Consequently, users need to be cautious about what the survey system provides for free, what services it bills for, and what the cost for each service is.

## FOCUS GROUPS: AN EXAMPLE

The next most frequent approach for determining community sentiment is focus groups. In some situations, communities may use both surveys and focus groups. Typically, the focus group explores issues, terminology, and key concerns over a period of time, while the survey is used to systematically gauge overall public opinion at a moment in time.

Focus groups should not be confused with the use of breakout sessions at large meetings or town halls. The primary agenda for the focus group is to collect data and develop an understanding of an issue from the perspective of stakeholders. General meetings and town halls are primarily to share information between the administration and stakeholders.

There are online survey systems such as *Survey Monkey* which may be used if the members of the population to be surveyed have email, if the systems can be accessed via the internet, and if the researcher has the URL, e.g., http://www.surveymonkey.com/

Survey research and focus group sessions may be employed for the same program assessment. Since jurisdictions need to understand the views of stakeholders, the initial process is a focus group. For example, the city of Pomona received federal funding from the Department of Justice which required that recipient jurisdictions establish oversight boards of residents, administrators, elected officials, and civic and nongovernmental agencies. These boards were to govern and participate in the implementation of activities, to develop cooperation between residents and police/safety officers, and to foster social service programs and beautification efforts. As an initial task in developing an understanding of the program in the community a focus group session was conducted with the oversight board.

The city administrators elected to employ a focus group session that included representatives of the board. The session was held during one of the board's normal evening meetings, scheduled each month.

The session began with introductions of the board members, facilitator, and notetakers. The objective of the meeting was to assess the oversight board members' expectations, concerns, and challenges with regard to the Department of Justice program in their community. As a group the participants discussed what would be meaningful outcomes for the target community. Once the goals/objectives were identified, members prioritized the goals on their own and shared their ratings with the group.

The participants had a general conversation about how success might be measured, for example, lower dropout rates, better crime statistics, and lower graffiti removal costs. Finally, participants identified the factors that presented the greatest challenges and those factors that were most promising. These topics were explored individually by participants and then discussed with the group.

Later analysis of the participants' comments indicated that participants held four distinct models of cause-effect relationships:

- A high incidence of blight (graffiti, trash) leads to high crime rates.
- Greater attention to youth (dropout rates, poor test scores) will lead to a revitalized community.
- The gap between new and old immigrants leads to conflict and disparity in demands on city services.
- Police involvement in community life will lead to greater effectiveness in stemming crime.

While one model did not rule out another, the diversity in perspectives reflected a disparity of views regarding which efforts would represent the best use of funds.

# A STEP-BY-STEP GUIDE TO CONDUCTING A FOCUS GROUP

## Step 1: Identify Specific Objective(s) or Outcome(s) To Be Achieved

While the focus group format is more fluid than that of surveys, the facilitator needs to have a clear understanding of how the focus group interaction will develop a deeper understanding of community needs and concerns and what the scope of the group's discussions and recommendations may and may not include. Identify what the outcomes should be, such as draft policies or guiding principles.

## Step 2: Identify Persons and/or Groups to Participate in the Focus Group Sessions

Generally, focus group participants represent a casual sample of the population. A school interested in parent concerns may recruit participants from its parent-teacher association or from volunteers for after-school programs such as booster groups for sports or music programs. A senior center might recruit persons who attend a senior lunch program or regularly scheduled fellowship events. Critics of programs should be included as well.

## Step 3: Send Invitations to Participants Indicating the Date, Time, Location, and Reason for the Meeting

Follow up on the invitations to determine how many and which persons will be present. Bring, or have on hand, an easel, butcher block paper, masking tape, and markers to note comments of participants. Also have name tags for everyone at the session and paper and pencils for respondents so that they can take notes before sharing ideas with others. Snacks and drinks for participants are recommended but not required. Test audio equipment for taping the session and/or train notetakers to capture the information and tone of comments. A group of six to 12 participants per session is ideal. It is large enough to spur conversation and discussion and not so large that it makes monitoring comments and sharing views unwieldy.

Technology provides options for focus groups as well. Members from diverse areas may be invited to a *Zoom* session via the internet. While in the Zoom session, participants may be broken into prearranged discussion groups. A notetaker can be assigned to each group as well. The process of the focus group remains the same, but the technology enables scholars and practitioners to accommodate a wide range of participants. As with survey technology, the obstacle may be to assure that everyone has a strong internet connection and the necessary computer and/or laptop equipment to assure they can fully participate in the process. It is also possible to electronically record Zoom sessions. However, this feature should be utilized with caution. To assure that what is said in the focus group session is confidential and anonymous, participants may prefer the session not be recorded. The wishes of participants should outweigh the convenience for the researchers.

## Step 4: Welcome Participants to the Session

Once the group is assembled the facilitator needs to introduce themself, welcome the participants, and define the focus group's objective and process. Why has this focus group been assembled? Who is interested in the information? What will be done with the information? How were participants selected?

Introductions should include a name and relationship to the issue under discussion, such as, "My name is Sally, and I have three children who have attended this school." When introducing themselves, facilitators often do icebreakers or share some fact or interest with the group. For example, an icebreaker might be, "What is the most unusual place you have ever been?" or "What about your life experiences makes you distinct from most others you meet?" Unusual places could be Fiji, Bora Bora, a submarine, or an Alcatraz prison tour. A unique aspect could range from having 13 brothers and sisters to having met a U.S. president. The objective of the introductions is to build some cohesiveness among the group members. If there are notetakers in the room, they should be introduced at this time.

Establish ground rules about the focus group process. For example, any opinion or idea is acceptable. Comments of participants will be respected and kept confidential. All comments should be directed to the facilitator. This is to ensure that the notetakers are not distracted with side conversations and/or to ensure that the audio equipment (if allowed) is able to capture all comments. Provide an agenda for the session and indicate that the objective is to adhere to the proposed timeline.

## Step 5: Proceed With the Session Outline and Agenda as Planned

If the topic is a particular service, the facilitator might want to open with a general question about what respondents see as most beneficial about its current operations.

This might be followed by questions regarding concerns or challenges facing the organization or facility. The facilitator's role is to solicit comments from all participants and ensure the session is not dominated by one or a few persons. The facilitator needs to summarize concisely what the group consensus is. The facilitator might indicate what he or she is hearing to be assured that it is the gist of the conversation.

The other role of the facilitator is to follow up on comments to get more specific information. For example, the public might perceive that an agency's response time is slow, but what does slow mean? Is the expectation that a response will be available within the hour? The day? The week? If there is concern about how the organization prioritizes its attention, then what priority would the respondents like to see? To draw out thoughtful considerations, a facilitator might have participants itemize as a group all the services and tasks the agency performs. Place a number next to each item, and then have participants take a few minutes on their own to prioritize these tasks from most to least important. When debriefing the group look for common items that were at the top of most lists and those that were at the bottom. Finally, ask participants to identify the first thing that they would like to see resolved or changed. Try to get members to be specific about what the change is and the difference they perceive it would make.

Listen closely for areas of agreement and disagreement among participants. Are the disagreements due to differences in language usage or to substantive differences of opinion and/or experience? Listen for new ideas, concepts, collaborations, and solutions. Take time during the session to summarize what is being said and identify areas of similarities and differences.

## Step 6: Take a Break

If the session will take more than an hour, give participants the opportunity to stretch, snack, and chat with one another for about 10 to 15 minutes after the first hour and a half.

## Step 7: Complete the Session Agenda

Have participants summarize what they liked about and/or learned from the session. Also have participants evaluate the focus group experience, the facilitator, and any materials or exercises used in the discussion. Thank all participants for their input and indicate how the information will be presented and provided to the community and/or community decision makers.

## Step 8: Transcribe the Minutes From the Meetings Immediately

Transcribe notes and clarify any areas where the discussion may have gone off track. Studies require two or more sessions; when transcribed notes from all the sessions are complete, the researcher should review all sessions thoroughly.

## Step 9: Compare and Contrast the Information

What were the areas of agreement and disagreement? What was the tone of the comments? What insights were reported from meeting and discussing concerns with others in the community? Overall, what was learned? If language and phrasing are important in conveying meaning, then language nuances should be identified and discussed.

## Step 10: Prepare and Present a Report on the Sessions for Decision Makers and Stakeholders

The report can take many forms but should include the following:

- the background in developing and designing the focus group sessions (that is, summarize the questions or issues the sessions were designed to address)
- the target population and the means used to develop representative public participation at the sessions
- the session agendas
- the findings regarding areas of agreement and difference (that is, place the focus group sessions in context with other information the agency may have based on surveys, commendations, complaints, and so forth)
- conclusions and recommendations (be specific regarding the next steps the stakeholders and decision makers need to consider and take and be conservative with the conclusions drawn from this process; the findings may be richer in detail and context but are less representative of the population than is survey research)

## CONCLUSION

Focus group studies are qualitative research wherein the primary objective is to explore what are the issues and questions to be studied. They provide the researcher with an understanding of how citizens view circumstances, outcomes, and processes. Focus groups help to define the language that is most appropriate for community surveys/questionnaires. This process provides depth of analysis, while surveys may address concerns for a broader scope of community views.

Survey research is a more quantitative approach that uses systematic means for selecting samples and analyzing data. This approach enables researchers to estimate from their data the views of a population with a high degree of accuracy. Surveys can inform decision makers of the public's needs, support, and concerns regarding the quality and quantity of public goods and services provided. Both focus groups and surveys are a snapshot in time and are most useful in providing information that can guide public policy and program initiatives. In the examples provided in this discussion, researchers would need to follow procedures that would protect participants, ensure the confidentiality of responses, and where possible ensure anonymous participation.

## PRACTICING PUBLIC ADMINISTRATION

1. Assume a community has a population of 150,000, of which 98,000 are 18 or older. The community wants to draw a sample of voters that will have a confidence rate of 95% and a confidence interval of 4%. Which size sample does it need?

2. Refer to the table below. Which are the proper sample sizes for populations of 2,500, 25,000, 250,000, 2,500,000, and 25,000,000 if the confidence level is 95% and the confidence interval is 3%? What difference does it make if you change the confidence level to 99%?

| Population Estimate | SAMPLE SIZE 95% Confidence Level 3% Confidence Interval | SAMPLE SIZE 99% Confidence Level 3% Confidence Interval |
|---|---|---|
| 2,500 | 748 | |
| 25,000 | | |
| 250,000 | | |
| 2,500,000 | | |
| 25,000,000 | | |

3. The Department of Motor Vehicles can provide a list of every motorist in the jurisdiction noted in Question 1. Should the community draw a systematic sample from the DMV's list or take a random sample of residents using phone numbers? Discuss the pros and cons of these options.

4. What is wrong with the following survey questions? How might they be correctly worded?

   a. Where did you grow up?
      i.  urban area
      ii. country
      iii. city

   b. Are you satisfied with your job?
      i.  ___ Yes
      ii. ___ No
      iii. ___ No opinion or refused to answer

   c. What was your AGI for (year)? _____

5. As a committee of the whole determine which groups should be polled regarding satisfaction with a master's in public

administration program. In small groups develop a brief questionnaire to assess how to poll these respondents about their satisfaction.

6. A recreation center is interested in determining which changes are needed to serve its changing population. How might you identify persons to participate in a focus group session?

7. As the facilitator for the public recreation center study, you are tasked with developing the focus group agendas. Which questions would you ask and in which order to understand the needs of citizens?

## BIBLIOGRAPHY

Asher, H. (2007). *Polling and the public: What every citizen should know*. Washington, D.C.: CQ Press.

Barbour, R, S., & Kitzinger, J. (1999). *Developing focus group research: Politics, theory and practice*. Thousand Oaks, CA: Sage.

Bloor, M., Frankland, J., Thomas, M., & Robson, K. (2001). *Focus groups in social research*. Thousand Oaks, CA: Sage.

Charmley, S. (2006). Evaluating public participation in environmental decision making: EPA's superfund community involvement program. *Journal of Environmental Management* 77 (3), 165–182.

Edmunds, H. (1999). *The focus group research handbook*. Chicago, IL: NTC Business Books.

Gadomski, A., Wicks, D., & and Abernethy, K. (1997). Providing preventative services in a rural area through a public-private partnership. *American Journal of Public Health* 87 (8), 1375–1376.

Greenbaum, T. L. (2001). *Moderating focus groups*. Thousand Oaks, CA: Sage.

Hays, R. D., Liu, H., & Kapteyn, A. (2015). Use of Internet panels to conduct surveys. *Behavior Research Methods* 47(3), 685–690. https://doi.org/10.3758/s13428-015-0617-9

Janssen, M., Wimmer, M. A., & Deljoo, A., Eds. (2015). Policy practice and digital science integrating complex systems, social simulation and public administration in policy research. Springer International Publishing. https://doi.org/10.1007/978-3-319-12784-2

Langer, J. (2001). *The mirrored windows: Focus groups from a moderator's point of view*. Ithaca, NY: Paramount Markel.

Longo, D., Kruse, R. & Kiely R. G. (1997). A framework for designing and implementing community benefit standards. *Journal of Health Care Finance* 23 (4), 71–91.

Manheim, J. B., Rich, R. C., Willnat, L., & Brians, C. L. (2006). *Empirical political analysis: Research methods in political science*. (6th ed.). Boston, MA: Allyn & Bacon.

Marshall, C, & Rossman, G. B. (1999). *Designing qualitative research*. (3d ed.). Thousand Oaks, CA: Sage.

Monette, D. R., Sullivan, T., & DeJong, C. R. (1998). *Applied social research: Tool for the human services*. (4th ed.). Fort Worth, TX: Harcourt Brace.

Neuman, W. L. (2006). *Social research methods: Quantitative and qualitative approaches*. Boston, MA: Allyn & Bacon.

Norris-Tirrell, D., & Clay, J. A. (2017). *Strategic collaboration in public and nonprofit administration: A practice-based approach to solving shared problems*. Boca Raton, FL: Routledge.

O'Toole, L. (2000). Research on policy implementation: Assessment and prospects. *Journal of Public Administration Research and Theory* 10 (2), 263–286.

Patten, M. L. (2001). *Questionnaire research: A practical guide*. Glendale, CA: Pyrczak.

———. 2005. *Understanding research methods: An overview of the essentials*. Glendale, CA: Pyrczak.

Rowe, G., & Frewer, L. (2004). Evaluating public participation exercises: A research agenda. *Technology and Human Values* 29 (4), 512–557.

Salway, S., Chowbey, P., Such, E., & Ferguson, B. (2015). Researching health inequalities with community researchers: Practical, methodological and ethical challenges of an "inclusive" research approach. *Research Involvement and Engagement* 1(1), 9–9. https://doi.org/10.1186/s40900-015-0009-4

Sonnega, J., Sonnega, A., & Kruger, D. (2019). The city doesn't sleep: Community perceptions of sleep deficits and disparities. *International Journal of Environmental Research and Public Health* 16(20), 3976. https://doi.org/10.3390/ijerph16203976

# 9

# Making Complex Decisions
# Multi-Attribute Utility
# Technique (MAUT)

Section 2 of this text began with a discussion of the need for jurisdictions and agencies to articulate a vision and mission to establish community-wide goals and objectives. Chapter 7 explored how administrators support the strategic thinking process, and Chapter 8 examined how discussions with community partners and stakeholders are augmented with surveys, polls, and/or focus groups to ensure a cross section of the community's views are incorporated into long-term plans and objectives.

The underlying premise is that the public, or surrogates for the public (e.g., advocacy groups, public interest organizations), is involved in the decision-making process. In these situations, external representatives may or may not be involved. The focus is on internal decision-making efforts.

Middle managers have greater discretionary authority, greater responsibility for organizational effectiveness, and greater accountability to upper management and to elected officials than their subordinates, who may be professionals, technicians, and/or rank-and-file public servants. How much discretionary power middle managers have, how it should be utilized, and what underlying approach should be employed has been debated for the past quarter century. The basic debate is about whether public managers are, or should be, entrepreneurial like their private-sector counterparts or if the context for public-sector management is unique, such that a private-sector comparison is artificial. Regardless of which side of the debate one is on, scholars and practitioners tend to agree that the old hierarchical command system was cumbersome and did not allow managers the latitude needed to effectively serve the public.

# CONTROL

The control and command administrative system developed by the Progressives in the early 20th century was reinforced by the systems employed by the federal government to combat the Great Depression and mobilize a nation to fight a war in Europe and the Pacific. The primary agenda items were to exercise control over the administration, ensure efforts were implemented, and shield administrators from politicians, war profiteers, and the unscrupulous. Administrative systems had deep hierarchies (executive, department, division, unit, area, etc.) in which information flowed upward and decisions flowed down. An engineer interested in pricing information for a benefit cost study of a toll road would request the data from his or her manager, who would pass the request up two or more layers of management in the engineering division before the question was passed to Finance. The finance director would then pass the information down his or her chain of command until it reached the pricing specialist who had the information; this person would pass it up multiple levels of management before it was transferred to Engineering and found its way to the person requesting the information. The consequences of this system are legendary: response times were slow, coordination of efforts was a chronic problem, miscommunication was the norm, and efforts were costly.

The Progressive reforms had two benefits: control and accountability. The head of the department/agency issued commands to subordinates and controlled communication between their area and those who were not under their chain of command. Employees in these systems spoke of units in the organization as being "siloed": isolated, unaware, and unresponsive to colleagues, citizens, and competing views.

Control, accountability, and responsibility continue to be core values of public administration but are not the only values. By the mid-1950s scholars questioned the rationality of Progressive reform systems, citing the need for an army of coordinators to get work done or an informal network of employees who would run the organization but not be overtly accountable for its operations.

## Challenges to Administrative Control Systems

By the 1970s state and local governments were being challenged by the public's unwillingness to pay for government programs. In addition, changes in technology (especially the computer) enabled persons to communicate with one another directly rather than going through layers of administrative hierarchy. Administrative systems began to change, and in the early 1990s David Osborne and Ted Gaebler discussed this evolving revolution in *Reinventing Government: How the Entrepreneurial Spirit Is Transforming the Public Sector*. This work and an array of publications that followed had a different view of the role and decision-making efforts of middle to upper managers.

- The manager in the public sector should operate using the same priorities and skills as his or her private-sector counterpart. The manager should seize on innovative opportunities to save money and expand/improve services. Frontline managers should allocate funds to be most responsive to customers and less attentive to rules or regulations. The middle manager should be accountable for decisions after the fact rather than (with permission from superiors) on an a priori basis. Seizing the opportunity requires more discretionary decision making about how money is spent and on what it is spent.

- The manager's focus should be on serving the customer, not upper management. Upper and middle managers should make mission-driven decisions.

- Government and its managers should create, encourage, and foster competition with private-sector providers, nongovernmental organizations, and/or other public providers. Instead of creating a new bureau for every new public demand, the government should look for ways to realize results without adding to the bureaucracy. For example, if communities want fewer greenhouse emissions, then the community should provide tax incentives for installing and documenting solar panels and energy-efficient appliances and driving hybrid vehicles. If these options are not well understood then communities should utilize existing education institutions, conservation consortiums, and/or private energy providers to educate, inform, and reward behavior that reduces the community's carbon footprint. If a service must be provided (e.g., disposal of waste water, sewage, or toxins) then communities should seek competitive bids and monitor effectiveness and costs through provisions in contracts or grants. The government should be the provider of last resort.

- Managers should operate in flat, self-governed teams and reward effectiveness, cost efficiency, and innovation rather than be rewarded for spending, hiring staff, and raising barriers to public involvement.

## Assessing the Reinventing Government Revolution

Osborne and Gaebler's book is a thought-provoking compilation of vignettes from a dozen or so cases interspersed with summaries of emerging trends and perspectives. However, it is not a systematic analysis of the decision-making conditions of public- versus private-sector managers. Scholars have sought to examine decision-making behaviors and identify competing and persistent differences that make entrepreneurial decisions more challenging in the public sector. Among the differences reported are the following:

Private-sector managers serve customers with relatively uniform goods/services demands. A private school's client is the student's parents. The public-sector manager's customers are overseers, each of whom are arguing for a different clientele: students' parents, taxpayers, teachers unions, and special interest groups with issues that may or may not be related to education. Among the issues that have been added to the public education agenda are immunization requirements, drivers' education, intramural sports programs, fellowship, and prayer.

The private sector's environment is competitive with incentives to get as many customers as possible from as broad an area as possible. In the public sector there are disincentives to offering programs to citizens outside the jurisdiction. An effort to capture clients from other jurisdictions is considered wasteful.

Private-sector managers allocate money to data collection and analysis as a cost of doing business. Public-sector managers have less data, and data gathering may be at the expense of providing some goods and/or services.

Private-sector managers may operate in secrecy; operational decisions are not open to public scrutiny. Public manager decisions are open to public review and scrutiny either directly or indirectly.

Private-sector managers have a limited, hierarchical chain of command with a relatively coherent and consistent operational definition of success (market share, increase revenue, profits, etc.). Public-sector managers have conflicting, turbulent, and competing operational definitions of success. The public-sector manager works toward integrating different attributes of success into some representation of the public interest.

The differences between the sectors have consequences. Public-sector managers are prone to having a consensus-building bias, seeking out views of elites and/or experts, and relying less on objective analysis and more on means that promote negotiation and balance among competing agendas. Public and private managers have similar efficiency agendas: the greatest output/outcomes at the least cost. However, they have different effectiveness agendas. The private sector seeks to maximize its market impact and can unilaterally abandon markets it finds unprofitable, while the public-sector manager seeks to make decision-making criteria explicit and apply criteria consistently while maintaining services to all citizens.

## THE PRACTICE OF INTEGRATING
## COMPETING AGENDAS INTO A COHERENT DECISION

Governments make hundreds of decisions on behalf of the public each day. Who is the best applicant for the job? Which contractor would provide the best service? Which recreation facilities should be expanded, merged, or phased out?

When there are multiple factors that affect a major decision (selecting the best contractor or the best candidate for a high-level position), managers seek out a methodology that enables them to address the diverse concerns in the environment, employ analysis about outcomes, and systematically assess available options. The factors are called "attributes." The systematic incorporation of these many factors is called the multi-attribute utility technique (MAUT). In some circles the process is called multi-criteria decision analysis (MCDA) or may go by another name. In practice, these are all using the same approach. For example, when selecting a police chief from among a number of candidates the important attributes might be:

* years in law enforcement,
* public relations/community involvement experiences,
* management skills,
* leadership skills,
* forensic expertise,
* education, and
* reputation.

While all factors are important, they are typically not of equal importance. Management and leadership skills may be more important than years of education. However, to make an informed decision one needs to identify and weigh all factors. Each attribute is a fraction of the whole decision, and the sum of these important pieces should total 100%.

If a factor has weight, then there needs to be a means to determine to what extent an attribute is present. What does the resumé indicate about the candidate's years of service and in which areas of public safety? What education and/or training does the candidate have? Some experiences will be more useful in meeting the demands of the job than will others. Twenty years of experience may have more utility than 10, but experience in both line and staff positions may be more desirable than a concentration of experience in one area. This approach requires that each valued attribute have some means to be observed and evaluated. Utility measures may range from 0 to 100. The range of utility for an attribute may be expressed in any number of ways. However, the easiest explanation may be that if there is no evidence of an attribute, the utility is 0, and if the attribute is fully realized, the utility is estimated at 100%. Based on this range, decision makers may determine what would constitute 25%, 50%, and 75% satisfaction or evidence of an attribute's being present.

Finally, each applicant, provider, or option needs to be assessed by tempering the evidence about each attribute (years of education, experience) against its relative weight, indicating importance. The decision to favor one choice among others typically involves selecting the option or options with the highest weighted score.

## PROS AND CONS OF MAUT

The pros:

- It makes explicit what is important and how important different factors are to the overall decision.

- It enables others to review the process and determine if they would have reached the same—or a similar—conclusion.

- It incorporates the expertise of many decision makers into a comprehensive whole.

- It enables decision makers to clearly identify what are the advantages of their chosen option and what are the limitations or deficiencies of other options.

The cons:

- It takes time and requires an experienced facilitator to manage the process.

- Some steps take more discussion and are contentious.

- Participants sometimes see MAUT as too subjective, while others see it as too impersonal.

- Not all decision makers are comfortable with techniques that involve math.

## MAUT TIMING

MAUT may help determine the importance of different attributes in a selection. In the public sector outlining attributes in advance of making a decision is necessary for ensuring transparency. If decision makers are seeking to select the best contractor to provide a public service, the MAUT process should be completed before the request for proposal or bid instructions are sent out. Similarly, if the objective is to find a new chief of police or to determine which programs are to be expanded, maintained, or cut, MAUT attributes and weights should be identified before advertising the position or asking managers and staff to provide information about existing operations.

# A Step-by-Step Guide to Conducting MAUT

## Step 1: Key Decision Makers

Prepare a list of all persons who will participate in the decision. The list would include the diversity of interests associated with the decision. For example, if the objective is to select a public works director, the participants might include private-sector entrepreneurs, minority entrepreneurs, user groups and associations, taxpayer associations, chamber of commerce, and so forth. Be sure the list of participants is based on the task at hand.

Once a task is defined and the participants are identified, a facilitator should be named. The facilitator will develop the agenda(s) and provide feedback to members as the process proceeds. The facilitator need not be from outside the agency but should be someone whose sole responsibility is to ensure that all participants are included in the process, key points are summarized, and meeting times and schedules are followed.

Not every participant and interest will be involved in every step, but participation by key decision makers is not voluntary. For MAUT to be effective the decision makers must be available and must participate in the process.

## Step 2: Developing Goals and Identifying Attributes

Identify the group's mission. What specifically is the goal of the decision-making process? What criteria or attributes do participants feel should be included in the decision? This requires facilitating an open discussion with participants in the MAUT process about the criteria they are using—or want to use—in valuing their options.

*Criteria* is a term that participants do not always understand. For example, participants might suggest promoting from within to boost morale or choosing a supplier who operates in the jurisdiction to support the local economy. While these features may be important and associated with one or more options, they are not criteria.

Criteria are broad concerns for which there is a range of responses. For example, consider your choice of shoes and the attributes you considered when selecting this pair. You might have considered price, color, comfort, and durability. These are criteria. It may be your shoes are black, and this is a feature of many of your choices. However, the criterion is color because while you choose black, you do so from a range of options: brown, blue, red, and so forth.

Criteria may be developed at a brainstorming session or facilitated meeting at which any and all relevant factors are open for discussion. Ask participants to suggest criteria and offer brief definitions of what they see as essential in the decision-making process.

The assumption that promoting an internal candidate for a high-level position will boost morale may be part of the criterion of a candidate's demonstrating an ability to promote a positive work environment. A desire to hire a local contractor may be subsumed under the criterion of expanding opportunities for local businesses and labor. There are limitations:

- Each criterion should be unique and not overlap with another criterion—if one criterion is management skill and another is efficient use of resources, these may be two ways of expressing the same concern or uniquely different factors.

- There should be less than 15 criteria in all—more than 15 criteria will dilute the effectiveness of this technique in distinguishing among weights assigned to different attributes.

- All the participants should agree on the list of the criteria. Agreement is critical. While some items will have more influence than others, all items need to be listed.

## Step 3: Prioritizing Attributes

After coming up with a unique list of criteria, participants need to organize the list in terms of importance, placing the items in descending order with the most important at the top.

Getting the list prioritized is an iterative process. Generally, there is some consensus among decision makers about where some items fall. It does not matter on which items decision makers initially agree. Typically, there is agreement at the top or the bottom rather than in the middle. Most of the discussion tends to focus on items in the middle.

The facilitator should begin by trying to get the participants to identify the importance of the criteria they generally agree on and define why those criteria belong in their relative positions. Once agreement has been developed on a few items the participants are able to discuss the remaining criteria in relationship to agreed-on criteria.

Important criteria when selecting a chief of police may include:

- community relations
- education
- forensic expertise
- leadership skill
- management skill
- reputation with peers
- years in law enforcement

Although the criteria are unique, they are linked. Wouldn't one's management and leadership skills be linked to the number of years of experience in law enforcement? Isn't one's reputation in law enforcement likely to be built on a candidate's leadership ability with fellow officers and his or her working relationship with community groups and citizens? Perhaps, but a candidate's many years of experience may mean little if there is no corresponding growth in responsibility and ability to handle challenges. Similarly, a relatively short tenure in a leadership position may reveal a candidate's mettle for handling adversity, whereas 20 years of service in a less contentious environment may not have tested one's leadership ability. Therefore, while the criteria are linked, each criterion provides a unique contribution to the overall decision and can be taken into account individually.

In our example the criteria were given the following relative priorities:

**Criteria**
1. Leadership skill
2. Management skill
3. Community relations
4. Years in law enforcement
5. Forensic expertise
6. Reputation with peers
7. Education

This step is complete when all participants agree about the order of the criteria.

## Step 4: Weighing Attributes

Having developed a prioritized list, each criterion needs to be rated in relationship to the others. To begin, select the least important item on the list and assign it a value of 10. Then proceed up the list asking participants if the next item up is of equal value or more value. If the higher attribute is of equal value, then give the item the same number. If the next item is of greater value, have the participants indicate the relative increase. For example, if the next item up were half again as important as the first (set at a base of 10), its value would be 15; if it were twice as important, its value would be 20; if it were two and a half times more important, its value would be 25; and so forth.

Participants may want to debate and "bargain" as to how much more important one factor is than another. Bargaining will not harm the analysis as long as the differences in assigned points do not violate the agreed-on order. This means that a group might decide to increase a lower attribute by five points and decrease a higher attribute by seven. This will narrow the distance between the attributes. However, the lower attribute should remain in the same relative position with regard to the other attributes in the array.

For example, let's assume the panel for selecting a police chief assigns the following weights:

| Attribute | Weight |
|---|---|
| Leadership skill | 90 |
| Management skill | 90 |
| Community relations | 45 |
| Years in law enforcement | 30 |
| Forensic expertise | 20 |
| Reputation with peers | 15 |
| Education | 10 |

This reveals the panel's understanding that leadership and management are of prime and equal importance, whereas community relations represents half the weight of these prime skills. In retrospect they may decide that community relations should be higher and is undervalued in this array. The increase in an attribute can go up to and include the same value as that for the attribute above it but should not exceed the value of the next higher attribute. In this example this could mean increasing community relations to 90 but not 91. If the increase is greater than the next higher item, it violates the agreement worked out in Step 3 and might require revisiting Step 3.

Assigning weights to the attributes is less contentious and time consuming than developing the criteria and prioritizing them. It is typically in these earlier conversations that a collaborative notion of the relative importance of the criteria has been formulated, and assigning numbers serves to reinforce norms developed earlier in the process.

Assigning numbers to values is difficult for some persons who assess factors in more qualitative than quantitative terms. This single step takes time and patience. It should not be rushed. If the assigning of numeric values proves to be an obstacle, then the facilitator may elect to provide the participants with MAUT experience by having them assign weights to criteria for selecting shoes, a movie, or any simpler decision. Participants will come to grasp how the numbers provide a shorthand representation of their more complex concerns about the attributes identified.

To normalize the weights as fractions of one, simply sum the values and divide each criterion by the total, as in the example on the following page:

**Table 9.1  Weighting Attributes in a Multi-Attribute Utility Analysis**

| Attribute | Weight | Percentage |
|---|---|---|
| Leadership skills | 90 | 90 ÷ 300 = 0.30 |
| Management skills | 90 | 90 ÷ 300 = 0.30 |
| Community relations | 45 | 45 ÷ 300 = 0.15 |
| Years in law enforcement | 30 | 30 ÷ 300 = 0.10 |
| Forensic expertise | 20 | 20 ÷ 300 = 0.07 |
| Reputation with peers | 15 | 15 ÷ 300 = 0.05 |
| Education | 10 | 10 ÷ 300 = 0.03 |
| Total | 300 | 300 ÷ 300 = 1.00 |

Once the prioritized and weighted list of attributes is normalized, this phase of the process is complete.

The next phase is to develop utility functions, sometimes called "utiles," to measure each factor. Using utiles ensures comparing like things and not comparing apples with oranges. For example, one attribute might be time measured in years or while another is measured in ratings from 1 to 10. Let's assume that experience is valued at 0.4. If expertise were measured along the rating system of 1 to 10, it could be valued from 0.4 to 4.0 ($0.4 \times 1 = 0.4$ to $0.4 \times 10 = 4.0$). If experience were measured in years, then responses from 5 to 15 years would be valued from 2.0 to 6.0 ($0.4 \times 5 = 2.0$ to $0.4 \times 15 = 6.0$).

Factors will be influenced less by their utility to the decision makers and more by the scale used to measure the attribute, such as raw ranks, years, square feet, and so forth. For this reason, raw data, or assessments of an attribute, needs to be translated into a uniform measuring mechanism. The utility system does not need to be from 0 to 100, but it does need to be some specified range.

Decision makers may or may not be area experts for one or more of the attributes identified as critical to the final decision. Persons not involved in Steps 1 through 4 may complete the development of utility functions.

## Step 5: Converting Attributes into Utility Functions

Utility functions are a concept borrowed from economics. Economists assume that the presence or consumption of a good or service has utility that users can identify. On a hot day, after you have spent hours in traffic with exhaust fumes and noise, you have the opportunity to stop at a local ice cream parlor. This particular parlor has facilities to serve customers from one to 15 scoops of ice cream at a single visit. The first scoop of ice cream is delightful and totally satisfying (100%), but the second scoop—while satisfying—is less so (about 75% of what was experienced with the first), and by the fifth or sixth scoop you are sick of ice cream and feeling nauseous. Its utility is zero.

You can plot the utility by placing the percentage of utility realized on the vertical axis (y) and the amount of ice cream consumed on the horizontal axis (x). The utility function would look like Figure 9.1.

**Figure 9.1    Utility Function for Scoops of Ice Cream**

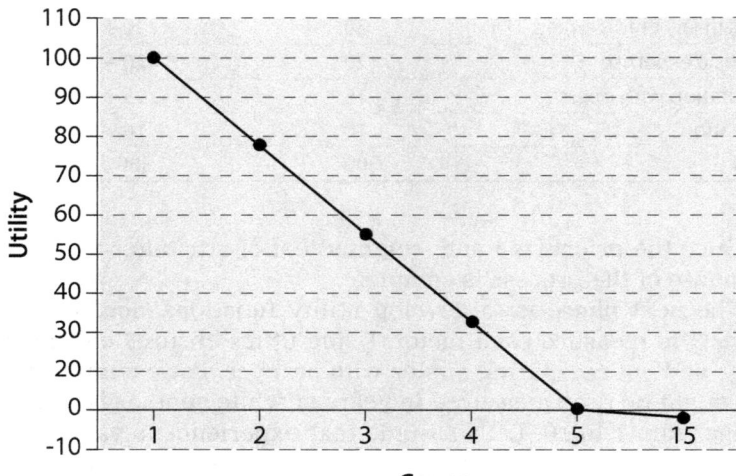

Utility curves can be built around any attribute. For example, an agency wants a police chief able to adapt his or her leadership style to meet a variety of demands associated with the position. Experts inside and outside the agency are looking and listening for the following information:

- candidate identifies different constituents related to the chief's role,
- candidate provides examples of using different approaches to motivating persons to work in concert,
- candidate explains conflict situations where he or she successfully resolved a situation, and
- candidate explains conflict situations where he or she could not successfully resolve a dispute but identifies what he or she learned from the experience.

How might this utility curve look? A candidate who scores high among all reviewers for all four circumstances would be the ideal (100%) candidate with regard to leadership, while a candidate who scores poorly on all four would have little to no (zero percent) utility regarding this position. More difficult to assign is what represents a midpoint or "mostly" good rating. High marks in most areas with a low mark in one might represent a 75% situation, while high marks in one aspect but low marks otherwise would represent a low score (25%). The utility curve might look like Figure 9.2.

**Figure 9.2    Leadership Utility Curve**

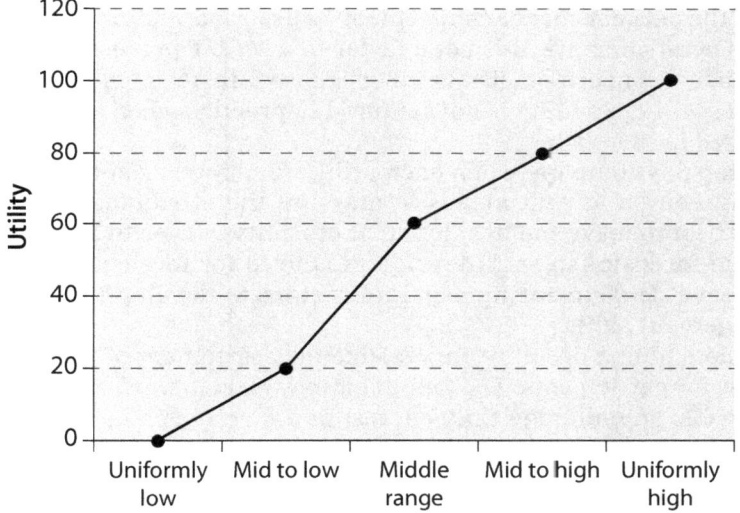

Reviewer Scores for Candidates' Level of Leadership

Utility functions are not exact measurements of an attribute but rather are agreed-upon standards for observing and evaluating what the decision makers mean when they speak of an applicant's ability with regard to an attribute.

One or more utility curves need to be developed for each attribute. If an attribute has more dimensions than can be represented on one curve, then the utility scores from two or more curves may be averaged to best represent the attribute of interest.

Utility functions are sometimes linear (composed of lines) like the ones above and sometimes curved. For example, as education rises the utility experienced may rise as well. However, that relationship may have limits for the position being considered. While someone with a graduate degree might represent 100% utility, a person with a PhD and law degree may represent less utility for the police chief position. In these circumstances the initial utility curve would rise as with the leadership curve above and then fall—or slope downward—with each additional degree.

The process of describing—in measurable terms—qualities, values, and concepts is unsettling to some decision makers. They might suggest there is just some "je ne sais quoi" or "I don't know what" quality—the final option must be acceptable. This elusive quality confounds description and measurement; as Justice Potter Stewart once quipped, I can't define obscenity, but "I know it when I see it."

If the decision maker cannot identify, describe, and/or express variations of an attribute, it is not a factor in a MAUT process. Nor should the elusive concern be dismissed or ignored. Instead, go through Step 6, and see if the quality is not captured in practice when each option is assessed individually.

Step 5 is complete when each utility function has been developed and agreed on as a fit means to measure the attributes. It is sometimes best to leave the development of utility curves to area experts. Let the forensic lab staff develop the curve for forensic knowledge, and leave department managers/directors to develop the curve for management skills.

The building of utility curves, like the assignment of weights, may be new for participants. The facilitator may elect to work with the group as a whole on building utility curves for a factor such as shoe comfort or restaurant ambiance. Once participants have experience with utility curves, they are able to apply curves to the situation at hand. However, analysts should note that developing utility curves is neither a science nor objective. It is a subjective representation of a creative and collaborative process that requires participants to translate imprecise values into concise and specific terms.

## Step 6: Applying the Utility Function to Each Alternative

Once the information is submitted the process of reviewing the information and assigning a utility value (0 to 100) begins. In our police chief example, Candidate B may have received high leadership scores from most reviewers but low scores by one. Candidate B's utility score is 85 on leadership. A utility score needs to be identified for each attribute (management, education, etc.) for each alternative (candidate). Finally, the identification of each utility score for each attribute for each option (candidate) is summarized on a matrix along with the agreed-on weights.

Each attribute's utility score is multiplied by its corresponding weight (e.g., leadership [100] × [0.30] = 30) to determine the weighted score. The boldface scores in Table 9.2 indicate the weighted scores for each attribute for each candidate, which are then added up to calculate the total weighted score for each candidate (88.2 for Candidate A and 91.6 for Candidate B). Can you compute a weighted and total weighted scores for Candidate C?

# Making Complex Decisions

**Table 9.2   Summary Matrix of Weight with Utility Scores for Candidates**

| Attribute | Leadership | Management | Community Relations | Years | Forensic | Reputation | Education | Total |
|---|---|---|---|---|---|---|---|---|
| **Weight** | **0.30** | **0.30** | **0.15** | **0.10** | **0.07** | **0.05** | **0.03** | **1.00** |
| Candidate A Utility Scores | 100 | 80 | 92 | 88 | 58 | 90 | 100 | |
| Candidate A Weighted Scores | **30.0** | **24.0** | **13.8** | **8.8** | **4.1** | **4.5** | **3.0** | **88.2** |
| Candidate B Utility Scores | 85 | 98 | 100 | 95 | 85 | 90 | 60 | |
| Candidate B Weighted Scores | **25.5** | **29.4** | **15.0** | **9.5** | **5.9** | **4.5** | **1.8** | **91.6** |
| Candidate C Utility Scores | 80 | 75 | 84 | 72 | 100 | 100 | 86 | |
| Candidate C Weighted Scores | | | | | | | | |
| **Maximum possible Weighted score** | **30** | **30** | **15** | **10** | **7** | **5** | **3** | **100** |

---

### Box 9.1   MAUT Math

The math requires multiplying each weight by its corresponding value (utility or utile) and summing the results. For example, a college syllabus indicates the following:
- 20 points will be based on the midterm,
- 30 on the term paper,
- 40 on the comprehensive final, and
- 10 on participation and attendance.

The list indicates the relative importance or weight attached to each task. The sum of these weights (0.2, 0.3, 0.4, and 0.1) is 1.0.

The evidence for each factor are the scores received on the midterm, on the final, on the project, and for participation. Therefore, a student who receives 60 on the midterm, 70 on the term paper, 92 on the final, and 80 for participation would have an overall score as follows:

Score = 0.2 (60 midterm) + 0.3 (70 midterm) + 0.4 (92 final) + 0.1 (80 participation) = 12.0 + 21.0 + 36.8 + 8.0 = 77.8 out of 100 points.

## Step 7: Selecting the Best Option

Based on the numbers alone, the most rational choice is B with an overall score of 91.6. However, the distance between the top score and the next best alternative is 3.4 points (91.6 – 88.2). Is this difference sufficient to rule out one candidate in favor of another? If not, what should be done?

Assuming the short list is the top two options, decision makers may elect to interview anew the top candidates to capture additional information about areas of weakness and strength. Candidate B appears to be the stronger manager, while candidate A seems to be a stronger leader. In other ways the candidates are quite alike, and/or the factors are of lesser importance. Consequently, if a second interview is held, the specific aspects of leadership and management should be the focus of the agenda. How significant is the deficiency? Does the candidate recognize the deficiency? Is the candidate working on improving their skills or abilities in the area? Finally, are there programs, staff, and resources in place in the city to provide leadership or management support until the best candidate is fully versed in the job?

It is likely that more contact and communication with candidates will clarify concerns about skills and abilities. After the second interview the decision makers may reassess the utiles assigned and see if the scores are unchanged. In light of the new information, decision makers should review the overall scores and select the best option based on the highest score.

## ETHICAL CONCERNS

It was the end of a long and arduous project. The project's managers and analysts were going to celebrate at a local restaurant. They could not agree on a restaurant but elected to vote on a few options. The majority of votes were for Bistro Café. The entire process took about 5 minutes. The project's consultant saw the restaurant discussion as an opportunity to utilize MAUT and proceeded through the steps with the team members. The highest-ranking score went to Bistro Café, and the process took nearly an hour. The team members were not impressed. What good is the process if one arrives at the same decision but it takes 10 times longer to get there? What is ethical about taking up everyone's time?

Technical processes do not substantively change the decisions of an organization. The processes will not change the options, the organization's needs, or its values. However, the processes enable all points of view to be heard, enable all options to be discussed, and make explicit what the values are and how they are incorporated into the decision. This integration of values and reason promotes ethical decision making in a range of concerns that administrators address daily. It supports community cohesion.

This cohesion saved the project's celebration. When the participants arrived at Bistro Café it was closed due to a family emergency. The team's members proceed to the second option without needing to reconvene, hold another discussion, or vote. They understood the options in the context of their community.

## CONCLUSION

This discussion has focused on using MAUT in a personnel function, but it can be used in any situation wherein there are multiple interests, such as selecting the best available contractor, allocating funds to multiple facilities, or allocating resources for multiple functions. Organizations may simplify some steps. For example, one could substitute expert assessments on a scale from one to five in lieu of formal utility curves. The mechanism need not be elaborate as long as it is understood and useful in weighing all factors that are essential to making an informed decision.

One may also use MAUT as a research tool. A researcher can assist the organization in developing weights for criteria and utility curves to measure outcomes. Based on these tools the researcher can assist the organization in evaluating the net changes in its decision-making process by identifying delays and/or deviations from the "best option" alternative supported by the MAUT process. The tools do not dictate solutions but provide decision makers with insight and understanding.

## PRACTICING PUBLIC ADMINISTRATION

1. Compose a list of criteria that would be appropriate for selecting new police cars, a high school history text, or a janitorial service for a five-story public office building. Prioritize your criteria from most to least important. Compare and contrast your list and priorities with a colleague. Can you derive a common list?

2. Based on your list of criteria, identify one means for observing the attribute and measuring it. For example, if a criterion is reliability, then a car's reliability might be judged by how auto experts rank its frequency of needing repairs and estimate its years of useful life, while a janitorial service might be rated based on positive and negative comments of current users.

3. Build utility curves for each of the top three criteria.

4. The educational subcommittee has prepared the following matrix regarding its criteria and review of four options.

| No. | Criteria | Raw Weights | Utility Scores for Four Options | | | |
|-----|----------|-------------|---|---|---|---|
| | | | A | B | C | D |
| 1 | Balanced treatment of current-event issues | 90 | 80 | 85 | 78 | 90 |
| 2 | Readability (based on student reviewer's comments) | 50 | 90 | 80 | 75 | 65 |
| 3 | Cost per student | 30 | 80 | 80 | 90 | 75 |
| 4 | Quality of faculty aids (e.g., test bank) | 20 | 90 | 90 | 100 | 80 |
| 5 | Scope of auxiliary materials (e.g., videos, online web resources) | 10 | 90 | 100 | 100 | 80 |

5. Complete the matrix below.

**Criteria Applied to Educational Materials Decision**

| Normalized | Balance | Readable | Cost | Faculty Aids | Auxiliary | Sum |
|-----------|---------|----------|------|--------------|-----------|-----|
| Weights | 0.45 | 0.25 | 0.15 | 0.10 | 0.05 | 1.00 |
| Option A Utility Score | 80 | 90 | 80 | 90 | 90 | |
| Option B Utility Score | 85 | 80 | 80 | 90 | 100 | |
| Option C Utility Score | 78 | 75 | 90 | 100 | 100 | |
| Option D Utility Score | 90 | 65 | 75 | 80 | 80 | |

Note: Chart is reoriented to reflect options in the rows and criteria in the columns.

6. Based on the analysis above:

  a. What is the best option?

  b. Why?

  c. What advice could the reviewers give to Option A to improve its score in future years?

## BIBLIOGRAPHY

Belton, V. T., & Stewart, J. (2002). *Multiple criteria decision analysis*. Boston, MA: Kluwer Academic.

Edwards, W. (1992). *Utility theories: Measurements and applications*. Boston, MA: Kluwer Academic.

Forman, E. S., & Gass, I. (2001). The analytical hierarchy process: An exposition. *Operation Research, 49*(4), 469–486.

Gass, S. I. (2005). Model world: The great debate—MAUT versus AHP. *Interfaces, 35*(4), 308–312.

Health Decisions Strategies. (2003). MAUT grapher and calculator. www.healthstrategy.com/mautgraph/mautgraph.htm.

Hitt, M., Ireland, R., & Hoskisson, R. (2003). *Strategic management* (3rd ed.). St. Paul, MN: West.

Keeney, R. L., & Raiffa, H. (1992). Decisions with multiple objectives. New York, NY: John Wiley.

McInnes, R., Smith, G., Greaves, J., Watson, D., Wood, N., & Everard, M. (2016). Multicriteria decision analysis for the evaluation of water quality improvement and ecosystem service provision. *Water and Environment Journal : WEJ, 30*(3–4), 298–309. https://doi.org/10.1111/wej.12195

Nutt, P. (1993). The formulation processes and tactics used in organizational decision making. *Organizational Science, 4*(2), 226–251.

———. (2005). Comparing public and private sector decision making practices. *Journal of Public Administration Research and Theory, 16*, 289–318.

Osborne, D., & Gaebler, T. (1993). *Reinventing government: How the entrepreneurial spirit is transforming the public sector*. New York, NY: Plume.

Saaty, T. L. (1982). *Decision making for leaders*. Belmont, CA: Lifetime Learning.

Shoemaker, P. J. (1982). The expected utility model: Its variants, purposes, evidence and limitations. *Journal of Economic Literature, 20*(2), 529–563.

Weimer, D., & Vining, A. (1999). *Policy analysis: Concepts and practice* (3rd ed.). Upper Saddle River, NJ: Prentice Hall.

# 10 ——◇——◇——◆

# Project Management
# PERT and Flowcharts

Over the past quarter century, the most dramatic change in organizational management has occurred at the supervisory level. This chapter discusses one way the shift from hierarchical to flattened organizations fundamentally redesigned the supervisor's role and responsibilities. In part the redesign of the frontline manager's role reflects the fact that multiple specialties are required to address new and complex projects on a large-scale basis—for example, the design and implementation of specialized computer software for operations and reporting. In addition, frontline management under early organizational models was held accountable for project schedules and budgets. The shift to organizations that use task forces, project management, and/or teams has meant that efforts that were once solely the concern of managers (performance evaluation and review or the charting of tasks) are now broadly held by both managers and staff. The tools discussed here are used as opportunities for training, for continuous improvement, and for facilitating communication, coordination, and cooperation.

## THE DISSOLVING AND EVOLVING
## OF FRONTLINE MANAGEMENT

Early in the 21st century positions that were primarily supervisory began to disappear in the public sector. As job functions were redefined, 1.5 supervisory positions were lost for every nonsupervisory position shed at the federal level. A similar elimination of supervisory positions occurred in state and local governments. In part the redesign of the organization was the consequence of several converging factors:

the application of social science theory and research, new technology, the rise of a more professional workforce, and greater sophistication and complexity in public programs.

## Theory X, Theory Y, and Theory Z

The hierarchical organization originated in antiquity and was used to mobilize and deploy the military throughout a political jurisdiction to maintain order and ensure obedience. This system of management meant information flowed up and orders flowed down a chain of command. Persons in these organizations were focused on obeying directions of superiors and enforcing compliance from subordinates. In the scholarly literature this became known as Theory X management. Social scientists in a range of disciplines from sociology and psychology to economics began to explore the relationship between organization structures and their productivity, stability, and adaptability. Did hierarchical, disciplined, command-control systems provide anticipated outcomes? Research findings varied, but there emerged a body of research that indicated Theory X management often stymied organizational goals. Douglas McGregor suggested in 1960 that work was as natural as play and that persons sought out opportunities to learn, be responsible, and contribute to group life. The high costs of administrative structures were due to systems failing to support employees rather than employees failing the administrative system. In practice the social science findings gave rise to new practices and/or experiments generally based on Theory Y management: cross training, quality circles, self-managed teams, psychological testing to identify personality predispositions (e.g., Myers-Briggs), and so forth. The dilemma was that the leaderless, or self-guided, teams lacked management skills, experience, career paths, and a reason for management responsibilities to be absorbed by nonmanagement employees who were neither recognized nor compensated for these responsibilities. Early difficulties with teams raised issues.

In part these issues were addressed by Ouchi's Theory Z, which suggested that to have viable self-guided teams, organizations needed to change the culture. Some aspects of Theory X management needed to be retained, such as authoritative relationships, performance evaluation, work specification, and the rational use of resources. However, to incorporate these attributes organizations needed to nurture collaboration on and consensus about tasks and deadlines. Organizations needed to have long-term commitments to employees rather than see them as replaceable cogs in the machinery of the agency. Career paths would be nonspecialized and would slowly evolve with the emerging managerial culture. As with Theory Y decades earlier, the scholarly findings about the performance of Theory Z organizations were mixed.

## The New Organizational Environment

Despite scholarly attempts to isolate and measure which organizational structures provided which behaviors and results, organizational redesign continued. In part, it was driven by technological changes such as personal computers, servers, the internet, and cell phones in the 1970s to early 2000s and the team management software and innovations, like Zoom, which came later. Persons in different parts of the world could be in contact with each other virtually instantly. Information was more widely available than ever before. The span of control of managers grew exponentially.

The new technology also meant that technical, engineering, and specialized skills were now involved in programs and policies that had once been the sole purview of teachers, health care providers, and police officers. Matrix teams of various specialized areas—technical, financial, operational, and so forth—rather than hierarchical structures were essential to get fundamental systems built and operational. Employees needed to see how their specialties and functions were integrated into a coherent whole to execute tasks and meet deadlines.

While the internal culture of organizations was changing, the external culture was changing as well. The workforce at the end of the 20th century was more diverse, with a significant influx of women, minority persons, and disabled persons. Earlier generations had sacrificed family life and personal time to climb the organizational ladder. Generations X and Y were less interested in organizational career paths per se and more interested in flexibility regarding the time and place they worked. Managing frontline employees required significant people skills: listening, advising, coaching, persuading, and so forth. These elements are discussed in Chapter 11.

In addition, frontline managers (team leaders, area directors) were to guide rather than execute plans and identify time constraints, resource utilization, and/or interactions with other functional areas. The management skills of performance evaluation reviews and/or charting out tasks and timelines became skills and tasks for teams. These tools were used for a variety of purposes: training, communicating, coordinating, and promoting continuous improvement and accountability in operations. These skills and tools have been formalized in the field of project management. Professional organizations have attempted to provide guides for managers and to train staff and managers at all levels. Tools have increased to allow for special circumstances in organizations and flexibility in tackling problems, especially complex programs involving multiple departments, disciplines, and vendors. While there are a variety of mechanisms used in organizations, this chapter will focus on three: Program Evaluation Review Technique, Gantt chart development and utilization, and flow charts.

# THE USE OF PERT

The Program Evaluation Review Technique (PERT) is a management tool for visualizing interrelationships among tasks so that they can be effectively coordinated and scheduled. PERT is especially useful when the component tasks are executed by multiple agencies or independent divisions with specialized expertise. A space launch requires the expertise of a rocket manufacturer, communications engineers, telemetry monitors and analysts, specialists in astronaut training and mission preparation, congressional relations personnel, media specialists, and so forth. For each area to see how its efforts are integral to the overall effort, a PERT network can display the sequence of steps and time frames required to achieve the larger effort. PERT also helps identify which sequence of tasks must be completed on time for the timely completion of the program and which tasks can take longer than planned and still not adversely impact program completion.

PERT analysis is commonly used to develop, design, test, and implement computer systems or engineering efforts. The cause-effect relationships tend to be clear, concise, and easily reasoned. PERT as used in the implementation of public programs sometimes lacks the clarity and conciseness of engineering systems but does permit managers to work out schedules and set milestones to ensure efforts are coordinated and effective.

PERT networks are a graphic representation of what occurs. They need to be detailed enough to depict what is done, by whom, and how tasks are concluded, but not as detailed as a job description or training manual—although they may be useful in both documents. While a PERT diagram is developed at the outset of a new program or effort, its major value is in being reviewed and updated regularly to reflect changing circumstances and to promote continual operational improvements.

There are many software programs that facilitate developing and implementing PERT, with some programs tailored to specific industries or applications. Many federal departments and some local governments and private agencies use a variation called Earned Value Management (EVM) which integrates the aspects of PERT described in this text with measurements of project costs, progress toward task completion, and technical accomplishments. This text covers only the general outline and processes of PERT; the reader should consult the software documentation for details of its use.

## PROS AND CONS OF PERT

The pros:
• It focuses attention on critical tasks.

- It helps to evaluate progress, identify problems, and facilitate decisions.
- It establishes milestones and enables disparate parts to operate coherently toward a single objective.
- It clarifies relationships among various participants.

The cons:
- The listing of tasks, sequence, and time estimates may be highly subjective. (For example, should the city attorney determine the legality of a program effort that is to be federally funded before or after the city finance officer determines if federal funding is available? The determination of whose expertise is to serve whose agenda is more a political issue than a technical question.)
- Time estimates are educated guesses that depend on experience with monitoring and ability to monitor tasks—the tendency is to err on the side of longer timelines to complete tasks but political pressure may be to err on the side of short timelines.
- Management of time and milestones is not analogous to containing costs.
- The weights assigned to time estimates and variance estimates assume a normal probability distribution,[1] but actual time periods for tasks and variations from expected time estimates may differ significantly.
- A PERT network needs to be simplified into a chart to clearly communicate start and end times for activities

## TIMING FOR PERT

PERT networks should be developed as program efforts move into the implementation phase, when multiple areas and resources need to share a common vision of how they will operate in concert with one another. At this stage participants typically know the long-term objective of the effort, the individuals or functional areas that are involved, and the proposed process that will enable the effort to realize its goal. PERT networks are developed and refined periodically during the program/process to monitor progress, identify problems, shift resources, and establish or reinforce target deadlines.

Table 10.1 is an outline of the implementation manual for the Weed and Seed Program (now called the Bryne Criminal Justice Innovation [BCJI] Program) funded by the U.S. Department of Justice. Participating communities seek to "weed out" crime activities in low-income areas by developing ties between residents and the police, instituting

---

[1] A normal probability assumes that over 60% of observations are clustered around the mean. The balance are symmetrically distributed above and below the mean.

community policing programs, and providing after-school programs at safe havens near schools. In addition, the program funds "seeding activities" such as beautification projects, cleanup efforts, and rehabilitation of homes.

**Table 10.1    Weed and Seed Implementation Manual: Phases and Steps**

| Stages | Recommended Steps |
| --- | --- |
| Organization of steering committee | 1. Meet with local officials to determine program commitment.<br>2. Create leadership group.<br>3. Select stakeholder organizations to participate in steering committee.<br>4. Determine roles and responsibilities of steering committee.<br>5. Develop decision-making process to govern Weed and Seed efforts. |
| Selection of sites | Determine sites based on local commitment, data, master plan, community potential with regard to economics, community organization, and resident interest. |
| Assessment of resources and needs | 1. Assemble assessment team.<br>2. Determine type of data to be collected.<br>3. Take inventory of neighborhood (selection site).<br>4. Develop crime and asset map.<br>5. Identify existing resources and formulate approaches for developing additional needed resources.<br>6. Document resources. |
| Planning for Weed and Seed | 1. Assemble planning team.<br>2. Identify resources.<br>3. Prepare to define specific goals and objectives.<br>4. Move from community needs to critical priorities.<br>5. Link priorities to goals and objectives.<br>6. Develop implementation plan.<br>7. Develop planning format for local strategy. |
| Management of Weed and Seed | 1. Establish organizational structure.<br>2. Develop action plan.<br>3. Develop open communication among all parties.<br>4. Establish consistent procedures for selecting staff.<br>5. Develop process for steering committee and subcommittee meetings.<br>6. Develop process for team building.<br>7. Provide training. |
| Community mobilization | 1. Secure resident commitment and involvement.<br>2. Encourage residents to help provide community focus.<br>3. Build community networks.<br>4. Create resident-led leadership structures.<br>5. Leverage internal and external resources.<br>6. Create additional communication vehicles. |

**Table 10.1    Weed and Seed Implementation Manual: Phases and Steps (cont.)**

| Stages | Recommended Steps |
|---|---|
| Law enforcement | 1. Establish Law Enforcement subcommittee. |
| | 2. Review needs assessment. |
| | 3. Establish goals, objectives, and tasks. |
| | 4. Identify additional resources for strategy. |
| | 5. Develop implementation plan. |
| Community policing | 1. Create a community policing partnership within designated area. |
| | 2. Determine community characteristics. |
| | 3. Develop information and communication network. |
| | 4. Assess and develop resources. |
| | 5. Develop an implementation plan. |
| | 6. Collaborate on problem solving—take action. |
| | 7. Monitor and assess success. |
| Prevention, intervention, and treatment | 1. Establish Prevention Intervention and Treatment subcommittee. |
| | 2. Review needs assessment, and develop action plan. |
| | 3. Develop plan for locating and staffing "Safe Haven." |
| Neighborhood restoration | 1. Create subcommittee. |
| | 2. Revisit needs assessment. |
| | 3. Formulate goals and objectives. |
| | 4. Develop activities to achieve goals/objectives. |
| | 5. Secure steering committee approval. |
| | 6. Adjust goals, objectives, and/or activities. |
| | 7. Evaluate restoration plan. |
| Evaluation | 1. Identify coordinator and members of evaluation team. |
| | 2. Agree on definitions of terms use in evaluation. |
| | 3. Review priorities to be measured. |
| | 4. Collect and analyze data. |
| | 5. Determine next steps. |

Source: U.S. Department of Justice, Office of Justice Programs. (2005).

## STEP-BY-STEP GUIDE TO PERT

There are six steps to PERT: listing tasks, sequencing tasks, developing a network diagram, determining time estimates, identifying the critical path, and monitoring progress. As part of this technique, managers typically use weighted averages to estimate the times along the network and examine variances associated with tasks to determine how reliable a task's expected time truly is.

## Step 1: Listing Tasks

There are numerous resources for developing a comprehensive list of tasks. PERT assumes that each task has a discrete beginning and a milestone or outcome that defines when the task is completed. Federal agencies typically outline with some specificity the tasks they expect local agencies to undertake with federal funds. For example, the Department of Justice provided a *Weed and Seed Implementation Manual* that listed every stage and step to be taken to progress from an approved proposal to the evaluation of program outcomes and effects (see Table 10.1). Other considerations are contract provisions with businesses and/or memoranda of understanding with private and non-governmental organizations and units within government (e.g., police unions). A schedule of activities is outlined either by the government agency seeking to contract for goods or services or by the responding organization. Few public efforts are without precedent either within a jurisdiction or in other jurisdictions in the state. Urban redevelopment plans and partnerships with private developers often require detailed plans of sequential steps, deadlines, and accountability measures. Prior experience and documentation are good references to use as one begins to conceptualize his or her task responsibilities toward the larger effort. Each participating functional area needs to develop initially its own comprehensive list.

## Step 2: Sequencing Tasks

Logic and reason will often dictate the sequencing of tasks; for instance, a house must have its foundation set before putting up walls before you can put on a roof. Sequencing is often an iterative process because it includes identifying which tasks must precede each task. Some tasks may have no preceding tasks, but most will have at least one precedent task. In the case of the Weed and Seed project outlined in Table 10.1 it is logical to assume that developing a governing body (A) and determining the geographical area to be served (B) will precede assessing the target area's strengths and weaknesses (C) and developing implementation plans. However, it is not necessarily the case that the assessment must be completed before assembling a planning team to prioritize and develop local strategies for executing program objectives (D) or developing the organizational structure needed to carry out tasks (E). However, both an organizational structure and a clear understanding of the area's challenges and assets need to be understood to mobilize and utilize residential participation (F). Finally, the tasks of law enforcement (G), community policing (H), prevention (I), and restoration (J) can be carried out simultaneously rather than sequentially. If tasks were addressed sequentially, a local program might never implement tasks or spend grant funds for all relevant areas. Finally, program tasks need to be implemented before they can be evaluated (K).

While there are no rigid rules as to what the sequence ought to be, logic and information needs will drive how functional areas are linked together.

Stage A is the organization of a steering committee. This step begins with individual and/or group meetings with local officials regarding their understanding of, and participation in, the proposed program and this step ends with the stakeholders on the Weed and Seed steering committee developing and approving bylaws and a system of procedures to govern their ongoing responsibilities to the program. In Figure 10.1 the start of an activity is noted with a node, and the line and letter indicate its timeline.

**Figure 10.1    Time Duration of an Activity as Measured from Node to Node**

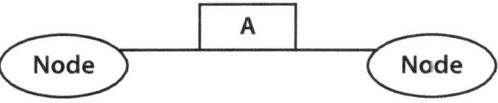

## Step 3: Developing a Network Diagram

The sequencing process permits managers and analysts to build a simple diagram of nodes and lines that links tasks in a manner that is consistent with the group's consensus and logical to a naïve reader who might view the diagram as an interested citizen, elected representative, or other person outside the organization. Like sequencing, developing the network diagram is often an iterative process. Figure 10.2 illustrates one possible network diagram for the tasks listed in Table 10.1.

**Figure 10.2    Depiction of Weed and Seed Task Network**

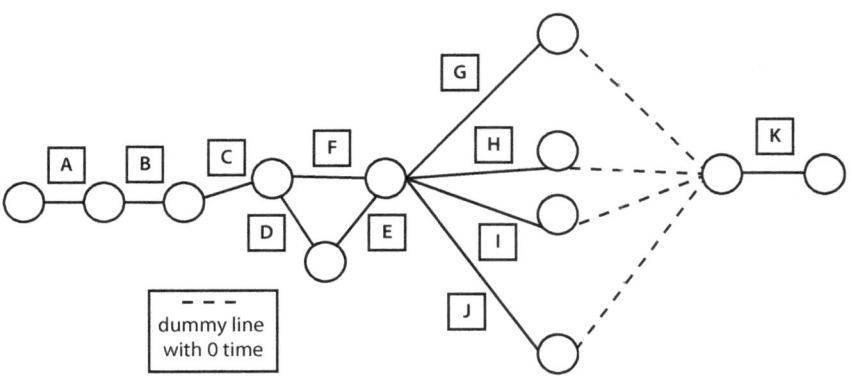

## Step 4: Determining Time Estimates

Before surveying the experts regarding time estimates, the program manager needs to consider which unit of time makes sense for monitoring and analysis. A mission to Mars that may take 17 years to execute might use 90 days as its time unit, while a hazardous spill response network might use time units of minutes rather than months. Since many public projects are executed during a 12-month fiscal year, months or weeks are often adequate time units. If a task takes less than a unit, then it is expressed as a decimal. An 8-day task using a 1-week unit of time would be 1.14 weeks (8/7), and in terms of months it would be 0.27 (8/30). Time estimates need to be represented using the same base unit.

If there are many experts and/or implementers involved in a task, then as many as feasible should be surveyed regarding time estimates. The estimates from various sources can be averaged and analyzed when determining what the final figure should most likely be for establishing time periods along the network.

For each task and/or step, the experts will be asked the following:

- What initiates the task? Does the agency or participant need an invoice, memo, or referral call?

- What milestone or outcome indicates the task is complete? Is there a monitoring report, an official authorization or inspection, and so forth?

- Which task must be completed before this task can start? Some tasks may have no preceding task, but most will.

- What is the typical time period associated with this task? Is the time frame documented? Time estimates are based on current funding, staffing, and resources. In the PERT literature this time estimate is called the "most likely" time period.

- What is the quickest or shortest amount of time spent to complete the task? What contributes to the shorter time frame? This is often called the "optimistic time" estimate.

- What is the longest time it has taken to complete this task? This is a tricky question because the program manager is interested in the maximum reasonable time needed to execute the task, not all possible delays. When estimating program tasks for a 3- to 5-year redevelopment project, a city attorney was asked, "What was the longest time it took to get a legal determination regarding the sale of a condemned property?" His response was, "15 years, depending on trial delays, court appeals, and so forth." However, a single, well-documented, extreme case is not useful in developing network times. In the 250-year history of the city, the 15-year delay occurred once, and the probability of its reoccurring over the next 3 years is 4 in 1,000. Instead, the project manager is interested in likely and repetitive delays in executing tasks and the reasons for the delays. If tasks require police support and their support is strained during peak holiday periods, then the extent of the delay and the reason for it are essential to note as one develops the network's timetable as a whole.

Having collected time estimates from all the experts/participants, the weighted time estimate formula (weighted time estimate = [*(optimistic)* + (4 × *most likely time*) + *(pessimistic)*] ÷ 6) is applied to each task, noted on the network diagram, and distributed to participants for review and verification. The weighted time estimate accounts for the different time estimates to simplify the planning.

The standard weighted time estimate formula gives the most likely time four times the weight as the most optimistic and the most pessimistic; thus, there are six time data points (1 optimistic, 4 most likely, and 1 pessimistic) which are averaged together to yield the weighted time estimate.

It is also helpful to note the variance associated with each task by applying the variance formula:

Variance = ([pessimistic or longest time – optimistic or shortest time] ÷ 6)$^2$

A summary sheet of the data might look like Table 10.2. However, unlike in Table 10.2, all time estimates and variances would be reported. Can you complete the information for tasks B and C above?

---

**Box 10.1    Calculating Weighted Time Estimate**

Weighted Time Estimate (T.E.) = [*optimistic* (shortest time) + 4 × *most likely time* + *pessimistic* (longest time)] ÷ 6

How long does it take to respond to a routine inquiry? You might determine that the quickest you were able to respond was 1 minute; on most days you respond within 3 minutes; and on rare occasions it has taken 5 minutes. The time estimate for this task would be T.E. = [1 + (4 × 3) + 5] ÷ 6 or 18 ÷ 6 = 3. Your time estimate would be 3 minutes.

---

## Step 5: Identifying the Critical Path

A path through a network begins with the initial node of the first task and ends with the ending node of the last task. The critical path is the longest time through the network. It is assumed that any delay along the longest path will delay the entire effort, and therefore these tasks are critical. Once the critical path is identified, the network diagram is often modified to highlight the critical path tasks.

> **Box 10.2 Defining and Computing Variance from the Estimated Time**
>
> How reliable is the 3-minute estimate? It depends on the amount of disparity between the optimistic and pessimistic times. The smaller the disparity, the greater is the reliability. The wider the differences, the less reliable is the estimate. The formula for variance is
>
> Variance = ([pessimistic or longest time – optimistic or shortest time] ÷ 6)$^2$
>
> In our case above, the longest time was 5; the shortest was 1. Therefore, the variance is ([5 – 1] ÷ 6)$^2$ = (4 ÷ 6)$^2$ = 0.66$^2$ = 0.44 (or a little longer than half a minute). A comparable time estimate of 3 with a variance of 1.98 would be far less certain and less desirable if the manager were seeking to get a project completed on time.

**Table 10.2   Implementation Summary Sheet (units in weeks)**

| Task | Preceding Task | Shortest (optimistic) | Most Likely | Longest (pessimistic) | Time Estimate | Variance |
|------|----------------|-----------------------|-------------|-----------------------|---------------|----------|
| A | — | 4 | 6 | 8 | 6 | .44 |
| B | A | 2 | 5 | 8 | 5 | |
| C | B | 3 | 6 | 11 | | |

Note: Dash indicates there is no preceding task.

In Table 10.1 (and Figure 10.2) there are eight possible paths through the network. The time estimates for these paths are summarized in Table 10.3 below. Using the information in Table 10.3, determine the critical path for the network by completing Table 10.4.

**Table 10.3   Times and Variances Associated with Table 10.1**

| Task | Predecessor/s | Time Estimate | Variance |
|------|---------------|---------------|----------|
| A. Organization of steering committee | — | 2.0 | 0.55 |
| B. Selection of sites | A | 0.5 | 0.33 |
| C. Assessment of resources and needs | B | 3.0 | 1.00 |
| D. Planning for Weed and Seed | C | 4.5 | 2.00 |
| E. Management of Weed and Seed | D | 5.0 | 1.66 |
| F. Community mobilization | C | 3.5 | 2.00 |
| G. Law enforcement | E and F | 2.0 | 0.33 |
| H. Community policing | E and F | 4.0 | 1.66 |
| I. Prevention intervention and treatment | E and F | 4.0 | 2.07 |
| J. Neighborhood restoration | E and F | 5.0 | 2.66 |
| K. Evaluation | G, H, I, and J | 1.5 | 0.66 |

Note: Dash indicates there is no preceding task.

**Table 10.4    Identifying the Critical Path**

| Path | Network | Time Estimates on Path | Total Time |
|------|---------|------------------------|------------|
| 1 | A, B, C, F, G, and K | 2.0 + 0.5 + 3.0 + 3.5 + 2.0 + 1.5 = | 12.5 |
| 2 | A, B, C, D, E, G, and K | 2.0 + 0.5 + 3.0 + 4.5 + 5.0 + 2.0 + 1.5 = | 18.5 |
| 3 | | | |
| 4 | | | |
| 5 | | | |
| 6 | | | |
| 7 | | | |
| 8 | | | |

Table 10.4 provides examples of two of the eight networks in Table 10.1 and Figure 10.2. The longest path through this network is 21.5 units. Can you identify th s path?

## Step 6: Monitoring Progress

The network manager's key concern is to track closely the tasks on the critical path. In our case the initial critical path totals 21.5 units. The difference between the critical path's total time and the total time of every other path is called "slack." Other paths and tasks may be important for other reasons (safety, cost) but are not critical to the network deadline. However, as a project progresses time estimates change and the PERT network must be updated.

Let's assume that Activity G, Law Enforcement, actually takes 6 units of time rather than 2 as originally estimated. Path 1's new time is now 16.2, but path 2's total time is now 22.5 and Path 2 represents the new critical path.

Any delay in Path 2 activities will delay the whole project. Path 2's total time of 22.5 compared to the initial critical path of 21.5 indicates the initial path now has 1 unit of slack time. Knowing that the project is off schedule and by how many units may suggest ways the manager may address the concern. For example, could funds, resources, or personnel be redeployed to make up for lost time? Should the project request a variance from the initial plan to address the delay? Are there steps in subsequent tasks that might be redesigned to keep the project on time? PERT can alert the manager to the time issues but does not provide the manager with specific viable alternatives. For this the network manager will need to rely on other management skills.

In Table 10.3 the coordinating manager developed time estimates for Table 10.1. The network diagram may be awkward for those who find diagrams too abstract to represent a process. Consequently, PERT networks are often translated into Gantt charts that display the data in a more readable format. There is Gantt chart software available from several sources as well as an add-on for Microsoft Excel.

The Gantt chart can be prepared on a spreadsheet or in a Word document. The chart has a column for each unit of time required by the project and a row for each task. If our project is 22 time units long, then the Gantt chart needs to have 22 time units in the columns. The transformation of Table 10.3 into a Gantt chart would look like Table 10.5.

Activity A has no prerequisite activities and therefore begins with unit 1, while tasks G, H, I, and J begin after both E and F are completed in time unit 16. Table 10.5 shows the Gantt chart at an early planning phase. When the federal funds are released and/or council approves participation, the time units would be replaced with specific dates, months, or days. A final Gantt chart should also include the agent (a manager, department, or agency) charged with executing the task. If more than one area is involved, all should be listed and a lead highlighted.

In PERT Exercise 3 in the Practicing Public Administration section, there are a network and time estimates. Can you translate this information into a Gantt chart?

## FLOWCHARTS

A flowchart is any graphic representation of a process that indicates the sequencing of steps and decisions made in a process; it may also indicate the persons or areas responsible for these steps. A Gantt chart is a specific example of a flowchart.

The advantages of flowcharts are the following:
- They foster an understanding of how tasks are interrelated.
- They improve communications and can be effective learning devices.
- They document what the processes are.
- They serve to foster process improvement and the efficient use of resources.
- They help identify missing and looping steps.
- The disadvantages of flowcharts are the following:
- There is no universal standardization of what their symbols mean, and those symbols vary from organization to organization or within an organization between operational areas.
- They need to strike a balance between too much detail and too little.

Persons with firsthand knowledge of the process need to participate in developing the flowcharts and in process improvement discussions.

Flowcharts are read from top to bottom and from left to right. Each shape has a specific meaning or use.

There are specialized flowchart software programs and symbols for areas (e.g., auditing, computer programming) with unique needs.

**Table 10.5  Gantt Chart for Weed and Seed Program**

| TASK | | PREDECESSORS | TIME EST. | MONTH NUMBER OF PROGRAM |||||||||||||||||||||
|---|---|---|---|---|---|---|---|---|---|---|---|---|---|---|---|---|---|---|---|---|---|---|---|
| | | | | 1 | 2 | 3 | 4 | 5 | 6 | 7 | 8 | 9 | 10 | 11 | 12 | 13 | 14 | 15 | 16 | 17 | 18 | 19 | 20 | 21 | 22 |
| A | Organization of steering committee | NONE | 2.00 | X | X | | | | | | | | | | | | | | | | | | | | |
| B | Selection of sites | A | 0.50 | | | x | | | | | | | | | | | | | | | | | | | |
| C | Assessment of resources and needs | B | 3.00 | | | x | X | X | x | | | | | | | | | | | | | | | | |
| D | Planning for Weed & Seed | C | 4.50 | | | | | | x | X | X | X | X | | | | | | | | | | | | |
| E | Management of Weed & Seed | D | 5.00 | | | | | | | | | | | X | X | X | X | X | | | | | | | |
| F | Community mobilization | C | 3.50 | | | | | | x | X | X | X | | | | | | | | | | | | | |
| G | Law enforcement | E & F | 2.00 | | | | | | | | | | | | | | | | X | X | | | | | |
| H | Community policing | E & F | 4.00 | | | | | | | | | | | | | | | | X | X | X | X | | | |
| I | Prevention intervention and treatment | E & F | 4.00 | | | | | | | | | | | | | | | | X | X | X | X | | | |
| J | Neighborhood restoration | E & F | 5.00 | | | | | | | | | | | | | | | | X | X | X | X | X | | |
| K | Evaluation | G, H, I, & J | 1.50 | | | | | | | | | | | | | | | | | | | | | X | x |

Note: X = full month; x = half month

**Table 10.6  Flowchart Symbols and Definitions**

| Definition | Symbol |
|---|---|
| A. Terminator or start and end point—typically the area or person responsible for the tasks | |
| B. Action or process such as a conversation with citizen, manual activity, data collection, or physical task | |
| C. Alternative task that could be undertaken in lieu of task symbol B, noted above | |
| D. Predefined process, for example, Mirandizing an arrestee or using triage protocol in an emergency room | |
| E. Document—multiple symbols of this type indicate a number of documents | |
| F. On-page connector—links task to another task on the same page | |
| G. Off-page connector—links task on one page to action/ output on another page | |
| H. Delay—indicates task is postponed or set aside to address priority task | |
| I. Decision point—typically outcomes are yes or no, and a decision is needed before subsequent tasks can be undertaken (only one question can be included in a single decision point). A decision point can go directly to another decision point. | |
| J. Stored data, typically electronically stored on a computer, server, or similar device | |
| K. Direct access to stored data or electronically stored material | |
| L. Data such as Excel spreadsheets or statistical information | |
| M. Lines indicating forward flow from top to bottom and from left to right | |
| N. Lines indicating backward flow process from bottom to top or from right to left | |

Note 1: The 14 symbols above represent typical symbols for a management flowchart and are not intended to be an exhaustive list. These symbols are readily available in Word, which is incorporated in Microsoft Office software.

Note 2: To use the symbols in Word, access Auto Shapes and Flowcharts. Access Draw, and set Grid to on. This enables the user to line up and connect symbols easily. Double click on a symbol to place it on a page, and click on a corner of the symbol to position it where it belongs. By right clicking on the symbol, one can access Add Text and place the narrative inside the symbol.

## A Flowchart Example—Policing

A number of city departments such as police, community development, public works, and housing are involved in Weed and Seed efforts. Each needs a flowchart of operations, but in our illustration we will look at police operations.

Figure 10.3 represents the sequence of steps from the initiation of a call to the dispatch center regarding a crime through the disposition of a case in court. From Figure 10.3 one can see that the dispatch center gives each call a number and a priority based on a predefined protocol before an officer investigates the incident. There are many steps to investigating a crime scene such as interviewing persons in the area and collecting evidence. However, this chart summarizes the whole police process rather than all the substeps of the process. A patrol supervisor might begin with this overall process and develop a more extensive chart to depict all the tasks associated with "Investigates call." From Figure 10.3 a reader can see that the next steps depend on whether a person is taken into custody and whether the offense is a misdemeanor or a felony. In addition to field work, officers in this system file a report that is reviewed by a supervising officer. Once an official report is filed, it is logged, indexed, packaged, and reported both internally to each police shift and externally to the Department of Justice in Washington, DC, and the state attorney general's office on a monthly basis. The case or file is not completed until it is adjudicated, closed, and filed electronically.

## Figure 10.3.1    Policing Process

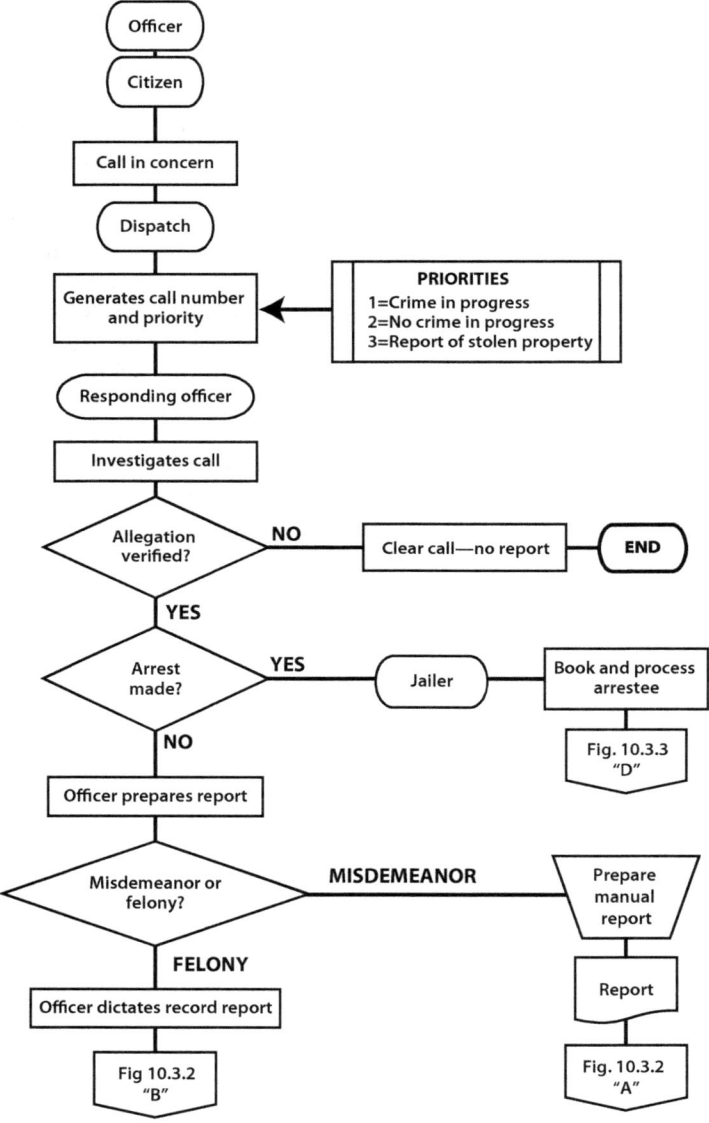

**Figure 10.3.2   Policing Process (continued)**

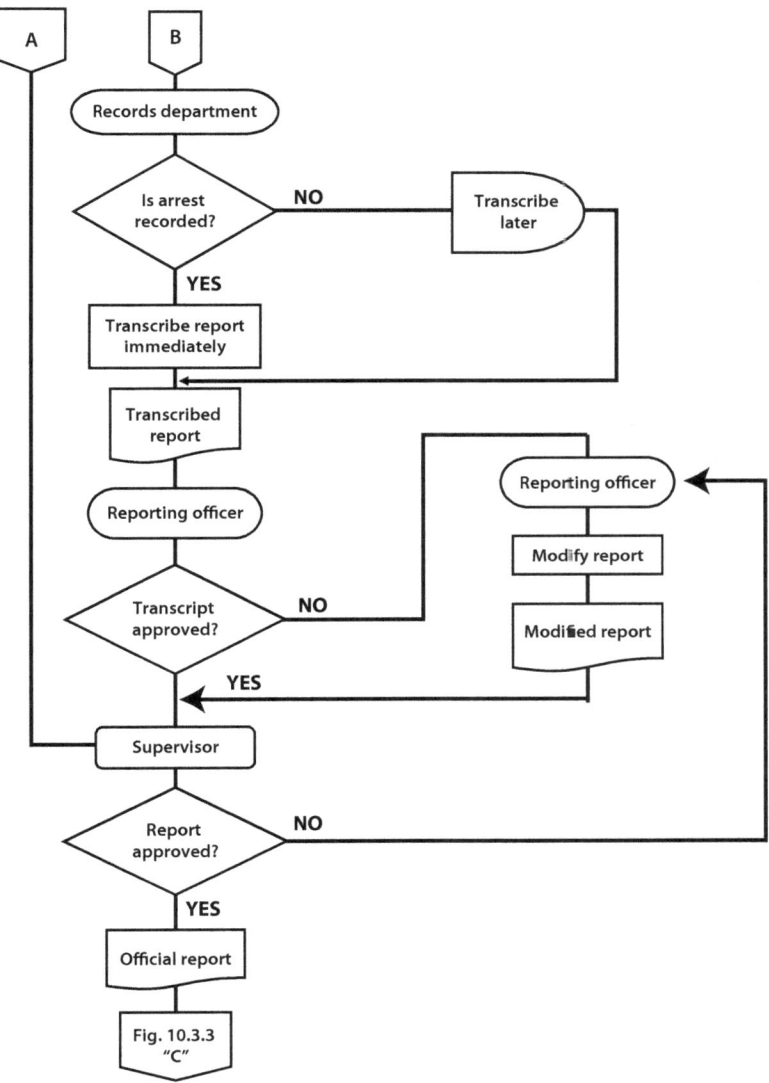

**Figure 10.3.3    Policing Process (continued)**

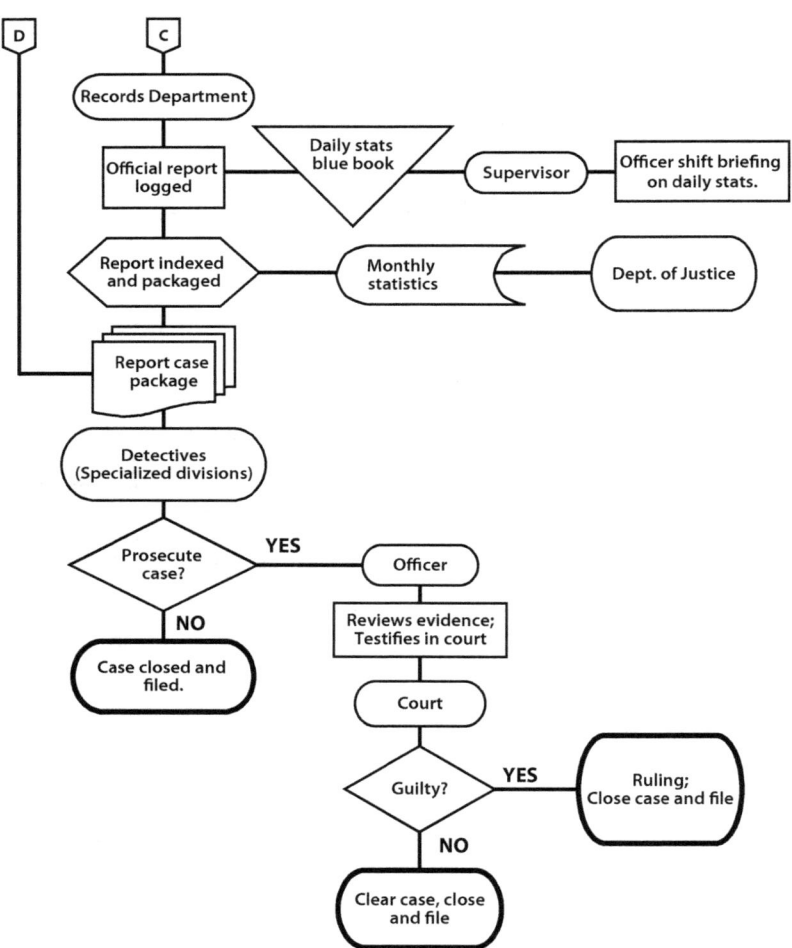

# A Step-by-Step Guide to Flowcharting

## Step 1: Define the Process to Be Developed and Determine the Boundaries or Audience the Flowchart Is to Serve

Ask what initiates an action and when it is complete. An area manager might require less detail, while the patrol supervisor's chart may need extensive detail as to where the responding officer's process begins and ends. Once the scope is defined, a person fully trained in each step needs to participate in the process of developing the chart.

## Step 2: Define What Each Symbol Means

See Table 10.6. If symbols are cumbersome, then assign participants sticky notes with different colors to represent different aspects of the chart. For example, you will need something to represent a manual task, a computer task, a decision point, the responsible area or person, and so forth.

## Step 3: Begin by Identifying What Initiates Action

What initiates action—is it a citizen call? Computer output? Media report? Council action? Identify what concludes the process, for example, a court decision, a payment, or a filed report. Which tasks by which persons/areas are linked to getting from the initiated action to the end result? Briefly identify who does what—with what—to resolve the concern and/or move the determination to the next area. During this process it is important that each area agrees to what initiates and concludes its part of the process and that the steps are in the order in which they occur. Link the tasks with lines and arrows.

## Step 4: Prepare an Overall Chart (See Figure 10.3, for Example) and Bring the Managers and Area Experts Together to Verify That the Chart Is Accurate and Complete

Analyze the chart and test its utility against actual operations.

* Look for "loops" wherein the flow moves from bottom to top and/ or from left to right. A loop may indicate a task is being done over, causing delays and higher costs. In Figure 10.3.2 transcribed notes may be reviewed and resubmitted by the initiating officer and/or his or her supervisor. These loops may indicate a need for training or closer coordination and communication between officers and recorders earlier in the process. A loop is a problem when there is no definable exit from the loop.

* Look for processes with no clearly defined end product or outcome. This may indicate where things fall through the cracks or remain unresolved. In Figure 10.3.1 an unsubstantiated

allegation is "cleared" without a report. If unsubstantiated allegations are rare, this may not be a problem, but if they represent a significant percentage of calls, officer time, and department resources, some ending report may be useful in determining how to minimize such calls in the future.

• Look for outcomes that are not optimal. The optimal outcome for a prosecuted case is a conviction. When conviction is not the outcome, identify the factors that contribute to a not-guilty ruling.

• Take a random sample of closed actions or cases, and look at time-in and time-out dates. When possible, look at costs or personnel time associated with each case. For each category (burglary, rape, assault) determine the norm and the disparity from the norm. The greater the disparity from the norm, the higher is the risk that the norm is not reliable. Do robbery cases get resolved (on average) within 3 months but vary significantly from 1 month to 15 months?

• Are there opportunities to reduce the typical time period and/ or the variation around the time period? For example, can the objective be completed with fewer steps and fewer decision makers participating in the process? Are there opportunities to redesign the process so tasks are done in tandem or to ensure bottlenecks are minimized?

• Will revising steps reduce costs?

• Will revising the process reduce errors or loops?

## Step 5: Share Charts With Managers, Supervisors, Employees, Clients, Citizens, and So Forth

Charts to guide citizens may need to be streamlined for clarity.

## ETHICAL AND EQUITY CONCERNS

To the degree that techniques clarify functions and accountability or promote the coordination of human efforts, they serve the purpose for which they were created. However, techniques are often embraced as solutions unto themselves. There are many who trust that some new means will facilitate communication or improve the quality of information. For a tool to be useful it must be understood and integrated into the fabric of human relations in the organization. The techniques discussed in this chapter are intended primarily to serve as guidelines for understanding and managing complex projects and as aids for collaboration, cooperation, or training. Ideally, they also enable public administrators to be accountable and transparent in the administration of public policies and programs.

# CONCLUSION

PERT's primary dimension of value is time. When time is a key issue, a PERT process clarifies time commitments, outputs, and inter-relationships among participants and tasks. The first challenge is to get reasonable estimates of the quickest, most typical, and longest times associated with each task. PERT relies on the subjective estimates of functional managers and/or the accuracy (or lack of accuracy) of the timekeeping. In addition, the decision about where a task belongs in the flow of events will depend on technical as well as subjective organizational concerns. Therefore, while the process is formula driven and logical, the data and policy issues that drive organizational culture provide unique challenges. Once the program starts, evaluation of each tasks' progress and actual costs help track overall progress and highlights where management may need to take action to stay on schedule and/or budget.

Flowcharts summarize complex processes to clarify the tasks, boundaries, decision points, and outputs/outcomes of a process. Building a flowchart aids managers and staff in clarifying activities and their consequences. A completed flowchart may serve as an instrument for developing processes of greater efficiency with fewer delays, errors, and costs. Providing flowcharts to new employees and citizens may improve coordination and communication. Flowcharts are especially useful for examining compliance with policies and regulations by businesses and other agencies.

Not all functions lend themselves to flowcharting. Crime investigations rely on witness testimony, forensic evidence, criminal history, environmental conditions, and the analysis of statements and evidence. Each case may have a discrete beginning and end, but the process is, in part, science, intuition, and educated guessing. Consequently, while a flowchart may provide a picture of the overall process, the subroutines may not readily fit into a flowcharting system.

## PRACTICING PUBLIC ADMINISTRATION

### PROGRAM EVALUATION REVIEW TECHNIQUE (PERT) EXERCISES

1. Imagine you are planning a major event (wedding, inauguration of officers, opening of a clinic); list and sequence the steps needed to execute the project on time.
2. Based on the steps above, draw a network of the interrelationships.
3. Based on the diagram and information below, estimate each task's expected time and variance. Which task(s) are you least certain will be completed on time?

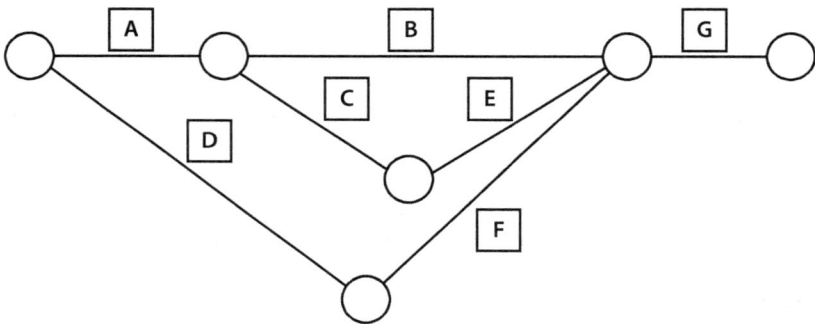

| Task | Preceding Task | Most Likely | Optimistic | Pessimistic | Expected Time | Variance |
|------|----------------|-------------|------------|-------------|---------------|----------|
| A | — | 3.0 | 2.0 | 4.0 | | |
| B | A | 6.0 | 4.0 | 8.0 | | |
| C | A | 5.5 | 4.0 | 7.0 | | |
| D | — | 5.0 | 3.0 | 7.0 | | |
| E | C | 2.0 | 1.0 | 3.5 | | |
| F | D | 8.0 | 6.0 | 12.0 | | |
| G | B, E, F | 6.0 | 4.0 | 8.0 | | |

Note: Dashes indicate there is no preceding task.

4. How many paths are there in the network described in Question 3? Which path is the critical path?
5. How much slack do paths A, B, and G have in this network?
6. Complete and discuss the chart for all paths in the network.

FLOWCHART EXERCISES

1. Convert PERT Exercise 2 above from a PERT chart to a Gantt chart. Use the following time estimates: A = 3.0, B = 7.0, C = 5.5, D = 5.0, E = 2.5, F = 8.0, and G = 6.0. Remember to allow one column for each time unit.

2. Simplify Figure 9.3 in this chapter, regarding the police process, to summarize the public safety effort so it can be shared with citizens.

3. Below is a draft partial flowchart of a child welfare agency's response process to an allegation of child abuse/neglect. Can you identify eight or more questions/concerns about this chart?

**Flowchart of Local Child Welfare Program**

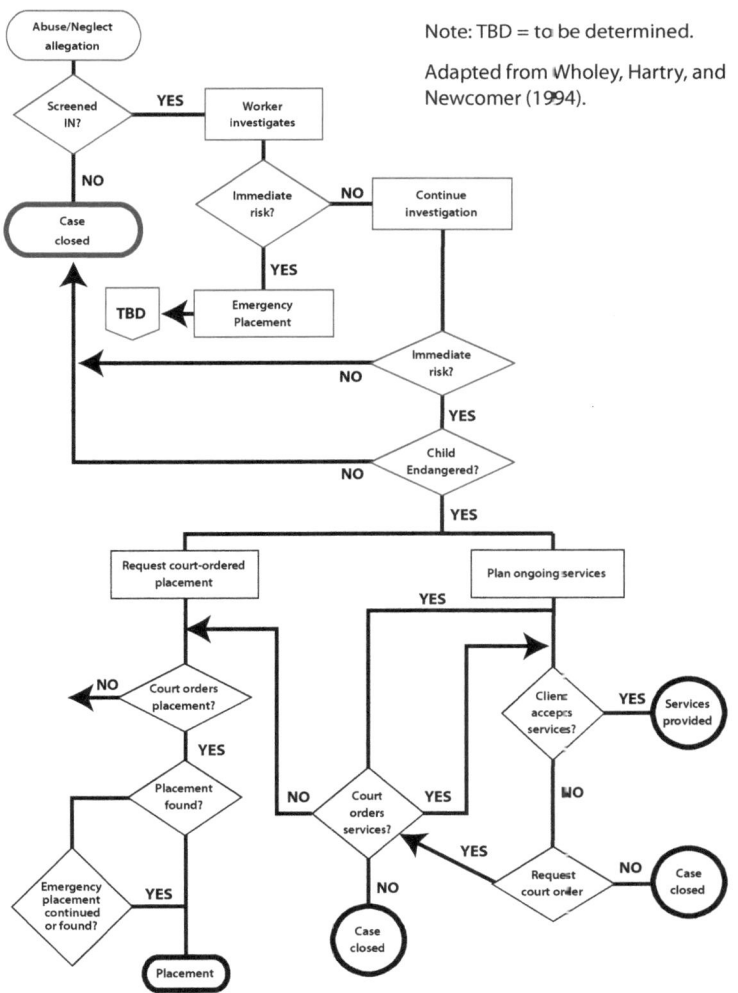

4. Flowchart a process in your organization or at your school. Where does the process begin and end? Describe the logical flow of areas, tasks, and outcomes that links the activities.

5. Which changes to the processes above can you suggest that might result in faster service, fewer errors, and/or less cost?

## BIBLIOGRAPHY

Ammons, D. (2009). *Tools for decision making: A practical guide for local government* (2nd ed.). Washington, DC: CQ Press.

Burns, M. (2007). Work in process. *CA Magazine, 140*(5), 16.

Carstens, D. S., & Richardson, G. L. (2019). *Project management tools and techniques: A practical guide* (2nd ed.). Boca Raton, FL CRC Press.

Cattanach, R. L. (1973). Audit planning: An application of network analysis. *Accounting Review, 48*(3), 609–11.

Eppen, G. D., Gould, F. J., Schmidt, C. P., Moore, J. H., & Weatherford, L. (1998). *Introductory management science* (5th ed.). Upper Saddle River, NJ: Prentice Hall.

Erikson, S. M. (1981). *Management tools for everyone: Twenty analytical techniques that are easy to learn and valuable to know.* New York, NY: Petrocelli Books.

Frame, J. D. (2003). *Managing risks in organizations.* San Francisco, CA: Jossey-Bass.

Gill, T. (2004). Teaching flowcharting with FlowC. *Journal of Information Systems Education, 15*(1), 65–77.

Groebner, D., & Shannon, P. (1992). *Management science.* New York, NY: Macmillan/Dellen.

Hubbard, L. (2005). Limits of process documentation. *Internal Auditor, 62*(3), 26–27.

Jackson, H. K., & Frigon, N. L. (1994). *Management 2000: The practical guide to world class competition.* New York, NY: Van Nostrand Reinhold.

Knechel, W. R., Salterio, S. E., & and Ballou, B. (2007). *Auditing: Assurance and risk.* Toronto, Canada: Thomson.

Modi, P. N. (2017). *PERT and CPM.* New Delhi, India: Standard Book House.

Nouri, H. (2006). A flowchart approach to vehicle donations. *National Public Accountant, 5*(2), 24–25.

Pope, T. R. (1979). A flowchart analysis of the federal income tax concept of earnings and profits. *Accounting Review, 54*(1), 163–169.

Project Management Institute. (2021). *A guide to the project management body of knowledge* (7th ed.). Newton Square, PA: Project Management Institute.

Render, B., & Stair, R. (1994). *Quantitative analysis for management* (5th ed.). Boston, MA: Allyn & Bacon.

ReVelle, J. B. (2003). Safety process analysis: Improving safety results with process flowcharts and maps. *Professional Safety, 48*(7), 19–26.

Richardson, L. (2006). *Improving your project management skills.* New York, NY: American Management Association.

Roman, D. D. (1962). The PERT system: An appraisal of Program Evaluation Review Technique. *Journal of the Academy of Management, 5*(1), 57–65.

Rubin, J., Hildreth, W.B., & Miller, G.J. (1998). *Handbook of public administration.* New York, NY: Marcel Dekker.

Russell, J. P. (Ed.). (2005). *The ASQ auditing handbook: Principles, implementation and use* (3rd ed.). Milwaukee, WI: ASQ Quality Press.

U.S. Department of Justice, Office of Justice Programs. (2005). *Weed and Seed implementation manual.* www.ojp.usdoj.gov/ccdo/ws/welcome.html.

Wholey, J., Hartry, H. P., & Newcomer, K. E. Eds. (1994). *Handbook of practical program evaluation*. San Francisco, CA: Jossey-Bass.

Wysocki, R. K. (2019). *Effective project management: Traditional, agile, extreme, hybrid* (8th ed.). Hoboken, NJ: Wiley.

# SECTION
# 3

# Human Resources, Planning, and Risk Management

Government accomplishes its mission through people, primarily employees, who are the largest source of expenditures for government agencies. This means that a key role of the public administrator is the management of human resources. Chapter 11 discusses the civil service system, including how positions are created, classified, and filled. It also discusses concepts and strategies for developing leaders in the public sector.

Chapter 11 also discusses the advantages and disadvantages of unions and introduces readers to the step-by-step process jurisdictions take in negotiating labor contracts with unions. While only a few managers will participate in labor negotiations, labor contracts influence how managers handle discipline, grievances, and employee complaints. Therefore, all managers are required to know and follow contract provisions on behalf of their political jurisdictions.

Among the most critical of labor contract provisions are those regarding employee pay and benefits. Chapter 12 discusses what is meant in the public sector by total compensation benefit packages, health, workers' compensation, safety measures, risk management, pensions, Social Security, overtime, compensatory time, training, and so forth. Due to the rising costs associated with benefit packages, there are new attempts to share costs or redesign benefits to better reflect the specific needs of employees and employers.

# 11 ◇ ◆ ◇ ◆

# Managing Human Resources

The most important resources in any organization are the people. Labor costs represent the largest percentage of local agency budgets, often as much as 80%. Government has some unique characteristics in the way it manages human resources—in particular the civil service system. However, there are many elements of managing human resources that are universal, and this chapter will explore both the differences and similarities. Unions have a significant role in the management of human resources, which this chapter will also examine.

## WHAT IS CIVIL SERVICE?

*Civil service* in the United States typically refers to government employment. A civil servant is a government employee who works for a federal, state, regional, or municipal agency. The federal civil service dates back to the 1880s and includes most nonpolitical appointed positions in the executive, judicial, and legislative branches of the government of the United States, except positions in the uniformed services. Although members of the U.S. military are not included at the federal level, public safety employees such as police officers, sheriffs, and firefighters are considered civil service employees. Elected officials at all levels of government are not part of the civil service, although they are certainly public servants.

Civil service replaced a system that was known as the "spoils" system, in which most government jobs were viewed as favors to be given out to political supporters in exchange for votes—and each time an election brought in a new administration there was workforce turnover. Civil service eliminated turnover with each new election and ushered in a concept in which jobs are based on merit and nonpartisanship. See Appendix C.

The exception has typically been appointees to high-level executive positions, which serve at the pleasure of the president, governor, mayor, or county or regional boards. Such employees are often identified as "at will." These high-level positions remain outside of civil service and are customarily given to persons in the executive's political party or to trusted supporters (in nonpartisan offices) to enable the executive to carry out the programs and policies for which he or she campaigned. Although appointees to these positions have a higher level of accountability to the administration, in the interest of checks and balances, their confirmation is often required by an elected body such as Congress, a legislature, or a city council to mitigate favoritism and partisanship.

Some agencies include nonexecutive employees in the at-will category. The public often includes these positions in the term *civil servant;* however, the employees are treated differently than those with traditional civil service status. While their hiring may not be subject to political patronage, these employees may serve at the pleasure of department management and be exempt from civil service tenure and the due process protections described in this chapter. Professional and technical experts, unskilled laborers, and part-time employees are commonly included in the at-will category.

Educational systems have a unique form of protection. While teachers are not part of the civil service systems common to other local government agencies, they have similar protections in the form of tenure. Most of the characteristics described below for civil service also apply to tenured teachers employed by school districts, colleges, and universities.

## PROS AND CONS OF CIVIL SERVICE

The pros:

- Avoidance of turnover of employees creates more stable and functional organizations; turnover often slows down the work of organizations as new employees are trained and come up to speed.
- Career employees develop experience and expertise that enhances their value and productivity.
- Merit-based examinations encourage professionalism and expertise.
- Job security enhances a career focus and job satisfaction.
- Civil service decreases political influence.
- Structured arrangements of classifications and salaries, although somewhat inflexible, avoid favoritism regarding awards of compensation.

The cons:

- The employment process may be slow and laborious, with delays causing some of the most highly qualified candidates for civil service jobs to be offered jobs in the private sector before the process can be completed.

- Formal examinations for broad civil service classifications are not always the best selection tool for identifying the most qualified person for an individual position, particularly in fields that require professional or technological expertise or in new fields.
- Use of special factors (e.g., seniority for promotions or layoffs, or military service in lieu of additional examination credits) may interfere with, or override, merit principles.
- Broad job classes, public disclosure of salaries, and limited ability to provide additional compensation make it more difficult to reward individual employees for outstanding performance or to discipline them for inadequate performance.

## MODERNIZATION AND REFORM OF CIVIL SERVICE

Because of perceptions that civil service systems may breed a culture of mediocrity and discourage productivity, there have been movements during the past 20 years to modernize and reform the system.

Some of the measures are relatively minor adjustments to the current system. For example, slowness in testing is being diminished by online testing or on-the-spot hiring, replacing written tests with interviews, training and experience evaluations, or selective certification to allow for more accurate filtering of candidates. Similarly, extending probationary periods to provide longer periods of initial evaluation is designed to enhance the quality of selection and testing. Once an employee has successful completed the probationary period, they become a permanent employee and terminating them typically becomes more difficult.

Other measures are directed more to the heart of the system, such as replacing seniority with performance as a criterion for layoff or broadening job classifications to avoid testing. The most extreme measure is removing civil service protection entirely and converting positions to at-will status, which allows an agency to hire and fire without many of the restrictions that have been mentioned above and will be discussed in further detail in this chapter.

Several states have adopted measures to "reform" civil service, and many local agencies have adopted these measures to some degree.

## A STEP-BY-STEP GUIDE TO HIRING
## AND RETAINING CIVIL SERVICE EMPLOYEES

The following paragraphs describe the steps involved in selection and what happens after civil service employees are hired. Additional details of the hiring process are discussed in Appendix C.

## Step 1: Identification of the Positions to Be Filled

Identification of the positions to be filled occurs at the operating-department level and includes both existing vacancies and new jobs. During the annual budget process, or on an interim basis, organizational units identify a need for resources. The supervisor of a unit may be required to prepare a *position description*, a document that describes the duties and requirements of a specific position, sometimes including the percentage of time required for each type of task. The organizational structure will have an impact on the duties, for example, whether the position has supervisory responsibility (line function) or it is a staff function. Supervision usually entails a separate group of skills and abilities. Position descriptions are usually submitted to centralized human resources and/or budget unit(s) that evaluates whether the requested position will be included in the budget for the entire department.

## Step 2: Classification

Upon submission of a budget request and position description, a central budget or human resources unit may determine whether the described position falls within an existing classification described in the *class specification*. A class specification describes duties, responsibilities, qualifications, pay range, and benefits for a group of positions that can be identified under a specific title. The criterion for inclusion of positions within a classification is that a common examination can be used to test qualified candidates. If the described duties do not fall within an existing classification, then the human resources department/civil service commission may develop a new classification. A new classification will require a salary-setting process along with a description of the duties.

## Step 3: Recruitment

Recruitment in the public sector is not materially different from recruitment in the private sector, particularly for professional and executive positions that focus on college recruiting techniques or use outside employment search firms. Like in the private sector, successful recruitment depends on whether wages and benefits are competitive with the local labor market in a community. Human resources professionals utilize compensation surveys as a mechanism to evaluate the marketplace. Recruiting applicants from all backgrounds is very important in the public sector to ensure fairness, equal opportunity, and transparency.

The internet has become an important recruitment tool, along with advertisements in professional/trade publications and participation at career fairs. Recruiting for specialized public-sector jobs, particularly public safety, has been a major challenge for many agencies. Intense advertising campaigns along with the targeting of specific demographic groups may be necessary to attract candidates to occupations with high demand or a limited candidate pool. For example, recruiters may use incentives such as signing bonuses and/or and housing or relocation assistance to facilitate hiring when necessary. Public agencies may partner with trade schools or community colleges to enhance recruitment for skilled trades or health professionals. Offering apprenticeship or internship positions is a method of attracting candidates and provides necessary training for permanent employment. On the other hand, there are many public-sector jobs, such as firefighter and unskilled laborer, that attract hundreds or thousands of candidates, and in a recessionary economy this category extends to many more occupations. In this case the challenges are to avoid overwhelming an agency with too many applicants and to close the application process quickly and as fairly as possible.

Civil service jobs have typically provided opportunities for traditionally underrepresented groups (e.g., women, minorities, and disabled people) to gain access to employment, particularly to middle-class jobs. The public sector was at the forefront of affirmative action initiatives beginning in the 1970s. Although the courts and ballot measures have invalidated the use of numerical goals to achieve greater representation, the public sector still takes a leadership role in outreach activities that provide employment opportunities for the entire population that it serves. Along with enhancing opportunities for racial minorities and women, outreach may include opportunities for disadvantaged youth or seniors, welfare recipients, and disabled people.

Government, like the private sector, is sensitive to economic and demographic trends. Because public-sector pay levels may not be as competitive during periods of economic growth, public-sector jobs may be less attractive. As the economy contracts and job opportunities become scarce in the private sector, the security and benefits associated with government jobs becomes more attractive. Currently the public sector faces many of the same challenges as does the rest of the nation while the generational shift continues and retirements increase. With the availability of generous retirement benefits, many agencies are beginning to experience significant gaps in their workforces. Agencies will be looking more to partnerships with educational institutions and the private sector to maintain continuity of service.

## Step 4: Examination

After a group of applicants is identified through the recruitment process, an examination process may take place. Examinations should be validated to ensure that the exam process adequately tests for all of the appropriate skills, abilities, and knowledge related to the position and does not test for unrelated skills, abilities, or knowledge which are unnecessarily discriminatory. This examination process varies greatly by the type of job. Exams may consist of an interview and a written exam, which could test either general aptitude, aptitude for specific job content, or both. For some occupations a performance test may be required. The most rigorous exams are typically required for public safety jobs such as police officer and firefighter jobs—their selection processes often include oral, written, and performance exams as well as psychological, background, and medical evaluations. Drug tests are commonly required for safety-sensitive jobs. In addition to experience and education, factors such as former military service and seniority may entitle a candidate to extra points on certain examinations.

An examination usually results in a list of eligible candidates with scores identifying their placement on the list. Agencies may be required to hire candidates based primarily or exclusively on the highest scores. The duration of these lists may extend from a few months to a couple of years, depending on whether the exam is for an entry-level or promotional job and how quickly the list is utilized. Exams may be given on a continual basis if the jobs are difficult to fill.

## Step 5: Interview and Hiring Process

Following the examination process, eligible candidates with the scores identified by their placement on the certification list are invited to interview with managers or supervisors for open positions. Depending on the level of position, there can be two or more interviews per open position with the hiring department. Since many large agencies conduct their own interview and hiring process, it is not uncommon to participate in the process several times with a large agency until a candidate is selected. The interview and hiring process is usually lengthy and can take as long as 6 to 8 weeks while references are checked and a background investigation is conducted if necessary.

Government interviews can be structured or semi-structured. A structured interview can follow the Uniform Guidelines for Employee selection where every candidate is asked the exact same questions in the same order; this ensures that everyone is treated the same and has the same chance for success. However, this rigid format can feel robotic. The departments will need to determine if this level of formality is important for the hiring position. In a structured interview, if a candidate indicates they do not understand the question, some interviewers will have one alternate form of the question to read as clarification. But they can only ask the prepared questions, and nothing else. In a semistructured interview, there may be prepared questions, but the interviewer(s) have freedom to ask additional questions in a more conversational style. Departments should work with Human Resources to determine the best option for each position to be hired.

Interviews, whether structured or unstructured, can be done one-on-one or in panels. The one-on-one interviews usual consist of the applicant and the hiring manager. In most government agencies, these are less common because most hiring departments want to ensure a high level of transparency and accountability. As a result, panel interviews (consisting or two or more interviewers) are common. It is important that the interview panels are given consistent guidelines for the process, and one person should lead the meeting. Questions can be divided among the panel members, and follow-up questions from each member (in semi-structured interviewed) can take place at the end. Good coordination of the panel is important to ensure the integrity of the hiring process.

There can be multiple interviews that take several forms. Interviews can be in person, on the phone, or using video. Early interviews of a larger group (for example, maybe 10 people) may be done by phone to obtain preliminary information and make the first cut. The next interview may be by video (for example, the candidate pool may be reduced to five people at this stage). Then the final interview (for example, the top three candidates), may be in person. Most hiring managers are well aware how to conduct professional in-person interviews. They may arrange for a conference room setting, and the panel will be professionally presented and well prepared. That same attention to detail should be given to video interviews as well. If each panel member will be joining remotely, attention should be given to the background seen in the camera (avoid aiming the camera at an un-made bed or sink filled with dishes). Instructions should be given to the panel ahead of time of how to stay muted until they are ready to talk, and protocols for asking questions. If the panel will be joining the interview from their office, ensure the area is free from clutter, lighting is appropriate to see their faces clearly, and background noise is kept to a minimum.

Post-interview etiquette may be important for a number of positions. Some departments will wait to receive a thank-you note from the candidates (via email, handwritten or both), prior to including the candidate in order to proceed to the next level. Other departments will eliminate any candidate who sends a thank-you note following an interview, usually for a few entry-level positions. Management and Department Head positions are usually look for the polite response. Be sure to check with the Human Resource Department for protocols in the department. Again, managers should work with Human Resources to determine if thank-you notes are an important part of the process.

## Step 6: Appointment and Probation

Following hiring, civil service employees serve a *probationary period*, which is a working test period ranging from 3 to 18 months. There are also some longer-term apprenticeship programs that may extend up to 5 years, such as those for the skilled crafts (e.g., electricians), and bridge-class programs, which help employees move from clerical and unskilled occupations into skilled or professional positions.

During the probationary period the new employee is generally more easily dismissed if their job performance is not up to expectations or part of their background is found to be falsified or many other reasons. Also, the probationary employee may not be entitled to some of the benefits (such as vacation, paid leave, etc.) or perquisites of the position.

## Step 7: Tenure

Following the conclusion of a civil service employee's probation, they become tenured and have a property right to the job. This means that the employee can be suspended, demoted, or discharged only for cause. Discipline may require due process hearings both before and after the action. This process is discussed in the Discipline section below. *Seniority* is a common characteristic of civil service organizations. As mentioned above, seniority may be used as a factor in the selection process, particularly for promotional positions. After employees have completed probation and become tenured, the initial date of appointment is typically used to determine eligibility for transfer, advancement to higher level positions, and benefits. In the event of a layoff resulting from a budgetary shortfall, reorganization, or other lack of work, seniority is often used to determine the order of layoff (although performance factors may also be considered).

## WHICH ISSUES ARISE ON THE JOB?

After employees are hired, various issues may arise that require the public administrator to conduct investigations and make recommendations regarding employees' status on the job.

## Discipline

Proper handling of discipline is a significant responsibility of supervisors, managers, and human resources professionals. The decision to discipline an employee is often a difficult one because of the processes required to ensure that the discipline is upheld—that is, agreed to at levels of appeal. Civil service employees are entitled to *due process*, which means that they have a right to a procedure that ensures that all of the facts are considered before they lose any pay or benefits (see Skelly vs. State Personnel Board, 1975). A pre-disciplinary hearing may be required before a disciplinary action is taken. After an employee is suspended or discharged for cause, they may have the right to appeal the action to a civil service commission or to an arbitrator. If the employing department cannot provide a sufficient basis for and written documentation to support the action, the appeal body may reinstate the civil service employee. An appeal to an arbitrator arises out of a *grievance* (discussed below).

There are distinctions between civilian employees' and public safety employees' discipline and appeals processes and their selection processes because of the paramilitary nature of public safety employees' occupations. For example, public safety employees' suspension and termination processes may be modeled after the military tribunal process, instead of the civil service appeals process, in an effort to ensure that other public safety employees are part of the adjudication process.

## Grievances

Employees may file grievances for a variety of reasons other than appealing discipline. A grievance is a mechanism for employees to address a variety of complaints with management, and it often involves an allegation that a provision of a collective bargaining agreement or working rule has been violated. It is typically a multiple-step process with its goal being to resolve the issue at the lowest supervisory level possible. Therefore, a grievance may initially be heard by a first-level supervisor, and if the grievance is not resolved, then it is appealed to higher levels in the organization up to the department head and/or an arbitrator. An arbitrator is an unbiased third party from outside of the organization, oftentimes a professional with a legal or labor relations background, who specializes in this type of work.

## Discrimination Complaints

Discrimination complaints arise when employees allege that an employer has violated laws that prohibit discrimination on the basis of race or national origin, age, gender, or sexual orientation. They differ from other complaints and grievances because of the role that may be played by outside agencies. Although the goal of public managers is to resolve these complaints within their own organizations, if employees are not satisfied, they may seek redress from federal or state agencies. Employees may also file their complaints directly with these outside organizations without notifying their employing agencies. At the federal level, discrimination on the bases enumerated in the 1972 amendment to Title VII of the Civil Rights Act (race, color, religion, sex, and national origin) are enforced by the Equal Employment Opportunities Commission. Other laws enforced by this agency include the Americans with Disabilities Act and the Age Discrimination in Employment Act.

Some states' laws provide additional levels of protection in certain categories. For example, the Department of Fair Employment and Housing, in California, handles complaints alleging discrimination based on race, color, religion, gender, pregnancy, sexual orientation, marital status, national origin, ancestry, physical or mental disability, medical conditions (including HIV and AIDS), and age (40 and older); denial of pregnancy leave or reasonable accommodation; sexual harassment; and denial of family and medical leave.

## INVESTIGATIONS

Public administrators are called on to conduct investigations and provide guidance in connection with proposed disciplinary actions or to resolve appeals or grievances arising out of these actions. They also may take an active role in resolving grievances or other complaints. This is a time-consuming task with many steps. It is important that the steps be followed to ensure due process for the affected employees and avoid political interference. The steps include the following:

1. researching the issue, including reviewing personnel files or similar cases or complaints;
2. interviewing witnesses, including supervisors, co-workers, and subject experts;
3. preparing reports and supporting documents (e.g., copies of employee records) and making recommendations for appropriate action;
4. discussing the issue with the employee's union representative and in some cases with legal counsel;
5. participating in a selection process for a neutral third party, in accordance with a union contract or personnel manual requirement, if the employee appeal is referred to a third party for resolution;
6. acting as a representative of or advocate for management during a grievance or civil service hearing;
7. testifying at the hearing or meeting with outside agency representatives (such as federal or state agency representatives who handle discrimination or safety complaints);
8. preparing post-hearing briefs or reports;
9. presenting reports or recommendations to upper management, a commission, or elected representatives; and
10. protecting confidentiality of complainants and witnesses to the maximum extent possible, particularly with respect to discrimination investigations.

## PERFORMANCE EVALUATION AND EMPLOYEE DEVELOPMENT

All employees participate in performance evaluation either as the subject of an appraisal or as a supervisor responsible for conducting the appraisal. Supervisors and managers at all levels in an organization are judged on their performance, whether by other managers, elected officials, or the citizens and electorate. Employees often view performance evaluation negatively or skeptically; but as an element of employee development, it should be a recognized also as a positive tool.

Performance evaluation is often thought of as a formal process in which supervisors fill out forms and/or engage in planned discussions with employees regarding a set of performance criteria. The most effective performance evaluation occurs daily in the form of ongoing communication and feedback, and the formal process merely serves as documentation and reinforcement of those ongoing communications. The core elements of performance systems include the following:

- *Evaluations are appropriate for the job.* They should begin with an analysis of the job requirements, similar to what occurs in the examination process. Along with determining the skills, abilities, knowledge, and traits needed for a job, the evaluation should establish criteria for determining the characteristics that constitute outstanding performance, average performance, or need for improvement. For example, some jobs demand high-quantity work output and timeliness and can be measured in objective terms, whereas the focus of other jobs may be on problem solving and critical thinking, which involves more subjective evaluation. Oral and written communication and interpersonal skills may be critical elements of jobs held by persons who interact with the public, whereas other jobs in fields such as information technology, engineering, or the skilled crafts require strong technical skills. Supervisors and managers are evaluated on their leadership abilities and effectiveness in planning, scheduling, delegating, training, and mentoring. Along with the job-specific traits, there are common characteristics that define performance in virtually all jobs. Employees who consistently get along with others—supervisors, colleagues, and customers—and who have a cooperative and pleasant disposition are valued in any job.

- *Evaluations should enhance employee development.* The objective of evaluation is to provide constructive feedback that motivates workers to achieve their maximum potential and contribute to their organizations. The evaluation process provides the supervisor with the opportunity to have a one-on-one conversation with their subordinate. Supervisors can point out the employee's strengths and opportunities for growth. Ideally it should improve morale, but that can be a challenge when a supervisor needs to identify shortcomings in an employee's performance, particularly when it is in writing. Written evaluations should include outstanding performance as well as substandard performance. Evaluation is particularly important in dealing with difficult employees who may require more diligent and regular monitoring. Although evaluation may not formally be part of the discipline process, it should support or at the very least not be contradictory to the discipline process, in case formal discipline becomes necessary.

## WORKING WITH DIVERSITY

One of the characteristics that agencies look for in employees and leaders is the ability to understand diversity and inclusion. Public organizations strive to be representative of the populations they serve. Changing demographics mean that people of various cultures, races, gender orientations, and ages are an integral part of the workforce as well as the clientele whom public organizations serve. Employees, managers, and executives are expected to be sensitive and demonstrate awareness of these diverse groups. On the most basic level this means compliance with equal employment opportunity laws and the Americans with Disabilities Act, but on a more subtle level it also means recognizing unique mores within the workforce/clientele and respecting all employees and clients. While these characteristics may come naturally to some employees and leaders, others may require more coaching and training, both formally and informally.

The goal of managing public-sector human resources is to produce a workforce that serves its citizens, its employees, and its community effectively.

## THE ROLE OF UNIONS

The role of unions is intertwined with many of the functions described in previous sections. Historically, private unions developed first and came under the jurisdiction of the National Labor Relations Board during the Franklin Roosevelt administration. Public unions and their collective bargaining rights developed later. In the early 1960s a presidential executive order established a program of "employee-management cooperation" under the supervision of the federal Civil Service Commission, and a few years later the Office of Labor-Management Relations was established under the jurisdiction of the commission. That organization led to statutes that granted exclusive recognition of employee organizations, representation elections, and agreements for payroll dues deductions.

Many state and local governments adopted mandatory collective bargaining legislation during the 1960s and 1970s, often modeling their statutes on those that applied to private-sector employees. For example, labor relations statutes may designate an agency, such as a state or local commission, to administer and enforce the labor laws,

or without such designations the courts assume the oversight responsibility for representation and collective bargaining issues. The early
laws granted employees the right to organize and recognized unions
but limited their activities to "consulting" with management. As the
laws evolved, unions were granted the ability to collectively bargain
wages, hours, terms, and conditions of employment. Many states have
adopted such laws.

## PROS AND CONS OF UNIONS IN THE PUBLIC SECTOR

The pros:

* Unions give employees a voice and protect their rights, as they do
  in the private sector.
* They serve as watchdogs by identifying waste and holding
  management accountable to the public as well as their members
  (e.g., teachers unions help educate the public about issues related
  to spending and quality).
* They support initiatives and tax increases that may help the
  public.

The cons:

* Unions exert undue influence over elected officials through their
  ability to provide campaign contributions and advertising funds.
* Their influence has resulted in higher wages and benefits than in
  the private sector.
* They can be an obstacle to efficiency by protecting certain work
  rules such as seniority and tenure.
* They may harm public health and safety during a work stoppage.

## THE NEGOTIATIONS PROCESS

Negotiations between union and management representatives are
complex, lengthy processes involving multiple steps. Not all the following steps occur during each negotiation. For example, Step 1 occurs
when unions are first recognized and allowed bargaining rights but
may not occur on a regular basis. Step 4 occurs only when the parties
cannot reach agreement during negotiations.

### Step 1: Unit Determination

Before negotiations begin, appropriate bargaining units are established. The process of unit determination is based on the agency's
classification structure. Separate bargaining units are typically established for public safety and civilian employees and for professionals
and blue-collar employees. The idea is that the employees within a
bargaining unit have at least generally similar job functions. Whereas

the private sector excludes management-level employees from collective bargaining rights, public-sector statutes often allow managers to join unions and collectively bargain. This can result in awkward situations because managers have conflicting allegiances, particularly in labor disputes.

## Step 2: Scope of Bargaining

Negotiators identify the subjects on which labor and management are required to collectively bargain—these are the issues that fall within the scope of bargaining. Statutes may define the scope, but the scope is often refined or interpreted through court or labor relations board decisions. In the most narrowly defined situations, unions may organize but may not have the right to negotiate wages. More expansive laws extend the scope of bargaining to wages, hours, and terms and conditions of employment, which may be broadly interpreted. Rights typically reserved to management include decisions regarding the mission of the agency, determination of the quantity and quality of service, and organizational structure required to maintain uninterrupted service to a community. The rights to hire, discipline, or lay off are also management rights, although the exercise of these rights does not preclude employees/unions from raising grievances or consulting about the practical consequences of these matters as they relate to wages, hours, and terms and conditions of employment. Provisions included in state or local laws or rules adopted by a civil service board may also be exempted from the scope of bargaining.

Although most public administrators and human resources professionals will not have the opportunity to negotiate a complete collective bargaining agreement, they are responsible for administering and interpreting such agreements on a day-to-day basis and for resolving disputes (grievances) arising out of such agreements. It is an essential responsibility of every supervisor to read and understand the provisions of agreements covering employees under their supervision and to recognize when to seek guidance from labor relations experts. Sensitivity to issues that have labor relations impacts is crucial to avoid situations in which operating practices may undermine written agreements. For example, providing employees with more compensatory time than is allowed in the agreement can ultimately cause an arbitrator to rule that the past practice has overturned the written agreement.

There are also many issues that may arise outside of those in the master agreement that may require negotiation. For example, individual departments or units within a department with a desire to change long-standing work schedule practices are often required to engage in a meet and confer process before they can implement the change.

## Step 3: Meeting and Conferring

Collective bargaining in the public sector is often referred to as "meeting and conferring" or "meeting and conferring in good faith." Either of these terms recognizes a distinction between private-sector and public-sector negotiations. Whereas negotiators in the private sector typically have authority to enter into a binding agreement, public-sector management representatives are agents of a governing body that retains the authority to approve a binding agreement. Usually the elected representative(s) is the legislative branch—a state legislature, city council, or county board of supervisors. When these elected representatives approve a memorandum of agreement or memorandum of understanding, it becomes a binding contract on the parties. The memorandum of agreement/memorandum of understanding may also require an enabling ordinance or law to become legally binding. Agreements on issues at departmental or smaller organizational unit levels may be codified with letters of agreement or letters of intent, which are supplemental agreements within the authority of individual managers.

*Interest-based bargaining*, sometimes known as "mutual gains" or "win-win" bargaining, has gained acceptance in recent years as a negotiations approach. It is a process that encourages the parties to collectively solve problems and minimize adversarial communications. While it is particularly effective in dealing with operational changes, it can also be used in negotiating full labor contracts.

## Step 4: Impasse Procedures and Strikes by Public Employees

Ideally negotiations result in agreements. However, sometimes parties to the negotiation are unable to agree on the contract terms and reach an impasse. This is sometimes known as an *interest dispute*. An impasse can be declared by either the union or management when it believes negotiations are no longer productive.

Traditionally in the private sector such disputes result in strikes. Exerting economic pressure by withholding services is an effective tool used by labor to get the attention of management. Government is not measured by profits, and therefore a strike has limited effectiveness in the public sector and also can result in significant harm to the public. The principle that public employees cannot strike has eroded, although it still remains in place at the federal level. Court decisions in many states have granted the right to strike subject to certain limitations, such as ensuring that work stoppages do not result in an imminent threat to the public health and safety. Therefore, public safety employees may be prohibited from striking even if civilians in the same jurisdiction have that right. A decision about whether a strike endangers the public is made by the courts, which must evaluate the specific evidence in each situation. Public administrators in individual agencies may be called on to provide information in support of such actions brought to the courts.

In the public sector, the effect of declaring an impasse means that management is prepared to impose its last offer in lieu of further negotiations; for the union the choice may be between accepting the final offer and striking. However, there are usually several steps before either of these actions is taken.

With or without the right to strike there are other mechanisms for dispute resolution, depending on the nature of the dispute. As an alternative to striking, state or local statutes may provide for mediation and/or nonbinding voluntary arbitration, also known as *fact finding*. This process utilizes a neutral third party or panel of neutrals to assist the parties when negotiations result in an impasse. Both arbitration and fact-finding proceedings involve formal hearings that require the parties to produce witnesses, present written evidence, and often to submit written briefs. Human resources professionals and other public administrators may be called as witnesses in such hearings; those who negotiate individual issues may have the responsibility to act as advocates as well.

Some agencies have legislated binding arbitration of interest disputes; however, this is controversial, and most agencies reject this form of dispute resolution. Although it may be considered preferable to a strike as the final step in the negotiating process, the objection is that arbitration inappropriately delegates the most critical public policy decisions involving tremendous financial resources to a third party who has no accountability to the electorate.

Another impasse resolution process is *mediation*, which may be used as an intermediate stage in the process or as the final stage, depending on the terms of the labor relations statute (law). Although mediation also utilizes a neutral third party, the process is considerably more informal than arbitration. The role of the mediator is to assist the parties while negotiations are still under way by providing a mechanism for them to communicate without direct contact. It is nonbinding or advisory. If unsuccessful, the parties may then seek fact finding, binding arbitration, or strike, depending on the terms of the labor statutes of their jurisdiction.

## Step 5: Administration of the Agreement/ Disputes Regarding Interpretation

Following an agreement, it is the responsibility of public administrators to understand and comply with its provisions and language. For example, it is important to ensure provisions are properly interpreted for such features as special compensation provisions for working in specialized positions or for working under unusual conditions. Violation of the

agreement or related working rules or a perception by employees of ineq-
uitable or disparate treatment may result in a grievance, also known as
a "rights dispute." The last step in the grievance process is usually *binding arbitration*. Because disputes over contract interpretation are less far
reaching (and may affect only one employee or a small group of employees), they do not raise the same public policy concerns as discussed in
connection with arbitration of impasses in the bargaining process. Grievances may also be submitted by the parties to mediation, which works
similarly to the mediation process described during negotiations.

Another type of dispute that may arise either during negotiations
or during the term of a contract is known as an *unfair labor practice
charge* or an *unfair*. These disputes may involve a charge of bad-faith
bargaining (by either party, although most frequently by unions) alleging a refusal to bargain; surface bargaining, that is, just going through
the motions; making unilateral changes without bargaining; interfering
with a union; or attempting to dominate a union. The most common
unfair charge that affects public administrators involves unilateral
implementation of changes to working rules. Unfairs can be avoided
by understanding the agreements that cover employees in their organizations. This type of dispute is typically adjudicated by an employee
relations board or the courts.

## UNION INFLUENCE

The pros and cons of unions were summarized earlier. There are
some related issues to be mentioned in closing this topic. The popular
press sometimes takes aim at public-sector unions as an obstacle to
governmental efficiency. Unions are clearly a potent political force as
major contributors to the election campaigns of the officials of agencies
that employ their members. One of the reasons is that unions are able
to take advantage of laws allowing for "independent expenditures" to
spend significant amounts of their dues money to buy advertising in
support of candidates or ballot measures. Independent expenditures
are not subject to campaign contribution limits that may affect individuals. Furthermore, unions can mobilize hundreds to thousands of
members to work or vote for candidates who have promised to protect
the job security, wages, and benefits of government employees. Unions
also typically support tax increases to help increase resources available for wages and benefits or may lobby against measures designed
to hold public employees more accountable (such as elimination of
teacher tenure systems). To this extent some argue that public-sector
unions exert influence not enjoyed by unions in the private sector.

On the other hand, the public-sector union watchdog role can act
to counterbalance private-sector corporate interests and monetary
contributions, such as those that may be exerted by insurance or the legal
professions (e.g., to oppose comprehensive health insurance reform).

Historically, under union agreements, employees were required to pay an agency fee to a union for representation services, even if they were not dues-paying members (Abood v. Detroit Board of Education, 1977). Agency shop arrangements guaranteed financial security for the union and increased its influence. Public employees were required to either be (1) a dues-paying union member, or (2) if they opted out of the union, they were required to pay an agency fee to cover the costs of collective bargaining. However, in 2018, Janus v. AFSCME was a landmark decision of the Supreme Court ruling that public employees can no longer be required to be a union member or pay an agency fee in order to work in the public sector. Public sector employers must notify all employees that they have a First Amendment right not to join a union or pay union dues or fees before they sign any membership application or dues deduction authorization. As opposed to private-sector unions, the Supreme Court ruled that public sector unions are inherently political and therefore, compelling membership dues or fees is a violation of First Amendment Rights.

## ETHICAL CONCERNS

Public-sector hiring often raises ethical issues and dilemmas. The testing process has the objectives of fairness and openness, often at the expense of efficiency. Tests alone may not evaluate the attributes most needed for the position. Treating prospective employees equally meets certain ethical standards; however, some would argue that it may not result in hiring the most talented and motivated public servants and that this does not serve the greater public interest. Similarly, reforms that seek to remove employees from extensive testing are controversial.

A similar argument can be made that the greater public interest is best served by protection of employees from inappropriate discipline or discharge. While these processes protect employees from political influence, they also make it more difficult for conscientious public managers to deal with unproductive employees who do not adequately serve the public. A process for documenting and coaching employees to be productive serves the ethical objective of fairness and due process.

Human resources administrators confront ethics issues frequently in connection with employee misconduct and discipline. An interesting situation arises in connection with whistleblowers, a case study of which was included in Chapter 4, "Ethics." Government agencies have laws and regulations in place to protect employees who disclose fraud, misconduct, or other ethical violations from retaliation by employers. Ideally, there would be an individual or organization outside of the whistleblower's agency who would hear and investigate complaints. This helps protect the employee's privacy, helps to ensure a more objective investigation, and helps to ensure that accused members of an organization cannot influence or thwart the outcome. However, human resources professionals sometimes see another side of whistleblowers. Sometimes employees attempt to use whistleblower protections to get attention and/or avoid discipline for poor performance or their own misconduct. Sorting out legitimate ethics complaints from complaints of employees seeking to protect themselves from threatened or pending discipline can be a challenge.

Another reality is the impact of ethics complaints on the entire organization. From time to time people make mistakes. When whistleblowers disclose these mistakes, there may be unintended collateral effects on people who one would not expect to be affected. For example, in the health care field, disclosure of inappropriate practices by health care personnel may result in the release of confidential medical information of patients and may jeopardize their privacy if privacy laws are not closely followed. Therefore, there may be unintended victims of the whistleblower's actions.

In the human resources field, it is not uncommon for complaints, grievances, or disciplinary actions that are not resolved at the agency level to be litigated in the courts. Once actions move to the courts, the issues become more adversarial and less amenable to compromise. Issues may rise to this level because the process itself is unfair and may not have provided the grievant with the expected forum or resolution. On the flip side, the threat of litigation can cause justice to be compromised in the interest of expediency. Because government agencies are seen as deep pockets, vulnerable to large judgments by judges and juries, some undeserving employees may receive settlements in discrimination cases so agencies can avoid battles in court that have the potential to cost more than pre-court settlements.

Unions are also involved with advocacy on a regular basis. Sometimes they represent their members regardless of the merits of cases, an obligation similar to that of attorneys representing clients. Does this advocacy role relieve the unions of accountability for solving problems and working in concert with agency management to serve the public interest? That is an interesting ethical question.

## CONCLUSION

Developing positive relationships with union representatives/leadership is an essential requirement for public administrators. In today's world partnerships with unions are integral parts of both managing resources and achieving policy initiatives.

## PRACTICING PUBLIC ADMINISTRATION

1. Review the following position description for John Doe, and create one for your own job by adapting the shaded items.

**Position Description**

| Name of Employee: John Doe | Job Classification: Analyst | Salary Rate: |
|---|---|---|
| **Reason for description** <br> New Position   Yes        Change in Position | | |
| **Department, Division, How long in position** <br> Public Works, Accounting, 3.5 years | | |
| **Name and classification of supervisor** <br> Jane Smith, Chief Accountant | | |
| **Description of Duties:** <br> Describe what is done, how it is done, materials, equipment, and percentage of time, and indicate whether the duties and responsibilities have changed | | |

| Percentage of Time | Duties |
|---|---|
| 40% | Provide administrative support for accounting division manager, coordinating hiring of personnel and preparing organization charts, position descriptions, accounting reports, and administrative paperwork; coordinate computer installation for staff |
| 15% | Maintain, update, and distribute approved policies and procedures relating to accounting operations, such as the purchasing card program, travel policy, and petty cash policy |
| 15% | Coordinate and prepare the division budget; assist and provide recommendations and justifications in writing for new positions and expense items |
| 10% | Procure supplies and materials for the division in accordance with purchasing and contract requirements and procedures; process requisitions to pay for services and items through a review of the budget and use of computer applications |
| 10% | Supervise two clerical employees (one senior clerk typist and one clerk typist), providing direction, training, and evaluation |
| 10% | Provide training for accounting operations staff on new policies and procedures |

| | |
|---|---|
| **List equipment used:** Computers, printers, fax machines | |
| **Physical requirements:** Light walking, mostly indoors; lifting and shifting up to 20 pounds | |
| **Machinery used:** Automobile to pick up and deliver supplies and visit employees in field | |
| **Responsibility for cash:** Petty cash up to $100 | |
| Signature of Employee: | Date: |
| Signature of Supervisor: | Date: |
| Signature of Department Head: | Date: |

2. A city council has assigned the task of developing an environmental czar position. Which issues and questions must be resolved?

3. A new supervisor has been assigned to a unit with personnel problems, including a complaint that resources such as vehicles have been improperly used by some staff. Identify the issues and steps to address the complaint.

4. A new manager assumes responsibility for a function in which employees are working alternative work schedules that result in inadequate public service on some days of the week (usually Monday or Friday). Which issues are involved in changing these schedules?

5. Group exercise: The city council has announced that employees must be furloughed to deal with a budget shortfall. Select participants to represent the union and management, and engage in a negotiation over the implementation of the furloughs. Each group should identify the issues and present its position.

## BIBLIOGRAPHY

Ban, C., & Riccucci, N. (2001). *Public personnel management: Career concerns, future challenges.* (3d ed.). New York, NY: Pearson Longman.

Bennett, J. T., & Kaufam, B., Eds. (2007). *What do unions do? A twenty year perspective.* New Brunswick, NJ: Transaction Publishers.

Cayer, N. J. (2004). *Public personnel administration.* Belmont, CA.: Wadsworth/ Thomas Learning.

Cropf, R. A. (2008). *American public administration: Public service for civil society in the 21st century.* New York, NY: Pearson Longman.

Golembiewski, R. T., Ed. (1976). *People in public service: A reader in public personnel administration.* Itasca, IL.: F. E. Peacock.

Hays, S. H., & Kearney, R. C. (2003). *Public personnel administration: Problems and prospects.* (4th ed.). Upper Saddle River, NJ: Prentice Hall.

Hickman, G. R. (2001). *Managing human resources in the public sector.* Fort Worth, TX: Harcourt College.

Ingraham, P. W., & Romzek, B., Eds. (1994). *Rethinking public personnel systems.* San Francisco, CA: Jossey-Bass.

Mosher, F. (1982). *Democracy and public service.* (2nd ed.). New York, NY: Oxford.

Najita, J. M., & Stern, J. (2001). *Collective bargaining in the public sector.* Armonk, NY: M. E. Sharpe.

Prynes, J. (2004). *Human resources management for public and nonprofit organizations.* San Francisco, CA: Jossey-Bass.

Riccucci, N. M., Naff, K.C., Shafritz, J. M., & Rosenbloom, D. (2007). *Personnel management in government: Politics and process.* (6th ed.). Boca Raton, FL: CRC.

Rice, M. (2005). *Diversity and public administration: Theory, issues and perspectives.* Armonk, NY: M.E. Sharpe.

Shafritz, J. M. (2001). *Personnel management in government: Politics and process.* New York, NY: Marcel Dekker.

Spengler, A. W. (1999). *Collective bargaining and increased competition for resources in local government.* Westport, CT: Quorum.

U.S. Merit Systems Protection Board. (2000). *Competing for federal jobs: Job search experiences of new hires.* Washington, D.C.: Office of Personnel Management.

## PROFESSIONAL ORGANIZATIONS AND GOVERNMENT RESOURCES

GovLeaders.org provides free learning resources to help public managers forge a more effective and motivated government workforce
www.govleaders.org

International Public Management Association for Human Resources:
www.ipma-hr.org

U.S. Department of Labor, Bureau of Labor Statistics:
www.bls.gov

# 12 ◇ ◇ ◇ ◆

# Benefits and Managing Risks

Chapter 11 addressed the subject of pay and benefits in the context of recruitment and the role of unions in negotiating compensation packages. In this chapter we will examine the total compensation package, specific types of benefits, and managing their costs and risks.

## WHAT IS A TOTAL COMPENSATION PACKAGE?

Compensation is an approach to providing value to employees in exchange for work performed. Some forms of compensation are received in money, for example, salary and overtime, and others in forms that have value but are not received as money, such as time off, benefits, and insurance. Compensation may be received immediately for performing work or deferred as in the form of pensions.

The first and most significant element of compensation is the basic salary or hourly wages. Embedded in the salaries for some jobs are bonuses for additional education, experience, and for hazardous or unpleasant working conditions that are not normally part of the basic requirement for a job classification. Other bonuses may be paid intermittently when unusual conditions arise (e.g., occasionally for nighttime work, work in noisy conditions, or work on aerial equipment). Another significant element of salary is overtime, which is premium compensation mandated by both federal and state laws for work beyond regular working hours. Some jobs also include uniform or tool allowances, which may be paid as amounts supplemental to salary on a regular basis or paid in a lump sum annually or semiannually.

After salary and related allowances, there are non-cash benefits that also have an ongoing and significant hard-dollar cost, often for both the employer and the employee. These benefits include various forms of insurance—health, dental, life, disability, and workers' compensation—as well as employee assistance programs, tuition reimbursement, and specialized training. Social Security, Medicare, and other government-provided pension plans also fit into this category. (See Chapter 14 "Operating Budgets," for specifics.)

Finally, there are benefits for time off, measured in terms of productivity or the loss of productivity, which are sometimes referred to as "soft-dollar" costs. Included in this category are employer-paid holidays, vacations, sick leave, family and personal leave, military leave, jury duty leave, and witness appearance leave. Some employers may also allow time off for charitable activities such as donating blood or helping in the community. Benefits have evolved into a major component of the compensation package of government employees to a large extent because government salaries were traditionally less competitive than salaries in the private sector. Benefits helped to bridge the pay gap and attract and retain employees, particularly in high-risk jobs such as those in police and fire departments.

Some of the earliest pension plans were developed for police officers and firefighters; they date back more than a century, before the establishment of Social Security and most private-sector pension plans. Similarly, some of the earliest employer-sponsored health insurance benefits were provided for uniformed safety employees not only as recruiting tools but also because private insurers were reluctant to insure employees in these high-risk professions. Historically, these benefits may have been provided by independent nonprofit benevolent associations, but later government agencies assumed responsibility for administering and/or subsidizing the benefits.

## ELIGIBILITY FOR BENEFITS

While the focus of this chapter is benefits provided to full-time civil service or classified employees, we should note that there are other categories of government employees who have different packages of benefits or who may be ineligible for benefits.

The packages of benefits provided to elected officials, high-level exempt executives, and other political appointees often look different than those provided to civil servants, particularly those who are represented by unions. High-level officials often have special perquisites such as automobiles or other special vehicles (even aircraft), personal drivers, their own retirement and time-off plans, travel, relocation and housing allowances, and/or expense accounts.

At the other end of the spectrum are part-time employees (often defined as those working less than half-time), seasonal or temporary employees, and contractors. These employees often are ineligible for many benefits or are eligible for a lesser package of benefits. It is common for employees who work between half-time and full-time to receive benefits that are the same as or similar to those of full-time employees, but on a prorated basis.

The Affordable Care Act (ACA), passed in 2010, was implemented to ensure all employees received access to health benefits. The "Affordable Care Act" refers to the comprehensive health care reform law meant to ensure health insurance is available and affordable to all. One of the other benefits to the ACA was the ability to reduce the costs of health insurance by mandating coverage and increasing competition among insurers. The long list of provisions includes employer annual reporting and a requirement that applicable large employers either offer acceptable coverage or make a payment to the IRS to subsidize individuals on government plans.

The range of benefits, from insurance coverage, leave benefits, to holidays and vacations, is addressed below.

## HEALTH INSURANCE

As medical costs continue to exceed other inflation indicators, health insurance has become the most significant part of benefit packages. Public employers typically subsidize a high percentage of employees' and their families' health insurance premiums, recognizing that health insurance serves a public policy purpose that extends beyond benefits to their own employees by lessening the burden on public hospitals and emergency rooms.

Employers may contract with one or more health insurance providers, usually providing employees with a choice of plans. Health insurance providers fall into two main categories, health maintenance organizations (HMOs) and preferred provider organizations (PPOs). HMOs emphasize illness prevention and are characterized by the requirement that primary physicians refer patients to specialists, that is, act as gatekeepers to help control medical costs. PPOs provide employees with more choices of physicians and hence are usually more expensive plans. Government agencies are more likely to subsidize the full cost of premiums for HMOs, which are less costly. PPOs are only partially subsidized, which increases the cost to the employee.

For much of the past decade health insurance costs have been exceeding the general rate of inflation and have expanded overhead costs for employers. Because of the increasing costs, health insurance is often a contentious issue during labor negotiations. The mission of unions is to secure benefits of greatest interest and need to its members, while employers look to control costs by seeking to share costs. Cost sharing is accomplished by limiting access to and/or choices of benefit providers (in other words, fewer plans); eliminating the types or number of covered medical procedures (such as physical therapy, chiropractic, or mental health visits); increasing employee co-payments for office visits, medical procedures, or hospitalization; or reducing the employer's dollar contribution to the subsidy.

However, any of these options evokes strong reactions from unions. For example, when the City of Los Angeles attempted to follow the lead of Los Angeles County by placing a cap on the health subsidy—setting a fixed dollar amount on coverage rather than continuing an automatic escalator based on increases in the family coverage premium for one of its HMOs—the city's unions threatened to strike. The City withdrew that proposal and maintained the subsidy without a cap, which has the effect of continuing to drive up health insurance costs.

Joint labor-management benefits committees can be useful in overseeing or managing health benefits issues. Going back to the example of the City of Los Angeles in the 1990s, when health insurance costs were escalating significantly, a joint labor-management committee stepped up to explore options for controlling costs along with providing benefits that better met employees' needs. The committee agreed to co-payments for doctor's office visits (which had the effect of freezing increases in the premium for a couple of years), and in exchange employees were offered more benefit options (discussed below). The theory was that new benefits would not cost any more and that the total employer subsidy for all insurance benefits would remain fixed or become a defined contribution. However, this concept of cost neutrality did not remain in place for long; within a few years health insurance costs again drove increasing costs in the benefit program. This issue contributed to significant policy changes, such as mandated insurance and the ACA.

Joint labor-management committees, which consist of union and employer representatives, can have significant responsibilities for the administration of a benefits program on an ongoing basis. Such committees are a democratic method of providing employees, through their unions, with a greater voice in their benefit choices and costs than if the human resources department were to make the decisions unilaterally. The committees may be empowered, through ordinances, labor contracts, and the committees' own bylaws, to design and approve benefit structures and to negotiate with health insurance companies (such as Blue Cross) or directly with service providers (HMOs such as Kaiser Permanente). They may issue requests for proposals for new plans or plan amendments and hire consultants to assist in analyzing and negotiating benefits. They also may be responsible for overseeing communications and enrollment as well as handling appeals when a health insurance company denies coverage. For a joint committee to be effective the union members must represent a majority of the affected employees, and the management representatives should include those who have knowledge of benefits and who are responsible for administration.

## RELATED INSURANCE BENEFITS

Other benefits offered by public employers may include dental insurance, life insurance, short- and long-term disability insurance, accidental death and dismemberment insurance, child care, wellness programs, and employee assistance programs (EAPs). Employee assistance programs aid employees with substance abuse as well as financial, legal, psychological, and family issues. These supplemental benefits may be subsidized in whole or in part (e.g., employee-only dental coverage or up to $50,000 in life insurance) but usually provide employees with the option to purchase additional coverage for themselves or their families at their cost.

Flexible benefit plans, which are used in some agencies, are structured to provide employees with a fixed amount of dollars to spend on benefits of their choice. One type benefit under a Flexible Spending Account (FSA) is the Health Care Reimbursement Account (HCA). This allows an employee to take money out of a paycheck on a pre-tax basis, which can be used on out-of-pocket health care expenses. Another benefit is a Health Savings Account (HSA), a tax-advantaged medical savings account that may be available to those who are enrolled in a health plan. The funds contributed to an HSA are not subject to federal income tax at the time of deposit. All of these plans are appealing to employees because they help address the different needs of employees who are single, are married, and/or have families.

## WORKERS' COMPENSATION

All employers must provide workers' compensation coverage for employees who are injured or become ill on the job. Benefits include a percentage of salary continuation for employees whose injuries/illnesses prevent them from working (temporary disability) and payment of medical and supplemental job displacement benefits. Once an employee's condition is stable, a permanent disability award may also be granted if the injury or illness results in a chronic condition or permanent impairment. Ongoing medical expenses may also be granted. While a basic level of temporary disability is mandated by the state, individual agencies may elect to provide a higher level of benefit and may choose to either purchase insurance or self-insure. Public safety employees typically have a different level of benefits, in recognition of the higher risk associated with their jobs. Workers' compensation benefits have generated controversy in recent years as a source of uncontrolled business costs. This has resulted in efforts to reduce medical costs by limiting the type or length of certain treatments.

Measuring workers' compensation costs can be a significant challenge in determining effectiveness in controlling costs. While employers may achieve success in limiting new claims, the impact of older cases and recurring claims may extend for many years. Current or former employees are often eligible for continuing payment of medical expenses related to an occupational injury or illness long after the initial date of injury. Therefore, even if future claims or benefits are reduced, there may be significant delays in cost reductions.

Workers' compensation may be provided through insurance companies or self-funded and administered by larger government agencies. When self-administered, it may be handled by individual departments or a centralized agency. If the administrative function is centralized, then costs may be charged back to the departments that incur the costs. Maintaining reasonable caseloads for claims adjusters and attorneys is one of the challenges in administering an effective program. In one case study, where an operating department took over the program from a central agency and reduced caseload, it was able to control costs more effectively by reducing work-related injuries and costs. Although costs increased for the first few years as a result of the acceleration in closure of cases and payment of new awards, over time the greater case management efficiency resulted in the department's holding costs constant although the number of employees increased.

## SAFETY

Occupational safety is the corollary to workers' compensation. In a perfect world, employees would engage in safe work practices and avoid all work-related injuries. However, even in the safest work environment employees are injured or exposed to illnesses. Although safety is a function that may be administered by different organizations, such as risk management, it is frequently a human resources function.

Federal (Occupational Safety and Health Administration) and state agencies enforce rules and regulations governing occupational safety. Safety experts use these as a framework for safety programs. Large agencies often employ safety engineers, industrial hygienists, and ergonomic specialists to investigate workplace injuries, analyze work spaces, monitor noise levels and chemical exposures, develop safe driving programs, provide fire protection and emergency response plans, conduct testing or audits, and provide safety training.

## RISK MANAGEMENT

Risk management encompasses a broad range of activities beyond safety. As well as managing liability arising out of employee injury, risk management experts analyze, monitor, and seek to prevent other types of liability, including those affecting the public. Liability claims include those related to employment practices; legal issues; equipment failures; slips and falls; falling objects; road, sidewalk, tree, and traffic hazards; and automobile accidents.

Workplace violence incidents and injuries are also a serious risk management concern for organizations. The Occupational Health and Safety Office (OSHA) defines workplace violence as "any act or threat of physical violence, harassment, intimidation, or other threatening disruptive behavior that occurs at the work site" ranging from threats and verbal abuse to physical assaults and even homicide. Workplace violence and other injuries is currently the third-leading cause of fatal occupational injuries in the United States.

The goal to mitigate all risk management is to hold managers accountable and implement preventive measures before an incident or complaint becomes a liability claim or litigation against an agency. Risk management involves looking holistically at operations to identify and analyze exposure to loss before it happens. Incidents, complaints by the public or employees, reviews of training and disciplinary procedures, interviews, and operational inspections are loss-prevention tools.

## PENSIONS AND DEFERRED COMPENSATION

Generous pension plans are characteristic of government employment. While many private employers have scaled back or eliminated their defined benefit plans, such pension plans are still prevalent in the public sector. Defined benefit plans are prefunded, meaning that funds are set aside for employees during their working careers, based on actuarial assumptions, to provide adequate benefits during their retirements. Because defined benefit plans guarantee a benefit based on a formula, the sponsoring agency assumes the risk of providing that benefit even if the plan has not been adequately funded or if enhanced benefits are approved without regard to future costs. There are also established legal principles that protect promised levels of benefits. Once an employee is hired and earns benefits under a pension plan, the benefits cannot be eliminated. Consequently, pension plans may cause agencies to accrue liabilities they cannot afford and, in extreme cases, drive agencies into bankruptcy.

Funding of defined benefit plans has been an ongoing challenge for the public sector for a variety of reasons. First has been the issue of the decision of some agencies not to contribute the entire amount identified by actuaries as required. Not all sponsoring agencies have had legal requirements to contribute the amount recommended by the actuary on an annual basis. For example, in the City of Los Angeles, the Police and Fire Pension plan was not funded for over 30 years, meaning the city was not required to prefund or set aside funds during the active life of employees but was required only to pay the pensions that became due each year. This pay-as-you-go policy resulted in hundreds of millions of dollars of unfunded liability by the 1970s until the city charter was changed to require the city to make the actuary's recommended annual payment. Similar issues have arisen with the State of California plan. Today, federal and state standards (Internal Revenue Code and other governmental accounting standards) have improved funding policies and helped to protect pensions for both government and private-sector workers.

Although strides have been made in funding policies and accounting standards, funding shortfalls have also arisen when agencies have increased benefits, particularly during periods of strong stock market experience. Today, a large percentage of pension plan assets are invested in the stock market, in contrast to the practice 30 years ago when cash, bonds, and other more conservative investment instruments were popular. A strong market increases the value of the assets to pay pensions, and in the late 1990s the increases were so dramatic that many plans became "super funded." This meant that some plans had more than sufficient assets (surpluses) to pay all of the promised benefits, and employer contributions were not recommended by the actuaries. This situation created political pressure to increase benefits and the ongoing costs of the plans without regard to the potential impact if the stock market would level off or decline. The downturn in the market in the first years of the new millennium was catastrophic for some agencies (e.g., the City of San Diego, which was threatened with bankruptcy). Related actions that create funding shortfalls are poor investment decisions unrelated to fluctuations in the market.

In 1994 California's Orange County attained notoriety for engaging in speculative investments in derivatives. Others reported that Orange County was not alone in its use of high-risk unregulated and speculative investment instruments. Many other public entities responded by changing their investment policies, closing the door on risky securities. Texas, for example, amended the Texas Public Funds Investment Act to restrict purchase of high-risk securities and adopted a more conservative approach to investing funds. In Michigan there were calls for reform as well, based on reports of pension systems' investing in high-risk initial public offerings and realty trusts. Concerns were also raised there about deficient disclosure requirements. These experiences heightened awareness of policy makers and bond-rating agencies and created a public demand for greater accountability in decisions related to pension plans.

In 2008–2009, after some years of recovery from recessionary losses earlier in the decade, pension plans faced enormous new challenges resulting from the severe national recession. Again, there were allegations of risky real estate, private equity, and hedge fund investments by the largest public pension fund in the nation, CalPERS, whose chief investment officer had gained a reputation for daring investment at the Washington State Investment Board. However, more alarming were reports that many public plans throughout the nation had serious long-term shortfalls resulting from billions of dollars of stock market losses from what had been considered prudent investments. These losses in market value of investments were compounded by increases in benefit levels that had been approved during the market boom in the late 1990s and resulted in new calls for pension reform.

In January 2013, the California Public Employees' Pension Reform Act (PEPRA) changed the way retirement and health benefits were applied under CalPERS (California Public Employee Retirement System), and placed compensation limits on members. The greatest impact was felt by new CalPERS members, those hired after January 1, 2013, which created a new tier of decreased benefits for employees.

Another significant factor affecting pension plan funding is demographic change, which affects virtually all plans, regardless of benefit and funding policies. This is a function of the large population bubble caused by the baby boom generation as well as by increased life expectancies for the entire population, which have changed career expectations and trends. Pension costs increase as more retirees live longer and as employees are hired and join retirement plans when they are older. As government employment has become less attractive to younger high school or college graduates and more attractive to mature adults seeking the security of the public sector as a second career, the average age of the employment pool increases. Employees who are hired in their 30s or 40s are more likely to remain employed until retirement age and collect their pensions. Employees who are employed soon after completing school are more likely to resign before retirement age, withdraw their pension contributions if there are any, and forfeit the contributions made to the plan by their employers.

Today a critical issue is inadequate funding of other post-employment benefits (commonly referred to as "OPEB") such as health and dental insurance. This is another problem with a variety of causes. Post-employment health insurance is a benefit that has been increasing during the past 30 years. While many public agencies provided pensions for years, subsidized health insurance benefits for retirees are a newer and evolving benefit and one that is particularly sensitive to people's living longer and utilizing more health care resources. The impact of increasing medical costs from new technologies and improved pharmaceuticals is even more exaggerated in the retiree population than among younger active employees.

Although many agencies promised retirees subsidized health insurance, very few prefunded this benefit, and as a consequence of continuing to fund on a pay-as-you-go basis, they are now facing tremendous unfunded liabilities. Governmental Accounting Standards Board (better known in the field as GASB) now requires these liabilities be recognized. Although a few progressive agencies have started to prefund these benefits, the situation has reached crisis proportions in many other agencies. Government agencies and business groups have commissioned studies to evaluate the impact of rising public employee benefit costs, and bond-rating agencies (which determine the credit worthiness of bond issuers) are closely monitoring the steps governments are taking to contain costs. The media have identified this issue as a ticking time bomb.

Public agencies may provide *defined contribution plans*, such as 401(k) or 457 plans (which refer to the enabling sections in the Internal Revenue Code), in addition to defined benefit plans and Social Security (FICA, Federal Insurance Contributions Act). Some agencies have discontinued their defined benefit plans entirely and replaced them with defined contribution plans, although this is still the exception. Defined contribution plans may include an employer match. Because the employee assumes the risk, these plans generate less liability for the agency but do not provide as much financial security to the employee. However, because they are portable to other employers, they may be advantageous for the employee who does not serve an entire career with one agency.

Defined contribution plans are lower maintenance for employers/ plan sponsors because employees assume all of the financial risk and actuarial funding is not required. However, because the assets belong entirely to the participants, who make the investment decisions and pay the fees, employees may pay closer attention to the administration of the plan. There is typically a board of trustees with oversight responsibility for the plan; the board includes agents of the plan sponsor as well as elected employee representatives. Since the financial fiascos of the 1990s (e.g., the Orange County bankruptcy) trust and fiduciary requirements for such plans have been enhanced, and participants have demanded more transparency. The trustees must be vigilant about political meddling or improper relationships between vendors and decision makers. To protect the plan sponsor from fiduciary exposure it is important to design a governance structure that inhibits political influence in the selection and awarding of contracts to administrators and/or investment managers.

## SOCIAL SECURITY AND MEDICARE BENEFITS

Social Security and Medicare benefits are provided to many public employees, although there are some agencies that were exempted from providing these benefits years ago. The three forms of retirement benefit—defined benefit, defined contribution, and Social Security—commonly constitute the "three-legged stool" that is designed to provide adequate benefits for retirement. For details about how Social Security and Medicare are funded, refer to Chapter14, "Operating Budgets."

## COMPENSATED TIME-OFF BENEFITS AND OVERTIME

Holidays, vacation, sick leave, family leave, military leave, and time off for jury duty, to serve as a witness, or to donate blood are benefits commonly provided to employees. Some agencies are now beginning to offer paid maternity leave. Effective January 2021, most employers in California were required to provide up to 12 weeks of unpaid family and medical leave to employees for qualifying reasons. This was in addition to the 4 months of pregnancy disability leave, which employers with five or more employees were already required to provide to qualifying employees.

Another type of leave passed by Congress in late 2019 was the Federal Employee Paid Leave Act (FEPLA) which establishing parental leave for most federal civilian employees. The new law provides up to 12 weeks of paid leave within 12 months after the birth, adoption, or foster placement of a child occurring on or after October 1, 2020. Policies and procedures for accruing and using these benefits are typically contained in employee manuals or labor agreements that are administered by labor relations professionals.

Flexible work schedules are also considered employee benefits, although they may also be beneficial to employers. Such schedules are usually variations of the traditional 40-hour week. For example, an employee may work a schedule of four 10-hour days in a week, or may work a schedule of eight 9-hour days, one 8-hour day, and one day off during a 2-week period. Less common is a 3–12 (three 12-hour days) schedule within a 36-hour week. Flexible schedules are advantageous to employees in accommodating family or educational schedules and may be advantageous to employers in saving energy, decreasing traffic, or meeting pollution-reduction goals. Flexible schedules may present challenges in ensuring that they do not result in unintended overtime.

Overtime administration is one of the most significant and challenging areas of benefits administration. Public employees at the state and local levels are covered by the federal Fair Labor Standards Act (FLSA) and may also be covered by state laws or local ordinances as well. Coverage by the FLSA was initially mandated by the U.S. Supreme Court in the early 1970s, was overturned a few years later, and was reinstated in 1985. Amending legislation and several phases of rulemaking by the Department of Labor have continued to guide overtime rules. However, litigation continues to present a liability for many agencies. Law suits challenge which employees are covered by overtime rules. For example, the FLSA exempts executive, administrative, and professional employees from overtime requirements, but employees often challenge whether they belong in these categories. Similarly, fire and police employees are eligible for special exemptions that allow overtime to be calculated over extended time periods and may challenge whether employees are qualified for these exemptions. Other subjects of litigation have included issues such as timeliness of overtime payments, denials of use of compensated time off, and whether certain hours are compensable as hours of work (e.g., time spent by police officers changing into and out of uniforms, pre- and post-shift preparation, training activities, or "volunteer" activities).

## EMPLOYMENT OPPORTUNITIES AND DISCRIMINATION

Beginning with the Equal Employment Opportunity Act in 1972, the federal government has been at the forefront of enhancing employment opportunities for traditionally underrepresented groups in the workforce by challenging standards that may mask biases in hiring and promotion. For example, height or weight requirements had the effect of discriminating against women, Hispanics, or Asians. Similarly, maximum age requirements for new applicants (previously common for public safety jobs) and most mandatory retirement ages that promoted age discrimination were also challenged and eliminated. Today, standards must be thoroughly justified as being necessary and related to the job.

Human resources professionals promulgate policies and procedures to prevent discrimination. At the federal level, laws and policies protect racial minorities, women, and older workers as well as prohibit sexual harassment by either gender. Depending on the jurisdiction, laws and policies may also protect same- and opposite-sex domestic partners—a subject of debate throughout the nation.

Employment discrimination complaints, particularly those that are unresolved at the agency level and become lawsuits, are costly to public agencies. A pattern or practice of lawsuits may result in consent decrees, which place an agency under the oversight of the courts or the Department of Justice for a specified time period until a specific goal is met or measure of progress demonstrates that the pattern of discrimination no longer exists. Such consent decrees may mandate that certain underrepresented groups be hired in percentages that approach the labor pool or that a particular process be established to ensure merit-based promotions and other employment decisions.

An ongoing challenge in the public sector is one of accountability for actions that result in costly payouts. Enforcement of policies and procedures and discipline of those who fail to comply are critical elements in minimizing and preventing future litigation. Accountability must start from the highest level officials and executive management and reach down to first-level supervisors and workers to create a culture of employment equality.

## TRAINING AND SUPERVISORY DEVELOPMENT

Training, which will be discussed more fully in Chapter 19 "Leadership for Administrators," is often viewed as a benefit, particularly tuition reimbursement for college courses or specialized training offered by consultants. Formal training to enhance occupational skills or develop supervisory skills needed for career advancement may be negotiated as part of the total compensation package. Because employees recognize that moving into supervisory or management positions requires skills and qualities that are different from those of a technician or professional worker, they may be particularly interested in courses regarding time management, writing skills, or supervisory skills that are needed to advance their careers (see Appendix A, "Writing and Speaking Effectively" along with Appendix B "Preparing and Making Presentations").

Formal training is often neglected and is one of the first items to be cut during budget reductions when resources are scarce. When this occurs, agencies may resort to on-the-job experience and mentoring by senior-level employees or cross training by supervisors. This type of training occurs every day as employees learn their jobs and become more skilled at their occupations, but is often not as effective or rigorous as formal training.

Training is often recommended as an approach to managing risk. When problems are identified in an organization, oftentimes as a result of litigation, training is mandated to avoid future liability. This may occur when employers are found liable of employment discrimination, negligent in protecting employees from occupational hazards, or in violation of labor codes. Online training can be helpful when training is mandated for an entire organization because it is more flexible and can be easily monitored (as in sexual harassment training).

## STEPS TO ADDRESS RISING BENEFIT COSTS

### Step 1: Identify the Source of Rising Costs

Some costs are identified by operating departments, and others by centralized budget or human resources departments. Line managers should regularly monitor costs arising from work-related injuries, workers' compensation costs, and overtime, as these are often controllable at working levels. Discrimination and harassment complaints may be reviewed at this level but are also monitored and reviewed by human resources departments. Identifying rising costs of pension or health insurance benefits is typically the responsibility of the centralized departments.

Data needs include identifying the areas of rising costs, which requires a baseline or benchmark for comparison purposes. This means that accurate records and data must be available to conduct an analysis. In some cases, particularly overtime, federal or state-mandated records must be maintained and available for inspection at any time (such as employee workweek and schedule records). If none exist, then the first step is to develop a record-keeping process and to obtain such data, using raw information from the agency (e.g., examining several years' worth of experience data). When reviewing benefits such as insurance or pensions, information from outside sources such as benefit consultants, who conduct and sometimes publish regular surveys, is useful.

## Step 2: Identify the Affected Employees/Organization

Rising benefit costs may be limited to a particular organizational group, particularly those costs related to occupational hazards or workload issues that drive overtime costs. The Occupational Safety unit or the organization's safety engineer should be brought in at this point. It may be feasible to develop options at that level; however, part of the analysis is to distinguish whether costs are rising because of legislative changes or operational issues. Pension and insurance cost increases normally affect all eligible employees.

## Step 3: Identify Options

At the operational level, options typically involve closer supervision and supervisory/employee training to minimize costs associated with injuries, excessive use of sick time, overtime, or employee complaints.

Options are more complex for benefits that affect the entire workforce. Several of the options for addressing health insurance costs were referred to in the preceding section, such as redesigning benefit structures to provide less generous programs by reducing plan choice (e.g., offering only HMOs), increasing co-payments and deductibles, and/or limiting employer subsidies of monthly premiums (for all employees or perhaps only for dependents). Other advanced approaches involve managing health care delivery, health maintenance and promotion of consumerism, and accountability. Specific options could include the following:

- wellness or fitness programs that reduce cost through the prevention of illness;
- health risk appraisals;
- claim and disease management in high-cost areas;
- development of value or high-performance networks of health care providers (based on consultant's evaluation of costs and outcomes for medical procedures); and
- collective pharmaceutical purchasing.

  Options to address rising pension costs may include the following:

- closing existing plans to new employees and adopting new plans (it is noted that many agencies are part of statewide plans, and this option may not be available);
- increasing employee contributions; and
- reducing employers' payments of employee contributions (sometimes negotiated as part of a pay package and known as "employer pickup").

Reducing pension benefits for current employees is not usually a viable option because of legal restrictions.

## Step 4: Evaluate the Impact of Options on the Organization and the Public

The practicality and feasibility of the options must be weighed against the impact on both the public and employees. If rising costs are threatening the ability of the agency to provide basic public services or the viability of the agency to continue to function, then drastic measures will be more politically acceptable. Absent a significant threat to services, the feasibility of reductions must also be weighed against the negative impact on employee morale and/or resistance from employee unions. Changes that increase benefits must be considered in the same context. To the extent that citizens view government employees as enjoying greater security and a compensation package that exceeds their own, increases are likely to generate negative reactions in the press and pressure on elected officials. Whether or not public perceptions reflect reality, they are always present during the decision process.

Another factor in determining feasibility is the ability of the agency to implement and administer changes, either in the short term or in the long term. If benefits have been negotiated as part of a multiyear agreement, then an agency may be limited until the contract expires. In other situations, legislation, charter, or constitutional changes may be required, and a long-term strategy will be needed to initiate changes.

Finally, technological and administrative issues must be considered. If benefit changes require system upgrades to a payroll or benefits management system, then the cost and timing may be affected.

## ETHICAL CONCERNS

Because public-sector benefits are typically more generous than those in the private sector, there is even more concern when they are misused. It is not uncommon to see internet or news headlines about workers' compensation or overtime abuses. These are benefit areas that must continually be scrutinized because they are susceptible to abuse. The abuse ranges from outright fraud in which individuals claim benefits to which they have no entitlement to more subtle cases in which employees extend their periods of eligibility, slightly pad their medical expenses, or add a few minutes or hours to their overtime timekeeping records.

Pension spiking is another area of potential abuse. It occurs when an employee, particularly a higher level one, is granted a promotion during his or her final year of employment for the primary purpose of increasing the salary base used to calculate his or her pension. While some of these promotions are legitimate, spiking is most alarming when used to encourage nonperforming employees to retire early. It may also be used to reward valued employees for career service who may not have been as successful in rising through the civil service system to higher pay levels that reflect their accomplishments and value to an organization. In either case spiking is a questionable use of public resources that drives up costs.

It is important for agencies to establish and maintain adequate controls to avoid these abuses, but even with good internal controls, abuse will occur from time to time. Then it is important to acknowledge and correct the problem quickly to reassure other employees and the public that the organization is back on track and public dollars are being appropriately spent.

## CONCLUSION

Managing employee benefits and risk is about providing an environment in which employees are motivated to thrive and achieve maximum productivity. Employers face an ongoing balancing act to provide benefits that attract and retain the best employees without creating costs that jeopardize service to the public.

## PRACTICING PUBLIC ADMINISTRATION

1. A city council has announced that a joint labor-management committee should be established to administer benefit programs. Determine how the committee should be organized and the appropriate questions, areas of concern, or discussion topics for the committee.

2. A benefits administrator and/or benefits committee must reduce health insurance costs to meet a projected budget shortfall. What are the options? Should cost sharing be an option to explore?

3. Liability claims related to employment discrimination have increased in your agency. Which steps would you take to reduce the claims? Which areas should be considered?

4. A small city with a declining tax base due to a downturn in real estate values is facing financial ruin. Benefit costs have been taking up a higher percentage of the city budget during the past 5 years. Which issues should be considered?

## BIBLIOGRAPHY

Boyken, G. (2007). *Funding the golden years in the golden state: An overview of public employee post-employment benefits and recent concerns about how to pay for them.* Sacramento, CA: California Research Board.

Chiappetta, T. O. (2005). Managing healthcare costs. *Public Personnel Management 34*(4): 313–320.

Freyss, S. F., Ed. (1999). *Human resource management in local government: An essential guide.* Washington, D.C.: International City/County Council.

Greenwald, J. (2008). Economic woes squeeze local governments' risk budgets. *Business Insurance 43*(22): 15.

Jasper, M. (2004). *Social Security law.* Dobbs Ferry, NY: Oceana.

Johnson, W. C. (2004). *Public administration: Partnerships in public service.* (3d ed.). Long Grove, IL: Waveland.

Kilgour, J. G. (2007). Public sector pension plans in California: How big is the problem? *Compensation and Benefits Review 39*(2): 16–26.

Maiorano, C. (1991). Government pension system needs reform. Mackinac Center for Public Policy. www.mackinac.org/article.aspx?ID=194.

Miller, G., et al. (1998). Public-sector defined contribution plans: Lesson from seven governments. *Government Finance Review 14*(6): 29–33.

Mitchell, R. (2004). The health care clash moves to the next aisle. *New York Times*, (October 10) sec. 3: 5.

Morris, C. (2006). *Apart at the seams: The collapse of private pension and health care protections.* New York, NY: Century Foundation Press.

Morrison, Scott. (2003). California strikes point to struggle on health benefits medical costs. *Financial Times*, (October 15), Americas: 2.

Nigro, L., Nigro, F., & Kellough, J. E. (2007). *The new public personnel administration.* (6th ed.). Belmont, CA: Thomson Wadsworth.

Odden, A. (2000). New and better forms of teacher compensation are possible. *Phi Delta Kappan 81*(5): 361–366.

Preston, M. (2005). Budget buster: Cities and counties can ill afford escalating health care costs. *American City & County 120*(5): 36.

Shafritz, Jay. (2001). *Personnel management in government: Politics and process.* New York, NY: Marcel Dekker.

Wiatrowski, W. J. (1994). On the disparity between private and public pensions. *Monthly Labor Review 117* (April): 3–9.

Willett, M. (2005). Increasing participation in your defined contribution pension plan. *Benefits and Compensation Digest 42*(11): 18–21.

Yu, H. H. (2021). Improving work–life balance for female civil servants in law enforcement: An exploratory analysis of the federal employee paid leave act. *Public Personnel Management.* https://doi.org/10.1177/00910260211046560

# SECTION
# 4

# Financial Resources

This section explores how the public sector identifies, utilizes, and monitors financial resources. The emphasis in this section is on how funds become available and how funds are spent with regard to public policies and programs.

Chapter 13 "Revenues," discusses the criteria for a *good tax* and the various mechanisms such as sales, property, and income taxes as well as user fees state and local governments use to raise revenues. It addresses factors (population, unemployment, etc.) that influence how productive a revenue source may be and mechanisms used to manage cash flow to ensure public needs are met without interruption. Chapter 14 "Operating Budgets," discusses budgeting approaches from traditional *line-item budgeting* to newer budgeting systems that emphasize policy objectives and program performance. Operating budgeting requires ongoing planning, implementation, and monitoring as well as communication and coordination with the legislature, typically on an annual cycle. In contrast, projects that commit resources for many years and require extensive financial commitments beyond a single fiscal year are discussed in Chapter 15, "Capital Budgeting." Readers are introduced to analytical concepts, including present value and internal rate of return, that enable decision makers to evaluate competing requests for financial resources. The resources available for capital projects and budgets often depend on a jurisdiction's access to financial markets. This access depends on a number of experts: financial managers, attorneys, tax experts, and bond-rating services, to name a few. Without adequate expertise, communities may place their financial well-being at considerable risk.

Like organizations in other sectors, governments use contracts and grants to provide goods and services and to implement programs.

Chapter 16, "Contracts and Procurement," discusses the unique and often conflicting objectives that control public contracts and summarizes the wide range of relationships state and local governments have with other governments, firms, and nongovernmental organizations. Contracting and/or procurement may take many forms such as competitive bidding, sole source, and *piggybacking* that frequently require extensive planning, evaluation, and monitoring to protect the public interest. An example of a contract that transfers funds and authority is a grant. Chapter 17, "Grants," discusses the role that federal grants have played in defining relationships among levels of government. *Grant administration*, which is the identification of grant opportunities, the application to funding agencies, program implementation, and monitoring, has become an increasingly vital effort by local and state administrators. In the months and years ahead, as federal and state funds for economic recovery become available, more effort will be devoted to grant administration.

# 13 ——◇——◇——◆——

# Revenue

# Raising Money for Public Purposes

He [king of England] has . . . given his assent to . . . acts of pretended legislation [and has imposed] taxes on us without our consent.

—Thomas Jefferson

Taxes are the price we pay for a civilized society.

—Oliver Wendell Holmes

## CRITERIA FOR TAXATION

Taxes have served as both an irritation that has brought down governments and the key resource needed to sustain civil society. Is there a distinction between a good tax system and a poor one? Generally speaking, scholars apply six criteria when assessing a tax system. A "good" tax:

- *Is a robust source of revenue.* This means the tax should have a broad base of contributors, as does a tax on income or sales transactions. A tax on ballroom dancing, even if it were fairly steep, would not yield sufficient revenue to make its collection worthwhile.

- *Enjoys popular acceptance by the public.* There tends to be broad support for sin taxes (on liquor, cigarettes) and taxes on luxury items (yachts, fur coats, private jets). There is popular support for high taxes on those with significant wealth and income. In addition, communities prefer to tax outsiders, such as tourists renting hotel rooms (transient occupancy tax), rather than levy taxes on residents.

- *Requires little effort by government to collect or administer.* Sales taxes are imposed on customers by businesses for each transaction at the time the sale occurs. The transaction does not require complex technology beyond what the business uses to record the sale. The tax collector is the business providing the good or service. The same is true for income taxes, wherein the employer serves as the tax collector. The advantage of having every salesperson and employer serve as a tax collector is that the tax is difficult to avoid.

- *Links the tax burden to the tax benefits.* Gasoline taxes are set aside to maintain and expand roads. Those who have vehicles recognize the connection between their use of public roads and the need to raise revenue to maintain them. Many states have taxes on alcohol that fund drug and alcohol rehabilitation programs. Those who are most likely to need such services pay for the services when they buy related products. A similar direct link is made by governments with user fees. Those who use public golf courses pay the fees to maintain the courses.

- *Is consistent with rational economic and social decisions.* Taxes should not distort rational decisions. Taxes on income should not be so high that persons elect not to work. Taxes on consumption should not discourage persons from buying needed products or drive markets underground. On the other hand, tax breaks allow people (and businesses) to reduce their income taxes when they engage in behaviors (such as insulating a home to cut energy costs or to support charities) that benefit the public without requiring government programs.

- *Ensures equal treatment among equals.* If the median income for a family of four is between $30,000 and $40,000, then a 10% tax on such a family's income would treat all persons in this group in the same way. It would have horizontal equity. While the government may want to make adjustments to this tax rate based on an individual's health challenges or property losses, it treats everyone in the group in the same way.

- *Ensures vertical equity or the equitable treatment of persons who are unequal.* Do we want to apply the 10% rule to all families of four regardless of their income? Based on the 2021 poverty guidelines for the U.S. Department of Health and Human Services, a family of four with an income of $26,500 is living at the poverty level. A 10% tax would raise $2,650 dollars but would also push the family deeper into poverty ($23,850). In this regard a flat tax (also called a "regressive tax") of 10% impoverishes low-income citizens and makes their households worse off. A "progressive" tax applies a higher tax rate on higher incomes, operating on the theory that high-income earners can afford to pay more.

A household earning $400,000 and paying a 10% tax would pay $40,000 dollars, which is ten times more than the median income group earning $40,000, but is this level of payment equitable for a household that has 10 times the income? How steep the tax increase should be is a controversial matter. In the current tax system, someone earning 10 times the median income pays approximately a 30% tax rate or roughly $120,000. Historically the maximum tax rate has been even higher, at the 50% to 60% rate. When there is a higher tax rate or tax burden on higher incomes, the tax is *progressive.*

If tax rates are equitable when based on the taxpayer's ability to pay, then some taxes are equal but not equitable. Sales taxes are an example. A 5% (.05) tax on $5,000 in purchases would translate into a $250 tax. However, for the family earning $20,000, the sales tax on the $5,000 purchase is 1.25% of their total income; while for the family earning $400,000 it is only 0.0625% of their total income, or only 1/20 of what it is for the low-income family. Taxes that place a greater burden on those with the least resources are called *regressive.*

Of all the issues that face governments the issue of tax equity remains the most difficult. The discussion below follows the evolution of taxation from the excise taxes of the colonial days to the payroll taxes authorized by the Franklin Roosevelt administration. It examines how managers make quick estimates of future revenues based on past collections and how population, income, and job markets are important factors to consider when estimating revenues.

## SOURCES OF REVENUE

There are four basic sources of revenue—sales tax, property tax, income tax, and user fees—that jurisdictions employ to generate revenues to meet the demand for public goods and services. The oldest of these is sales tax, and the most recent is income tax.

### Sales Taxes

The British imposed sales taxes (called "tariffs" or "excise taxes") on the purchase of sugar, stamps, tea, paint, glass, paper, and so forth. Since nearly all imports were from Britain, the Crown could raise revenue from importers and citizens buying manufactured goods from abroad. The appeal to the Crown of sales taxes on imports was that the taxes:

- were easy to collect given the few points of entry to monitor,
- were stable sources of revenue, and
- provided sufficient revenues.

However, the taxes were not equitable. Whether one was a wealthy merchant like John Hancock or a struggling farm worker, one paid the same tax rate. The tax treated everyone equally but was not equitable. The British taxes on basic goods spurred piracy, smuggling, and the American Revolution. The regressive nature of sales taxes remains a problem to this day.

There are two types of taxes that are typically collected at the time of a sale: *sales tax* is a percentage of the total sale, and excise tax which is a fixed amount per unit sold. The *excise tax* is applied to specific products such as gasoline, cigarettes, and telecommunications. For example, an excise tax of 18 cents per gallon of gasoline would mean that for each gallon purchased, the buyer would pay 18 cents. If the buyer filled the tank with 20 gallons of gasoline, the excise tax would cost the buyer 18 cents per gallon × 20 gallons = $3.60. It would not matter whether the price of a gallon of gas were $1.00 or $10.00; the excise tax revenue collected would be the same, although the total purchase cost would vary. In some states (Hawaii, for example) the excise tax is levied against the seller rather than the consumer. In theory, the retailer pays the excise tax as a business expense in the same way it pays the light bill, water fees, and sewage fees. However, in practice the excise tax is paid by the consumer. The amount of the tax that is absorbed by the consumer depends on the *elasticity* of the good being consumed.

Goods that are elastic are ones for which there are many providers and many alternative goods to select. Ballpoint pens are elastic goods because there are many producers and many substitutes (crayons, pencils, electronic devices). For these goods passing on the tax to the consumer is difficult and will be largely absorbed by the business. However, other goods such as gasoline and processed foods are inelastic. Consumers have few firms to choose from when buying the goods, and there are few substitutes. When a merchant sells an inelastic good the ability to pass on the tax to the consumer is far greater.

Retail sales taxes are based on prices in the marketplace. If there is an 8% sales tax on a bottle of soda that sells for $1.00, the total cost of the soda is $1.08. If the price of soda rises to $4.00 a bottle, the same sale will cost the consumer $4.32 ($4.00 × .08), but the buyer consumes the same volume of soda.

Currently sales and excise taxes constitute 2.9% of federal revenue. Most retail sales taxes are raised by states. Some states have no sales taxes (e.g., Alaska, New Hampshire, Delaware and Oregon) while others (e.g., Arizona, Louisiana, and Tennessee) derive over 40% of their state revenues from sales tax. The national norm is that sales taxes constitute about 23% of state revenues. In addition, local governments raise revenue from sales taxes. The national norm is that 6.5% of revenue from sales taxes is raised locally, but the disparity among localities is significant.

State governments are ideally suited to raise revenue using sales taxes. They are close enough to businesses and citizens to impose and enforce uniform rules and practices and far enough away to absorb the criticism that the tax adversely affects the poor and persons on fixed incomes. To mitigate the criticism that sales taxes are regressive, state laws typically exempt "essentials" such as unprocessed foods such as vegetables, meats, and produce from retail sales taxes.

Sales taxes have customarily been applied to tangible property or products rather than to services, but this is not the case for all states. One special type of sales tax is the transient occupancy fee that is levied against customers of hotels, inns, and other tourist accommodations. Area residents are supportive of these taxes because they are levied against outsiders and produce funds for the community to provide services, such as police, to the travelers. However, the rate needs to be low enough to be acceptable to customers and high enough to produce needed revenue. As with all taxes, it is the balance between interests that is most difficult to calculate. Taxes on other services vary widely around the country. A 2018 U.S. Supreme Court decision allowed states to charge sales taxes on internet purchases. By December 2019, 43 states started doing so. Legislatures seek out new taxing areas typically as the demand for public services and goods begins to exceed the revenues from other sources.

Despite sales taxes' inequity, they remain popular with citizens and government. This popularity with governments is due to the fact that they are a productive source of revenue. The level of consumption remains relatively constant over time. In addition, the merchant, not a government agent, collects the taxes, and they are difficult to avoid. Citizens see sales taxes as more controllable than other taxes. The citizen can elect not to consume certain goods and thereby reduce or avoid the tax.

## Property Taxes

After sales taxes the next major source of public revenue is property taxes. The first federal property tax was passed in 1798; however, states and counties taxed real property such as land, equipment, and buildings prior to the federal tax. The assessment of property is determined in a number of ways:

1. the productivity of the property, for example, sales from the use of property;
2. the value of the property at the point of sale;

3. the estimate of the value of the property based on its inventory; and

4. the value of property sales in the immediate area.

Farms and some extraction properties (mines and drilling) are assessed based on the productivity or income generated from the properties. However, the major sources of property taxes are residents and businesses.

Real property taxes remain a core source of revenue for local governments. Property taxes on average across the United States constitute about 30% of all local tax revenues and less than 1% of all state revenues. The lowest property tax rate for local governments is in Delaware, and the highest rate is in New Jersey. In 20 states there is no property tax contribution to state revenues—all of the property tax revenues go to local governments—and the highest contribution to state revenue is in Vermont.

Property taxes are less desirable than sales tax from the government and citizen's point of view. They are more difficult to administer and often require a staff of real estate assessors to update the market value of properties on the tax rolls. Based on the estimated market value of the property, assessors assign an *assessed value*, which serves as the basis for determining the tax bill.

For example, a house may have been bought for $250,000 5 years ago. At that time the assessed value of property was determined to be $37,500, and the county ordinance sets the property tax rate at 10% of assessed value or $3,750. The $3,750 is 1.5% of the market value of the property ($3,750 ÷ $250,000). However, over time the value of the land and improvements to the property increase its value. Assessors use current market data to determine the rate at which property values are changing and adjust the assessed value rates of all properties in the area accordingly. However, the general market value of homes in an area may not reflect the true market rate of a specific house, so assessed values are estimates, at best. As a general rule the value of land and buildings rises over time, and local governments are able to derive more revenue from the properties in their areas. The frequency of reassessing property values varies from state to state. Reassessment may be done annually or at other regular intervals or only at the time of sale of a property.

Homeowners typically get property tax bills twice a year, and while they may be delighted with the higher market values of their homes, they are unhappy about the higher assessed values and taxes that accompany a rising market. When market values are falling, there is a drive for assessors to lower taxes but little incentive to do so quickly because of the loss of revenue to government. Homeowners who initiate requests to lower their assessments may experience delays from assessors.

The change in the tax bill is based on the value of the property and not the ability of the property owner to pay the tax. While there is a rough relationship between the value of property and the owner's ability to pay, it is tenuous. The elderly who have paid off their homes and now live on a fixed income are disadvantaged by property tax assessments that raise their taxes while their incomes remain unchanged. In 1978 during an unprecedented rise in market value and assessed taxes on housing, the disparity between taxes and income gave rise in California to a taxpayer revolt called Proposition 13. Under this voter initiative the property tax rate was set at 1% of market value at the time of sale. The $250,000 home would mean a $2,500 tax bill annually for as long as the current owner retained the house with a maximum possible annual 1% increase to adjust for inflation.

The 1% tax rate based on market value at time of sale introduced significant inequity among homeowners in the same area. For example, in the *Nordlinger v. Hahn* court case two residents in tract housing paid significantly different property taxes to the same government. Nordlinger, who was the more recent buyer in the area, was paying $1,701.00 in taxes, while her neighbor, who had bought a decade earlier, was paying $358.00. Over the next 5 years the 1% inflation rate allowed under the law would raise the neighbor's tax to $395.26, an increase of $37.26. Nordlinger would be paying $1,878.04, an increase of $177.04; Nordlinger's tax increase was 4.7 times greater than the next-door neighbor's. The 1% at time of sale standard tends to be disadvantageous to first-time buyers, the poor, and working-class buyers seeking to improve their housing situation by taking their equity out of a starter home and moving up. Despite the long-term inequity in taxes, the U.S. Supreme Court found that the constitutional provision for equal treatment under the law had not been violated. Court challenges to similar property tax measures in Oregon (Measure 5) and in Massachusetts (Proposition 2 ½) are unlikely.

Outside of tax-revolt states the inequity issue in property taxes has been addressed differently. One method is *circuit breaker credits*. Under the circuit breaker credit policy, persons pay the increased assessed value on their properties to the local government. The tax bills trigger credits for taxpayers when they pay state income taxes. Elderly and/or low-income homeowners compute the *overload* between the tax bills and their family incomes. A percentage of this difference is deducted from taxpayers' state income taxes as tax credits. Without cutting local tax revenues or creating significant disparities among neighbors, the circuit breaker policies enable governments to address the disparity between a property's value and the owner's ability to pay the tax. Other programs enable selected homeowners to defer the tax payment until the sale of the property. The government forgoes the tax increase for designated low-income and/or elderly homeowners and collects the tax when the property is sold.

Communities prefer home ownership to rental of residences because it is assumed that owner-occupants are more responsible, more involved, and more civic minded due to their economic stake in the community. The qualities of personal responsibility and an economic stake are based on the assumption that persons buying housing have the income to pay the mortgage and taxes and have an investment (a down payment) in the value of the property. Over time as equity in the property increases owners will have an incentive to see that public services, schools, and infrastructure are maintained and improved because these improvements contribute to the value of their properties.

On the plus side property taxes are usually a stable source of revenue and may provide a robust source of income for a community. However, a crisis in the subprime mortgage market will adversely affect property tax revenues for many communities. During a housing boom new and existing homes are sold at higher and higher prices. Since the market price of housing is the basis for property taxes, higher market values translate into increased revenues.

During the 1990s, as housing prices rose the number of qualified buyers with down payments and qualifying income declined. Financial institutions developed subprime (less than desirable) loans based not on borrowers' ability to pay but on the market value of the property. By the early 2000s, it was apparent that when the initial subprime rates expired, the revised and significantly higher mortgage rates were beyond the income levels of borrowers to pay. Homeowners began to walk away from their properties by the millions, leaving the secondary mortgage market, Freddie Mac and Fannie Mae, with billions if not trillions of dollars in outstanding debt. Banks holding the loans did not pay investors the principal and interest on the mortgages and were strapped for funds to pay taxes on the properties on which they foreclosed.

As market values began to decline there was a commensurate decline in property tax revenues. The decline came at an inopportune time. Property revenues fell just as investments in community revitalization, schools, and parks were most needed, making dependency on property taxes risky as the primary source of local revenue. The housing market has recovered markedly since the 2008 recession. Lenders tightened qualifications and prospective buyers were better advised of loan costs.

Property tax revenues may also fall if local communities compete to attract businesses/industries by allowing generous tax abatement (forgiveness) programs. Abatements may be offered for a limited start-up period of typically 10 to 12 years. Jurisdictions trust that the loss in property revenue will be more than compensated for by sales and/or income tax revenues generated from developing the area's economic base. Competition between areas that are geographically close, however, may not be productive. In any given retail market area, the demand for goods and services is limited in the short run. Adding strip malls or megastores does not generate new and expanded economic activity but redistributes activities from one geographic area to another. In such cases a jurisdiction may get caught up in a downward-spiraling bidding war with a neighboring jurisdiction, resulting in deeper and deeper cuts in commercial property tax revenues for longer and longer periods. If the overall expected economic boom does not materialize, localities may find themselves with less revenue and greater debt.

Local property taxes are also affected by financial institutions' practices over which state and local governments have little to no authority. The federal government has considerable influence over these practices but is not subject to either revenue gains or revenue losses based on its ability to adequately regulate the mortgage/banking market. Property taxes at the federal level are limited to estate and gift taxes, which are about 1% of federal revenues.

A tax related to property taxes is the real estate transaction or documentary transfer fee. While technically a user fee for a service provided by the government to record property transfers, this fee is directly related to activity in the real estate market. As property values and sales increase there is a concurrent increase in this revenue source; as sales decline this source of revenue declines too.

Finally, citizens may be subjected to *use* taxes. A *use tax* is a **tax on the storage, use, or consumption of a taxable item or service on which no sales tax has been paid.** For instance, when someone buys a car or airplane in one jurisdiction and registers it in another without paying sales tax, a tax on that property's *use* may be assessed. Such taxes seek to discourage persons from buying outside the state's jurisdiction in an attempt to avoid paying sales taxes. Some user taxes are easy to avoid. For example, if one buys a refrigerator in another state with no sales tax, the home state may levy a use tax. However, collecting the use tax on the refrigerator depends largely on an honor system wherein the resident self-reports and pays the use tax.

## Income Taxes

The major source of federal revenues is the individual income tax, which constitutes 45% of all revenues collected at the federal level. The other major income sources are corporate income taxes and payroll taxes. Income tax policies were established by the 16th Amendment (ratified in 1913), and payroll taxes are the consequence of the New Deal policies of the 1930s.

An early attempt by the federal government to directly tax citizen income occurred in 1861. However, the Constitution did not allow the federal government to directly tax citizens; that privilege was reserved for state governments. Prior to the 16th Amendment the federal government raised revenue primarily from imports and duties. The balance of the money was raised by allocating federal costs to the states. If the federal government needed $80 million, it would pass the costs—in equal proportions—to the states. States with large populations and significant agricultural or manufacturing resources could pay their shares. States with limited populations and fewer economic resources would struggle to meet those obligations.

The disparity among the states and the significant disparity among citizens led to the passage of the 16th Amendment, which enabled the federal government to tax citizens' income from whatever source derived. There is no test of one's ability to pay. Persons who were able to avoid state income taxes by moving to a state with no income tax could not as easily avoid the federal tax.

Income tax rates in 1913 started at 1% for the lowest-income groups (earning less than $20,000) and rose to a high of 7% for those earning in excess of $500,000 per year. Less than 1% of the population paid income taxes in 1913. With the outbreak of World War I, Congress was faced with enormous costs and made the income tax more progressive and more regressive. From 1918 to 1924, the highest tax brackets ($500,000 and greater) paid a tax rate of about 63.5%, while the lowest tax bracket (less than $4,000) paid about 4.4%. The highest income group's tax rate was over 14 times greater than the lowest bracket. The lowest tax bracket would never again see rates as low as they were during World War I, but the upper tax bracket would see *marginal income rates* rise to 91% during the 1950s.

Today the lowest tax group rate is 10% while the highest income rate is 37%. While the progressive nature of the federal income tax has plummeted, the differences in income have grown. The poorest or first 20% earn just 5.2% of all income; the second 20%, earn 9.7%; the middle 20%, about 15%; and the fourth 20%, 21% of all income. Therefore, 80% (20 × 4) of the American people earn 51.2% of the nation's income, while the remaining 20% command the other 48.8%. So, while the ability to pay has risen significantly among the top 20%, that group's tax rate has dropped from 70% in 1977 to 35% in 2006.

Forty-two state governments also raise income taxes. Among states with income taxes, the lowest proportion of revenue is realized by New Hampshire at 1.5%, and the greatest amount is realized by Oregon at 42.8%. State income tax systems often piggyback off the federal system. This means that the tax codes and tables used by the federal system (although not the tax rates) are adopted by state governments in computing state income tax. The net effect is that federal tax breaks often result in state tax breaks in roughly the same proportion. In 13 states local governments collect income tax. Generally speaking, this source of revenue is a very small percentage (0.4%) of the jurisdictions' total revenue.

The advantage of income tax is that it is easy for governments to collect since the collection is undertaken by employers. Generally speaking, it is a robust and productive source of revenue. However, while it has the potential to provide equity among unequal groups, there needs to be political will to balance taxpayers' ability to pay with the tax rate applied to different income groups. Income tax rates can distort economic decisions regarding leisure, work, savings, investing, and consumption. However, the most persistent citizen criticism of the system is that it is too complicated and riddled with loopholes that are neither fair nor just.

Finally, state and federal governments collect estate and inheritance taxes. While these terms are often used interchangeably, they are not the same. An estate tax is paid by the executor of a will on the *net value* of property left by the deceased. An inheritance tax is paid by the beneficiary who receives cash value from his or her assigned share of property as defined by the will.

Federal inheritance taxes are paid by very few since an estate's net value must exceed $22.8 million (2019) before federal taxes are applied. Eighteen states have inheritance taxes, and these are typically not as generous as the federal tax. State programs are applied to estates prior to beneficiaries receiving their shares. In some states the share of estate taxes may be as high as 20% of the estate's net value. Inheritance taxes tend to be higher. The levels of estate and inheritance taxes vary from state to state and vary based on the beneficiary's relationship to the deceased. For example, surviving spouses and children may pay no additional taxes, while others may pay based on graduated income tax rates as described above.

## Payroll Taxes

Besides individual income taxes, the next largest source of revenue at the federal level is the payroll tax for social insurance programs such as Social Security and Medicare. Using a very narrow definition, these programs are not tax programs but intergenerational arrangements by which one generation cares for another. The current workforce funds the costs for elderly, disabled, and retired persons. These are entitlement programs: what is spent is not determined by the revenue raised but by eligibility criteria established by law. Consequently, the system depends on the size and productivity of the current workforce being sufficient to shoulder the costs for those no longer in the workforce. When these programs were launched in the 1930s there were approximately 10 workers for each retired individual (10:1). However, with the retirement of the baby boomers in the current decade the ratio of employed to retired is 4.6:1; this ratio is forecasted to decrease to 1.9:1 by 2100. This demographic shift has caused policy analysts to be concerned about the long-term viability of these programs. However, the ratio of workers to retired persons is not the only factor that determines whether there are

sufficient funds for Social Security. In the 1930s there were no computers, robots, or internet technologies; the productivity of a single worker
was limited. Over the past 80 years the productivity of individual workers has increased significantly, and it is this expanded growth in gross
domestic product that suggests there is an economic capacity to fund
Social Security until about 2037 (down from 2047 forecasted in 2009).

Since social insurance programs are based on entitlements rather
than designated funds/revenue sources, there are no comparable programs at the state or local level. These tax programs are uniquely federal.

## Corporate Income Taxes

The last major source of revenue for the federal government is the
corporate income tax, which constitutes about 7% of federal revenue.
While it is called an income tax, it is actually not a tax on corporate
revenue. Instead, it is a tax on net corporate resources after the cost of
doing business is deducted. Consequently, who pays how much depends
significantly on how expenses are accounted for by corporations. The tax
is applied to chartered corporations and not to partnerships or sole pro-
prietorships which are taxed as individual owners. The most persistent
criticism of the corporate income tax is that it taxes the same income
twice. The argument is that this resource is taxed initially as corporate
income and taxed again when the funds are distributed to owners as dividends. A second criticism of the corporate tax is that it encourages firms
to favor debt over investment, because interest payments on debt are tax
deductible, while dividends paid to investors are not. However, despite
these arguments the corporate tax remains popular with the public, who
believes corporate CEOs and investors do not pay a fair share of taxes.

Corporate income taxes are practically nonexistent at the local
level. In fact, only six states raise corporate taxes locally. With the
exception of the case in New York, these corporate income taxes constitute less than one half of 1% of jurisdictions' tax revenues. State
governments have been more successful at tapping into this revenue
source. In general, corporate income taxes constitute 3.4% of state revenues and range from a low of 0% in Nevada, Texas, and Washington to
a high of 24.9% in New Hampshire.

As with individual income taxes, state and local governments often
piggyback their systems on the federal system. Consequently, the
advantages and failures of the federal system get repeated at state and
local levels.

## User Fees

User fees are almost entirely a revenue source for local governments. In this instance a government operates in a manner similar
to that of a private enterprise: selling a good or service for exclusive
use. Examples of user fees are licenses, lotteries, parking/meter fees,

bridge tolls, and water and sewage fees. The rise in user fees has been an incentive to privatize public services. Governments contract with private enterprises to implement programs and/or policies of government for a prearranged fee. In some instances (e.g., water and sewage) the government collects and distributes the revenue, and in other cases the government creates a monopoly operation based on a competitive bid process. The employment of user fees is limited because many public goods are not available on a transaction-by-transaction basis.

However, where user fees are practical, jurisdictions need to ensure the following:

- The fee covers direct and indirect costs for a particular service.
- Paying the fee is convenient, for example, one can pay by credit card or via the internet.
- There is minimal delay in depositing revenues.
- The public understands how fee costs are derived and what fees support.

In some states the establishment of, or an increase in, user fees requires voter approval. Approval may be a simple 51% majority or a supermajority of 66.6%. A change in user fees may be placed on the ballot as an initiative and generally follows the same process as that applied to a change in taxation.

## Other Revenue Sources—Grants

Although grants are not taxes or fees, they serve to transfer income from one governmental agency to another. They are a significant source of revenue, particularly to local governments, and are discussed in detail in Chapter 17, "Grants."

## Revenues Summarized

There are many ways governments collect revenues; however, no single tax or revenue approach is ideal. The main sources of public revenues are income taxes, sales taxes, property taxes, and user fees. The main obstacle to taxation is equity. Does a tax or fee treat people in the same economic situation the same and treat persons in different situations differently? Table 13.1 summarizes the discussion.

## BALANCING TAXES WITH EXPENDITURES

Historically governments made expenditures and then raised revenue to cover their costs. The Constitution requires that "money shall not be drawn from the Treasury but in consequence of appropriations made by Law; and a regular Statement and Account of the Receipts and Expenditures of all public Money shall be published from time to time" (U.S. Constitution, Article 1, Section 9). There is no requirement that Congress first raise the revenue before spending it.

**Table 13.1   Summary of Concerns Regarding Tax Sources**

| Tax | Primary User | Equity | Administration | Compliance | Citizens Can Avoid | Stable and Productive |
|---|---|---|---|---|---|---|
| Income tax | Federal | Potentially can be very equitable | Easy to collect, harder to administer | More difficult for citizens | Difficult to avoid at federal level but not at local level | Modestly stable and productive |
| Sales tax | State | Treats like groups the same but cannot treat unlike groups differently | Easy, done by retailer | Yes | Possible | Responsive to economy but generally productive |
| Property tax | Local | In part, to the degree that ownership reflects difference in income | Difficult | Somewhat, depending on assessment process | Difficult to avoid | Historically stable but may be under stress due to subprime crisis |
| User fee | Local | Treats all the same, cannot treat unlike groups differently | Easy, especially if done by a contractor | Yes | Difficult to avoid | Stable but limited use |

Notes:  Equity = treating like groups similarly and unlike groups differently.
Administration = easy to collect revenue and administer.
Compliance = citizens can comply and understand rate and process.

The same is not true of state and local governments. Typically these governments have the chief executive prepare and present an estimate of future revenues and a detailed description of expenditures.

State legislatures argue over the budget when there are surpluses and when there are deficits. However, the treasurer or the jurisdiction's finance officer makes reasonable projections based on past performance. Operating departments add and delete expenditures to meet demand within the limitations permitted by the budget. The most enduring challenge for state and local governments is to meet needs when public demand or circumstances (floods, fires, and/or economic recession) result in public expenditures exceeding revenues. Gaps between revenue and expenditures affect the next fiscal year and need to be addressed either by changes in policies (e.g., limiting eligibility for services, hours of service, etc.) and/or by identifying additional revenues.

## ESTIMATING FUTURE REVENUES

The most common approach to estimating the future is identifying trends from prior years. The formula discussed below is the same formula applied in Chapter 6 to revenue projections. For example, assume a department raised $3 million 5 years ago for parks and recreation services and raised $7 million last year. The rate of growth is:

$$(\text{Current year} \div \text{prior year} - 1) \times 100 \quad \text{or}$$
$$([7 \div 3] - 1) \times 100$$
$$= (2.33 - 1) \times 100$$
$$= 1.33 \times 100 = 133\% \text{ increase over 5 years.}$$

Annually, that would be:

$$[\text{Current year} \div \text{prior year}]^{1/\text{number of years}} - 1 \quad \text{or}$$
$$([7 \div 3]^{1/5} - 1)$$
$$= ([2.33]^{1/5} - 1)$$
$$= (1.1847 - 1) = 18.47\% \text{ per year.}$$

On a standard business calculator, one selects $X^y$ or $Y^x$ and then selects the left bracket, enters $1 \div 5$, and closes with the right bracket to look like $[1 \div 5]$. In this case the results are 1.18466, from which 1 is subtracted, leaving 0.18466 or an 18.47% change per year. The estimated rate of change allows one to project into the future. For example, if the manager is projecting over the next 2 years, based on prior experience what is the most likely cost figure?

$$Y = \text{most likely cost in the future}$$
$$X = \text{current cost}$$
$$1 + r = \text{rate of change}$$
$$n = \text{number of years into the future to be estimated}$$

In our example, $Y = 7 (1 + .18)^2$     or
$$7 \times (1.18)^2 = 7 \times 1.3924 = \$9.75 \text{ million.}$$

These quick estimates are called "back-of-the-envelope" calculations. They are simple to compute and are based on a wide range of assumptions:

- Changes in the past are indicative of changes in the future.
- The rate of change is incremental.
- Whichever factors (e.g., population, technology) contributed to the expenditures in the past are included in future estimates.

While these assumptions are not unreasonable, they are assumptions, and budget analysts and managers need to be aware of economic and demographic changes that may make these assumptions less viable. However, managers typically have little influence regarding the revenue side of the budget equation. Their primary responsibility is developing the expenditure figures and justification.

## PROJECTING REVENUES: THE CITY OF LOS ANGELES

Which factors contribute to estimating future revenues? The primary attributes that determine future revenues for a political jurisdiction are changes in population, employment, and income. Table 13.2 reflects some basic figures regarding population and employment.

From Table 13.2 one can see that the city's and the county's population growth are quite similar. Projected revenues depend significantly on growth in population and the ability to pay sales and property taxes. Neither the city nor the county raises revenue through income tax. Consequently the budget also describes which sectors of the economy are growing and which are in a state of decline (see Table 13.3).

From Table 13.3 one can see that the most significant drop in employment has come from the loss of over 50% of agricultural, natural resources, and manufacturing jobs. The growth areas for the city and county have been in leisure, hospitality (tourism), education/ health, and government. Overall the composition of the labor force has changed though the size is barely larger.

The city has a total budget of $11.2 billion. Nearly two-thirds (65.3%) goes into the general fund, and the bulk of the balance goes to *restricted funds*. It is relatively easy for governments to move funds from one area to another in the general fund. If the city's population is aging, then general fund money can be moved from youth programs to assistance for senior citizens. This is not the case with restricted funds, which are designated to an expenditure area regardless of the relative demand. While the city lists twenty sources of revenue, these sources can be clustered into the categories listed in Table 13.4.

The balance of the city's money is drawn from 55 special funds. The city's extensive listing of special funds represents a trend in revenue collection. Using referenda and ballot initiatives, voters have sought to raise money from specific sources that would go to pay for particular

**Table 13.2 Demographic and Economic Changes in the City/County of Los Angeles**

| Year | City Population | County Population | County Employment | County Unemployment Rate (%) |
|---|---|---|---|---|
| 2000 | 3,694,742 | 9,519,338 | 4,413,200 | 5.4% |
| 2005 | 3,747,800 | 9,691,600 | 4,532,900 | 5.3% |
| 2010 | 3,792,621 | 9,818,605 | 4,318,700 | 12.6% |
| 2015 | 3,946,487 | 10,126,423 | 4,641,100 | 6.7% |
| 2020 | 4,101,684 | 10,172,951 | 4,921,500 | 12.8% |
| Change (2000 to 2020) | +11.0% | +6.9% | +11.5% | + 137.0% |

Note: n.a. = not available.

Source: Los Angeles City Proposed Budget. (2020–2021). *Los Angeles Almanac.*

**Table 13.3 Los Angeles County Employment and Labor Force (1990 and 2020)**

| Sector | 1990 Labor Force | 1990 Percentage of Total | 2020 Labor Force | 2020 Percentage of Total | Percentage Change over 30 Years |
|---|---|---|---|---|---|
| Agriculture | 13,700 | 0.3% | 4,400 | 0.1% | −67.9% |
| Natural resources | 8,200 | 0.2% | 1,700 | 0.0% | −79.3% |
| Construction | 145,100 | 3.5% | 149,500 | 3.6% | +03.0% |
| Manufacturing | 811,600 | 19.6% | 313,800 | 7.6% | −61.3% |
| Trade/transportation | 794,700 | 19.2% | 787,300 | 19.0% | −0.9% |
| Information | 186,200 | 4.5% | 185,800 | 4.5% | −0.2% |
| Financial | 280,300 | 6.8% | 211,500 | 5.1% | −24.5% |
| Professional and business | 541,900 | 13.1% | 593,300 | 14.3% | +9.5% |
| Education/health | 384,700 | 9.3% | 820,900 | 19.8% | +113.4% |
| Leisure and hospitality | 306,600 | 7.4% | 394,400 | 9.5% | +28.6% |
| Other services | 136,700 | 3.3% | 127,000 | 3.1% | −7.1% |
| Government | 539,800 | 13.0% | 565,600 | 13.6% | +4.8% |
| Total | 4,149,500 | 100.0% | 4,151,000 | 100.0% | 0.0% |

Source: California Employment Development Department, Labor Market Information Division and LA City Proposed Budget. (2020–2021).

**Table 13.4   Revenue Sources for City of Los Angeles by Category for General Fund (65.3% of Total Budget)**

| Property Tax 22.4% | Sales and Excise 14.1% | User Fees 13.6% | Miscellaneous 15.2% |
|---|---|---|---|
| Tax on property | Retail sales | Permits, fees | Parking fines |
| | Occupancy tax | Business | Interest income |
| | (hotel rooms) | Documentary (real | Transfers from |
| | Parking user tax | estate) transfer | other funds |
| | Utility tax | fee | Grants from |
| | Motor vehicle | Franchise fees | outside city |
| | license tax | Motor vehicle | |
| | | license fees | |

programs. For example, a half-cent sales tax is applied to improve public transit services and reduce gridlock, and the solid waste revenue fund is paid for from fees for refuse collection that are spent on equipment and resources needed to collect and dispose of waste. Proper accounting practices require that revenues flowing into the fund and expenditures charged to the fund are reported on a fund-by-fund basis. The advantage to the fund approach is that revenues are raised from sources that may most benefit from the expenditure of the funds for these specific purposes. In this regard the taxpayer may be more disposed to support the tax knowing that the monies raised can be used only for specific purposes. However, a fund system limits the legislature's and administrator's discretion in moving money around to where it is most needed. For example, if a technological breakthrough in disposing of solid waste reduced costs significantly, the savings could not be spent on public transportation. This leaves a critical need unfunded in one area while special funds remain idle in another.

## CASH FLOW CHALLENGES

In some instances the government spends money it has not yet received. While it may seem that the government is collecting money continuously, the fact is that revenue collection is uneven. Property taxes, which represent a significant source of money for cities and counties, are collected once every 6 months. Sales and income taxes are processed daily, weekly, or monthly but paid to the government only every quarter: in October, January, April, and July. There is a gap between when the money is collected and when it reaches the public treasury to pay for government programs that run 24 hours a day, 7 days a week. To smooth out the gap between the peaks and troughs in public revenue, governments offer *notes* to banks and lending institutions for 12 months or less to cover costs. These temporary, short-term notes against revenues that will be available in the future are called revenue anticipation notes or tax and revenue anticipation notes.

In good economic periods there is little concern about short-term loans against anticipated government revenues; in difficult times banks are more wary about making loans based on anticipated revenues. Despite the critical role that revenue projection plays in the budget, very little attention is spent on the revenue side of the budget equation. Revenue projections vary significantly depending on the optimism of the revenue model. However, government budgeting tends to focus on expenditures, which are discussed in Chapter 14, "Operating Budgets." For a discussion of long-term borrowing see Chapter 15, "Capital Budgets."

## ETHICAL AND EQUITY CONCERNS

This chapter began with a summary of the criteria for a good tax: productive, popular, easy to collect, and equitable. Not all features of a good tax are features of ethical taxation.

Ethical taxes are those that treat taxpayers equitably and fairly but may or may not be popular. An equitable tax treats persons in similar situations in a similar manner and taxes persons with dissimilar resources differently. In this regard progressive taxes are more ethical than regressive taxes. An income tax that can place little or no burden on persons with limited income but a higher burden on those with significant income would be more ethical than a flat tax or sales tax of 3% for everyone.

Do progressive taxes serve as a disincentive to those who are more creative and productive, or are those who benefit the most from the current system obligated to be its largest supporters? Such issues vex government decision makers. Taxes are not punishments but mechanisms for citizens to secure goods and services collectively that would not be possible through markets or individual effort (e.g., roads, justice, and public welfare). Consequently, governments should promote vertical and horizontal equity as key features of an ethical tax system.

Another challenge in tax system equity is tax expenditure programs, sometimes called "tax loopholes," that reduce taxes for individual or corporate expenditures that are deemed beneficial to the economy or society; such loopholes include such things as charitable contributions or individuals' mortgage interest payments or businesses contributions to employee pension programs or health insurance for employees. These programs tend to forgive taxes for those who have more resources rather than those with fewer resources. Consequently, while they are legal and popular, the ethical objective of equity and fairness to all taxpayers remains a persistent challenge.

# CONCLUSION

The government relies on four major sources of revenue: sales taxes, income taxes, property taxes, and user fees. Each of these sources of revenue has advantages and disadvantages to taxpayers and their governments. While some are more equitable and ethical, they are less popular. Governments struggle with balancing equity and public support.

Historically governments made expenditures and then raised revenues to balance accounts. Today, governments try to accurately estimate revenues and pare expenditures to fit within revenue projections. However, revenues are difficult to estimate because they depend on factors (population, business growth, employment trends) outside government control. Also, there is a data gap. Population and economic data often lag forecasting of revenue needs by several years. Revenue projections are most reliable when trends are slow and steady. Significant and radical shifts in the economy make accurate projections far more difficult. Revenues are but one part of public budgeting. The following chapter discusses the bulk of public budgeting: expenditures.

## PRACTICING PUBLIC ADMINISTRATION

1. A local city wants to provide WiFi access to all businesses and residents in the community. How should the service be funded: by sales taxes, property taxes, or user fees?

2. Four years ago, city B raised $2.4 million through sales taxes, and last year it raised $4.7 million. What is the rate of growth in sales taxes for city B? If the area's revenues continue to grow at the calculated rate, then what is the projected sales tax revenue for 5 years from now?

3. Sixty-five percent of Boston revenue is derived from property taxes, which are set at 2.5% of full market value with some limited increases over time. The city has a local sales tax, but an income tax would not be feasible. State revenue support is limited. However, Boston is a historic city with an extensive public transportation network and a well-educated population. Given these limitations and possibilities, which revenue strategies might Boston use in tight economic times?

4. Which factors should a manager consider when estimating future sales tax revenues that support his or her program's operations other than past sales tax receipts?

5. Examine the revenue discussion in your local city or town budget. Where does the majority of the revenue come from: sales taxes, property taxes, or user fees? Are there gaps between public demand for goods and services, and if so, how might the jurisdiction raise additional funds?

# BIBLIOGRAPHY

Aronson, J. R., & Schwarts, E., Eds. (2004). *Management policies in local government finance.* (5th ed.). Washington, D.C.: International City/County Management Association.

Bahl, R., Martinez-Vazquez, J., & Youngman, J., Eds. (2010). *Challenging conventional wisdom on the property tax.* Cambridge, MA: Lincoln Institute of Land Policy.

Bell, M. E., Youngman, J. M., & Brunori, D., Eds. (2010). *The property tax and local autonomy.* Cambridge, MA: Lincoln Institute of Land Policy.

Brunori, D. (2020). *Local tax policy: a primer.* (4th ed.). New York, NY: Rowman and Littlefield.

Department of Taxation (Hawaii) (2000). Tax facts 96–1 general excise vs. sales tax. http://hawaii.gov/tax/taxfacts/tf96–01.pdf.

Department of the Treasury. (n.d.). History of the U.S. tax system. www.ustreas.gov/education/fact-sheets/taxes/ustax.shtml.

Gupta, S., Karayan, J., Neff, J., & Swenson, C., Eds. (2020). *State and local taxation: Principles and practices.* (3rd ed.). Plantation, FL: J. Ross Publishing.

Mikesell, J. L. (2003). *Fiscal administration: Analysis and application for the public sector.* (6th ed.). Belmont, CA: Thomson.

Norton, R. (2002). Corporate taxation. The concise encyclopedia of economics. www.econlib.org/LIBRARY/Enc/CorporateTaxation.html.

Phillips, K. (2002). *Wealth and democracy.* New York, NY: Broadway Books.

Piketty, T., & Saez, E. (2007). How progressive is the U.S. federal tax system? A historical and international perspective. *Journal of Economic Perspectives 21*(1). 3–24.

Rubin, I. S. (2020). *The politics of public budgeting: getting, spending, borrowing and balancing.* (9th ed.). Thousand Oaks, CA: Sage.

Rosen, H. (2002). *Public finance.* Boston, MA: McGraw-Hill.

Tax Foundation. (2021). Tax maps. www.taxfoundation.com/publications/tax-maps.

Vallianatos, A. (2016, April). Measure R oversight committee annual report on FY15 audits. *METRO.* https://www.metro.net/about/measure-r/

# 14 ◇ ◇ ◆

## Operating Budgets

## Funding Programs and Policies

Budgets are perhaps the most important documents that governments produce. They put goals and policies in place and clearly illustrate priorities. They guide governmental management and decision making. They are some of the most widely used and read documents of government, providing valuable information to policy makers, managers and staffs, investors, regulators, and other governments.

This chapter outlines general models of budgeting. Terminology may vary from government to government, and the exact method used in budgeting may borrow elements from different models to make a hybrid unique to a particular jurisdiction.

## TYPES OF BUDGETS AND THEIR GOALS

There are two basic types of budgets: operating and capital. This chapter will cover operating budgets, and the next chapter will cover capital budgets. Operating budgets deal with routine expenses of government, usually for 1 to 2 years at a time. A recreation and parks department's routine expenses, for example, would include salaries and benefits for employees, office supplies, facility upkeep, craft and sports equipment, and so forth.

The goals of budgets, regardless of the type, are fourfold according to the Government Finance Officers Association:

1. Budgets explain general and financial policies for the short and long term.

2. Budgets describe financial plans (trends in revenues and expenses).

311

3. Budgets act as a guide to operations (by outlining goals/objectives and specific budgets of organizational units and programs).

4. Budgets communicate priorities and policies to those inside and outside government.

## BUDGETS AND POLITICS

Budgets of any type are plans made by public managers and politicians. A budget is generally prepared by the top elected or appointed official in a jurisdiction and presented to the elected legislative body for approval. These parties may have vastly different perspectives on priorities and how they are translated into the approved budget. One group may delete a pet program from the budget or approve a program in principle but provide insufficient funding.

## OPERATING BUDGET FORMATS

Budgets are presented in a variety of ways. The traditional approach has been to present each type of expenditure, such as salaries, supplies, contracts, and equipment repair, on a separate line in a spreadsheet. These *line-item budgets* can provide much or relatively little detail, depending on whether the components are summarized in larger categories. For example, salaries and benefits can be shown as one line, or they can be broken into components such as regular salaries, overtime, medical benefits, dental benefits, and retirement contributions. Line items are usually shown for the entire government as well as for its departments or divisions.

Producing services in the public sector is labor intensive with few, if any, opportunities to substitute capital for labor. A local government, for instance, must provide lifeguards at its pools and cannot provide just video surveillance. Because of this, a government's largest expense is usually salaries and benefits. Developing the specifics for a line item requires looking at costs on a person-by-person basis for each factor that contributes to the employment salary and benefits package. See Table 14.1 for a hypothetical personnel worksheet for a Department of Recreation with six full-time salaried employees and 20 part-time and seasonal employees. What is reported for personnel costs to the public is a summary. See Table 14.2.

Other line-item costs are nonpersonnel costs sometimes called "operating costs." These include fixed costs such as machine maintenance contracts, and rental space. Fixed costs remain constant whether the department serves 100 or 10,000 residents. In general, operating costs, such as office supplies, training, uniforms, and contracted labor, are variable. The cost of postage, mileage, and office supplies will rise and fall depending on the population being served and the staffing levels needed to serve the population.

**Table 14.1  Personnel Worksheet for Department of Recreation**

| | Personnel Wages | | | Benefits ($) | | | | |
|---|---|---|---|---|---|---|---|---|
| Personnel | Number of Positions[a] | Salary/ Wages ($)[b] | Overtime ($)[c] | Medicare[d] | Health[e] | Dental[e] | Pension[e] | Social Security[f] |
| **Full-time** | | | | | | | | |
| Recreation manager | 1 | $60,000 | 0 | $870 | $7,206 | $900 | $9,600 | $3,720 |
| Recreation supervisor | 1 | $42,000 | 0 | $609 | $5,040 | $900 | $6,720 | $2,604 |
| Recreation coordinators | 4 (@ $32,500) | $130,000 | $16,000 | $2,117 | $15,613 | $4,500 | $19,200 | $9,052 |
| **Part-Time and Seasonal** | | | | | | | | |
| Recreation aides | 20 (@ $18,240) | $364,800 | 0 | $5,290 | 0 | 0 | 0 | $22,618 |
| Sum | 26 | $596,800 | $16,000 | $8,886 | $27,859 | $6,300 | $35,520 | $37,994 |
| **Subtotal** | | $612,800 | | | $116,559 | | | |
| **Grand total** | | | | $729,358 | | | | |

[a]  Includes salaries for both (1) full-time year-round employees and (2) part-time and/or seasonal workers.
[b]  Salaried employees receive fixed amount regardless of hours worked and/or overtime.
[c]  Overtime pay must be justified by productive working hours.
[d]  Employer contributes to retirement funds as a .0145 wage tax. An equal amount is deducted from employee pay.
[e]  Employer may contribute to variable employee health insurance and pension fund benefits. Employees may contribute to a benefit plan via pay deductions.
[f]  Employer contributes to social security as a .062 wage tax, capped for 2021 at $142,800. An equal amount is deducted from employee pay.

The estimates for these fixed and variable costs should be derived from the prior year's experience and documented changes in rates. If the manager with a staff of six spent $1,800 on phones last year and there is no change in personnel, there is a high probability that $1,800 will cover the costs this year, all things being equal. If the department hires two new employees who will be using phones in the coming year, the manager can estimate the new cost to be about $300 per person ($1,800 ÷ 6 staff) or an additional $600 in the coming year. Operating costs support personnel activities and can be estimated based on actual costs from the prior year at a per-employee rate.

During the course of the fiscal year, managers often learn that membership fees, maintenance contract rates, or postage rates change. The cost estimates for these items should be based on the revised price information multiplied by the quantity used in a prior period, all other things being equal. If projected costs vary significantly from one fiscal year to another, it will draw attention from citizens and elected representatives. Managers need to be prepared to provide information to support cost estimates.

## Budget Guidelines

Managers need to understand what work and/or which outcomes are produced by each employee or categories of employees and budget for the salaries and benefits attached to these positions.

## Salaries and Wages

Budget worksheets begin with salaries for two categories of employees: full-time, year-round employees and part-time, and/or seasonal workers who are supervised by others on a regular basis. The budgeted salaries should (1) be for both approved and pending positions—if pending positions are not approved, budget figures can be adjusted accordingly—and (2) reflect pay increases anticipated for the upcoming fiscal (budget) year.

Salaried positions are paid a fixed amount on a regular basis regardless of the number of hours worked and they do not receive overtime pay; thus, they are also called "exempt" employees. "Non-exempt" (or hourly) positions are paid for the actual number of hours worked and must be paid at overtime rates when they work extra hours as defined by state laws and contractual agreements. To estimate salary and wage costs, managers consult the prior year's budget and variance reports (periodic reports of actual expenditures). If a manager were developing a budget for a new program, then the manager would need to identify the appropriate number and level of staff needed. Since there would not be a prior year's budget or variance reports for a new program, the best estimate for salary and wage costs would be the midpoint of the pay range for each budgeted position.

Pay for overtime is often a contentious item for local policy makers who fear employees do not work diligently to complete their work during the regular day to justify working overtime and getting extra pay. If overtime is needed, the manager should include a justification in the budget request. A recreation program may be well staffed for 9 months out of the year but have extra demands for serving residents during the summer. These program needs may justify paying overtime, which is less costly on a yearly basis than hiring additional full-time staff or hiring extra part-time seasonal employees.

## Benefits

Medicare is a tax that provides a benefit upon retirement. The tax rate is 0.0145 on all income earned during the course of a year, paid by the employer. This amount is matched by the employee. The employee's share is not reflected in the budget since it is accounted for under salary.

Health and dental insurance and pension costs in the budget may vary on an employee-by-employee basis. For example, premium charges vary based on age, number of dependents, and scope of coverage selected. The manager may not have this information on an employee basis, but it should be available from the human resources (personnel) and/or payroll office. Some benefit costs may be shared with employees. The budget should reflect only the employer's contribution; the employee's share is deducted from salary or wages.

Social Security is another tax equally shared (.062) by employees and employers. The budget shows only the employer's share of the tax since the employee's share comes out of their pay. Social Security is capped, which means that income in excess of a certain statutory amount is not subject to the tax. For example, in 2021 the cap was set at $142,800. If an employee earned $160,000, the employer's share would be .062 × $142,800, or $8,854, only. The balance of the employee's earnings ($17,200) would not be subject to the tax. For information about rates and caps, visit the Social Security website. Some governments have opted not to participate in the Social Security program.

**Table 14.2  Department of Recreation: Personnel-Related Costs (in dollars)**

| Personnel Wages and Benefits | Prior Year's Proposed Budget | Prior Year's Actual Expenditures | Next Year's Proposed Budget | Next Year's Approved Budget[a] |
|---|---|---|---|---|
| Regular salaries | $220,400 | $227,360 | **$232,000** | |
| Part-time wages | $346,560 | $353,856 | **$364,800** | |
| Overtime salaries | $4,000 | $15,900 | **$16,000** | |
| Fringe benefits | $116,679 | $114,797 | **$116,558** | |
| Personnel subtotal | $687,639 | $711,913 | **$729,358** | |

[a] Final figures are recommended by the chief executive, such as the city manager, board supervisor, or mayor, and approved by the city council or legislature.

## Nonpersonnel

The balance of an annual budget consists of nonlabor costs. Personnel and nonpersonnel costs should be linked to both the projected workload and the department's goals. For example, a manager may determine through analysis of department operations that it takes two recreation coordinators and two recreation aides to run an after-school program for 50 children. If the goal is to enroll 100 children, it might take four coordinators and four aides total, resulting in a 100% increase in salary costs. This manager might also determine that a program for 50 children takes $1,000 in supplies (arts and crafts supplies, sports equipment), so a program for 100 children could be estimated to cost an additional $1,000 in supplies (see Table 14.3).

**Table 14.3   Department of Recreation: Nonpersonnel Cost Summary (in dollars)**

| Operating Costs | Prior Year's Budget | Prior Year's Actual Expenditures | Next Year's Proposed Budget | Next Year's Approved Budget[a] |
|---|---|---|---|---|
| Memberships | $670 | $945 | $1,700 | |
| Printing and postage | $6,400 | $4,069 | $5,000 | |
| Office equipment maintenance | $350 | $400 | $520 | |
| Electricity | $17,400 | $30,000 | $32,000 | |
| Miscellaneous[b] | n.a. | n.a. | n.a. | |
| Operating subtotal | $171,910 | $179,370 | $183,905 | |
| Total | $859,549 | $896,850 | $919,525 | |

Note: n.a. = not available.

[a] Final figures are recommended by the chief executive, such as the city manager, board supervisor, or mayor, and approved by the city council or legislature.

[b] Allowances for miscellaneous or unknown costs are often calculated as a percentage of the total of the other costs.

Line-item budgets can obviously provide much detail, maybe too much, distracting from programs and their intended results. This type of budget presentation remains popular because policy makers and citizens often find it easy to relate to the specific line items. For example, they know how much a car costs and find it easy to evaluate whether a car proposed as part of a budget is priced higher or lower than they would expect. Recognizing this, some governments have adopted other presentation approaches.

Another approach, the *performance budget*, organizes the budget information around results or outcomes. Measures of performance, to be covered in Chapter 18, can focus on inputs, outputs, processes, or results. Desired results or outcomes for fire prevention could be shown with all costs that contribute to producing these results, such as salaries, equipment, and maintenance. In recreation and parks, desired results might be increased park use or higher attendance at sports events. With this budget presentation, salaries, supplies, and other details may or may not be shown separately (see Table 14.4).

**Table 14.4 Department of Recreation: Performance Budget (in dollars)**

| Performance Objective | Prior Year's Budget | Prior Year's Actual Expenditures | Next Year's Proposed Budget | Next Year's Approved Budget[a] |
|---|---|---|---|---|
| Goal 1: Decrease juvenile crimes/misdemeanors (35% of budget) | $300,842 | $313,898 | $321,834 | |
| Goal 2: Provide adult programs rated at least "good" in satisfaction surveys (25% of budget) | $214,887 | $224,212 | $229,881 | |
| Goal 3: Increase participation in youth sports programs (40% of budget) | $343,820 | $358,740 | $367,810 | |
| Total | $859,549 | $896,850 | $919,525 | |

[a] Final figures are recommended by the chief executive, such as the city manager, board supervisor, or mayor, and approved by the city council or legislature.

Another approach, the program budget, categorizes departments and divisions into meaningful programs. A program may be, for example, public safety, which could include fire, police, animal control, and emergency preparedness (see the discussion about government functions in Chapter 2, "Government Functions and Organization"). For recreation and parks, programs might be classified as adult programs, youth sports, after-school programs, and so forth. Budgets for each program can be shown in line items, with less or more detail. A key to this approach is obviously how programs are defined. If they do not align easily with government departments, this approach may not serve as a valuable tool (see Table 14.5).

**Table 14.5 Department of Recreation: Program Budget (in dollars)**

| Program | Prior Year's Budget | Prior Year's Actual Expenditures | Next Year's Proposed Budget | Next Year's Approved Budget[a] |
|---|---|---|---|---|
| Adult services | $214,887 | $224,212 | $229,834 | |
| Youth services | $644,662 | $672,638 | $689,644 | |
| Total | $859,549 | $896,850 | $919,478 | |

[a] Final figures are recommended by the chief executive, such as the city manager, board supervisor, or mayor, and approved by the city council or legislature.

Tables 14.1 through 14.5 are examples. It is, of course, possible to combine the approaches into hybrids. For instance, a performance or program budget may include line-item detail. Many program budgets include goals for each program, adding an element from performance budgeting. A popular budget term, *zero-based budgeting* (ZBB), is not actually a presentation approach. It refers to a budgeting method, which will be discussed later.

These formats correspond to different budget reform movements. Performance and program budgets evolved to focus decision making on the outcomes or results of budgets instead of the line-item inputs. Both performance and program budgets are used in management-by-objective models of public management; they can help focus attention on objectives. ZBB can be used with any budget format; this reform involves starting each budget item at zero and justifying all values instead of looking principally at changes to prior years' budgets.

Following are some pros and cons of the three major ways to present operating budgets.

## Line-Item Budgets

Some pros:

- They are understood by many readers.
- They can match accounting records, making it easier to use these records in analysis.
- They provide legislatures with a high degree of control.

Some cons:

- They can provide too much detail, drawing attention away from results and programs.
- They focus on means rather than ends or outcomes associated with programs.

## Performance Budgets

Some pros:

- They focus attention on results.
- They look at workload issues and activities.
- They attempt to measure what is provided to the public in terms of efficiency.

Some cons:

- It may be difficult to develop performance measures that departments can actually control.
- It is difficult to know if what is being provided is what the public wants.
- It is difficult to know if what is being measured is the most important aspect of the effort.

## Program Budgets

Some pros:

• They focus attention on organizational units that are responsible for meeting goals/objectives.

• The goals and objectives are based on policy agendas.

• They enable citizens and legislatures to see links among agencies and departments.

Some cons:

• It can be difficult to come up with clear classifications (e.g., would driver's education be in the education program or the public safety category?).

• It is more difficult to hold managers accountable for funds and outcomes that are jointly authorized.

## THE FISCAL YEAR

Public fiscal years are built around the legislative cycle. The federal fiscal year is from October 1 through September 30. The California fiscal year is from July 1 to June 30, which is typical of many states. However, Alabama's and Michigan's fiscal years parallel the federal timetable and begin in October, while New York's fiscal year begins in April. The fiscal-year period for a political jurisdiction is specified in the jurisdiction's constitution, charter, or incorporation document. Localities (counties, cities, towns, special districts) typically have fiscal years that parallel those of their states.

As a general rule the executive branch prepares a budget that estimates revenues and projects public efforts and expenditures. For example, the federal budget, which is presented to Congress during the first week of February, takes about 8 to 9 months to prepare. The Office of Management and Budget prepares general guidelines that reflect the president's agenda. The departments and agencies prepare budgets around these guidelines, and the Office of Management and Budget prepares the budget message and detailed document for Congress. In February, the president delivers the budget message to Congress.

Congress has 9 months to discuss and deliberate on budget matters. Congress breaks up the president's budget into 13 parts that represent the 13 separate appropriations bills that Congress will pass. In this regard the national budget is unique. At the state and local levels, the executive budget may be debated and deliberated on for 6 to 8 months, but a single budget or appropriations bill is passed by the legislature.

Once the legislature has passed the budget it is sent to the executive for his or her signature. At the federal level the president can either accept the appropriations or veto them. At the state and local levels, an executive may have a line-item veto power. This allows the governor or mayor to delete some items in the budget that he or she feels are inappropriate. The president does not hold a similar power. Budget authority at the federal level rests with Congress, while budget power at the state and local levels tends to favor the executive branch. Regardless of whether the budget is a single document or thirteen separate documents the budget period is typically 12 months.

Once the budget year has been completed the legislature typically requests that agencies report on their programs and that the auditors review the books to ensure that the legislative programs have been faithfully implemented. The auditing process usually lasts about 6 months. The typical budget cycle looks like Table 14.6.

**Table 14.6  Typical Timetable for Budget Process**

| Preparation (3–4 months) | Legislative Review (2–5 months) | Implementation (12 months) | Auditing (6 months) |
|---|---|---|---|
| Agencies/ departments prepare budgets with oversight from the executive budget/finance office. | Federal or state budgets are reviewed by each chamber. Local budgets are reviewed by committees comprised of councilmembers (legislature). | Funds are released to departments and agencies. Allocations are made. | Auditing agency reviews expenditures and reports to legislature. |

# A STEP-BY-STEP GUIDE TO THE OPERATING BUDGET PROCESS

Some of the steps in budget preparation take place in the government's central budget office, which might be located in the city manager's or director of administrative service's office, or in finance, and others take place in departments and programs. There is some evidence of a trend toward preparing 2-year budgets, but most budgets are prepared for 1-year periods.

## Step 1: Establish Priorities

To establish priorities elected officials and senior management may use a strategic-planning process, described in Chapter 6, "Strategic and Other Types of Planning." Planning of this type may take place less often than annually, with priorities updated annually to guide the budget process. Increasingly governments are using internet surveys and community meetings to help set budget priorities separately from a formal strategic-planning process. Once priorities are established, specific goals/objectives are sent to department and program managers as guides for them to use in developing their own priorities for the coming fiscal period.

## Step 2: Forecast Revenue

The government examines its revenue sources and forecasts revenue available for the budget period. Typical revenue sources include property taxes, sales taxes, and user fees and charges. In recreation and parks, revenue might come from fees charged for classes or activities, grants from other levels of government or private organizations, or the government's general fund (which includes tax revenue). Government analysts monitor these sources periodically, closely examining trends. Analysts may use one or more of a wide variety of forecasting methods:

- statistical models that relate growth in different types of revenue to factors like population growth;
- statistical models that focus on trends and patterns only, without relating them to other factors; and
- rules of thumb that relate revenue to growth (e.g., park revenues increase 1% for every 10% increase in the school-age population).

Analysts may review other regional economic forecasts, often done by local universities and investment institutions, and use these to validate their own models.

## Step 3: Issue Budget Instructions and Guidelines

The department charged with preparing the budget solicits requests from department and program managers for expenses in the budget year. A senior manager, such as the city manager or finance manager, usually initiates this budget-preparation process by issuing guidelines and manuals. Based on the revenue analysis and forecasts, these guidelines may severely limit or allow some increase in expenditures from prior years. For example, the guideline may be a 1% increase, no change from prior years, or a 5% decrease. These increases or decreases could reference prior years' budgeted or actual expenditures. See the earlier discussion about estimating personnel and operating costs.

Budget preparation might involve using a ZBB method. This involves justifying all budget requests, rather than assuming that a particular steady-state level will be approved. Some governments assume that there will be a certain level of fixed costs for programs and staffing that will not vary much from year to year. In this case, analysts review these fixed or baseline costs rather than just assessing requests for new or higher expenses.

Steps 1, 2, and 3 are preparatory steps in developing a logical, rational, systematic approach to creating budgets and related documents for policy makers.

## Step 4: Prepare Requests

Department and program managers prepare their budget requests using formats required by the department assembling the budget. These managers look at new staffing required, considering factors such as existing vacancies and the workloads of current staff. They estimate which equipment and supplies new and current staff may need. Managers also determine if they will need to supplement staff with contractors who provide special expertise needed for particular types of programs or who may supplement staff in peak workload periods.

## Step 5: Evaluate Budget Requests

Analysts evaluate requests. Following are some questions that are asked in the materials provided by program and department managers:

- Does the request fit into the overall government goals and priorities?
- Is the projected workload consistent with prior years' workloads?
- Are the requested levels of staff, supplies, equipment, and other types of expenses related to the projected workload?
- What is the impact of not funding the requests?
- Does the request aim to improve current services? If so, who asked for the improvement? How will the improvement affect other services? Does the improvement have future costs and benefits?
- Is this the appropriate department or program to run the new service?
- Will a new or improved service generate revenue? How much? How was the projection made?
- Are there alternative means for providing the goods or services such as contracting with other levels of government, with private nonprofit organizations, or with for-profit companies?
- Does a new program request fit into an ongoing program? If so, how did the department do without this request in the past?

In doing this analysis, analysts may hold budget hearings with department and program managers to get answers to these questions. These hearings are a way for the managers to strengthen their cases in favor of including their requests in the budget.

## Step 6: Assemble the Budget for Decision Makers

Finance and/or budget analysts assemble the budget, matching revenues forecasted with expenditure requests. Some revenue sources, such as particular grants, may be available only for specified types of expenditures. For example, a transportation grant can be used only for the types of transportation programs specified in the funding measure (the law, ordinance, etc.). A grant for youth recreation services can probably be used only for a specific program or target population. This step allows analysts to determine whether the budget is balanced and whether revenues cover requested expenditures. If revenues are lower than expenditures, forecasts and assumptions can be examined to see if revenue forecasts are unrealistically low. This step is often iterative, including many small steps to match revenues and expenses. The assembled budget goes to the next step in the form of a printed preliminary budget.

## Step 7: Present the Budget

Senior managers present a recommended balanced budget to policy makers. Whether they are elected or appointed officials, these policy makers review recommendations and make decisions about what to reduce, eliminate, or increase. They may ask the same questions as the analysts who reviewed the requests. They may ask analysts for additional reviews and answers to more questions. Policy makers may hold more hearings with department and program managers to get answers to their questions and to give managers another chance to explain their requests. Policy makers often invite the public to make comments and suggestions during these public hearings.

## Step 8: Make Recommendations

Policy makers then make their recommendations to the mayor, county executive, or anyone else with ultimate responsibility for approving the budget. The legislature passes the budget as an appropriations bill. Depending on the government, this executive may be able to veto major or minor parts of the budget. Any changes may need to be referred back to the policy makers.

## Step 9: Adopt the Budget

The budget is adopted when it is in its final form. There is typically a first reading of the final draft of the budget, which is followed by a second reading when the budget is adopted as an ordinance or resolution. The government publishes an adopted budget and uses this as a policy and operations guide throughout the fiscal year.

## Step 10: Monitor the Budget

An essential step in budget management involves close monitoring of the budget. After the budget is adopted, the finance or accounting department enters the budget figures into the government's accounting system. Part of the accounting system involves organizing the accounting records based on the source of funds. Funds are of several types, with the general fund's being the largest. There are a number of special funds. These funds must be segregated from the general fund to ensure the money is spent for a designated reason. For example, sales taxes for transportation purposes must be set aside in a separate fund. Refuse collection fees may be used only for sanitation purposes. Special funds are self-balancing, which means the revenues and the expenditures are reported in the same fund.

Departments are given a maximum amount for the fiscal year divided into accounts and sometimes monthly allotments. Often a government will use a secondary set of processes to provide another check on spending. For example, budget analysts might check purchase requests to make sure that funds are available and that the type of expenditure (such as the purchase of a computer) was approved in the budget discussions.

During the fiscal year, budget managers prepare and distribute variance reports to help department and program managers monitor their budgets. These reports usually are in the form of spreadsheets, with columns for actual expenditures, budgeted expenditures, and the difference between actual and budgeted expenditures expressed as dollar amounts and as percentages. The rows can be line items, outcomes/results/goals, programs, or some combination of these. There are several ways to compute variances, depending on whether the government wants to show rows in which actuals are larger than budgeted amounts as positive or negative numbers. Regardless of how variances are computed, they are valuable tools to manage budgets. Where actuals are much higher than budgeted amounts, a natural question is whether there are controls in place to properly limit spending to amounts authorized in the budget. Where actuals are lower than budgeted amounts, there may be a delay in making a particular expenditure or starting a new program.

Table 14.7 presents a sample variance report for a line-item budget. Variance reports can also be presented for performance or program budgets.

In this example, the Department of Recreation is under budget by 2.5%. This illustrates another part of monitoring budgets, which involves adapting to changing circumstances. Priorities obviously can change after a budget is adopted, or estimates might be found to be too high or too low. In these cases, governments have procedures for budget transfers which move allocations from one place to another in the budget. Some procedures may allow finance or budget departments to make transfers without asking the governing body's approval if the transfer is less than a certain amount of money.

**Table 14.7   Department of Recreation: Variance Report (in dollars)**

| Operating Cost | Budget Approved by Legislature | Year's Actual[a] | Dollar Variance[b] | Percent Variance[c] |
|---|---|---|---|---|
| Personnel | $729,358 | $717,480 | $11,878 | 1.6% |
| Memberships | $670 | $945 | −$275 | −41.0% |
| Printing and postage | $6,400 | $4,069 | $2,331 | 36.4% |
| Office equipment | $350 | $400 | −$50 | −14.3% |
| Electricity | $17,400 | $30,000 | −$12,600 | −72.4% |
| Other operating | $165,347 | $143,956 | $21,391 | 12.9% |
| **Total** | **$919,525** | **$896,850** | **$22,675** | **2.5%** |

[a] What has been spent/accounted for, to date, in the current budget year.
[b] The dollar amount difference (variance) between the approved budget and the year's actuals. Sometimes the variance is calculated as actual minus budget so that a negative variance shows under-budget spending while a positive shows an over-budget spending.
[c] The percentage of authorized budget dollars represented by the variance.

The example Table 14.7 also indicates that the department was significantly under or over budget in different line items. Each of the differences might be questioned by analysts, focusing more on the larger variances such as memberships and electricity.

When reviewing variances, it is also important to account for when the variance is calculated and when expenditures will occur. Some expenditures, such as personnel, may be expected to be fairly uniform throughout the year. Others, such as office equipment, will tend to occur sporadically, perhaps only two or three times during the year. Therefore, sometimes the budget is broken down into quarterly or even monthly budgets so that the corresponding variance reports will be easier to use as a control tool.

## BUDGET ADJUSTMENTS

During any budget period priorities change and/or emergencies occur. In some cases managers and/or the executive department may move funds from one line item to another to meet changing needs and circumstances. However, when administrators and the executive branch determine funds need to be reallocated between departments and/or programs, legislative action is needed. At the federal level Congress and the executive branch request rescissions. A rescission bill repeals a previously authorized appropriation. Once funding approval has been removed the legislature is free to authorize expenditures through a new appropriation.

Central budget offices at the state and local government levels review budget and expenditures about 3 to 6 months into the fiscal year. Based on their analysis of the budget plan compared to actual expenditures they propose transfers, cuts, and/or increases to the legislature. The legislature then approves, rejects, or amends these requests.

The legislature has significant authority over how public revenues are raised and spent. However, the executive is not without resources. Executives may impound public money. This means the executive may elect not to spend the appropriated funds. These unspent funds may be placed into rescission bills for the current year or included in the proposed budget for the coming year.

## ETHICS, EQUITY, AND OPERATING BUDGETS

Budgeting succumbs to two ills. One is to be "a-ethical" or to have a technocratic view that perceives budgeting as highly specialized and process driven. The second ill is to see budgeting as the ultimate arena of bargaining, pluralism, and interest group politics. Neither of these perspectives is particularly satisfying because neither addresses the core values of the democratic republic: transparency, inclusiveness, compromise, and consideration of others.

Legislators have been classified in texts as being either "delegates" or "trustees." Delegates are those who serve their constituents even when they personally hold different views, and trustees are those who vote independently of popular sentiment based solely on their own judgment of the facts. In the first case the elected representative is a slave to public sentiment, and in the second he or she is aloof from it. Both views fail ethically because the role of the representative is not only to advocate a point of view but to educate constituents about broader concerns and interests of the community. The trustee view and delegate view are deficient because each fails to engage in discussion and enhance the understanding of the sovereign—the people. Each appears to use discretionary decision making in an arbitrary and inappropriate manner.

Developing budgets for governmental operations involves making choices. Ideally strategic plans provide goals that are translated into specific items in a budget. But goals may be compromised by special interests. As Chapter 4, "Ethics," points out, firms seeking government contracts may make contributions to politicians in the hope of changing priorities. Politicians may earmark or attempt to ensure that funds go to their favorite areas of interest and/or their political districts. Because of this possibility, transparency in budgeting is essential.

Transparency starts with having clear steps for setting goals, policies, and procedures for government staff to follow in developing and managing budgets. Chapter 5, "Informing and Involving the Public," discusses several mechanisms to encourage the public to be involved in budgeting, such as participating in surveys about budget priorities, attending public meetings, and serving on boards or councils that approve budgets. Ethical decisions and choices are best made in the overall context of the government's responsibilities to all citizens over time rather than as a discussion of specific interests during a budget cycle. Building ongoing, long-term relationships with citizens as co-owners of the budget remains a core challenge in ensuring ethical budgetary decisions.

A challenge for managers in assuring equity is that there is often more space and options in prosperous communities than in low-income areas. Consequently, a manager may look upon these inequities as opportunities for prosperous communities to participate in planning and funding of programs for their neighborhood and use public monies to enhance options in less prosperous areas. Equity to some extent is customization to meet specific needs rather than providing the same program and design uniformity in all areas.

## Conclusion

Operating budgets are critical documents used by governments to fund goods and services provided to citizens while ensuring resources are efficiently and effectively employed. Budgeting involves a coordinated effort by public executives, department managers, and the legislature to ensure that each year's expenditures are consistent with community goals, objectives, and projected revenues. Since public goods and services are labor intensive, a primary concern for management is linking department outputs and/or performance to personnel. Consequently, operating budgets focus on personnel costs (pay and benefits) and nonpersonnel costs (fixed and variable) that are essential to executing the responsibilities assigned to the department.

Finally, budgeting is a year-round effort. While political jurisdictions are required by law to provide budget documents at a specified time, managing the budget is an ongoing necessity. To assist in ensuring funds are not squandered or left idle, periodic budget updates, called variance reports, are produced to track monthly or quarterly expenditures. These updated reports, along with evolving circumstances, are the basis for budget adjustments or reprogramming funds during the fiscal year.

Spending the community's money requires difficult choices both about what government will do and how government will raise revenues. It is important in raising revenues and in spending appropriations that managers address issues of both efficiency and equity.

## PRACTICING PUBLIC ADMINISTRATION

| J. P. Morgan Community Library Personnel | | | | | Benefits ($) | | | |
|---|---|---|---|---|---|---|---|---|
| | | | | | | Health | | | Social |
| Position | Number | Salary ($) | Total ($) | Medicare | Insurance | Dental | Pension | Security |
| **Full-time** | | | | | | | | |
| Head librarian | 1 | $48,000 | $48,000 | | | | | |
| Reference librarian | 1 | $42,000 | $42,000 | | | | | |
| Assistant librarian | 1 | $30,000 | $30,000 | | | | | |
| Circulation clerk | 2 | $22,000 | $44,000 | | | | | |
| Maintenance worker | 1 | $18,000 | $18,000 | | | | | |
| Subtotal | 6 | | $182,000 | | | | | |
| **Part-time** | | | | | | | | |
| Reference librarian | 1 (1/2 time) | $21,000 | $21,000 | | | | | |
| Assistant librarian | 1 (1/2 time) | $16,000 | $16,000 | | | | | |
| Clerk | 4 (1/2 time) | $10,000 | $40,000 | | | | | |
| Page | Estimated 3,200 hours / year | $8.00/hr. | $25,600 | | | | | |
| **Total** | **9 FTE +** | | **$284,600** | | | | | |

Note: FTE = full-time equivalent. See notes to Table 14.1.

1. Compute the benefits for the J. P. Morgan Community Library.
   Apply .0145 for Medicare and .062 for Social Security taxes. For
   the purpose of this exercise apply a 16% rate for health insurance,
   a 6% share for dental coverage, and an 8% share for pension
   coverage for all full-time employees based on their salaries. A
   salary of $10,000 with a 16% rate applied to it would be a cost of
   $1,600. What are the total personnel costs for this library?

2. Based on your computation of all salaries and benefits, which
   percentage of compensation to the J. P. Morgan library staff
   comprises benefits?

3. Personnel costs represent 82% of the library's overall costs of
   $440,208.41. The city manager and council are desperate to cut
   costs. They are looking for 5% savings in all departments. A
   councilperson has suggested cutting the circulation clerk staff
   ($22,000 each) to one full-time position and employing three part-
   time clerks ($10,000 each) rather than four. What are the actual
   budget savings of the council proposal? If this is the only change,
   will it meet the 5% total reduction desired?

4. The J. P. Morgan Community Library serves predominately
   preschool children, kindergarten through grade 12 students,
   summer tourists, local businesses, and retired residents. In which
   ways might the library either cut costs ($22,010) or raise revenue?

5. When taking into consideration across the board cuts to programs
   and services (see Question 4 above), what ethical and equity
   considerations might the director of public libraries consider
   when proposing the cuts?

6. The Optics Corporation sells equipment that allows users to
   check out books and materials without the assistance of clerical
   help. Each machine costs $8,000. The customer slides his or her
   magnetized library card through a slot and then passes each
   book's bar code under the infrared light. In response the machine
   logs the card name and each book's identification number. It
   produces a list of the books and the due date for the customer. It
   also allows customers to demagnetize the books once the receipt
   is generated. The optic scanner has been successfully employed in
   a number of community and college libraries in the area. Which
   questions should a budget analyst ask regarding the purchase of
   these scanners?

7. The J. P. Morgan Community Library has a line-item budget
   (see next page). With this money it provides library services
   from 10:00 a.m. to 8:00 p.m. Monday through Thursday and
   from 10 a.m. to 6 p.m. on Fridays and Saturdays and is closed on
   Sunday. In the past year it served 8,200 customers and circulated

| $360,970.90 | Personnel |
| $45,000.00 | Acquisition costs for books, periodicals, and so forth |
| $22,000.00 | Office supplies |
| $7,000.00 | Utilities |
| $3,200.00 | Maintenance |
| $2,037.51 | Other related programs |
| $440,208.41 | Total costs |

65,874 books and materials including videos, CDs, DVDs, and posters. It provided special programs to new readers, the visually impaired, kindergarten through grade 12 schoolchildren, and the elderly. Last year the staff assisted patrons with 1,100 reference questions. Which type of budget format, other than line item, would best represent the library? Why?

8. Obtain a budget from your local community. Which kind of budget format is being used? Which questions about revenue generation, expenditures, and service does the budget adequately address? Which areas are not adequately addressed and why?

## BIBLIOGRAPHY

Alexander, J. (1999). A new ethics of the budgetary process. *Administration & Society 31*(4): 542–565.

Aronson, J. R. & Schwartz, E., Eds. (2004). *Management policies in local government finance*. (5th ed.). Washington, D.C.: International City/County Management Association.

Axelrod, D. (1995). *Budgeting for modern government*. (2d ed.). New York, NY: St. Martin's.

Baker, D. (2008). *Government budgeting workbook: Bridging theory and practice*. San Diego, CA: Birkdale.

Bland, R. L. & Overton, M. R. (2019). *A budgeting guide for local government*. (4th ed.). Washington, D.C.: International City/County Management Association (ICMA).

Botner, S. B. (1985). The use of budgeting/management tools by state government. *Public Administration Review 45*(3): 616–620.

City of Los Angeles Administrative Office. (2002). *Department manual for the budget system*. Los Angeles, CA: City of Los Angeles

Emerson, S. M. (2008). California. In *Proceedings from Annual Western States Budget Review Roundtable*. Salt Lake City, UT: Center for Public Policy and Administration, University of Utah.

Forsythe, D. (2004). *Memos to the governor: An introduction to state budgeting*. Washington, D.C.: Georgetown University Press.

Frank, H. A., Ed. (2006). *Public financial management*. Boca Raton, FL: CRC Press.

Hyde, A. C., & Shafritz, J. M. (2002). *Government budgeting: Theory, process and politics*. (3rd ed.). Belmont, CA.: Wadsworth.

Kelly, J. M., & Rivenbark, W. C. (2020). *Performance budgeting and local government*. (2nd ed.). New York, NY: Routledge.

Kleine, A. (2018). *City on the line: How Baltimore transformed its budget to beat the great recession and deliver outcomes*. New York, NY: Rowman and Littlefield.

Lee, R., Johnson, R. W., & Joyce, P. G. (2008). *Public budgeting systems*. (8th ed.).Boston, MA: Jones and Bartlett.

Menifield, C. (2017). *The basics of public budgeting and financial management*. (3rd ed.). New York, NY: Hamilton Books.

Mikesell, J. L. (2003). *Fiscal administration: Analysis and application for the public sector*. (6th ed.). Belmont, CA: Thomson.

Musell, R. M., with Yeung, R. (2020). *Understanding government budgets: a guide to practices in the public service*. (2nd ed.). New York, NY: Routledge.

Nice, D. (2002). *Public budgeting*. Belmont, CA: Wadsworth.

Perry, J. (1996). *Handbook for public administration*. San Francisco, CA: Jossey-Bass.

Rubin, I. S. (2005). *The politics of public budgeting: Getting and spending, borrowing and balancing*. (5th ed.). Washington, D.C.: CQ Press.

Thompson, J. A., & Felts, A. A. (1992). Politicians and professionals: The influence of state agency heads in budgetary success. *Western Political Quarterly 45*(2): 153–168.

Wildavsky, A., & Caiden, N. (2004). *The new politics of the budgetary process*. (5th ed.). New York, NY: Longman.

# 15

# Capital Budgeting

# Funding Major Projects

In the last chapter, we looked at how governments pay for programs and for ongoing responsibilities such as law enforcement, trash pickup, and other services. Governments have another type of responsibility—building government facilities (such as city halls, sports arenas, and water treatment facilities) and building general infrastructure (such as roads and bridges). Building these resources usually takes years and costs hundreds of thousands to billions of dollars. Once facilities and infrastructure are constructed, they have to be maintained. This type of undertaking is different from planning and paying for ongoing services or short-term projects. Governments often do not have the millions of dollars that longer-term projects require without looking for outside resources. While money for projects is available, there is never enough to fund everything. Governments must carefully weigh the merits of each project and look for funding outside of their own resources.

## What Do Governments Buy and Build?

Local governments invest in assets of many types. They build facilities to provide public services. These may include civic center complexes with city halls and other buildings, sewer and water treatment facilities, harbors, airports, water and power systems, computer hardware and software, and so forth. They also purchase large pieces of equipment for their use in providing regular services. These can include street sweepers, fire engines, and police mobile laboratory vans. Local governments invest in infrastructure, such as roads and bridges, that is used by everyone who lives in or visits their jurisdictions and is vital for economic development.

Examples of typical capital projects are the following:

- municipal auditoriums,
- police and fire stations,
- highways,
- parking structures,
- public parks,
- streets and freeways, and
- schools.

All of these capital investments have common characteristics. They have benefits that last many years into the future. They can be purchased over time and are funded over time since they are very expensive. For planning purposes and to distinguish what goes into the operating budget from what belongs in the capital budget, governments usually set a minimum dollar amount for capital investments. For example, a city may have a policy that purchases over $500,000 are considered capital investments. Another city may decide that its capital budget includes only items with values greater than $100,000.

Some projects, such as sports arenas or water treatment facilities, may generate revenues eventually in the form of user fees. Most capital efforts will require some ongoing operating costs once the projects are operational. Staff and supplies will be needed, for example, to run a treatment facility. One may think of these revenues and expenses as *streams*.

A major issue in the early 21st century is the inadequacy of capital investments by governments at all levels. Governments made significant infrastructure investments during the 1950s through 1970s in highways, airports, colleges, buildings, and other areas, and in the early 21st century many of those investments are nearing the end of their useful life. Interest in cutting taxes has meant less spending on infrastructure, infrastructure maintenance, research and development, education, and other areas.

## PROS AND CONS OF CAPITAL BUDGETING

The opportunities inherent in capital budgeting include the following:

- It allows governments to rationally plan their long-term projects. Most capital projects take years to plan and build, and they produce benefits only after their completion. By separating decisions about these long-term projects from the operating expenses discussed in the previous chapter, governments can look at criteria and priorities.

The resources available to pay for projects included in capital budgets allow matching of costs and benefits. Projects such as new schools take years to plan and construct, but they have long useful lives. By using grants and debt (as we will see later in this chapter), the costs of these projects can be spread over many years. A government can secure financing to pay for the planning and building stages, when there are no students enrolled and no state education payments, and then repay the costs when the school is fully operational.

The challenges of capital budgeting include the following:

- It is very difficult for governments and other organizations to foresee the future. Needs may change, making capital projects that once looked good seem to be bad investments. For example, the nation has invested large amounts of money in interstate highway systems that have benefitted citizens and businesses. But when oil prices go up and interest in rapid transit grows, this large investment looks like it might have been misplaced.

- It is also difficult to balance sources of funding for capital projects. Governments can use their current tax revenues, raise new tax revenues, sell bonds, or seek grants. Raising taxes may shift the burden of payment for the capital project to future taxpayers who had no say in the investment. Selling bonds obligates the government to set aside future money to repay the bondholders; this shifts the payments to future residents who and businesses that may benefit from the investment, but it also limits the funds the government can use for operating budget needs in the future.

## STEP-BY-STEP GUIDE TO CAPITAL BUDGETING

The capital budgeting process is usually separate from the operating budget process, but decisions about capital projects affect the operating budget. Labor and maintenance costs for a completed project should be included in the future operating budget. To show this linkage, some information about capital projects from their earliest stages should be included in the operating budget. The information included in the budget document can be the complete capital budget, if a separate document is not prepared, or a summary list of projects.

A variety of departments are involved in developing capital budgets. Operating departments such as public works may identify bridges that need to be replaced. The fire department may want to build a new fire station to serve a new housing development. The recreation and parks department may want to expand a youth center. The government's principal engineer often estimates costs for proposed projects. The finance department then identifies funding. A committee made up of these departments' representatives usually participates in making a prioritized list of projects that is submitted to the governing body for approval.

Looking at the process in more detail, it typically has five main steps.

## Step 1: Asset Inventory

The first step in deciding which projects to do is assessing the current situation. City staff, often in public works or engineering departments, list and assess all assets (e.g., building, vehicles, and equipment). They note the age, capacity, and replacement costs of each asset.

Governments may hire engineering consultants or use their own engineering staff to conduct detailed analyses of facilities. These analyses may include assessments of structural and other hazards, interior and exterior walls, elevators, mechanical and electrical systems, fire/life/safety systems, and environmental hazards such as the presence of lead paint and asbestos.

## Step 2: Capital Improvement Plan

The next step is to list and describe possible capital projects. Staff will typically identify projects for 5 or more years into the future. They will describe each project in detail, including a map of its location and its cost data. At this step, all possible projects are considered. These may include construction of new facilities, major remodeling or expansion of existing facilities, major maintenance projects that are not included in the operating budget, and large equipment purchases (such as fire engines and specialized trucks).

An evaluation committee will consider each project. Key factors usually include linkages with other plans and projects, such as the city's general or master plan, as well as scheduling and the overall priorities of the legislature or governing board. Based on these considerations, the evaluation committee and staff will program projects, or schedule them for each of the next few years. The committee usually includes representatives from engineering and public works who can evaluate feasibility in terms of operations, construction, costs, and planning and who can check conformity with the city's general plan. Some techniques used in analyzing and prioritizing projects are discussed below.

## Step 3: Long-Term Financial Plan

The next step is matching projects with sources, costs, and timing of funding. Each funding source has special requirements that need to be considered, and some are limited by law or custom to particular types of projects. It is good to have the financing term be shorter than the expected life of the capital investment. It would not be a good idea, for example, to finance the purchase of a trash truck that is expected to last for 10 years using a 30-year municipal bond. In the example displayed in Table 15.1 the city has identified five projects with differing construction periods and funding sources.

**Table 15.1  Summary of Proposed Projects and Potential Funding**

|  | Total Cost Estimate ($) | Time Period | Funding Source |
|---|---|---|---|
| New park in the Uptown area | $10,000,000 | Years 1 and 2 | Bond |
| Community center remodeling | $2,000,000 | Year 1 | General fund |
| Sewer upgrade | $15,000,000 | Years 2, 3, and 4 | State funds |
| Main Street bridge repair | $5,000,000 | Years 3 and 4 | Federal funds |
| New fire truck | $500,000 | Year 1 | General fund |
| **Total** | **$32,500,000** |  |  |

## Step 4: Capital Component of Annual Budget

The first year of a long-term capital plan becomes one part of the annual budget, which is often payment on principal of the debt. This portion of the capital budget might receive greater attention in the budget presented to the public and legislative body. In Table 15.2 the jurisdiction is reporting that the first-year budget commitment is $7,500,000.

**Table 15.2  Summary of Funding Commitment over Four-Year Period**

|  | Year 1 | Year 2 | Year 3 | Year 4 |
|---|---|---|---|---|
| New park in Uptown area | $5,000,000 | $5,000,000 | $0 | $0 |
| Community center remodeling | $2,000,000 | $0 | $0 | $0 |
| Sewer upgrade | $0 | $5,000,000 | $5,000,000 | $5,000,000 |
| Main Street bridge repair | $0 | $0 | $1,000,000 | $4,000,000 |
| New fire truck | $500,000 | $0 | $0 | $0 |
| Total | $7,500,000 | $10,000,000 | $6,000,000 | $9,000,000 |

## Step 5: Execution of Capital Budget

The last step is to put the capital plan and budget into effect. Governments have policies about how to procure services such as project design and management and about how to select contractors to build projects or vendors to provide major pieces of equipment. The government's priorities, construction costs, and other factors may change over the long time periods needed for planning and constructing projects.

Governments may need to negotiate *change orders* with their contractors to formally amend contracts. See Chapter 16, "Contracts and Procurement," and Chapter 17, "Grants," for more information.

Managers and staff also need to put in place ways to ensure that projects are on schedule and on budget. See Chapter 10, "Project Management, PERT and Flowcharts," for more information. Besides careful monitoring and frequent communication with contractors, contract performance is often handled by structuring a contract's terms so that payments are made only after certain milestones are reached and government managers have approved parts of the project.

## PROJECT ANALYSIS AND RATINGS

Ideas can come from a number of areas. Recall that the first step in developing a capital budget is evaluating the inventory of assets owned by a government. Applying standards for the length of useful life expected from a piece of machinery or carefully assessing the condition of a bridge or other type of infrastructure can produce a list of projects. The government may have a strategic-planning process that sets priorities and produces ideas for projects and programs. Politicians and key stakeholders may have ideas for projects as well. In some areas, such as environmental protection and homeland security, federal and state government agencies may mandate that local governments undertake certain projects.

Suppose there are several projects vying for scarce resources. The following are three widely used methods for evaluating capital projects and deciding which to include in a capital budget. All of these methods can be used easily with spreadsheet software.

### Payback Method

This method computes the number of years required to recoup an investment, with the goal of minimizing this period. For example, suppose $10,000 is available to spend, and there is a choice of two projects with different streams of revenue (see Table 15.3).

Project A generates $10,000 in revenue in 2 years, so the payback period is 2 years. Project B generates $10,000 in revenue in 3.5 years, which is the payback period. Project A would be selected because it has the shortest payback period.

The payback method is easy to understand and emphasizes a quick return, which reduces risk. But this method ignores revenue received after the end

**Table 15.3  Payback Comparison of Two $10K Capital Projects Over 5 Years**

| Year | Project A Revenue | Project B Revenue |
|------|-------------------|-------------------|
| 1 | $5,000 | $2,000 |
| 2 | $5,000 | $2,000 |
| 3 | $2,000 | $2,000 |
| 4 | $0 | $6,000 |
| 5 | $0 | $6,000 |
| Total | $12,000 | $18,000 |

of the payback period, when project B will generate most of its total revenue. This method also does not consider the time value of money, which is discussed below in the Net Present Value section.

The next two methods take into account the timing of flows of expenses and revenues.

For background, consider why $100 a year from now is not the same as $100 now. One hundred dollars now can yield a flow of valuable services throughout the year, such as interest. A person must be compensated if they sacrifice current use of resources for future use. At the end of one year, someone could have $100 plus interest, so $100 now has greater value than $100 at the end of one year.

Discounting is a way to convert a stream of revenues and expenses over time into a single present value. It is a way to compare revenues and costs that occur at different times. Compounding is related to discounting, which adjusts sums to be received in the future to the present value equivalent, or to the amount to which sums may grow if invested at the prevailing interest rates.

## Internal Rate of Return (IRR)

The IRR method determines the yield on investments (interest rate) that equates the cost stream to the revenue stream. For a simple example, if an investment of $100 yields (earns) $120 in one year, the IRR is 20% (120 ÷ 100). In practice, however, since the return (yield) on the investment takes place over several years and may vary from year to year, the calculation is a bit complicated, although spreadsheet programs can do it quite easily.

Using projects A and B,

- IRR for project A is about 11.16%, and
- IRR for project B is about 18.23%.

## Net Present Value (NPV)

The NPV method discounts the revenue anticipated over the life of the project to determine whether the revenue is equal to or exceeds the initial investment. The basic discount rate is the cost of capital, or the amount of interest paid by the government for money borrowed.

Present value = current dollar ÷ $(1 + \text{discount rate or } r)^{n \text{ (time period)}}$

or

$1 a year from now at a 10% discount rate =
$$1 \div (1 + 0.10)^1 = 1 \div 1.1 = .9090$$

Therefore, $5,000 a year from now = $5,000 × 0.9090 = $4,545.

Assuming the discount rate is 10% and the investment is $10,000, what would be the values of the two competing projects, A and B? (See Table 15.4)

**Table 15.4 Revenue Flows for Two Competing Projects with $10,000 Initial Cost**

| | Project A[a] | | | Project B[a] | | |
|---|---|---|---|---|---|---|
| Year | Revenue | Discount Rate | Present Value | Revenue | Discount Rate | Present Value |
| 1 | $5,000 | .909 | $4,545 | $2,000 | .909 | $1,818 |
| 2 | $5,000 | .826 | $4,130 | $2,000 | .826 | $1,652 |
| 3 | $2,000 | .751 | $1,502 | $2,000 | .751 | $1,502 |
| 4 | $0 | 0 | $0 | $6,000 | .683 | $4,098 |
| 5 | $0 | 0 | $0 | $6,000 | .621 | $3,726 |
| Total | $12,000 | | $10,177 | $18,000 | | $12,796 |

Therefore:

| | | |
|---|---|---|
| Present value of revenue | $10,177 | $12,796 |
| Present value of cost | −$10,000 | −$10,000 |
| Net present value | $177 | $2,796 |

[a] The factors used to discount the revenue streams come from standard statistical tables. Spreadsheet programs such as Excel also have net present value functions.

| | Project A | Project B | Recommendation |
|---|---|---|---|
| Payback | 2 years | 3 ½ years | A (quick payback) |
| IRR | 11.17% | 18.23% | B (higher yield) |
| NPV | $177 | $2,796 | B (higher NPV) |

Note: IRR = internal rate of return; NPV = net present value.

For this example, project B has both a higher IRR and a higher NPV than project A. These methods are compared above.

There are complications to using these techniques. How, for example, can you take into account costs and benefits that do not have monetary values? Costs and benefits can be identified through careful descriptions of projects. Which groups are served? What are the intended results? Benefits can be estimates and be valued through pilot projects, simulations, and market studies. Costs should include construction, financing and operating costs, and the opportunity costs of resources used in the project. The *opportunity cost* of $10,000 may be the foregone interest the government could have earned if the funds had been placed in the bank. If the interest rate earned were 10%, then the opportunity cost of $10,000 ($10,000 × 0.10) in year 1 would have been $1,000.

Cost estimates should include externalities, costs that are not directly associated with the project but that have unintended consequences to third parties. A cost of a highway repair project that diverts traffic may be lost revenues to area businesses. This cost is an externality of the project and should be included in the project's cost estimates.

How is a discount rate selected? One can see from the calculations above that discount rates are important. A commonly used discount rate is the cost of borrowed funds (or the interest rate that government pays).

Which kinds of decision criteria can be applied to these calculations? You can see that results vary with the discount rate used and with assumptions about costs and benefits. One may test the effects of different assumptions by conducting a sensitivity analysis. Simply change the assumptions and compare results for one project using all four methods. The changes in assumptions should be as realistic as possible. For example, one set of assumptions may suppose nothing can go wrong and be a best-case scenario. An alternative view might be to assume that everything will go awry (bad weather, labor strikes) and be a worst-case scenario. The midpoint between these two scenarios may be the most reasonable estimate to use for comparisons with other projects. One can also establish *hurdle rates*, minimum acceptable ratios for each technique, such as the following:

- IRR = 20% or more
- Payback = less than five years
- NPV = greater than 1 (NPV must exceed 0 so revenues exceed costs)

These criteria can be used along with the more quantitative measures to rank or grade projects.

## HOW TO SET PRIORITIES

Like project ideas, priorities can emerge from conflicting interests and different viewpoints. Ways to set priorities usually look at several factors, such as the severity of problems identified and the availability of funding, and give numerical scores or letter grades to projects based on these factors. The projects with the highest or lowest scores or grades, depending on how the scales are constructed, become the top priorities for funding.

When setting priorities and evaluating projects, it is always good to ask questions such as the following:

1. Can this project be delayed? What would be the consequences if it were delayed?

2. How sensitive is the analysis to major changes in population, technology, prices, and so forth?

3. Who and what does the project affect? Who benefits? Who bears the costs of all types (monetary and non-monetary)?

4. Are capital costs realistic? (They can be compared to those of similar projects in other cities.)

5. Are all of the costs included?

6. How will operating costs change when the project is completed?

7. Are there other options, such as remodeling, renovation, leasing, and contracting?

8. Does the project generate revenue?

9. Does the project protect lives and property? Does it promote safety?

10. Does the project stimulate or depress other development?

11. Does the project mitigate environmental effects of other projects?

12. Is the project mandated by some other level of government or by a lawsuit?

# How Do Governments Pay for Capital Projects?

A key part of capital planning, and the part that literally turns a capital plan into a capital budget, is matching a list of projects to funding sources. Money for capital projects, both construction and equipment, can come from a variety of sources.

## Revenue

The most obvious source of capital funding is operating revenue. Governments generate money from property taxes, income taxes (most states, the federal government, and a few cities), sales taxes, fees, and charges. In some cases, governments can use this pay-as-you-go source for capital projects. But most of current revenue is usually needed to pay current bills, such as staff salaries, supplies, and minor equipment. Revenue is discussed in more detail in Chapter 13 and expenditures in Chapter 14.

## Tax Increment Financing

Within defined and approved redevelopment districts, another type of financing is available—tax increment financing. In this method, the assessed value used for computing property taxes for the properties in the redevelopment district are frozen at a particular moment in time. Any increases in the assessed value and the resulting increase in the property taxes are set aside by the redevelopment agency until it has enough money to undertake improvements. Tax increment financing can be combined with other types of financing to cover the total cost of a project.

## Assessment Districts

Another financial method has some similarities to tax increment financing. Governments may allow residents and/or businesses to set up assessment districts and tax themselves to finance improvements, such as street lighting, that benefit only those in the assessment district.

The government organizes and manages the district, residents vote on participation, and if a majority favors it, the district is formed. The government collects the tax, invests the proceeds, and then undertakes the project or service.

## Grants

Grants are transfers of spending power from one level of government to another or sometimes from a private foundation or corporation to a level of government. Grants are discussed in detail in Chapter 17.

## Debt

Another major source of funding is debt or borrowing money. Bonds represent this debt, or a long-term promise by the borrower (the bond issuer or government) to the lender (the bondholder) to pay the bond's face amount (par value or principal) at defined maturity date(s) and to make contractual interest payments until the loan is retired (loan is paid in full). The borrower is committed to pay debt service (interest payments and periodic repayments of principal) through the life of the loan.

There are several major types of bonds. *General obligation bonds* pledge the "full faith and credit" of a government, or in other words, its taxing power. These types of bonds are usually paid out of the government's general fund. Because of the stability of revenues that go into this fund, there is a high likelihood of on-time payments and, consequently, lower interest rates. *Revenue bonds* are repaid out of special revenue funds and are not backed by the taxing power that contributes to the general fund. These types of bonds are generally issued by revenue-producing departments or enterprise funds, such as airports, harbors, or other governmental authorities. A third type of debt is a short-term (less than one year) "note," in accounting and finance parlance. Tax and revenue anticipation notes help smooth out receipts of major revenue sources and are repaid out of these sources; these are discussed in Chapter 13, "Revenues."

A best practice is to have a debt policy adopted by the government's elected council or board. The debt policy specifies reasons for issuing debt and sets key guidelines. It may, for example, indicate that debt should not be issued for maturities longer than the financed project's useful life and is not used at a later time for operating expenses.

## A STEP-BY-STEP GUIDE TO ISSUING DEBT

The process of issuing debt can be long and usually involves a large group of government staff as well as key consultants, who have fiduciary (acting in a role of trust for another) responsibilities to investors and the general public as well as to the government. The following are the typical steps taken with regard to incurring debt.

## Step 1: Identify a Need to Issue Debt

The need for financing arises out of capital planning and budgeting. Other sources of funds, as described above, are considered, as is the government's debt capacity or the ability to borrow. There is no formula per se for determining debt capacity. Factors considered include expenditure levels and growth, revenue growth, growth of the tax base, potential for new revenue, and revenue to be generated by the project.

## Step 2: Hire Advisors (The Financing Team)

Key advisors include financial advisors, bond counsel, and underwriters. Financial advisors are consultants who conduct analyses, help write documents, and work with rating agencies and others to describe the government and why it wants to sell bonds. Bond counsel are attorneys who write technical documents and render an opinion about whether bonds are exempt from federal or state taxes. Underwriters are banks or investment companies that will buy and then resell the government's bonds. They can be hired at the beginning of the debt process to advise on marketing or when the bonds are sold.

## Step 3: Make Decisions (Structuring the Financing)

The government, advised by its consultants, makes a number of decisions:

- Type of bonds: the possible types include general obligation, revenue, refunding, and so forth.
- Amount of funds needed: this may include capitalized interest (payment of interest on the bonds until the project is finished and producing revenue). This is called the par value (total stated value) of the bonds.
- Forecasted interest rate(s): this is an estimate of borrowing costs for planning and analysis purposes.
- Maturity of debt: this is the term of the bonds or the number of years over which they will be repaid. This affects the amount of debt service (principal plus interest) that will be paid.
- Credit enhancements: the government must consider whether to buy insurance to protect the bondholders and boost the bond ratings. Credit enhancements come from state credit guarantees, bank letters of credit, and municipal bond insurance companies.
- Debt service coverage ratio: rating agencies and investors may want a particular ratio for security. This ratio measures the relationship between net income (income from operations before nonoperating revenue such as interest income) and the principal and interest required for debt payments. The formula is:

(Net operating income) ÷ (Principal + Interest on all outstanding bonds)

A higher debt service ratio means more security regarding whether the principal and interest will be paid. Acceptable ratios may be 1.25, 1.50, 2.00, or higher.

## Step 4: Market the Bonds

This marketing campaign requires preparation of some complex documents:

- The *preliminary official statement* is a marketing document that describes the government and its ability to repay, the scope of the project, and other key facts. It is called an *official statement* when it is updated after the bond sale with all of the information from the sale (interest rate, etc.).

- The *bond indenture* is a contract between the issuer and bondholders. Particularly important are the repayment provisions and the flow of funds, which provide guarantees of repayments to the bondholders and set restrictions on the government.

- The legal opinion of bond counsel is a certification that the bonds are exempt from taxes. This decision depends on the type of project being financed. Under most circumstances, projects must be for the government's use and not for use by private companies to be tax exempt. For example, airline terminals to be operated by a government agency for the use of the general public are usually tax exempt, but a rental car facility constructed by the agency for the use of private rental car companies is not. Governments can sell taxable bonds for projects that benefit private companies.

An important part of the marketing campaign is obtaining a rating of the bonds from one or more of the credit rating agencies. The major agencies are Moody's Investors Service, Standard & Poor's, and Fitch Ratings. These organizations evaluate the bonds for possible purchasers by looking at the regional economy, the government's outstanding debt, the government's management history and policies, and the advisors' financial analysis. In addition, the rating agencies do their own analyses of revenue trends and related factors. Based on their analyses, they issue letter ratings, with higher ratings usually translating into lower interest rates. See Table 15.5.

Standard & Poor's and Fitch Ratings use the same rating indicators. Ratings in the C range (also called "junk bonds") from any rating agency are not considered investment quality by most investors and are harder to sell at lower interest rates.

## Step 5: Sell the Bonds

Bonds can be sold competitively or through negotiations. Competitive sales mean that the underwriter is not known until the sale is made. With negotiated sales, the underwriter is selected before the sale and works with the government and its advisors on marketing the bonds. Bonds are usually sold to the underwriter who resells the bonds to investors (individuals, mutual funds, banks, and private companies). The underwriter's gross profit, or underwriting spread, is the difference between the price it pays for the bonds and the price it receives when it sells the bonds to investors.

Why are government bonds attractive to investors? Government bonds are usually exempt from state and federal taxes, something that the bond counsel certifies.

After the sale is executed, documents and funds go to a trustee, who checks everything and releases money to the government.

**Table 15.5   Rating Systems of Major Bond Agencies**

|  | Moody's Investors Service | Standard & Poor's | Fitch Ratings |
|---|---|---|---|
| Best quality | AAA | AAA | AAA |
| High quality | Aa1 | AA+ | AA+ |
|  | Aa2 | AA | AA |
|  | Aa3 | AA– | AA– |
| Upper medium quality | A1 | A+ | A+ |
|  | A2 | A | A |
|  | A3 | A– | A– |
| Medium grade | Baa1 | BBB+ | BBB+ |
|  | Baa2 | BBB | BBB |
|  | Baa3 | BBB– | BBB– |

## Step 6: Manage the Bonds

The trustee also makes the principal and interest payment to bond-holders on behalf of the government during the term of the bond.

Governments must be careful to abide by the requirements of debt. Bonds have restrictions on their use. If they are issued to fund capital projects, spending must begin within a few years of the bond sale. Projects cannot be delayed, and interest earned on the idle cash (also called arbitrage) is significantly restricted by the federal government. There are also continuing disclosure requirements. The official statement must be updated annually for use in the secondary market for the bonds. The government must monitor the debt service coverage ratio required in the initial bond agreement; bonds are technically in default if the ratio is below the level included in the original financing contracts.

Governments must provide ongoing disclosure materials. Bonds are traded on markets after their initial sale, and prospective buyers want information about the current financial conditions of the government. Laws require that governments provide annual updates to information about finances and any other key facts that were contained in the official statement.

Some governments organize bond oversight committees to review the progress of bond-funded projects and to help ensure that the requirements of the bond indentures are met. These committees are often composed of community members and sometimes finance experts not employed by the government. These oversight groups may review and make recommendations to the governing body about bonding practices and related matters.

## CREATIVE FORMS OF FINANCING

In addition to the forms discussed above, governments may use a variety of creative forms of financing. A leading form involves setting up a separate not-for-profit entity controlled by the government that can sell bonds to finance equipment and construction projects. This equipment and these projects are then leased back to the government, the advantage being that these entities can operate without some of the requirements that apply to government and that the principal and interest payments on the bonds do not appear on the government's financial statements.

## MANAGING FUNDS

What do governments do with the money they raise from bond sales? Capital projects can take years to complete, so there can be a significant amount of idle cash to manage carefully so that it is available when needed. Of course, other sources of operating and capital funds, such as property or sales taxes, also can produce cash that is not immediately needed.

Like individuals and private companies, governments invest money to make money. This is generally handled by the government's treasurer. The treasurer is usually guided by an adopted investment policy as well as state laws that cover which types of investments are permitted. The investment policy typically covers areas such as

- the types of funds that can be invested, such as short-term operating funds, bond proceeds, or pension funds;
- the types of investments permitted, typically including federal government securities, certificates of deposit, investment-grade obligations of other government agencies, money market mutual funds, and local government investment pools;

- requirements for diversification and maximum maturities of investments;
- requirements to consolidate all funds into a single pool to be invested;
- general objectives such as minimizing risk, maintaining liquidity, and achieving certain rates of return or yield from investments;
- standards of performance such as prudence, ethics and conflicts of interest, and delegation of authority;
- standards for safeguarding funds, including standards for authorized financial dealers and institutions with whom the treasurer will work as well as internal controls to be maintained by the government (this may include having written policies and procedures and adequate training for personnel, using wire transfers and electronic accounts to avoid the handling of physical copies of securities, and other controls); and
- reporting requirements, treasurers are required to report investment results to oversight committees and to governing boards on a regular basis.

Managing funds starts with developing a cash budget. This is a spreadsheet showing each of the 12 months of the fiscal year and when revenues are expected to be received and when expenditures are anticipated. Laying out this information for each month tells the treasurer how much money is needed each month. This helps determine how much money to invest and which maturities are needed.

The treasurer works with other government officials, often the director of finance and the controller, to make sure that the government gets all the revenue it expects.

The following are some principles of cash management:

- Accelerate collections: deposit any revenues received quickly, using devices such as bank lockboxes and wire transfers. Accept credit cards.
- Control disbursements: develop and monitor cash budgets. Pay bills as late as possible to get the benefit of investing the money, but pay soon enough to avoid penalties or interest charges.
- Consolidate balances: invest money placed in different government funds together rather than separately, by fund, to the extent possible.

## ETHICS, EQUITY, AND CAPITAL BUDGETING

Capital budgeting is where the big bucks are in government. While operating budgets may be larger in size, they are generally composed of smaller components, such as salaries of particular departments

**Box 15.1 Investment Pools and Orange County, California**

Investment pools can be advantageous to cities and are used routinely by groups of smaller cities that participate in county or state pools. The Orange County, California, bankruptcy in 1994 was a lesson in how important it is to carefully watch pools and investments in general and the dangers of assuming a particular trend in the economy and not being prepared for a downturn.

Robert Citron served as the elected treasurer–tax collector in Orange County. He managed the Orange County Investment Pool for 187 public entities (cities, school districts, water and sanitation authorities, and pension funds). At its peak the pool managed over $20 billion and got yields of 8% to 9%, in contrast to the California state treasurer's yield of 5% to 6%.

Mr. Citron achieved these yields by investing in securities whose yields were inversely related to interest rates. He borrowed more money, using borrowed money as collateral. The pool's participants welcomed the high yields and high interest income. In the early 1990s, the Federal Reserve Board increased interest rates. Mr. Citron's investments relied on interest rates going down. The pool lost significant amounts of money in 1994 and had insufficient funds to pay pool participants who wanted their money. The county declared bankruptcy on December 6, 1994.

Orange County immediately developed a recovery plan. It involved selling securities and cutting budget and staff. It was not able to come out of bankruptcy until June 12, 1996.

and purchases of office supplies. Capital budgets, in contrast, involve expenditures of thousands and often millions of dollars on construction of new highways, airports, and other public facilities. Sometimes politicians use the lure of possible work on capital projects as a way to get campaign contributions from firms that would benefit from the projects (construction firms, financial firms, etc.).

All of the issues discussed in Chapter 14, "Operating Budgets"—setting priorities, observing policies and procedures, involving the public in oversight—also apply to capital budgeting. Transparency in developing and managing capital budgets, therefore, is very important. Federal and state regulations also govern capital projects and the management of public funds. There are federal regulations against use of tax-exempt capital projects by governments for solely private purposes, such as buying a facility for a private firm. In addition, the Orange County bankruptcy case, as well as other public investment cases, has brought stricter requirements for oversight of capital fund management.

Like other types of government expenditures, there are concerns about who benefits from capital expenditures and projects. Governments have sometimes used large projects to clear sub-standard housing that is beyond the means of current residents to upgrade and without providing sufficient replacement housing. Major highway projects have cut thriving minority communities in half, causing negative financial consequences for local businesses and greatly reducing community cohesion. Because capital projects are often huge with very large impacts, it is important to consider all the positive and negative impacts in the analysis and monitoring phases of the projects.

## CONCLUSION

This chapter has discussed how the capital budget is put together and how projects are funded and managed. The capital budget process has five steps and results in a prioritized list of projects with sources of funding. Sources of funding include operating revenue, grants, tax increment financing, assessment districts, grants, and bonds. Bonds were discussed in some detail, including the typical steps taken by governments in issuing bonds. Debt through the use of bonds is the most typical means for raising revenue for capital projects. Since capital projects take years to plan and construct, governments need to manage effectively the funds they collect from bond sales and other sources.

## PRACTICING PUBLIC ADMINISTRATION

1. Why should capital expenditures be distinguished from operating expenditures in budgets?
2. What are the characteristics of capital expenditures?
3. Besides government staff, which other parties are important when issuing debt? Why?
4. What information would you need to evaluate the merits of two alternative capital projects? Which methods would you use?
5. You are a budget analyst in a small city. Your city council has listed a number of projects, and you are assigned to evaluate two of them:

   **Project A:** Modernize the convention center with improved electronics and lighting, and paint and carpet the interior. The cost is $500,000. The center manager estimates she will be able to increase fees and market the center more effectively once the modernization has been finished. The modernization will take one year.

   **Project B:** Expand the city-owned parking lot in the downtown business area. The cost is $200,000. The project will take about one year because the property for expansion needs to be purchased. This lot will increase parking revenues, but the increased revenue will be achieved in the first year of operation and will not increase much after that.

| Stream | Year | Project A | Project B |
|--------|------|-----------|-----------|
| Costs | 1 | −$500,000 | −$200,000 |
| Revenues | 1 | $0 | $0 |
| | 2 | $100,000 | $100,000 |
| | 3 | $150,000 | $100,000 |
| | 4 | $200,000 | $100,000 |
| | 5 | $250,000 | $100,000 |
| | 6 | $300,000 | $100,000 |
| Total | | $1,000,000 | $500,000 |

   Evaluate these projects, and make a recommendation to the city manager and council. The analytical approaches to be addressed are: payback periods, internal rate of return, and net present value, using discount rates of 3% and 6%.

## BIBLIOGRAPHY

Aronson, J. R., & Schwartz, E. (2004). *Management policies in local govern-ment finance.* (5th ed.). Washington, D.C.: International City/County Management Association.

Bartle, J. R., Hildreth, W. B., & Marlowe, J., Eds. (2012). *Management policies in local government finance.* (6th ed.). Washington, D.C.: International City/County Management Association.

Beckett-Camarata, J. (2003). An examination of the relationship between the municipal strategic plan and the capital budget and its effect on financial performance. *Journal of Public Budgeting, Accounting and Financial Management 15*(1): 23–41.

Block, S. B., & Hirt, G. A. (2000). *Foundations in financial management.* (9th ed.). Burr Ridge, IL.: McGraw-Hill.

Calia, R. (2001). Are public spending programs equal? Setting approaches for government budgeting. *Government Finance Review 17*(4): 18–23.

Carey, J. P., & Mucha, M. J., Eds. (2008). *Capital project planning and evaluation.* Chicago, IL: Government Finance Officers Association.

Chapman and Cutler LLP. (2016). *Municipalities in distress? How states and investors deal with local government financial emergencies.* (2nd ed.). Chicago, IL: Chapman and Cutler LLP.

Cohen, S. (2004). Governing New York City: Progressive government reforms hiding in plain view. *Public Performance and Management Review 27*(4): 67–90.

Daun, M. (2004). Managing major capital projects. *Government Finance Review 20*(3): 33–38.

Davis, T. R. (2005). Budget blowback. *Governing 18*(5): 106.

Engel, E., Fischer, R. D., & Galetovic, A. (2014). *The economics of public-private partnerships.* New York, NY: Cambridge University Press.

Fisher, R. C. (2015). *State and local public finance.* (4th ed.). New York, NY: Routledge.

Gianakis, G. A., & McCue, C. P. (1999). *Local government budgeting: A managerial approach.* Westport, CT: Quorum Books.

Jenkins, D. (2021). *The bonds of inequality: debt and the making of the American city.* Chicago, IL: University of Chicago Press.

Johnson, C. L., Luby, M. J., & Moldogaziev, T. T. (2014). *State and local financial instruments: Policy changes and management.* Northampton, MA: Edgar Elgar.

Jorion, P. (1995). *Big bets gone bad: The largest municipal failure in U.S. history.* San Diego, CA.: Academic Press.

McElravy, J., & Liang, L. Y. (2004). Debt capacity analysis for local government. *Government Finance Review 20*(5): 16–22.

Mikesell, J. L. (2007). *Fiscal administration: Analysis and applications in the public sector.* (7th ed.). Belmont, CA: Thomson Higher Education.

Miller, G. (1998). *Investing public funds.* Chicago, IL: Government Finance Officers Association.

Millionzi, K. A., Ed. (2018). *Introduction to local government finance.* (4th ed.). Chapel Hill, NC: University of North Carolina School of Government.

Mintz, J. A., & Rosenberg, R. H. (2020). *Fundamentals of municipal finance.* (2nd ed.). Chicago, IL: American Bar Association.

Pagano, M. A. (2007). Capital budgets: The building blocks for government infrastructure. *Government Finance Review 23*(3): 1–20.

Ritz, B., & McDermott, B. (2018). Ending America's public investment drought. Washington, D.C.: Progressive Policy Institute. https://www.progressivepolicy.org/wp-content/uploads/2018/12/PPI_Public-Investment-Drought_2018.pdf

Rivenbank, W. C., Vogt, J., & Marlowe, J. (2009). *Capital budgeting and finance: A guide for local governments.* (2nd ed.). Chapel Hill, NC: University of North Carolina School of Government.

Salwa, A., Duncombe, W., & Wright, R. (2001). Evaluating capital management: A new approach. *Public Budgeting and Finance 21*(4): 47–69.

Sapp, D. (2004). Estimating capital costs. *Public Works 135*(13): 38–39.

Sigal, R. L. (2020). *Shades of public finance, volume 1: Illicit bankruptcies, innovative municipal bonds and why the Patriots didn't move to Hartford.* Sonoita, AZ: Dudley Court Press.

Sigal, R. L. (2020). *Shades of public finance, volume 2: More inside stories of the municipal bonds that built America.* Sonoita, AZ: Dudley Court Press.

Srithongrung, A. (2008). The impacts of state capital management programs on state economic performance. *Public Budgeting and Finance 28*(3): 83–107.

Wood, L. (1998). *Local government dollars and sense: 225 financial tips for guarding the public checkbook.* Rancho Palos Verdes, CA.: Training Shoppe.

# 16 ──◇──◇──◇──◆

# Contracts
# and Procurement

Contracts are used by all sectors of the economy at all levels for purposes ranging from procuring supplies and equipment to hiring specialized professional staff. Typical items purchased with contracts include fire trucks, asphalt machines, office desks, and computers; typical services include systems development or engineering design and construction of major capital improvements. Contracts allow for the acquisition of goods that government does not produce or the accomplishment of work that can be performed more economically and feasibly by a contractor than by public employees.

Although the components of a government contract may be similar in nature to those used in other sectors, the governmental contracting process often includes additional steps and complexity to achieve a variety of goals that are not applicable to other enterprises. Some of these goals may appear contradictory. While the contracting process is normally designed to obtain goods and services at a fair and reasonable price to protect tax dollars, it also may have goals to maximize competition in the community, maintain procedural integrity and transparency, and accomplish socioeconomic objectives.

Some considerations when deciding to contract are ensuring that a contract does not diminish the agency's capacity to respond to emergencies, protects confidential information, does not result in reliance on a sole contractor, and does not infringe on the proper role of the government.

Contracts may be for a very short term—days or weeks—or for many years. Government agencies may work through other entities, such as the state and public authorities, to contract for goods and services to facilitate and expedite the contracting process. This chapter will explore types and methods of contracting, the process for selecting contractors, determining cost effectiveness, and administering approved contracts.

## PROS AND CONS OF CONTRACTING

There are clearly some government services that must be provided by government alone (police protection) and some for which contracts are almost always used (purchase of vehicles or equipment). However, there is also a range of possibilities wherein contracting with the private sector may be considered. During the 1980s and 1990s there was a strong push to privatize government functions, with the attendant advantages and disadvantages of contracting traditional government services.

The pros:

- potential to lower costs since direct salaries and fringe benefits are often lower in the private sector;
- ability to handle seasonal tasks, such as recreation services or snow removal, which are needed only periodically—government hiring practices may make it cumbersome to hire employees who are needed for only short periods of time;
- ability to handle specialized tasks by highly skilled professionals and technicians such as architects, engineers, and equipment repair specialists;
- greater managerial expertise and accountability for private-sector managers who work under pay-for-performance or other monetary incentives that encourage keeping up with technology and the latest practices;
- greater flexibility in private-sector staffing, which is not constrained by civil service procedures;
- new equipment in the private sector, in which there are tax incentives for purchasing new equipment; and
- mobilization of volunteers for human services, which may be contracted through nonprofit agencies (e.g., the Salvation Army) with long-standing commitments to certain communities and clientele.

The cons:

- reduction of government employment opportunities, particularly in urban areas where there may be high unemployment, where government may be the "employer of last resort," and/or where government has helped to create a middle class among its unskilled workforce;
- management of the contracting process, which is complicated and requires skills that may not be developed in the contracting agency;

- contracting of personal services, which adversely affects employee morale and may cause labor unrest, particularly if it results in layoffs or reduced employment opportunities;
- reduction in direct government control, making it more difficult to respond to citizen complaints;
- contracting for personal services, which may limit the ability of government to develop in-house capabilities in key areas; and
- excessive dependence on sole providers of services, which can result in higher costs and problems if a contractor goes out of business.

When governments make the decision to contract there are important considerations to keep in mind.

## CONSIDERATIONS IN THE PROCUREMENT PROCESS

The following are some of the concerns in the process of procuring goods and services through contracts:

- Quality: Organizations need to specify exactly what they want to purchase. This may mean developing a detailed list of desired features (or specifications) in a new police vehicle or transit bus or a detailed scope of work for an architect hired to design a new building. To ensure they get what they want, organizations also need to develop acceptance standards and performance measures.
- Cost: Organizations increasingly want to consider all of the costs of a purchase, including the initial acquisition cost, operating costs, and disposal or replacement costs. Considering only the initial cost may open the organization up to purchasing an inexpensive copier, for example, that needs significant ongoing maintenance and needs to be replaced sooner than a more expensive model.
- Risk: Purchases of goods and services entail some risks for organizations. Organizations may inadvertently depend too heavily on the contractor to provide goods or services that turn out to be unsafe, opening the organization up to possible lawsuits by users. Contracts may also be politically risky. They may be driven by public sentiment or fear rather than by analyses of needs and abilities.
- Competition: Public-sector procurement attempts to consider all possible sellers so the organization can get a good product or service at a fair price. This usually involves seeking *bids* or *proposals* (defined below) from two or more suppliers.
- Integrity and Transparency: Organizations develop processes to help them deal with suppliers fairly and in good faith so that they

may remain impartial and avoid any appearance of conflict of interest.

- Public Policy Objectives: Some organizations incorporate public policy objectives into procurement by, for example, giving preference to local businesses.

## WHO IS RESPONSIBLE FOR CONTRACTS?

As the preceding list illustrates, contracts may be used in all government operations. Purchasing may be assigned to finance or administrative departments, to a specialized department, or be decentralized throughout many departments. Centralized purchasing is often used to achieve economies of scale in obtaining goods and warehousing. It may also facilitate more efficient salvage/resale activity, and personnel who deal primarily in contract development and administration may be more familiar with the ins and outs of the process than someone who primarily has other tasks. Other types of contracts (noted below) are normally handled by the functional department and often require authorizations by a central agency or elected officials for the budget and/or for the contract itself. Since contracts are legal documents, they usually must also be approved by attorneys. Agencies often assign contract administrators as the individuals responsible for the process.

In Chapter 1, we noted that a significant amount of public work is provided by America's emerging *shadow government:* nonprofit and for-profit organizations that provide a wide range of public services and goods. Managers often must weigh the advantages and disadvantages of using personnel and resources outside of government to accomplish a policy objective. In addition, managers are more and more challenged to integrate their in-house efforts with those of contractors. Some common practices and issues are described below.

## TYPES OF CONTRACTS

There are a wide range of goods and services that are contracted for by governments. They range from small items such as office supplies to large construction projects such as building schools and highways. Similarly, highly skilled experts and lower-skilled maintenance crews may be under contract with governments depending on the jurisdictions' specific needs. The diversity of uses is extensive. Below are some typical contracting situations.

### Purchasing Contracts

Governments typically contract for commodities or tangible goods such as supplies and equipment. Purchasing contracts are also used to acquire vehicles, construction equipment, office equipment, supplies, and fuel.

## Personal Services Contracts

Contracts with private individuals and firms are used to obtain services that cannot be provided by regular staff or that can be provided more economically or feasibly by contract because: (1) the work is very specialized and the current civil servants lack the expertise; (2) the work is of an emergency or temporary nature, and it is not practical to hire permanent staff; (3) the work must be provided by individuals with proprietary knowledge of a system or piece of equipment or with independence (e.g., to perform audits).

Many personal service contracts are for professional, scientific, expert, or technical work. It is common for agencies to contract with systems specialists to design, implement, and maintain major technology programs; with individuals or firms for specialized engineering design; with individuals or firms for specialized legal services; with bond counsel; with real estate experts; and so forth. However, services such as security, maintenance, and temporary skilled and unskilled labor (e.g., construction forces or tree trimming) are also contracted.

## Labor Contracts

Contracts with employee groups within the governmental unit are unique forms of contracts developed and processed quite differently than other contracts, particularly in agencies operating under state or local labor laws. These are discussed in more detail in Chapter 11, "Managing Human Resources."

## Construction and Repair Contracts

Construction of major capital infrastructure projects such as roads, police or fire stations, libraries, and parks is often provided by contract, as are smaller-scale improvements, remodeling, and repairs. Equipment repairs or supply of parts in which a manufacturer is an exclusive agent is often provided by contract.

## Intra- and Intergovernmental Contracts

Intergovernmental relationships are implemented through contracts, sometimes in the form of memoranda of understanding (MOU) or memoranda of agreement. Grant contracts are some of the most common forms and are discussed in more detail in the following chapter. Other government contracts may involve the sharing of services or facilities. For example, counties may provide a variety of services to smaller cities within their jurisdictions, such as police or fire protection, or two jurisdictions might share a crime lab or provide forms of benefit reciprocity. All of these functions require some form of contractual arrangement.

## Concession Agreements

Government agencies that engage in enterprise operations often contract with private merchants for operations that are not typically provided by government but are on government property. Examples include food services at parks, zoos, or airports, and golf course management.

## Real Property Lease and Purchase Contracts

Contracts are used to lease and rent property for office space or other facilities and for realty services related to the sale or purchase of government property.

## Franchises

Agencies may grant franchises, which are implemented through contractual agreements, for the construction and operation of transportation, communication, and utility services. Common franchises include taxicab, cable television, power distribution, oil and gas pipelines, and bus services. These contracts allow a particular company exclusive privileges to operate within a particular jurisdiction, usually for an extended time period.

## Patented Articles Contracts

Contracts are required to utilize patented or copyrighted items or sources such as computer software or security devices (e.g., badge systems).

# PROCUREMENT METHODS

Each of the types of contracts described above can be negotiated in a number of ways, depending on the laws of the jurisdiction and the type of goods or services being obtained. There are a number of mechanisms used, including competitive bidding, sole-source contracts, and cooperatives. These are defined and discussed below.

## Competitive Bidding

A competitive effort ensures that all interested parties are provided an opportunity to participate in the process, encouraging competition between contractors and suppliers. It is typically used for commodity procurement contracts, standard construction contracts, general supply contracts, and routine service contracts where licensing requirements can be used to determine minimum acceptable qualifications and where differences in quality of goods are not a major factor. Competitive bidding is common when there are many parties with the potential capability to provide the commodity or service.

The objective of competitive bidding is cost savings, better product quality and reliability, and timely delivery. These are possible because

competitive bids typically contain exact requirements and specifications as well as clearly identified cost and delivery schedules for goods
and services.

The concerns associated with competitive bidding are that it may
be time consuming, may result in less flexibility for government action,
may jeopardize quality if specifications are inadequate, and may have
high administrative costs associated with preparing, disseminating,
and evaluating the bids.

The requirement that a contract be awarded to the lowest responsible bidder may limit the administrator's capacity to select the person
or company with the best experience or ability to perform tasks and/or
provide specified products. Bids based on a company's lowest-priced
product to meet the specifications can result in lower quality and lead
to change orders (contract revisions) during the life of the contract that
may increase the price.

A variation of open and competitive bidding is the competitive
sealed proposal method, which allows negotiations after proposals
have been received to allow clarifications of and changes in the proposal but still requires the final proposal to have the lowest ultimate
cost compared to any other responsive proposal.

What does it mean to award a contract to the lowest responsive and
responsible bidder? A responsive bidder is one whose bid responds to
all of the questions in the bid specification document (to be discussed
below), and a responsible bidder is one who can meet all of the requirements. For example, a bidder who does not furnish information about
the principals in the firm that will be doing the work or whose price
does not cover all of the elements of the project is not responsive. A
bidder who lacks the staff, who has not had experience in the type of
project described in the announcement, or who has a history of complaints about contract completion is not responsible.

Competitive bid contracts allow an agency to reject all bids if that
is to the advantage of the agency or to reject the bid of a bidder or
proposer who has previously failed to satisfactorily execute a contract. Bidding opportunities must normally be advertised in a form that
reaches the largest number of potential bidders, such as publication in
a daily newspaper. Other requirements may include furnishing bid or
performance bonds or affidavits of non-collusion.

Competitive bids have limitations and may not always be the best
mechanisms for securing goods or services. In these cases, other procurement methods are used.

## Limited Competition

Contracts for the performance of professional, scientific, expert, or
technical services of a temporary or occasional nature typically use a
modified form of competition to provide the opportunity for an agency

to evaluate qualitative factors such as experience and competence to perform a task and when quality rather than price is a key element. Contractors are normally solicited through a request for proposal (RFP) or request for qualifications (RFQ).

## Sole-Source Contracts

It is not always feasible to engage in a competitive bidding process. Although sole-source contracts are discouraged and often raise public concern, the following are examples of situations in which sole-source contracting may be allowed and appropriate:

1. when continuity and accountability in professional services (such as those of an architect) are necessary, when it is necessary to continue a project to completion, and when the underlying contract was awarded to a firm through a competitive process;
2. when only one company or person has the specific skills or knowledge to perform the work;
3. when contracting with other governmental agencies;
4. when there is only one manufacturer or authorized distributor for equipment or replacement parts;
5. when a critical patent or copyright is involved;
6. when the contract is determined to be of urgent necessity to preserve life, health, or property (e.g., demolition or construction after a disaster); and
7. when the cost of a bid/RFP would be excessive compared to the cost of the contract.

## Blanket Contracts

These arrangements are used for small purchases such as occasional office supplies or are managed with purchase cards (similar to debit cards). They are negotiated for a maximum amount, and once they are in place users can use petty cash or credit cards for the actual purchases.

## Cooperatives

Several governments may form a cooperative to obtain lower prices through volume discounts, to lower administrative costs, to increase competition, and to create more favorable terms and conditions. Governments may also join cooperatives to enhance services where there is jurisdictional overlap and/or where there are costly systems or capital costs required for implementation. For example, local 911 services or crime labs are opportunities for cooperative agreements between adjacent cities or between cities and counties.

As mentioned in Chapter 15, "Capital Budgeting," governments may form private, not-for-profit entities composed of only one or more than one jurisdiction. These entities can purchase equipment and contract for services without complying with normal government contracting guidelines.

## Piggybacking

The piggybacking approach uses contracts negotiated by other agencies or governments to meet a local need. An example is when a state negotiates computer hardware and software contracts and makes a list of qualified firms (including the prices as well as terms and conditions) available to lower levels of government within the state.

## STEP-BY-STEP GUIDE TO CONTRACTING

There are several basic steps in a contracting process irrespective of the procurement method. These include the following:

1. planning for the contract or procurement,
2. developing and releasing the solicitation document,
3. evaluating bids or proposals,
4. negotiating and awarding the contract, and
5. managing the contract.

### Step 1: Planning for the Contract or Procurement

The jurisdiction's strategic plan and annual operating budget form the basis for contract or procurement planning. They outline the government's goals and specific actions to meet objectives. They often translate the actions into specific contracts and bids that are needed during the fiscal year. In addition to the analysis that takes place during budget formulation, analysis is needed to prepare for specific contracts and bids.

*Determine the Scope of Work.* It is important to determine exactly what type of work is needed. Does the jurisdiction need to purchase desks and computers? Does it need to ask an independent consultant to evaluate its user fees and suggest possible increases? Does it want to build a new sports arena? Which of the contractor's staff will be required to do the work? Does the government have a right to approve use of particular staff? Administrators and managers responsible for particular functions such as engineering, finance, and other areas generally work together to specify the type of work needed in great detail. For routine and standard purchases, the government's purchasing staff may have specifications for purchases and related equipment; for nonstandard purchases, staff needs to create exacting specifications that will need the agency's needs.

*Determine Whether There Is a Need for An External Provider.* For equipment and supply purchases, the obvious choice is to purchase from a major supplier. Ideally major suppliers have sufficient quantities available and can offer products at lower prices. There are more choices when it comes to professional services. Alternatives are providing the service in-house, contracting out, leasing, or privatizing (i.e., giving up the function to the private sector entirely).

For procurement of equipment or supplies, either a central procurement office or an operating department may make the purchase. In either case consider inventory records to determine whether items can be obtained from existing stock or whether a request can be bundled with similar purchases throughout the organization to obtain volume discounts. Also carefully identify supply sources and determine if there are opportunities for cooperative purchasing.

For personal services, determine whether the service is normally provided by the agency or is a new service, if this has not been analyzed during budget formulation. Facility maintenance and security services are examples of services that might be provided both by an agency and by contract, depending on location and staffing level demands.

A determination should be made about whether it is more practical to hire additional staff or to contract. This review should evaluate:

- whether there are employees with the expertise to perform the work;

- whether employees who have the expertise are available to perform it within the time required;

- whether hiring new employees for a limited duration would result in layoffs at the completion of the project;

- whether a contractor has the proprietary knowledge needed;

- whether the need is for a long or short term (a longer-term need may indicate that additional government staff should be hired);

- whether the service is central to the mission of the organization (if it is, it may be beneficial to provide the service through government means and to build capability in-house to provide the key service); and

- whether a reliable pool of potential contractors exists (sufficient competition will be to the government's advantage in keeping costs low).

*Conduct a Cost-Benefit Analysis.* For purchases of equipment, life cycle costs should be evaluated to determine if purchase or leasing is more cost effective. Availability of funds may also enter into this analysis; although purchase may be less expensive in the long run, leasing may be the more practical alternative if funds are scarce in a particular fiscal year.

For personal services, it is important to evaluate whether it is less expensive to use existing staff or to contract out. This can be a complex process. It requires a comparison of the contract cost with that of the government agency resources/personnel. This means that the cost of each agency position that could do the work must be identified, including salaries and appropriate overhead rates. The more challenging part can be determining which overhead costs to include. Direct benefit costs, such as employer-provided insurance benefits and pensions, are usually applicable. More problematic are overhead costs such as services provided by other department staff (e.g., accounting, or human resources) and their office equipment and utilities, since these may or may not be required depending on the scope of the contract. If the contract is for a short duration, then the calculations must be prorated for the appropriate time period. The analysis is not always clear-cut and may be a subject of debate with bidders or labor unions whose members are affected by the contract. A sample form for a contract cost analysis is exhibited as Tables 16.1 and 16.2. An outline of how a cost-benefit analysis is conducted is discussed in Chapter 15, "Capital Budgeting."

*Determine Whether Budgeted Funds Are Adequate.* Are there funds available for contractual services in the agency budget, or is a separate appropriation required? Funding may come from the operating budget or capital budget. If it comes from the operating budget, there may be a line item in the budget for contracts without specific contracts itemized, or alternatively, each contract may need to be requested, justified, and approved as part of the annual budget process or through an interim budget adjustment.

*Notify Affected Unions.* If there is a labor component to the proposed contract, there may be a requirement that the agency notify unions that represent current employees when proposals are solicited or before the contract is finalized. The typical concern of the unions is that contracting out will eliminate union-represented jobs or diminish promotional opportunities. If the unions object, following notification, the contracting department may be required to negotiate (meet and confer) before the contract is finalized. (The specific requirements of this process are discussed in Chapter 11.)

*Review and Apply Laws, Policies, and Procedures.* Charters, ordinances, and procedures manuals specify basic requirements, such as competitive bidding requirements for types of contracts or for contracts of a specific duration or dollar amount. They identify entities or persons with authority for approving and executing contracts and the amount and duration of the authority. For example, a department head or governing commission might have approval authority up to $25,000 or $100,000 and/or for a contract not to exceed 3 years. Contracts above a monetary threshold or for a longer duration may require approval by a manager and/or a specified level, a mayor, or a legislative body. Attorney approvals are usually required as part of the final contract execution.

**Table 16.1　Contract Cost Analysis: Part 1**

| Department: | Contact Person: |
|---|---|
| Division/Section: | Phone: |
| | Email: |
| **Work To Be Performed:** | **Contract Start and End Dates:** |
| | __/__/____　to　__/__/____ |
| **Type of Contract:** | **Source of Funds:** |
| New _____　　Amendment _____ | If amending, indicate amount of original contract and all prior amendments: $_____ |

**Cost of City Forces Required to Perform Proposed Contracted Work**

a. Positions Required / Salary and Overhead Costs

| A | B | C | D | E | F | G | H |
|---|---|---|---|---|---|---|---|
| Position Title | Number in Position | Monthly Salary | Total Monthly [B × C] | Overhead Rate [per month] | Benefit Costs [monthly] | Duration (months) | Total [(D + E + F) × G] |
| | | | | | | | $ |
| | | | | | | | $ |
| | | | | | | | $ |
| | | | | | | | $ |
| | | | | Total Salary and Overhead Costs: | | | $ |

| | |
|---|---|
| b. Other Pertinent Nonpersonnel Costs (list) | |
| | $ |
| | $ |
| Total of Other Pertinent Nonpersonnel Costs: | $ |
| c. Total Estimated In-house Costs (lines a + b above) | $ |
| d. Total Estimates of Revenue Generated by City Forces (if applicable) | $ |
| e. Net In-house Costs (line c – line d) | $ |

*Incorporate Special Social, Economic, and Environmental Requirements.* Agencies may have special requirements of all contractors, of only firms of a certain size, or concerning awards exceeding a specified dollar amount. Examples are nondiscrimination policies, outreach to minority-owned businesses or small businesses, and the requirement that firms pay their employees a living wage or provide domestic partner benefits and child care to their employees. Living wage requirements entail the payment of salaries above minimum wage and may also include the provision of health insurance and compensated time-off benefits. Preference may be given to contractors that use businesses within the political jurisdiction. There also may be restrictions on contractors' business with operations in certain countries (e.g., South Africa and Darfur in the past). For some purchases, there may be preferences for companies that use recycled products or engage in environmentally conscious programs. Some contracts may require a review

**Table 16.2   Contract Cost Analysis: Part 2**

**Contractor Labor Costs and City Cost to Administer the Proposed Contract**

a. Total Proposed Contractor Labor Costs   $ \_\_\_\_\_

b. Total City Contract Administration Costs (Total Pay + Overhead)   $ \_\_\_\_\_

Calculation of Total Pay and Overhead Costs:

| A | B | C | D | E | F | G | H | I |
|---|---|---|---|---|---|---|---|---|
| Position Title | Number of Positions | Hourly Pay (per position) | Estimated Average Number of Hours per Position per Month of Contract | Total Monthly Wages Cost [B × C × D] | Administrative Overhead Rate* (*Table 16.1) | Monthly Benefits Cost [B × D*] (*Table 16.1) | Duration [months] | Total [E + F + G) × H] |
| | | | | $ | $ | $ | | $ |
| | | | | $ | $ | $ | | $ |
| | | | | $ | $ | $ | | $ |
| | | | | | | Total Pay + Overhead Costs:: | | $ |

c. Other Contract Costs (list)

$ \_\_\_\_\_

$ \_\_\_\_\_

Total of Other Contract Costs:   $ \_\_\_\_\_

d. Total Proposed Contract Costs (a + b + c)   $ \_\_\_\_\_

e. Total Estimated Revenue Generated by Contractor   $ \_\_\_\_\_

f. Net Cost of Contract (d – e)   $ \_\_\_\_\_

of the environmental impacts and associated mitigation measures and costs. The contract administrator must include these provisions in any bid/proposal and recognize that it might disqualify some potential bidders/proposers.

*Decide on the Type of Solicitation Document.* There are several types of solicitations.

- *Requests for Bid* (RFBs) are used in open and competitive selection processes when price is the only factor (after bidders meet specified minimum performance requirements).

- *Requests for Proposals* (RFPs) are usually used for professional services when price is just one factor and is evaluated along with the experience of the proposer and the quality of services.

Two other forms of solicitation may be used.

- Request for Quotation (RFQs) are often used to establish a list of vendors and their prices for specific goods or services. Once the list has been reviewed and approved, departments or agencies in the jurisdiction can place orders for those goods or services without having to go through a bidding process for each order.

- Requests for Information (RFIs) are less commonly used but help government agencies and departments develop specifications, particularly in preparation for contracting for complex technology or engineering projects. RFIs may be followed by either RFBs or RFPs when the exact work desired can be specified.

## Step 2: Developing and Releasing the Solicitation Document

After the planning process has been completed there are several steps needed to prepare and release the solicitation document. The discussion below is representative of the process but may vary by jurisdiction and by agency.

*Prepare the Document.* After planning is completed, the government's purchasing department or appropriate department will prepare the RFB or RFP or RFI.

RFBs may include the following:

- design specifications, spelled out in writing, often in great detail;
- physical characteristics or features of a piece of equipment;
- performance requirements (speed or other functionality);
- brands, models, or other quality indicators;
- logistical requirements such as when and where delivery should take place;
- maintenance requirements by the vendor;
- packaging requirements (e.g., environmentally friendly); and
- payment schedules (e.g., at project milestones).

RFPs, especially those for professional services, typically include the following:

- introduction/background;
- desired qualifications/capabilities of proposers—both firms and the individuals that will be providing the service (i.e., experience as well as financial and organizational capacity);
- references, including professional/customer references and financial references;
- detailed description of project/services needed;
- deliverables, such as the product or service;
- project schedule/deadlines;
- intellectual property requirements;
- constraints such as security requirements;
- evaluation process, including a description of each factor to be used and the weight of the factors;
- responsibilities of each party (office space or preparation of part of the work), insurance, and indemnification;

- administrative requirements (forms and reports);
- description of how to submit the proposal and a response format;
- cancellation and amendment procedures;
- protest process—description of the protest process if there are disputes over the selection process;
- standard contract provisions such as breach of contract, nondiscrimination/Americans with Disabilities Act compliance, workers' compensation and liability insurance requirements, indemnification (not holding the government agency legally responsible for certain actions by the contractor), bonding requirements, discount terms, business tax registration (if applicable), and so forth; and
- payment provisions (advance payments may be appropriate in some cases; interim payments are common for lengthy and complex service contracts and are often based on acceptance of deliverables; there may be retention provisions in which a percentage of each payment is withheld until acceptance of the final deliverable; final payment is provided after a product or work is delivered, tested, inspected, and or installed).

*Release the RFB or RFP.* Once the solicitation document is completed it must be communicated. It may be mailed to potential bidders/proposers and/or published in newspapers, in trade journals, or on an agency/department website (e-procurement). Some governments may accept bids and proposals online. The government may also notify local chambers of commerce and conduct a pre-proposal or pre-bid meeting to explain the scope of work and allow smaller firms to meet larger firms and answer questions from the bidders.

Project managers may be asked to anticipate subcontracting opportunities in their RFPs or RFBs and help with outreach to smaller businesses that can subcontract. During this solicitation process, provisions should be made to respond to inquiries by telephone and/or email. It is important for fairness to provide the same access to information to all potential bidders/proposers. This usually means limiting the number of people who can be contacted directly to answer questions distributing answers to all questions to all parties, and refusing to meet privately with bidders/proposers. Not following rules such as these can mean that the entire procurement process must be invalidated and redone.

## Step 3: Evaluating Bids or Proposals

Evaluating bids or proposals is a part of the process that is often subject to scrutiny and controversy. It is essential that the evaluation be fair and impartial without the appearance of favoritism or political influence. Proposals should be evaluated against the criteria stated in the RFP and fully documented. Ideally, several evaluators should participate in the process, using a form with numerical values attached to the criteria. Each evaluator should come up with an independent score, and then a summary document should be prepared to justify the final recommendation. The Multi-Attribute Utility Technique is one example of a multifaceted approach to decision making (see Chapter 9).

Interviews with all of the proposers (if there are only a few bidders/proposers) or more commonly the top three to five finalists are often used as part of the evaluation process, particularly for professional services. Interviews allow the evaluators to ask questions and clarify the responses in the written proposal and for the proposers to elaborate on the written document. The evaluators may be required to ask the same questions of all proposers to help ensure equitable treatment. The interviews are valuable tools for evaluating the qualifications and credibility of the key individuals identified to do the work.

## Step 4: Negotiating and Awarding the Contract

Contract documents are typically developed by the government's legal counsel in whole or in part. Operating departments may write the scope or statement of work, with the attorney contributing standard clauses such as insurance requirements and indemnification.

Many RFP/RFB processes allow for negotiation after the initial proposals are received but before the contract is finalized. It is important for the negotiator to have sufficient technical knowledge to understand each side's position and be able to prepare a thorough cost and price analysis. Negotiators should understand how much competition exists for the good or service; more competition places the agency soliciting the service at an advantage, while less competition helps the bidders. Finally, all issues (terms, conditions, prices, quantities, payment schedules, and liabilities) must be identified.

Preparation of the final contract involves incorporating most of the information from the RFP/RFB with any modifications resulting from the negotiations. The document should be carefully reviewed by appropriate supervisors and legal counsel before submission to the individual or body authorized to approve it. An accompanying report to a commission, mayor, administrative office, or city council may be required to explain and justify the contract. Any applicable waivers of standard requirements would be considered at this point.

Sometimes firms or individuals may protest the contracting process in cases of very competitive situations or allegations of irregularities during the process. Those responsible for the process should be prepared to justify their actions and decisions in a public forum.

Final execution of the contract involves obtaining the signatures of the principals authorized to sign on behalf of the contractor and agency, including legal counsel, and filing the contract with the appropriate department, such as a controller's or city/county clerk's office.

## Step 5: Managing the Contract

Managing the contract includes monitoring costs, timeliness, and quality as well as paying the invoices submitted by the contractor. It is important to ensure that all parties are meeting their responsibilities for adhering to the budget and schedule, producing deliverables of expected quality, dealing with change orders (if applicable) and contract disputes, and ensuring timely and appropriate payment. Generally, governments appoint a contract or project manager who is charged with enforcing all sections of the contract.

*Payments.* The contract administrator may receive several requests for payment during the contract period, in accordance with the payment schedule outlined in the contract document. Some governments use their websites, with password access, to allow vendors to track the processing of their invoices. For personal services contracts, the hourly billings and expenses should be carefully scrutinized to ensure they are appropriate and not padded by the contractor (e.g., with items such as research or training of their own staff and travel or administrative expenses that were not agreed to in the contract). Final payment should occur only when all deliverables have been received, terms and conditions have been met, and the administrator is satisfied that the product or service is complete and of appropriate quality.

*Subcontractors.* Large contracts are rarely handled by just one contractor. A prime contractor may hire specialist firms or subcontractors to handle parts of a project requiring specialized expertise. For example, a general engineering firm may hire another firm with expertise in seismic engineering to assist in building a new city hall. A firm doing a study of how to improve community acceptance of a new program may hire a specialized survey research firm to conduct a community survey. Opportunities to subcontract on a larger project give owners of small and minority firms a chance to build their businesses, and the contract may require that subcontractors be small businesses and/or minority owned.

Even if there are subcontractors, the government's contract is with the prime contractor. The terms and conditions also apply to subcontractors. In some cases, the government will approve changes in subcontractors. The prime contractor is responsible for managing the subcontractors, including approving their work product and paying their invoices. The government, however, should monitor this process and be aware of any problems so that subcontractors do not impede progress on the work and are paid by the prime contractor.

*Independent Contractor Status.* It is important to determine whether a personal service contractor is truly independent or has the characteristics of an employee. While employees may be hired on contract, independent contractors must meet certain requirements identified by the IRS in its Employer's Supplemental Tax Guide (publication 15-A; see http://www.irs.gov/publications/p15a/index.html). An employer must withhold income taxes and pay Social Security and Medicare for employees but is not required to do so for independent contractors. The Tax Guide contains a lengthy list of characteristics that identify an independent contractor. Employers who violate these rules may be subject to penalties for failure to withhold the taxes. Some states have more stringent rules on who can be classified as an independent contractor.

Contract administrators should be careful about independent contractors hired for long-term projects or projects that are extended, especially those who work on the employer's premises and who become subject to their rules and financial control. Such individuals may start off as independent contractors, but their status may change and cross the line into employee status if contract administrators are lax in monitoring the contract provisions.

*Final Evaluation or Closeout.* Some agencies require a closure document when all requirements are met. Closure may include packaging and archiving all documents and sending a formal letter notifying the contractor of completion of the contract along with the final payment. This document may be used to evaluate the vendor's performance for future consideration on contract awards.

## SPECIAL CIRCUMSTANCES

### Considerations in Construction Contract Management

Generally, the contracting process for construction projects is not different from the process outlined above. One difference, however, is that the procurement may be divided according to major phases of construction: design and construction. Another difference is how the payment terms are structured in the contract. The following are several major types of payment methods:

- Fixed Price/Lump Sum: The organization sets a not-to-exceed price for the project with a contractor who is at risk for going over the price. Some exceptions or leeway may be specified.

- Time and Materials: The contract pays for billed time devoted to the project and materials required, sometimes with a not-to-exceed amount specified.

- Cost Plus: This method is similar to time and materials but allows explicitly for a profit to be paid to the contractor.

There are several ways to manage a major capital project:

- Design/Build: The contractor handles both the design and the construction phases of the project. This may be controversial for public-sector projects because it allows fewer opportunities for other contractors, but can shorten the time it takes to complete the project by starting construction before every detail of the projects has been designed.

- Project Management: The organization contracts with a project management firm to oversee the work of the organization's staff and its other contractors. Alternatively, the organization itself handles the project management and other tasks with its own staff, contracting out only specialized design and construction phases to contractors.

Construction contracts of any type may include incentives for completing projects ahead of schedule. These incentives usually take the form of small percentage increases to the total cost, perhaps 10%. The objective is to address two key complaints about public projects: that they are too costly and not timely. Therefore, contract incentives serve to reward timeliness while keeping costs under control.

## Small Purchases

While this chapter has focused on procurement requiring contractual arrangements, governments purchase a variety of goods and services without contracts for items involving small dollar amounts, such as occasional office supplies or parking reimbursements. Small purchases may be made from vendors on a list resulting from an RFQ without having to get bids from several vendors. Governments may use petty cash or purchase cards (debit cards issued by banks) for these purchases. Strong controls on access to these funds or cards and on the dollar limits are essential. There is also middle ground between this approach and a formal contract, sometimes known as an authority for expenditure. These accounting documents are intended for single transactions in which there is no discretion, such as travel expenses, phone bills, or training expenses.

# ETHICAL AND EQUITY CONCERNS

As explored in Chapter 4, "Ethics," contracting is often a focus of ethics lapses, investigations, and reforms. This is a process wherein conflicts of interest are most evident and troublesome. Bids, RFPs, and other means of sharing information described in this chapter are designed to protect against bias and favoritism and ensure transparency. However, regardless of how diligent administrators and public officials are in adhering to these processes, there is no totally foolproof, unbiased mechanism, and government agencies remain vulnerable to

ethics violations because there is always some subjectivity and judgment involved in making these critical decisions. While bids may be
considered the most objective approach because cost is the only evaluation factor, there is still a potential for price fixing.

Bribes to favor certain contractors, kickbacks, collusion, and price
fixing by contractors as well as undue influence by politicians are
examples of what can go wrong and jeopardize the public trust. The
contracting process continually raises the ethical dilemma of balancing transparency with efficiency. Complaints by both the participants
and the public of inadequate information and/or inordinate delays are
commonplace. Being aware of these issues, having clear policies and
procedures, communicating them through training, and ensuring that
everyone is following the policies are steps that may help to prevent
problems. An internal audit, in which the process is evaluated after
contracts have been completed, also promotes integrity in developing
and sustaining ethical contracting and procurement processes.

Many local governments have an interest in promoting diversity
and equity in contract awards. These interests may be formalized in
a policy to award as many contracts as possible to businesses located
within the government's boundaries. To do this, the government may
discount the local contractor's bids on potential contracts so they are
awarded more points in an evaluation process. In analyzing their use
of local businesses, some governments have recognized that relatively
few contracts have been awarded to these businesses. Regular analysis of contract awards helps identify these patterns. To promote use of
local businesses and encourage them to bid on contracts, some governments conduct active outreach efforts to identify and educate the businesses on the process.

**Box 16.1   Example of Process—Parking Meter Contract**

Maple City has been using coin-operated parking meters in its city-owned
parking lots for decades. Recently the city's administrators have noticed articles
in industry publications about meters that can be paid using cell phones or credit
cards rather than coins. In researching this new technology, Maple City's traffic
engineers found that users of the new meters in other cities are very satisfied
with the change, that the cities' staff and managers feel that the meters are easier
to maintain, and that other problems, such as collecting and handling coins, are
eliminated. Maple City's engineering department has included the transition to
new meters in next year's budget.

Working with the purchasing department, Maple City's engineers develop
a set of specifications for the new meters based on their research and information from other cities. They determine that they should use an RFP that will allow
them to purchase the meters for a fixed price and use company consultants to

install the meters and train city staff to maintain them. The RFP sets milestones for the contractor's work and states that payments will be based on achievement of certain milestones, such as delivery of equipment, installation, completion of testing, completion of training, and final acceptance. The city intends to hold back 10% of each payment to ensure completion, and it requires a completion bond in case the company selected cannot complete the work.

Maple City receives three proposals from companies with experience installing meters of this type. Each company, though, recommends using a different type of meter. Maple City assembles a committee to evaluate the proposals; the committee is composed of the city engineer, a representative from finance, a representative from maintenance, a representative from the city manager's office, and the chief traffic engineer from a city using another type of meter. The committee reads each proposal, interviews each proposer's staff, and views demonstrations of the meters. It also checks references provided by the proposers and uses directories of professional associations to find other references. Other departments verify each company's insurance information and forms as well as their attempts to include minority- and women-owned businesses in the work. Based on their analysis, the committee recommends to the city manager and city council that one company be selected and awarded a contract.

As the company completes the contracted work, a manager in Maple City's engineering department serves as the project manager. She has daily contact with the company and receives and reviews status reports. She communicates with the city engineer and with an oversight committee. She receives invoices from the contractor, determines whether the work is complete, and approves payments. Upon completion of the project, she prepares a formal report to the city manager and council that includes an evaluation of the contractor's performance and a recommendation to release the amount retained.

# CONCLUSION

As mentioned at the beginning of this chapter, requirements are sometimes included in contracts that do not specifically relate to the work of the contract but that satisfy other socioeconomic objectives of governments. Preferences for or outreach to local businesses, requirements that contractors maintain certain human resources policies, or prohibiting contractors from certain business relationships can add to the complexity of the contracting process, discourage bidder participation, reduce competition, and increase the costs of goods and services. However, to the extent that government has broader social goals—to expand opportunities to underrepresented groups, stimulate the economy, and improve the community—reducing the efficiency of the contracting process may be considered a reasonable price to pay to advance its civic agenda.

## PRACTICING PUBLIC ADMINISTRATION

1. You have been assigned the task of determining whether your department should enter into a contract to relieve the backlog of tree-trimming work. Your agency currently performs tree-trimming work with existing employees, and they are represented by a union. What are the issues? How do the issues affect the contracting process?

2. You have been assigned the task of developing a contract to purchase specialized equipment used by street-cleaning crews. What are the likely costs and benefits?

3. Your city wants to expand its convention center to bring in larger conventions. It is considering options for structuring the construction contract. What are the advantages and disadvantages of each major type of procurement approach that the city manager might wish to consider?

4. Review your local government's contracting practices, which should be available on their website. How do they encourage equity in contracting?

## BIBLIOGRAPHY

Brown, T. L., & Potoski, M. (2003). The influence of transactions costs on municipal and county government choices of alternative modes of service provision. *Journal of Public Administration Research and Theory 13*(4): 441–468.

Brudney, J. L., Herbert, E. T., & Wright, D. S. (1999). Reinventing government in the American states: Measuring and explaining administrative reform. *Public Administration Review 59*: 19–30.

Chi, K. S., & Jasper, S. (1998). *Private practices: A review of privatization practices in state government.* Lexington, KY: Council of State Governments.

Curry, W. S. (2016). *Contracting for services in state and local government agencies* (2nd ed.). New York, NY: Routledge.

Curry, W. S. (2016). *Government contracting: promises and perils.* (2nd ed.). New York, NY: Routledge.

Dekel, O. (2008). The legal theory of competitive bidding for government contracts. *Public Contract Law Journal 37*(2): 237–268.

Hefetz, A., & Warner, M. (2004). Privatization and its reverse: Explaining the dynamics of the government contracting process. *Journal of Public Administration Research and Theory 14*(2): 171–190.

Osborne, D., & Gaebler, T. (1992). *Reinventing government: How the entrepreneurial spirit is transforming the public sector.* Reading, MA: Addison-Wesley.

Potoski, M. (2008). State and local government procurement and the Winter Commission. *Public Administration Review 68*: 58–69.

Savas, E. S. (2000). *Privatization and public-private partnerships.* New York, NY: Chatham House.

Shick, R. A., Ed. (2015). *Government contracting: A public solution handbook.* New York, NY: Routledge.

Warner, M. E., & Hebdon, R. (2001). Local government restructuring: Privatization and its alternatives. *Journal of Policy Analysis and Management 20*(2): 315–336.

# 17 ◇——◇——◆

# Grants

In 2020, during the first year of the COVID-19 pandemic, the U.S. Department of Health & Human Services allocated $726.1 billion in awards along with an additional $263.7 billion in Coronavirus Aid Relief & Economic Security (CARES) funds. Funding was allocated for a variety of programs including direct payments to the public, unemployment, funding to state and local government agencies, along with research funding to the private sector. One of the many mechanisms for getting billions of dollars into the economy was the extension of massive federal grants. While some federal funds flow into an area once a disaster has been declared by the state's governor, other funding was allocated using *grants*.

This chapter defines and discusses what a grant is—its historic roots and partisan politics—and the administrative tasks associated with developing, writing, and administering grants. Economic recovery depends not only on spending billions of dollars but on the efficient, timely, and effective implementation of programs that will employ millions of workers, provide classrooms, and reduce the nation's dependency on oil imports, among other policy objectives. *Cooperative federalism*, which relies on grants, is the practice of moving revenues from taxes, tariffs, and fees derived often from the state's residents and business and reallocating the funds back to state and local governments for priorities the current federal administration deems most worthy.

## WHAT IS A GRANT?

Grants are one of the sources of revenue for governments. A grant is an award of financial assistance from one agency (the grantor) to a recipient agency (the grantee) to carry out a public purpose. It transfers spending power from one level of government to another and sometimes from a government to a nonprofit, tribal government, or business.

Grants may make up for disparities between regions of the United States that have dissimilar resources for raising revenue from taxes or other means. They may encourage particular types of programs. Grants usually come with specified requirements from the grantor. The donor government or organization may require particular types of management, staffing, or service delivery as well as special record keeping.

There are several major types of grants. *Categorical grants* finance specific programs. They may have a matching or "maintenance of effort" requirement that requires the recipient government to pay a portion of the total program cost or continue a specified level of spending so the grant supplements rather than replaces a preexisting level of support. Categorical grants can be complex to administer and, because of these requirements, may duplicate other programs and/or distort local priorities. *Block grants* are usually distributed to recipient governments based on a formula such as population with certain income levels. In contrast to categorical grants, these grants are designed to finance programs in broadly defined areas and give the recipient government some discretion in funding particular programs. Grants can also be classified by whether they are discretionary or entitlement grants. *Entitlement grants* award funds depending on a general indicator such as population or number of aircraft flights. *Discretionary grants* usually require a government to apply for funding for specific projects. There are also hybrids of the above types of grants. Examples of each are described in this chapter.

Grants are distinguishable from other forms of intergovernmental fund transfers. They are not benefit entitlements, such as Social Security, GI Bill veterans benefits, or government pensions, which are entitlement programs through which government benefits are earned by individuals through service on a job or in the government. They are also distinguished from another type of entitlement relationship between government jurisdictions that involves no application process and is based on a formula. For example, the state of California has entitlement relationships with school districts in the state; its school districts are entitled to 40 cents per dollar of all revenues for kindergarten through grade 12 education. Similarly, localities are entitled to sales tax monies for local public transportation. The localities do not get this money by applying for it but are entitled to the money based on the school-age population enrolled and attending classes, the gross sales that take place within a given jurisdiction, the general population of the area, and so forth.

Governments may act as both grantor and grantee agencies. Grantors provide funds, and grantees are the recipients of the funds. In the United States, the primary grantor agency is the federal government, although state governments may also be a source of funds. Today, about 32% of local government funds come from state and federal governments, while 30% of state revenues come from nonstate proceeds. As of 2021, the five states with the highest total federal funding were: California ($43.61 billion), Texas ($26.90 billion), Florida ($23.77 billion), New York ($22.06 billion), and Virginia ($17.68 billion).

Since the focus of this book is local government, the emphasis of this chapter will be the agencies seeking and receiving federal or state grants and the process for obtaining and administering such grants. The process is similar to that used by those seeking grant funds from local governments, such as nonprofit agencies that receive grants to construct or operate facilities or implement programs on behalf of governments.

## BACKGROUND

Federal grants have a long history and are an instrument of federalism, as described in Chapter 1. During the 19th century, grants, financed from sales of public lands, were used for roads, education, and forest fire protection. Those early grants were donations without federal supervision or matching requirements. Public assistance grants began during the depression of the 1930s with work relief and public works projects. Grant activity slowed during the Second World War and then accelerated during the 1950s, particularly for highway construction. In the 1950s, grants amounted to less than 20% of state/local revenues.

Anti-poverty programs of the 1960s resulted in a tremendous growth in categorical grant activity, that is, grants approved for very specific activities or programs. By the end of that decade there was a backlash against the increasing number of grants and the complexity of the process by which categorical grants were awarded. In 1972, during the Nixon administration, the concept of grants changed. Congress enacted revenue sharing using formulas based on population and income in an effort to redistribute federal funds to the states without the burdensome control of the categorical grant process. Because the objective was to return more control to the states, most of these unconditional grants went directly to state governments, without requirements that funds be passed through to local governments. Nevertheless, through specific formulas a considerable amount was made available to local governments. This experiment was short-lived because Congress did not want to give up control and relinquish its ability to earmark funds to satisfy political objectives.

As the 1970s progressed categorical grants began to give way, in part, to block grants, which consolidated specific grants into broader categories and gave more discretion to states and local governments. Community Development Block Grants (CDBGs) and housing grants are two of the more established categories of block grants. When the money was placed in the CDBG system, communities thought they were getting the same amount of money but fewer restrictive regulations. When the CDBG grants came through, Congress bundled a wide range of programs together with roughly the same requirements but reduced the funding. A CDBG is both a grant and an entitlement. It is not a competitive grant in the same sense as a categorical grant for a specific purpose, which requires competition for each project. However, CDBGs have a need-based formula and an annual application/ renewal process. The program is discussed in more detail in a following section.

Some of the grants administered by the U.S. Department of Homeland Security have evolved into block grant/categorical grant hybrids. The Urban Areas Security Initiative program distributes blocks of federal funds to groups of metropolitan areas that are deemed to be at highest risk for terrorist attack. Within the group of high-risk metropolitan areas, individual cities and their surrounding urban areas compete for a portion of the group's block of funds. The federal funds are awarded based on an analysis of each urban area's risk (risk being determined by threat, vulnerability, and consequences) and the effectiveness of that urban area's proposed use of the grant funds. The State Homeland Security Grant Program distributes federal funds to all 50 states using a minimum allocation formula set by statute and a competitive process that takes into account the risk and effectiveness scores for each state's grant application.

According to the U.S. Government Accountability Office (GAO), Department of Homeland Security (DHS) grants are the federal government's primary tool for enhancing state, local, and tribal governments' emergency preparedness and response capabilities. The DHS grants risk-based awards to assist state, local, tribal and territorial efforts in preventing, protecting against, mitigating, responding to, and recovering from acts of terrorism and other threats. In 2021, there was $1.2 trillion available for grant programs for preparedness activities, including planning, organization, equipment purchase, training, exercises, and management and administration across all core capabilities and mission areas.

## POLITICS OF GRANTS

The battle over the appropriate level of government to control grants changes depending on which party is in control of the White House and Congress. Republicans have tended to favor less federal supervision and more delegation of spending discretion to state and local governments, consistent with a party philosophy of less federal government control. Therefore, Republican-controlled congresses have given higher priority to the creation of block grants. Democrats have favored more detailed, federally supervised spending, in the form of categorical grants. However, there have been exceptions. During the Democratic administration of President Bill Clinton, congressional Republicans were successful in getting presidential support for the transfer of responsibility for welfare programs from the federal government to the states. The Personal Responsibility and Work Opportunity Reconciliation Act (PRWOR) of 1996 ended the 61-year-old program of Aid to Families with Dependent Children, which was a federal guarantee of welfare support to mothers and children. PRWOR substituted welfare block grants to each state as opposed to individual grants to households. It also put another federal child care program into the block grant form: the Child Care and Development Block Grant. These welfare block grants gave states flexibility in how they provided for welfare but retained some federal restrictions on welfare recipients (e.g., a 2-year limit on welfare without working and a 5-year lifetime limit for benefits). In addition, Congress required that the states spend 75% of what they had previously been spending on welfare to be eligible for their full share of PRWOR federal dollars. Although the pendulum has shifted back and forth over the years, today welfare services are paid for using a combination of block and categorical grants.

## PROS AND CONS OF GRANTS

Money received from grants is money that governments and/or nongovernmental agencies do not need to generate through taxes and fees. While grants are a valuable source of funds to state and local governments, there are disadvantages to accepting these funds. Aside from specific conditions in the grants themselves, federal grant programs have led to other forms of control over states and localities through *cross-cutting* requirements in which a condition of one federal grant is extended to all activities supported by federal money regardless of the source. The Civil Rights Act is an example; it extends nondiscrimination requirements to all activities receiving any level of federal support. A related form of federal control is *crossover sanctions* which force the implementation of federal requirements in one area or the recipient will risk losing money in another, generally similar area. For example, states may lose highway grants if they fail to follow certain health or safety requirements imposed by the federal government.

Unfunded mandates are another disincentive to localities for accepting grants. Whenever the federal government gives money through grants (e.g., highway funds, education programs), there is a dollar amount awarded and an output or outcome specified. However, sometimes Congress wants something done but does not want to pay for it. In the opinion of Congress, communities ought to be implementing certain policies without federal money. For example, the Clean Air and Clean Water Acts are federal policies that require localities to have plans for protecting the air and water. In some cases, the federal government has funds for catastrophic events such as a major oil spill in Alaska or a nuclear meltdown at Three Mile Island. However, for the design and development of ongoing standards and programs, Congress specifies which plans and practices local government must have to comply with the Clean Air and

Clean Water Acts but does not fund any efforts. Instead, Congress with-holds federal highway money or community redevelopment money until environmental plans and means for enforcement are in place. This policy of "do the federal bidding but don't get a cent for the effort" is called an *unfunded mandate*. These unfunded mandates are tied to federal grants, and consequently many communities balk at taking federal grants and then having to incur expenses for a range of programs and policies that are imposed but not federally funded. The conventional wisdom is that federal money is many things—but free is not one of them.

## WHO IS ELIGIBLE FOR GRANTS?

State and local governments, cities, special districts, school districts, institutions of higher learning, public housing authorities, and nonprofit organizations with 501(c) status with the IRS, as well as small businesses, are eligible for a wide variety of federal grants. Grant categories are numerous: arts, business, community development, disaster prevention and relief, education, employment, energy, environment, health, housing, information technology, legal services, natural resources, public safety and homeland security, regional development, social services, and trans-portation are only some of the categories of services for which grants are available. As of 2020, there were 900 grant programs offered by 26 dif-ferent grant making agencies. Some public policy areas, such as disaster relief and recovery, receive both state and federal government grants.

In state and local governments, there may be entire programs or departments funded by grants, such as those that administer CDBGs or housing grants. More commonly there are specific programs within departments that are primarily supported by local tax dollars but with categorical grants providing additional services. Examples are crimi-nal justice or homeland security grants to police departments and clean water grants to sanitation agencies. The following section describes CDBGs, one of the oldest sources of block grant funds, and how these funds are distributed.

## COMMUNITY DEVELOPMENT BLOCK GRANTS

The Community Development Block Grant Entitlement Program was originally authorized by the Housing and Community Development Act of 1974, Public Law 93-383, and has been amended several times by Congress. In 2010 funding was cut in half, but since then Congress has continued to fund this effort as a general block grant to state and local governments. CDBG seeks to provide decent housing, a suitable living environment, and expanded economic opportunities for all Americans. There are three national objectives: (1) benefiting low- and moderate-income persons, (2) preventing or eliminating slums and blight, and (3) meeting urgent needs.

The rules governing the grant are contained in the Code of Federal Regulations, and the program is funded through the federal Department of Housing and Urban Development (HUD). The HUD *Guide to National Objectives and Eligible Activities for Entitlement Communities* states that public service programs include, but are not limited to, child care, health care, job training, recreation programs, education programs, fair housing, public safety, senior citizen services, services for homeless persons, drug abuse counseling and treatment, energy conservation counseling and testing, homebuyer down payment assistance, and welfare (excluding income payments).

HUD funds are awarded annually to eligible grantees as follows. Metropolitan cities with populations of at least 50,000 and qualified urban counties with populations of at least 200,000 (excluding population-entitled cities) are eligible. The funds are awarded based on a formula that uses objective measures of community needs including the extent of poverty, population, housing overcrowding, age of housing, and population growth lag in relationship to other metropolitan areas.

Each year each eligible grantee must submit a Consolidated Plan (Con Plan) to apply for its CDBG entitlement grant, which covers four grant programs:

- CDBG,
- HOME Investment Partnerships,
- Housing Opportunities for Persons with AIDS, and
- Emergency Shelter Grants.

The grantee must identify its goals in the Con Plan, which is used by HUD to evaluate the plan's performance. The Con Plan also requires certifications that not less than 70% of the CDBG funds received over a 1-, 2-, or 3-year period will be used for low- and moderate-income persons and that the grantee will further fair housing efforts and enforcement. The Con Plan must be consistent with the National Affordable Housing Act.

The program requires citizen participation by persons of low or moderate income, particularly from slum and blighted areas. The grantee must:

- hold public hearings to obtain citizen views, respond to proposals and questions, and review performance;
- provide public access to local meetings, information, and records about the use of the funds;
- allow written complaints and grievances and provide timely written answers; and
- accommodate participation by non-English-speaking residents at public meetings (U.S. Department of Housing and Urban Development; www.hud.gov/).

The eligible local entities in turn distribute and monitor the funds. The entities that receive the funds are grantees. Subrecipients, sometimes called subgrantees, are provided with CDBG funds by a grantee for their use in carrying out agreed-on eligible activities. The grantees and subgrantees may contract with others to deliver programs. The following types of activities may be eligible for funds:

- acquisition of real property;
- rehabilitation of structures—residential and nonresidential;
- construction of public facilities and improvements such as neighborhood centers, water and sewer facilities, and streets;
- energy conservation; and
- assistance to businesses in creating jobs and carrying out economic development efforts.

CDBG funds cannot be used to acquire or construct general government buildings, to construct new housing by local governments, or for any political activities. Figure 17.1 demonstrates the flow of funds from the time Congress appropriates the money to HUD through a range of conduit public agencies to program providers and beneficiaries.

# A STEP-BY-STEP GUIDE TO APPLYING FOR COMPETITIVE GRANTS

Local governments apply for competitive categorical grants in addition to the funds they receive under block grants. The following section describes the process for obtaining these grants. As mentioned in the preceding chapter, a grant award is a type of contract. It spells out the responsibilities of the grantor and grantee, the work to be done, funding, and reporting requirements. The following sections describe how a grant contract is developed and implemented. Specific requirements may vary by grant, and applicants must pay close attention to the format required by the grantor.

## Develop the Proposal

*Step 1: Get Ready.* Check the sources within the agency to determine who has authority to negotiate, approve, and execute grants. These sources may be contained in a charter, ordinances, administrative codes, or procedures manuals. They will specify the officials who may approve grant awards, such as a mayor, city or county manager, or legislative body. They may also stipulate that different officials or bodies have approval authority for grant awards up to a specific dollar amount or for a specified time period.

In addition to approval of the actual grant contract, there may be requirements that the grant proposal be reviewed before a department

**Figure 17.1    Flow of Federal CDBG Funds to Local Providers and Beneficiaries**

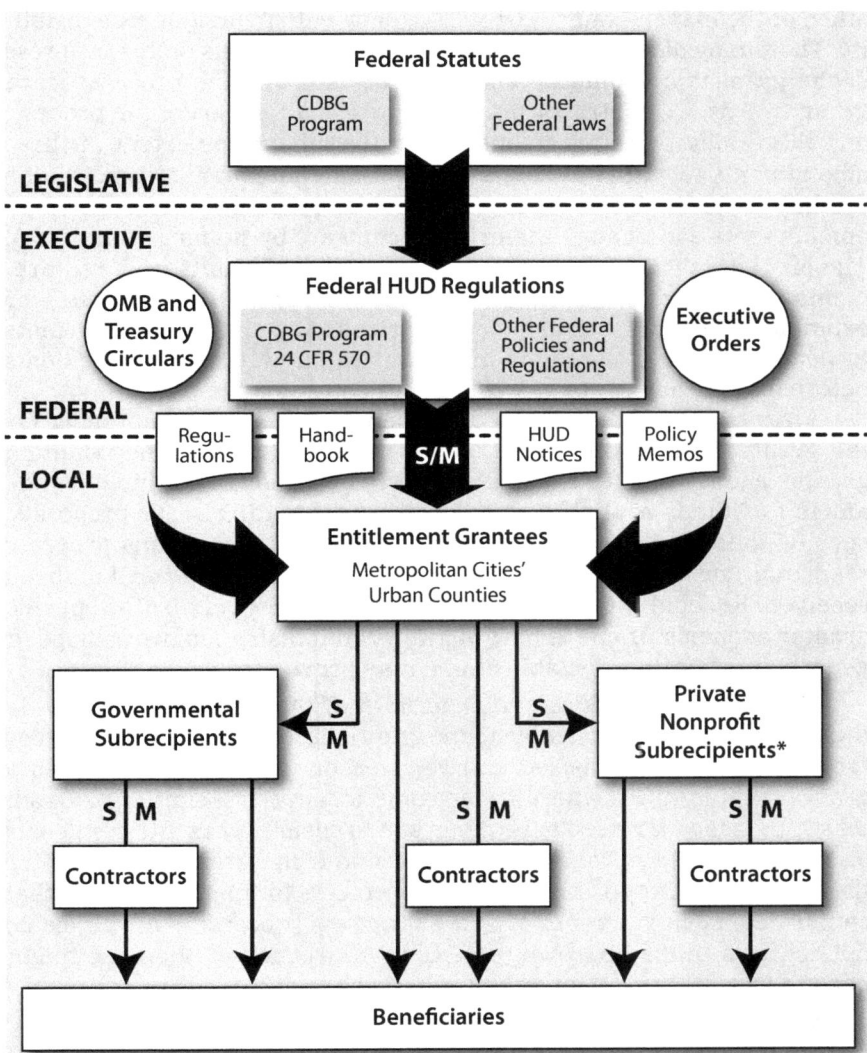

Abbreviations:
CDBG = Community Development Block Grant     OMB = Office of Management and Budget
HUD = Housing and Urban Development          CFR = Code of Federal Regulations
S = funds provided                           M = monitoring required
*includes §204(c)(2), for-profit community-based development organizations.

Source: U.S. Department of Housing and Urban Development. (2005, 8-7).

enters into negotiations or submits a proposal to a grantor agency. Thus, the department interested in the grant may be required to submit documentation and recommendations regarding the grant proposal to an office of the mayor, council, or staff agency with oversight responsibility. There may also be internal reporting requirements on the progress of the grant that should be known before starting the process. Since grant awards are contracts, amendments are often part of the process, and there may be requirements about the amount or extent of these amendments (e.g., that a single contract amendment can increase the funding level by 25% annually or that the cumulative amount of all amendments can change the original contract by no more than 50%). The procedures may also exempt certain types of grants from requirements or specify a different process for different types of grants—for example, a city engineer may be authorized to execute all amendments to a clean water grant. It is important to know these requirements before making any contacts with potential grantor agencies.

After understanding the requirements of the agency applying for the grant, the next step is to obtain information from the potential grantor agency about its requirements. This information includes the amount of funds available, deadlines for submitting grant proposals, specific guidelines for submitting applications, and various progress reporting and financial reporting required once the grant has been received. Recognize that the forms and procedures vary by the specific grantor agencies. If one is new to grants administration, workshops or general information available online may prove useful.

*Step 2: Develop Ideas and Determine If the Grant Is Feasible.* Is the grant feasible and saleable to the granting agency? Find out whether the idea has been proposed and rejected or whether it duplicates a grant being done elsewhere in the same locality. If a similar program exists, the idea may need to be reworked to ensure it has different goals or an innovative approach. Also determine if the grant is feasible for the recipient agency. If there are requirements for matching funds that cannot realistically be met or if the grantor's processing deadlines do not conform to the approval process in a jurisdiction, then one might need to look elsewhere or rethink whether the grant is practical.

*Step 3: Develop Community Support.* Explore whether there are political, academic, or professional groups within the community that are willing to advocate for the grant-funded project. Letters of support describing community commitment are particularly persuasive to grantor agencies when the grant is providing a service to the community (e.g., funding a health clinic, senior citizen center, or youth center). This process may require several months of effort. Some grantors require agreements between agencies to share resources, such as office space. Meeting with top decision makers and community leaders may be necessary as part of the mobilization of community support.

*Step 4: Obtain Program Requirements and Funding Information.* Once a potential grantor agency is identified, contact the agency and get to know the personnel who are responsible for processing the application. Request a grant application kit, carefully review all of the grant and application requirements. Some grantors allow sending a proposal summary requesting initial review; others will only accept complete application packages. Seek suggestions for improving the application or meeting the eligibility requirements to determine if the original concept needs to be modified. Be aware that there may be requirements such as services to particular client groups or involvement of specific institutions that may cause the grant to be impractical. If the grantor agency provides an unfavorable response to this initial review, the requirements are too onerous, or funds are unavailable, ask the grantor to recommend another agency that might be a better source of financial support.

If a decision is made to proceed with the grant proposal, carefully watch the deadlines, which are usually strict and not negotiable. There may be multiple deadlines within a fiscal year.

*Step 5: Write the Proposal.* Carefully review the grant application kit to ensure that all required components are included and are in the required sequence and are in the required format. Applications with missing or incomplete sections may be summarily rejected. When writing the various sections be aware that the application is often divided among several individuals for review; one person rarely reads the entire application. Some information may need to be duplicated in different sections of the proposal to ensure the reviewer has the information they need in the section they review. There are generally eight components to a good grant proposal:

1. Summary and outline of goals
2. Description of the organization
3. Problem statement
4. Project objectives
5. Project methods
6. Project evaluation
7. Future funding
8. Budget

*1: Summary and Outline of Goals.* A brief two- or three-page summary, in the form of a cover letter, is the best approach to outlining the project goals, getting the attention of the grantor agency, and making a good first impression. It could be the only part that is carefully reviewed before a decision is made to consider the project any further. It is often most useful to write this portion after the rest of the proposal to ensure it covers all of the key points. Identify how the funds will meet local needs and the influence the project will have both during and after the funding period.

*2: Description of the Organization.* Most proposals require a description of the organization that will be completing the project. Identifying the key administrators, the organization's goals, and its track record with other grants helps establish the applicant's credibility. Brief biographies of the key staff members may also be provided and/or required. Changing key personnel identified in the grant often requires the grantor's approval.

*3: Problem Statement.* Areas to cover in the grant proposal include the following:

- the purpose of the proposal,
- who will benefit,
- the nature of the problem (supported with evidence such as census or statistical data),
- how the organization became aware of or involved in the problem,
- what is currently being done,
- what will happen when the funding is exhausted, and
- how funding resources will be used.

Historical, geographic, statistical, and philosophical information is relevant to a well-crafted needs assessment.

*4: Project Objectives* Outcomes of the project should be measurable, verifiable, and relatable to the problem statement. If the program is funded, these objectives will be used to evaluate the progress of the program, so they should be realistic. A program for supervision of elementary children may eventually result in higher high school completion rates, college attendance, and self-sufficiency; but those outcomes can't be measured until several years after the supervisory program was implemented. However, in the short term it could foster greater parent involvement in school activities and perhaps better attendance rates among the targeted youth population.

*5: Project Methods.* Methods refer to activities that will occur and the resources and staff needed to accomplish the project. A Program Evaluation Review Technique (PERT) diagram or flowchart might help to describe the project steps and where personnel and support services are needed. For example, the diagram might show the number of staff required, a description of the daily operations, and what the project is expected to produce, such as the number of clients served. Specifics about PERT and flowcharts are found in Chapter 10, "Project Management."

The specific course of action should be described in the narrative and should identify the associated expenses. It is important to consider the time and money required for implementation. Whenever possible, highlight the features of this project that distinguish it from other proposals under consideration.

Appendices should be used to provide supplementary data and references and to avoid detracting from the readability of the proposal. Timetables, work plans, schedules, methodologies, technical specifications, legal papers, and letters of support are examples of documentation that should be included in appendices.

6: *Evaluation.* Project evaluation addresses how the project will meet its objectives, and process evaluation addresses the effectiveness of the activities in the action plan. This section should include a description of how the grantee will measure achievement of the program objectives. It is strongly suggested that the agency applying for funds submit an evaluation plan at the start of the project to identify the data that must be collected before and during the grant period. However, it is not always feasible for the agency to provide an impartial assessment of its own efforts. Agencies might partner with local colleges and educational institutions with research capabilities to assist in meeting this requirement of the granting agencies. Sometimes a pilot study is needed to begin the identification of facts and relationships that support the grant proposal.

Evaluations may be conducted by internal staff or an outside firm. The applicant should state the timetable, how the feedback will be communicated among the proposed staff, and a schedule for review and comment.

7: *Future Funding.* Identify resources for sustaining the program effort after grant funds have been expended. For example, if the grant is for construction, the agency must be able to provide funding for maintenance, equipment, and possibly for staffing the facility once it is built.

8: *The Budget.* Budgeting is a critical part of the process. The availability of funds in federal assistance programs changes annually, and understanding what has been available in the past is useful.

A grant is rarely the only source of funds for a project. An agency may need to commit to providing a percentage of the project by using new or existing personnel and resources such as work space, office equipment/supplies, and vehicles. This percentage is called "the match" and may consist of a *soft match* and/or *hard match*. Soft matches are usually in-kind services that do not require additional appropriation of money but are already authorized and may be used for the grant program, such as supervisory staff, office space, and utilities. A hard match is typically earmarked local funds specifically dedicated to the joint effort. In either case, the match is a share of the program that the local agency is required to contribute to the intergovernmental effort. The match helps stretch limited grant dollars, helps promote the success and sustainability of the program, and is a measure of community support and organizational capacity. In a multiyear program the matching requirement may be phased in, for example, ranging from 10% for the first year to 50% for the fifth year.

If new staff must be hired, then the budget should consider the possible need for additional space and equipment. If space must be rented, insurance may be required. Salaries should be reasonable; that is, grant-funded personnel should not cost more than those funded by agency funds. Some grants include *maintenance of effort* rules. That is, the agency seeking the grant must continue to fund and maintain the existing level of service and not use (federal) grant funding to substitute for the (state/local) agency funds. In these situations, it is usually the purpose of the grantor to provide net new value over and above the level traditionally funded by the agency. Equipment should be consistent with that allowed by the grantor. If matching funds are required, the contributions of the applicant and grantor should be identified in the budget plan to the grantor. It is important to consider both the implementation and phase-down costs. Do not fail to include costs for leases, audits, systems development, accounting, expenses for utilities, administrative supplies, fuel, and salary increases for personnel. If an indirect cost rate applies, it should be prepared and used according to guidelines contained in the federal OMB Circular A-87, *Cost Principles for State, Local, and Indian Tribal Governments* at https://www.whitehouse.gov/wp-content/uploads/legacy_drupal_files/omb/circulars/A87/a87_2004.pdf

Some grantors may impose limits on the amount of indirect cost that can be charged. Be sure to identify any such limits that may apply to the grant the agency is seeking.

A good budget provides justification for each expense consistent with the proposal narrative and with the government-wide circular requirements applicable to the federal program (see Catalogue of Federal Domestic Assistance, www.grants.gov ).

Three Office of Management and Budget (OMB) circulars provide budgetary, audit, and administrative guidance for recipients of federal grants.

- OMB Circular A-87, *Cost Principles for State, Local, and Indian Tribal Governments*, establishes principles and standards for determining eligible costs;
- OMB Circular A-102, *Grants and Cooperative Agreements with State and Local Governments*, explains administrative requirements; and
- OMB Circular A-133, *Audits of States, Local Governments, and Nonprofit Organizations*, explains audit requirements.

The federal government recognizes that state and local government agencies incur both direct costs and indirect costs when operating federally sponsored grant programs. Direct costs are typically the actual personnel required to carry out the programs. Indirect costs (also called overhead) are expenditures that are related to executing the grant program but are not exclusively or primarily dedicated to the program, such as motor pools, computer centers, general accounting, purchasing, and personnel administration.

Before the development and publication of OMB Circular A-87, federal grantors often did not pay the costs of providing the indirect support services necessary to carry out grant programs. The OMB circular defines "cost principles" for federal grant programs and states that federally assisted programs should bear their fair share of total allowable cost, both direct and indirect, except where prohibited by law.

It is vital to remember that a grant budget must be consistent with federal cost principles and must include estimated indirect costs based on a cost allocation plan (CAP), as defined and described in OMB Circular A-87, if the grantee intends to bill the grant for indirect support costs.

A grantee may be required to submit a CAP for review and approval by the oversight federal agency or may be required to simply maintain its CAP on file, available for review by federal auditors. A CAP must be certified by a high-ranking financial officer of the grantee, such as the chief financial officer or controller. The certification must include statements by the grant recipient agency that all costs included in the agency's CAP are allowable in accordance with OMB Circular A-87, all costs in the CAP are allocable to the federal grant based on a beneficial or causal relationship, the same costs have not been treated as both direct costs and indirect costs, and similar types of costs have been accounted for consistently.

There may be laws pertinent to specific grants that limit the amount of administrative or indirect cost allowed by that grant program. This information will be available from the federal agency administering the grant. The general principles in OMB Circular A-87 state that "amounts not recoverable as indirect costs or administrative costs . . . may not be shifted to another Federal award, unless specifically authorized by Federal legislation or regulation."

Federal agencies are required to report their efforts to Congress and consequently want local agencies to utilize funds efficiently, effectively, and in a timely manner. Delays in implementation are often met with reduction of funding support by federal agencies.

## What to Do if the Grant Is Not Approved

If the grant is not approved, several avenues are open. The applicant may be able to appeal the grantor's decision and ask for reconsideration, perhaps after providing additional information. The government can look for other grants, which might require rethinking the project's design and revising the application. The government can also look for other funding, such as its own tax revenues and debt. Without funding, some projects may need to be postponed, redesigned, or abandoned.

## Administering the Grant

Once the grant has been approved, a number of steps are required to satisfy most grant requirements. These involve establishing strong fiscal controls, careful monitoring, and detailed record-keeping. Grantees (and subgrantees) are audited or monitored annually. Audits consist of two types: financial and programmatic. Financial audits investigate accounting systems and requirements, and programmatic audits focus on the program's efforts and the population served. Being prepared requires a clear audit trail, as described in the following steps.

***Step 1: Track Program Progress.*** Develop simple periodic reporting forms to ensure that timetables are met, services provided, clients served, and results achieved as promised by the grantee. It is important to retain accurate intake sheets so the monitoring agency can verify the program is providing the services as stated in the grant award agreement.

***Step 2: Establish Accounting Controls to Distinguish Allowable Costs.*** The cost of a federally supported program comprises the allowable direct costs of the program plus its allocable portion of indirect costs. OMB Circular A-87 establishes principles and standards for determining costs applicable to grants, contracts, and other agreements with state and local governments. A checklist can be used to prepare for a financial audit visit. The grantor will normally provide a specific list of what is expected in advance of an audit. The key to success is to have all of the administrative documentation in place from the beginning of the program year. Consequently it may be useful to have the audit checklist at the outset while designing the implementation effort rather than waiting for the postaudit review at the end of the grant period.

***Step 3: Monitor Expenditures.*** Three practices for monitoring spending are the following:

1. Separate funds (and accounts) in the agency's accounting system to track revenues and expenditures. Federal funds may be disbursed on a reimbursement basis for actual expenses after they are incurred, which requires having backup documentation for payments to vendors and others.

2. Identify and designate a specific person to prepare required financial and program reports that must be completed on a regular basis.

3. Verify records for proper justification of expenditures, following rules and regulations. These records will be the focus of grantor auditors.

*Step 4: Understand and Use the Procurement Procedures Required by the Grant.* The procurement procedures may include requiring competitive bids for goods or services, or may require some purchases to be from GSA-approved vendors. Review Chapter 16, "Contracts and Procurement," for descriptions and definitions of contracting practices. The grantor might not reimburse the grantee (or may require repayment) if the grant's required procurement procedures are not followed.

*Step 5: Ensure the Grant Funds Are Spent.* Having separate accounting and reporting requirements for the grant ensure that the grant funds are being spent properly and expeditiously. Delays in implementing projects may jeopardize receipt of approved funds or continuation of grant projects. Consequently, localities may assign budget analysts and monitors within the accounting or finance department to assist agencies in meeting special federal or state reporting requirements and in monitoring accounting transactions associated with grant money.

*Step 6: Provide Periodic Reports and Respond to Audits.* In addition to the expenditure monitoring described above, grants require that recipients report regularly on expenditures and on progress toward achieving the project goals and objectives. Producing these reports often requires considerable effort by recipients since tracking these measurements may not be part of the recipient's regular management-reporting system. In addition to regular reports, federal auditors often visit recipients to conduct more in-depth studies of grant funding. Working with the auditors can be a time-consuming task for the recipient agency.

# HYPOTHETICAL CASE STUDY OF INSUFFICIENT GRANT FUNDING

A major city is experiencing an increase in domestic violence calls handled by its police department. Three years ago, the number was 50 per month, and it grew to 71 and 82 calls in subsequent years. The police chief is concerned that officers have little training in handling these calls and that there are few local nongovernmental agencies that can help meet demand for counseling of this type. The city's health department, which has experience with grant applications and funding, is asked to design a counseling program that will both offer counseling to victims and provide training to police officers. The program will cost $2 million over 2 years to cover salaries of staff, office space, and training materials. The state grants for these types of programs require a 25% local match. The city can either meet the match through a budget allocation (hard match) or use in-kind services (soft match), depending on the specifications outlined by the grant. The city defines its goals (reducing domestic violence calls to its police department by 10% in 2 years) and develops an action plan, which calls for a 2-year pilot program. It applies for the grant but tentatively receives only half of the grant funds it believes are needed to implement the program. The city must decide whether to accept the grant and increase its match or abandon the program because sufficient matching resources are not available.

Are the benefits of using external funds worth the city's efforts?

## ETHICAL CONCERNS

Ethics issues arise in the grants process in connection with the rules of grantors for the use of their funds. This chapter discussed in depth the issue of grants between government agencies and concerns about the strings (reports, matching funds, procurement policies) attached to federal funds provided to local governments. The sometimes onerous task of complying with grant-reporting requirements may pull scarce resources away from other tasks. Deciding to offer grant-supported services may also distort local government priorities by placing funded programs ahead of other community needs.

Grants between government agencies and private agencies raise even more ethical concerns.

Whether these issues are political or ethical may be open to debate, but many would argue the concern is principally an ethical one. Prime examples are federal policies regarding grant funds for family planning, abortion, and stem cell research. There have been significant changes from one federal administration to another that are based on strongly held beliefs, which may underscore the view that there is no single, universally held set of values in the country. Ethical questions may arise when religious organizations receive federal funds to provide public services such as day care, food distribution to the needy, or medical services. Should these program providers and recipients of federal funds be allowed to refuse to provide services that violate their religious convictions, such as family planning services at their health clinics? Similarly, should religious grantees be permitted to engage in discriminatory employment practices toward persons of different religious affiliations, which would be illegal in a public or secular organization? These are questions that raise both ethical and legal challenges when local governments seek and secure outside funds.

As federal and state grant funds become scarce in periods of economic hardship, ethics issues arise when governments accept grant funds from corporate entities. Corporations may be expected to finance programs or studies that serve their interests—but may or may not serve the public interest. For example, the federal government has a public interest in food and drug safety, and its agency, the Food and Drug Administration (FDA), has regulatory and oversight functions. There is concern that the FDA cannot adequately oversee and evaluate research conducted by private pharmaceutical companies that have a self-interest in the findings of the research and in the FDA's approval process. Likewise, public universities that have typically received research funds from the government are relying more heavily on corporate funds, which have agendas related to what is most important for their markets. Does this distort the public agenda? Perhaps there is a need to establish standards for accepting private money for public purposes, but where the lines should be drawn is a daunting task.

## CONCLUSION

This chapter has provided an overview of a very complex subject. Although many public administrators encounter the need to apply for a grant or use grant funds for a project here and there, grants administration is a specialty. Some administrators will make an entire job or career out of grants administration, becoming experts in the field of grant development and management. They will need to acquire more in-depth knowledge of the myriad of rules and regulations promulgated by the many grantor agencies. These specialists serve as staff resources for operating-department personnel who apply for and receive individual grants to supplement their programs.

## PRACTICING PUBLIC ADMINISTRATION

1. An agency is seeking grant funds to assist in reducing crime, particularly to fight gang activity. Which steps should be taken to obtain these funds?

2. Suppose an agency is writing a grant application for a new after-school program. What are examples of local contributions to the grant?

3. An agency has been provided grant funds but has not spent them according to the plan. What steps should agency staff take to address this problem?

## BIBLIOGRAPHY

Brewer, E. W., Achilles, C. M., & Fuhriman, J. R. (2005). *Finding funding: Grant writing and project management from start to finish*. Thousand Oaks, CA: Corwin Press.

Bunce, H. (1979). The Community Development Block Grant formula: An evaluation. *Urban Affairs Review 14*: 443–463.

Carter, C. (2003). *How to write a grant proposal*. Hoboken, NJ: John Wiley.

Collins, B. K., & Gerber, B. J. (2006). Redistributive policy and devolution: Is state administration a road block (grant) to equitable access to federal funds? *Journal of Public Administration Research and Theory 16*(4): 613–632.

Government Accountability Office. (2008). *Homeland security, DHS improved risk-based grant programs' allocations and management methods but measuring programs' impact on national capabilities remains a challenge*. GAO-08-488T. Washington, D.C.: Government Printing Office.

Hall, J. (2008). Assessing local capacity for federal grant getting. *American Review of Public Administration 38*: 463–479.

Logan, C. (2004). Politics and promises. *Governing 17*(10): 10–12, 14–15.

Preston, M. (2007). Wanted: Grant writers: Without earmarks, local must seek other funding sources. *American City and County 122*: 2, 26.

Rectanus, K. (2007). Grant-winning plans: Early measures of grant process is the key to success. *American City and County 122*: 5, 28.

Ruskin, K., & Achilles, C. M. (1995). *Grant writing, fund raising and partnerships: Strategies that work!* Thousand Oaks, CA: Corwin Press.

Stone, A. (2003). Housing advocates are seeing red. *Journal of Housing and Community Development 60*(3): 19–33.

U.S. Department of Housing and Urban Development. (2005). *Playing by the rules*. Washington, DC: Office of Community Planning and Development.

U.S. Department of Housing and Urban Development, Office of Community Planning and Development. (2007). *CDBG, guide to national objectives and eligible activities for entitlement communities*. Washington, D.C.: Government Printing Office.

## WEB SOURCES

American Association of Grant Professionals.
http://grantprofessionals.org/

Foundation Center.
http://www.foundationcenter.org/

Government Accounting Office.
https://www.gao.gov/federal-grants-state-and-local-governments

TAGG.
https://taggs.hhs.gov/

# SECTION
# 5

# Performance and Leadership

In the last analysis public agencies are valued based on their ability to provide goods/services and leadership. In both cases it is easier to describe what is provided than to assess the value that is realized from promoting the public interest. Consequently, these areas are both more controversial and more subjective than concerns discussed in earlier sections of this text.

Chapter 18, "Performance Measures," examines how to measure the value of public goods and services of government agencies. While inputs and costs may be readily identified and measured, output and benefit measures are more challenging. A brief discussion of the metrics process and challenges is provided.

Chapter 19, "Leadership for Administrators," discusses the evolving efforts to define what leadership is, how it is used, and what difference context, follower's needs, follower's expectations, and a leader's behavior have on the performance, decision making, and culture of the organization. We explore the practical tools of mentorships, cross training, special projects, etc., as means to identify and foster leadership competencies in public employees. While leadership in a private organization is similar in many ways to leadership in a public organization, it is the demands of the public outside the confines of an organizational setting that set public leadership apart from other sectors.

# 18 ━━━◇━━◇━◆━●

# Performance Measures

The private sector began to explore the use of quantitative methods to measure results against established standards in the mid-1950s. The new movement was called Total Quality Management and was associated with the work of Deming, Juran, and Crosby. In the public sector, efforts to identify measurable processes and outputs were linked to budget reform efforts such as the Program Planning and Budgeting Systems of the 1950s and Zero-Based Budgeting of the Carter administration in the 1970s. It was relatively easy to identify and measure both *inputs*—typically costs such as money and personnel time—and *processes*—which could be the number of service hours or program participants served. Measuring *outputs* (police patrols, taught classes, or inoculated residents) and *outcomes* (safer streets, educated and healthy residents) proved more of a challenge. The other core challenge in the public sector was connecting outcomes (safer streets) to public policies and programs. Did crime decline because more police were visible in an area, or did criminals move operations to areas with less surveillance? If a greater police presence resulted in crime reports' rising, did that indicate that crime was escalating or that community residents were now more willing and supportive of police efforts?

"Be thankful," Will Rogers quipped in the 1930s, "that we are not getting all the government we are paying for." What is the public getting for its tax dollars? In the early 1970s new demands for efficiency and effectiveness were championed by Tom Peters, David Osborne, Peter Plastrik, and E. S. Savas. A popular movement to contract out public services to the private sector forced governments to reexamine both their processes and the productivity of their efforts. Performance measurement, which had been introduced initially after World War II, again reemerged as a core responsibility of public administration.

This chapter discusses the advantages and disadvantages of performance measurement efforts in the public sector and describes one performance measurement approach: benchmarking. Using examples from policing, library services, and other areas, this chapter discusses how performance measurement is conducted step by step. Other quantifiable methods are available, such as gap analysis and scorecards, but the primary focus of this chapter will be on benchmarking.

*Benchmarking* seeks to improve performance by identifying and defining quantifiable empirical measures of performance. These metrics are then employed to compare operations to what is an industry or accepted norm or to more idealized standards, that is, best practices of efficiency and effectiveness. *Gap analysis* is a subset of benchmarking. Assuming one can benchmark performance, the next task would be to monitor success from where one starts to the goal. Scorecards present the key indicators of a set of performance measures in an easy-to-read, graphic format. *Scorecards* usually begin by developing specific quantifiable goals that reflect an organization's mission statement. In this system, progress toward these goals is typically measured in terms of costs, client/customer satisfaction, innovation efforts, employee satisfaction, and employee retention. Regularly scheduled updates enable organizations to assess their progress.

Performance measurement systems such as benchmarking attempt to make the comparison of two or more organizations systematic with regard to processes, practices, outputs, and outcomes. Based on comparisons to better performers, managers, and organizations can modify their approaches, processes, and methods to achieve greater effectiveness and/or productivity at less cost. While there is little disagreement about the objectives of performance measurements, there is considerable debate about the means.

## PROS AND CONS OF PERFORMANCE MEASUREMENT

There is an almost an innate need for individuals, groups, and countries to compare themselves to others. Students compare grades and faculty compare course evaluations. Humans need to gauge their success and/or lack of progress; we are by nature curious, adapting, and learning beings. What is true for the individual is true for organized groups of individuals. Performance measures provide the tools for addressing this most basic need to watch, compare, and learn to do better.

There are pros and cons of performance measures. Performance measures contribute to quality improvement in organizations when the measures are carefully developed and utilized. These measures:

- enable organizations to track productivity;
- empower employees to take on greater responsibility for operations and customer service;
- enable management to address emerging trends with long-term strategies rather than with short-time tactics;

* encourage learning and flexibility; and
* promote citizen understanding, support, and participation.

Despite their impressive benefits, performance measures have significant limitations. Performance measurement and management do not always produce the anticipated results because in some cases they:

* compare not excellence in organizations but differences in culture and circumstances;
* measure what is easy and available rather than what is needed;
* divert attention away from important issues;
* use performance measurement as an opportunity to assign blame rather than design improvements;
* settle for superficial interpretations of the data that send the organization in the wrong direction; and
* operate as though performance measures are a quick fix for propping up productivity rather than as a long-term commitment to continuous improvement, self-evaluation, and experimentation.

## MEASUREMENT

Measures are sometimes difficult to identify, develop, collect, analyze, and interpret. Performance management needs to determine how to do each of the following:

* validate the data,
* assess its reliability,
* analyze the data,
* determine the appropriate frequently to convert the data to report information,
* report information, and
* distribute information.

Consequently, performance measures require not only technical skills but also insight and interpersonal savvy. The ability to measure an effort is not the same as the ability to measure its value. There is a telling story about a public manager who passes her symphony tickets to a Schubert concert to her performance management director.[1] The morning after the concert, the manager asked the director if he enjoyed Schubert's *Unfinished Symphony*, and instead of hearing a few comments, she was handed the following memorandum:

---

[1] The story is an adaptation of "Schubert Considered by an Efficiency Expert."
http://www.classicalmusicguide.com/viewtopic.php?t=31938

1. For a considerable period, the oboe players had nothing to do. Their number should be reduced and their work spread over the whole orchestra, thus avoiding peaks of inactivity.

2. All 12 violins were playing identical notes. This seems unnecessarily duplicative, and the staff of this section should be drastically cut. If a large volume of sound is really required, this could be obtained through the use of an amplifier.

3. Much effort was involved in playing the demisemiquavers. This seems an excessive refinement, and it is recommended that all notes be rounded up to the nearest semiquaver. If this were done, it would be possible to use trainees instead of craftsmen.

4. No useful purpose is served by repeating with horns the passage that has already been handled by the strings. If all such redundant passages were eliminated, the concert could be significantly reduced, from 2 hours to only 20 minutes.

In light of the above, one can conclude that had Schubert given these matters proper attention, he would have had the time to finish his symphony.

In this chapter we will explore how performance is measured, how best to use measurement, and various complications that may arise regarding what is efficient and what is effective. In a perfect world, solutions would be both efficient and effective, but in public service the ideal balance may be difficult to find. The tendency is to favor efficiency over effectiveness, since it is easier to understand, document, and compute.

Performance measurement is an ongoing effort and should be part of an organization's regular reporting protocols that are used to account for personnel and funding. Consequently, performance measurement programs tend to parallel the jurisdiction's budget cycle. The discussion below examines how performance measurement may be addressed during a funding cycle.

# A Step-by-Step Guide to
# Performance Measurement

## Step 1: Goals and Objectives as Means for Determining What to Use as a Standard of Performance

In Chapter 6 there is a discussion of the role of mission statements, visions, goals, and objectives in public policy and programs. A mission is what the organization is chartered or created to do. Departments and agencies do not create themselves but are authorized by legislatures that set the public agenda about what government will provide with tax revenues the legislature raises. The statements are broad, imprecise, and all-encompassing since legislatures develop policies that are acceptable to competing political parties and interest groups with dissimilar goals of their own.

One of the most widely debated and sweeping policy goals was articulated in the Housing Act of 1949, which declared its objective to be "a decent home and a suitable living environment for every American." The functional dilemma with the policy goal was that Congress did not define what it meant by "decent," "home," "suitable," or "living environment." The primary procedural problem with the goal was that Congress could not directly implement the Housing Act of 1949 but has depended on the cooperation and capabilities of state and local housing and redevelopment authorities to carry out its will.

In practice, legislatures depend on the executive branch and public administrators to translate legislative intent into specific, operating programs. Congress is not alone in this regard. County and city councils engage in the same broad, all-encompassing language. One city's police department has its mission statement stenciled on its patrol cars: "to protect and to serve."

If the director of housing, chief of police, or public manager is to be held accountable for the implementation of public programs using appropriations from the legislature, these statements need to be expressed in terms that are unambiguous, are specific, and can be understood the same way by citizens and taxpayers. The first task of performance measurement is determining how legislative intent will be expressed in concrete terms.

What do we want a police department to do? The answer includes the following:

- reduce the crime rate in the community;
- be accessible 24 hours a day, 7 days a week;
- respond to calls quickly;
- investigate reports of wrongdoing;

- detain and arrest alleged perpetrators;
- provide prosecutors with evidence and testimony needed for convictions;
- prevent crime in a community;
- educate residents about steps to protect lives, homes, cars, and valuables;
- alert residents to potential problems and illegal activities in the area;
- know and work cooperatively with area residents;
- develop neighborhood watch programs; and
- build a civil society.

Table 18.1 lists some of these expectations along with their means of implementations and how the expectation might be measured. Some of the metrics are outputs (response to calls per hour, patrols per hour) while others are outcomes (resolved cases, convictions, crime rates). Given the importance of and emphasis on public safety at the local level, the issue is not the availability of data but the benchmark to be employed. Against which standard should a department be compared?

## Step 2: Resource Identification and Establishment of Reasonable Comparisons

Core areas of comparison include population, median income, ethnic composition, and so forth. Some of this information is available from federal or state sources (for example, governmental agencies, research organizations and universities), and some is developed or available locally.

If cities and counties require federal and/or statewide crime data, then the data are available either through such services as the FBI (of the Department of Justice) or through the state's attorney general's office. Jurisdictions report statewide and federal data about the same crime, in the same manner, to the same data collection agency, using the same timetable. Therefore, the measurement instrument is comparable. A 300-violent-crimes rate means there are 300 violent crimes per year per 100,000 persons in the population. The California index is based on approximately 450 counties, cities, and towns.

In addition to crime statistics, state and federal data are available about employment, education, airport operations, housing stock, and air quality, to name a few. The issue is not the metric or data collection process but determining what a community should be compared to. For example, Pomona, California, is located at the eastern border of Los Angeles County and has a population of about 153,000. The conventional wisdom is that Pomona should be compared to similar cities (by population, e.g.) in determining how well it provides police services.

**Table 18.1    Police Department Attributes and How They Might Be Measured**

| Attribute | Implementation | Metric (How It Is Measured) |
|---|---|---|
| Accessibility | Staffing of 911 call center<br>Number of patrols cars in operation | Calls per hour<br>Patrols per hour per area |
| Response rate | Staff and skill of 911 operators<br>Deployment of cars to site<br>Arrival of cars at site | Delay time to pick up call<br>Time to secure basic information (audit data on taped calls)<br>Arrive – deploy = response time |
| Report resolution | Officer reports per patrol hour<br>Report closed | Reports per hour<br>Resolved cases/all reports opened |
| Arrests | Bookings and detentions | Rate of cases cleared by an arrest |
| Convictions | Guilty adjudications | Court convictions/all court cases |
| Community education programs | Attendees<br>Follow-up actions | Number of persons at presentations<br>Requests for presentations and information |
| Neighborhood watch | Neighborhood groups organized | Number of groups<br>Number of citizens participating |
| Reduction of crimes of violence | Murders, rapes, assaults, kidnappings reported | UCR number of reported crimes per 100,000 population |
| Reduction of crimes against property | Burglary, robbery, arson, fraud, embezzlement, drug reports, and so forth | UCR number of reported crimes per 100,000 population |
| Reduction of misdemeanors | Vandalism, gambling, drunkenness, vagrancy complaints, and so forth filed | UCR number of reported crimes per 100,000 population |
| Reduction of traffic violations | Speeding, procedural violations, parking, and so forth police reported | UCR number of reported crimes per 100,000 population |
| Reduction of complaints against officers | Cases before Internal Affairs | Favorable resolutions / all Internal Affairs cases |
| Other services | Get cat from tree, give directions, find lost child, assist disabled pedestrian, and so forth | Customer surveys |

Note: UCR = Uniform Crime Reports.

National data would indicate a clear relationship between population and rate of crime. See Table 18.2.

While population and incidence of crime are not perfectly correlated, there appears to be a relationship between the two. As a population cluster's size decreases, there is a decline in the incidence of violent crime. The relationship is similar for property crimes. However, looking at cities of similar sizes does not provide the same clarity. To which cities could Pomona be compared that have the same population size, economy, and social system? Even if one could find a city with exactly the same population, gross domestic product, and political system, would that city be a fair comparison? See Table 18.3.

Pomona stands out in comparison to other cities of similar size in the area. Factors other than population may influence crime reports. Pomona is 64.5% Latino, has a large immigrant population, and has a median income of $49,765, which is below the median income of the county ($52,461). By comparison, Torrance has a median income of $70,262 (33% higher than the county median), and 52.4%

**Table 18.2   Crime Rates in the United States (2019)**

| Population | Violent Crimes | Property Crimes |
|---|---|---|
| 1 million or greater | 874.1 | 3,870.9 |
| 500,000–999,000 | 991.0 | 5,675.6 |
| 250,000–499,000 | 1,015.0 | 5,584.9 |
| 100,000–249,000 | 616.2 | 4,648.4 |
| 50,000–99,000 | 474.4 | 3,895.1 |
| 25,000–49,000 | 374.1 | 3,632.7 |
| 10,000–14,000 | 303.0 | 3,327.8 |
| Less than 10,000 | 330.0 | 3,645.7 |

Source: Federal Bureau of Investigation, Department of Justice. (2019, Table 16).

**Table 18.3   Pomona, CA, Compared to Similar Cities by Population 100,000 to 250,000 (2019)**

| City | Population | Violent Crimes (per 100,000 population) | Property Crimes (per 100,000 population) | California Index |
|---|---|---|---|---|
| Burbank | 103,738 | 189 | 2,617 | 168 |
| Norwalk | 105,067 | 432 | 1,571 | 258 |
| West Covina | 106,335 | 260 | 2,369 | 269 |
| Inglewood | 109,386 | 671 | 2,321 | 404 |
| Downey | 112,330 | 352 | 2,473 | 318 |
| El Monte | 115,830 | 304 | 1,787 | 262 |
| Pasadena | 141,913 | 613 | 2,866 | 256 |
| Torrance | 144,183 | 280 | 2,835 | 117 |
| **Pomona** | **152,776** | **940** | **4,208** | **393** |
| Lancaster | 159,335 | 1,359 | 3,346 | 378 |
| Glendale | 202,601 | 231 | 3,305 | 79 |
| Santa Clarita | 218,103 | 277 | 2,059 | 93 |
| Sum | 1,671,597 | 5,908 | 31,757 | 2,995 |
| Mean | 139,300 | 492 | 2,646 | 250 |
| Median | 128,872 | 328 | 2,545 | 260 |

Source: OPEN_JUSTICE, Crimes and Clearances from the Office of the CA. Attorney General at https://openjustice.doj.ca.gov/exploration/crime-statistics/crimes-clearances

of its population is white. Lancaster has a median income of $51,139, close to Los Angeles County's norm, and like Torrance is predominately white (52.4%), but Lancaster's violent crime rate is the highest for cities with populations between 100,000 and 250,000. In setting a benchmark it is not always clear which factors should be included in determining a like environment among political jurisdictions.

Norms can be developed from data by, for example, computing averages and medians. The average, or mean, is the sum of all observations (e.g., violent crimes per 100,000 rates) divided by the number of observations (12 cities in this category). In this example, the mean is calculated as follows: 5,908 ÷ 12 = 492. The median calculation requires that the 12 observations be arranged from lowest to highest and the middle point be selected. In the case of violent crimes, the array would look like the following: 189, 231, 260, 277, 280, 304, 352, 432, 613, 671, 940, 1,359. The middle point of 12 observations is halfway between observation six (304) and observation seven (352), therefore we calculate the median as 304 + 352 = 656 ÷ 2 = 328. The standard deviation is a measure of how reliable the mean is by indicating how little or how much the observations differ from one another. A small standard deviation signifies that the mean is a good indicator, and a large standard deviation signifies that the mean is a weak indicator of the norm. While the math is cumbersome, it may be computed on an Excel spreadsheet. Enter the raw data in a column from the first cell, A1, to the last cell, A12. In the function area ($f_x$) entry field on the Excel worksheet enter "=STDEV A1:A12" to calculate the standard deviation. A standard deviation of 351.9 indicates that if the average is 492, then two-thirds of all observations will be around the mean, +/−1 standard deviation, or from 844 to 140.

Note that Lancaster is comparable to Pomona with regard to population but has a much higher violent crime rate. The communities one selects to use for comparison will skew one's perceptions. In comparison to Lancaster, Pomona looks good; but compared to Torrance it looks terrible.

Downey's violent crime rate of 352 may differ from the mean of 492 due to random chance, while Pomona's 940 crime rate is beyond what is expected to occur at random. That is, Downey's violent crime rate is within one standard deviation of the mean while Pomona's is not. All other factors being held constant, the rate of violent crimes might be considered one benchmark to address in the coming years. While all the attributes listed in Table 18.1 are important, outcomes are valued above outputs. A lower crime rate is more desirable than increased patrols. The patrols are valued to the degree that crime rates fall. While all crimes have adverse effects, crimes against persons (violent crimes) are considered more threatening than crimes against property or public annoyances. Therefore, performance efforts typically focus on outcomes over outputs and more serious consequences over less serious ones.

In practice, all the attributes, implementation mechanisms, and metrics would be worked out in detail as was done above for violent crimes. The preceding discussion is an example of how this might be addressed in one case. Senior management typically determines how many and which attributes are included in the performance measurement effort, in which order, and over which time period.

Benchmarks limit our range of focus to what is the norm (or mean) and therefore limit the level of effort made to stay at, or just above, the norm. Minimum standards (adequacy) are as necessary as standards of excellence. If governments are not able to provide a minimal level of service, it may be an indication that the government needs to direct residents to services provided by other levels of government, develop a special service district, and/or develop partnerships with public, private, and/or nongovernmental organizations on behalf of the public.

A variation on benchmarking is identifying organizations that demonstrate best practices. For example, which police force has a reputation for community service, quick response times, and high rates of convictions and closed cases? How do its operations, budgets, personnel practices, and so forth compare, and which consequences arise from these differences? Best practices, like benchmarked data, need to be scrutinized. Are the best practices of the organization truly responsible for the consequences, or are external or synergistic factors responsible? Adopting the best practices of another organization is fraught with hazards. It is rare that a change to one or a few factors will turn an organization's performance around in the short run. Often getting significant and lasting improvement requires changing the organizational culture, implementing new leadership, and adapting over many years. A decision to employ best practices may mean a fundamental shift in orientation for an organization regarding its mission, goals, objectives, operations, and policies. Often officials and administrators underestimate the cost, time, and scope of change needed to bring operations to the standards of a high performer. In part, this is because change may be met with opposition from within the organization. Adopting best practices may also mean changing processes and interactions with community members. This may lead to resistance from outside the agency and delay implementation until new relationships and expectations can be established.

## Step 3: Information Needs

Being able to quantify one's objectives is not the same as knowing how to get from 940 to 492 violent crimes per 100,000 population. Identifying how current performance differs from the preferred is what is referred to as "gap analysis." Improving operations means identifying funding sources for new approaches to policing from the state and national governments, identifying area experts in the field, and collaborating with police organizations and associations on similarities and differences in processes. Are there differences in police operations (recruiting, training, deployment, follow-up, promotions, community efforts, and so forth) that seem to influence the department's crime rates? How can efforts be adapted to meet the needs of the evolving organization? Observations of other programs and discussions about proposed changes and their consequences are part of the learning process needed to introduce and sustain changes that enhance and inform performance.

## Step 4: Norms of Performance and Best Practices

In the policing example, the benchmark was an area norm (crime rates for cities of like size in the political jurisdiction). This is a feasible option due in part to the availability of data about outcomes. However, an area's norm is not the only yardstick. For example, in the case of library services there are no local, state, or national outcome data about how library books are educating residents and enhancing their lives. Nor are there outcome data for the quality of meeting minutes prepared by city clerks or the quality of public parks and play areas. Nonetheless, the absence of comparable data does not mean there is an absence of standards. Standards may derive from a variety of sources such as professional organizations and civic or public service associations.

Nearly every public function has a professional organization that seeks to substantively identify the value added by employees in the field and the outputs and potential outcomes that serve urban, suburban, and rural communities. The Public Library Association and the American Library Association have developed benchmarks on circulation of materials per capita, turnover rates of materials, new acquisitions, document delivery, and hours of operation from years of data collection.

The Texas Library Association developed standards in the late 1990s and revised them in 2014. Table 18.4 presents some selected standards.

In a similar manner the Parks and Recreation Department of San Diego regularly reports on the compliance of its assets with city standards regarding playgrounds, landscaping, fields, outdoor courts and roads. (Kitchell 2021). The metrics allow the department to determine how well it is providing an enriching physical environment in an environmentally friendly and fiscally responsible manner. As with library services, the value of programs is measured in both inputs (books, periodicals, operating hours) and outputs (circulation, reference questions resolved, volunteer hours).

Public services such as the maintenance of a jurisdiction's trucks and cars, purchasing services, and property management may be benchmarked against private-sector operations and/or professional standards. Another source of benchmarks are measures from other governments. For example, the City and County of San Francisco's charter requires the City Services Auditor to monitor the level and

**Table 18.4    Texas Library Association Selected "Accessibility" Standards**

| City Population | Enhanced (50th Percentile) | Exemplary (75th Percentile) |
|---|---|---|
| 1 to 4,999 | Library is open at least 35 hours per week | Library is open at least 40 hours per week<br>Library has a website |
| 5,000 to 9,999 | Library is open at least 40 hours per week<br>Library has a website | Library is open at least 45 hours per week<br>Library has a website |
| 10,000 to 24,999 | Library is open at least 45 hours per week<br>Library has a website<br>Library has a social media presence | Library is open at least 50 hours per week<br>Library has a website<br>Library has a social media presence<br>Library provides remote access to online catalogue<br>Library provides remote renewals for materials |

Source: Texas Library Association, *Public Library Standards*, 2014 Revision.

effectiveness of services by comparing San Francisco's measures to those of other cities. San Francisco collects information from a number of peer jurisdictions, including Baltimore, MD; Boston, MA; Chicago, IL; Denver, CO; Long Beach, CA; Los Angeles, CA; Miami, FL; Minneapolis, MN; Oakland, CA; Philadelphia, PA; Portland, OR; Sacramento, CA; San Diego, CA; San Jose, CA; Seattle, WA; and Washington, DC. The City Controller selected the peers based on a "likeness score" methodology based largely on population and population density. Benchmarking topics include transportation, public safety, livability, demographics, homelessness, public health and finance.

Other services are unique and have few comparable equivalents. The city clerk performs numerous tasks: developing and publishing the legislature's agenda, recording meeting minutes, logging documents, and coding documents for identification and retrieval. While city clerk responsibilities have existed for as long as there have been self-governing councils, only recently have professional associations (e.g., City Clerks Association of California) begun the task of setting and codifying standards. A number of cities have established their own standards for the posting of city agendas, accuracy of city clerk minutes, user-friendliness of archival records, and document indexing and retrieval.

## Step 5: Implementation and Trade-offs

Implementing performance measures poses two distinct challenges. The first is to identify reliable and consistent measures that contribute to the organization's information but are not costly and cumbersome to collect. The second measurement challenge is to have a measurement system that collects essential information about the organization's outcomes.

In 2001 Congress passed the No Child Left Behind (NCLB) Act that introduced extensive standardized testing to public schools using federal funds. It linked test scores to federal funding and was both expensive to implement and controversial. In 2015, NCLB was replaced by Every Student Succeeds Act (ESSA) which in 2021 received $16.5 billion in federal funding for education. ESSA kept some standardized test scores as metrics but expanded metrics to include percent of student population suspended annually, percent of graduating seniors having completed courses needed to attend a state university program, physical fitness scores, and dropout rates. A school's performance is now displayed on a dashboard enabling the public to assess how well a district and/or school was performing on specific tasks and if the school in the past three years had improved, declined, or remained unchanged. While the new approach tracks short term (e.g., suspension rates) and long term (e.g., graduation rates) metrics along with academic test scores, it misses critical attributes of education, such as creativity, fostering curiosity, and developing social and communication skills to promote civic life. While less draconian in consequences to public schools and more inclusive in measuring what performance is, ESSA is limited in its ability to capture those critical attributes that comprise the outcomes of K–12 education.

Persons are reluctant to change established practices. "If it ain't broke," goes the saying, "don't fix it." In addition, change means altering the use of scarce resources such as funds and personnel. An existing labor contract, supplier contract, or provider agreement may not allow changes in operations. Constraints on public manager discretionary decisions are sometimes seen as a resistance by public managers to making sweeping and needed improvements. However, public managers also have less discretionary authority than their private-sector counterparts. So while experimentation and change may be desired, creating the circumstances for implementation requires more preparation time in the public sector.

Returning to the violent crime example, a chief of police may wish to introduce community foot patrols, neighborhood watch programs, citizen cadets, and joint outreach efforts with schools, recreation programs, and youth groups. These efforts may provide more trained eyes and ears in the community to help identify and/or avert violent acts. To execute this effort some sworn officers may need to be reassigned to walk a beat or patrol on bicycles and meet with neighborhood groups. However, moving staff and resources may require deviating from labor contracts and/or legislative guidelines. Performance management requires that managers indicate how current efforts will not be sacrificed while agency improvements are being tested and refined. Two-person car patrols may need to be maintained in peak hours but relaxed at other times, thereby freeing scarce labor resources for a new initiative. Coverage of areas by foot and by bike may lower capital and maintenance costs for dedicated patrol cars, but the officers will not have the computer access they have in a vehicle. High school and college cadets may provide additional labor resources at a nominal cost for training and uniforms, but insurance, liability, and absence issues may be very high.

At every step the manager needs to determine the trade-off between existing efforts with an established track record and proposed and untested efforts to improve performance.

A private business adds capital and/or labor to the production of goods and services up to the point where the last dollar spent (marginal cost) is equal to the last dollar of revenue earned (marginal revenue). The firm continues to adjust inputs and processes to the point where the marginal cost does not exceed the marginal revenue. A firm might hire a new employee to produce 100 widgets a week at a cost of 8 cents per widget; this increase is acceptable up to the point where revenue for the last widget earns at least 8 cents of additional revenue. Private investors understand that returns on investments for new products or services may take years to develop. They forgo earnings in anticipation of significant revenues in future years.

In the public sector there are two challenges to this model. First, revenues are not directly linked to services. If an additional police officer is added to the violent crimes program it is not related to the property tax, sales tax, or income tax collected. Second, there may be no way to determine the market value benefit from the public effort. If rapes decline from five to three, what is the value of the decline? For some residents the improvement is immeasurable, and for others the difference is insignificant. Whatever the value is, it is not as easy to assess in the public arena as it is for private firms operating in markets.

The public manager makes an educated guess as to where the line is between efficient use of inputs (costs) and effectiveness to customers. For example, it may cost $60,000 per year to educate 30 third graders, or $2,000 per student. Raising the class size from 30 to 35 reduces the per-child cost to $1,714 and is a *more efficient* use of resources, but the larger class size may result in poorer education. How many third graders in a class is the optimal number to be educated for the lowest cost? This metric (the marginal benefit divided by the marginal cost) is not known and makes efforts to benchmark services more difficult for public managers.

The public is risk averse. Parents are unwilling to forgo their children's education in the third grade in hopes of catching up in the eighth or ninth. Balance in the public sector between efficiency and effectiveness is the balance between the public's acceptance of and opposition to perceived consequences in terms of outputs and outcomes and not an objective marginal analysis of tangible benefits to costs.

## Step 6: Feedback and Learning

Given the public aversion to taking risks with safety, education, or even leisure services, public program measures are often met with a wait-and-see attitude. Will the new metrics improve program administration, improve follow-up by decision makers, and result in better performance?

In Table 18.1 four of the attributes are part of the Uniform Crime Reports system. Staffing levels for phone banks and patrols may be monitored by the payroll department, while response times may be electronically captured by the police communication system and/or supervisors providing information and support to field operations. Due to the demands of courts for compliance with *due process* provisions of the Constitution, police processes and outputs (arrests, detentions, and investigations) are already extensively documented. In only a few areas (community efforts and outreach) would new monitoring be required. In an ideal learning environment these new functions would be incorporated into the existing reporting forms and system to minimize paperwork and the need for training.

Performance reporting needs to be incorporated into the jurisdiction's annual reporting cycle. For example, public budgeting is an annual event, and legislators may insist that expenditures be linked to performance. A parallel challenge in performance management is consolidating information from a range of sources (Uniform Crime Reports, Internal Affairs, phone banks, community services) into a coherent whole that can be understood by legislators and the public. It is important that the evaluation process indicate what the metric objectives have been, why the metric is significant or appropriate, what progress has been made and measured, and which improvements the data suggest. Data without context are meaningless.

The numbers do not speak for themselves but require interpretation. If violent crime rates are the same today as in prior years, is that indicative of success or failure? If the rate is constant as the population rises, then no change may indicate success. If neighborhood watch groups and community police establish strong ties in the community, citizens' initial response may be to report more suspicious behavior, resulting in higher crime reports rather than lower ones. Since police depend on citizens' reporting behavior before they can take action, higher reporting rates may represent better police-community relations and safer neighborhoods rather than rising criminal activity.

Concerns regarding interpreting data arise with library services, education, and recreation. Are higher test scores indicative of better-educated youth or more relaxed standards and familiarity with multiple-choice tests? Is greater use of public parks indicative of greater satisfaction with public services or less disposable income to buy recreational services in the private sector? How much change in the metric is representative of the mission being sought is difficult to assert unequivocally.

## Step 7: Continuous Improvement and Consequences

Metrics enable managers to more accurately observe, measure, and assess change. However, short-term changes are difficult to interpret. Long-term trends are more reliable. A rise or fall in crime rates, test scores, or book circulation from one year to the next may be due to chance variations in the monitoring system, short-term changes in consumer tastes, or environmental circumstances beyond the control of the agency or its management. Long-term changes over five to ten years may provide a clearer picture of program outputs and outcomes.

Examine the fictional case of Sunny Trails Recreation Program in Table 18.5.

**Table 18.5  Sunny Trails Recreation Program**

| Variable | Year 1 | Year 2 | Year 3 | Year 4 | Year 5 |
|----------|--------|--------|--------|--------|--------|
| Service hours | 1,400 | 1,500 | 1,580 | 1,680 | 1,700 |
| Rate of change (%) | n.a. | 7.14% | 5.33% | 6.33% | 1.19% |
| Patrons | 700 | 750 | 790 | 825 | 865 |
| Rate of change (%) | n.a. | 7.14% | 5.33% | 4.43% | 4.85% |
| Note: n.a. = not applicable. | | | | | |

Between year 1 and year 2 there was a 7.14% increase in both service hours and patrons. However, the change between years 1 and 2 is not repeated over any of the next 3 years. The average growth rate in patrons parallels the city's growth rate in hours of service. How does having this data help in determining metrics, program changes, and mission/goal accountability? The department's overall program metric comprises participation in tennis, field sports, Jazzercise, and after-school events. An examination of participation by subareas may reveal whether public use is greater for some programs than for others. A comparison of participation rates will enable the program director to move resources from low-growth areas to high-growth areas, all other factors being equal.

While immediate changes may be addressed through the operating budget, long-term trends need to be identified for capital projects. If Sunny Trails began as a bedroom community serving young families in the 1980s, service demands may be very different today as the population changes. Performance measurements and projections of demographic and user trends can make a compelling case for future capital expenditures.

## Step 8: Public Scrutiny, Budgets, and Evolving Objectives

Performance measurements are fraught with opportunities and pitfalls. This is most evident when program efforts, outputs, and outcomes are tied to budget projections and appropriations. For this reason, performance measures need to be fully vetted. If a change has occurred, how much of it can be laid at the doorsteps of the program, of random chance, and of demographic or economic trends outside the control of the public administrator? The objective is to make the best use of resources, to be accountable for program/policy operations, and to be transparent in the management and execution of efforts on the public's behalf.

Performance measures are not an administrative end or goal unto themselves. They are a means to an end. The end is better informed decision making and greater public accountability from administrators. To the degree that performance measures meet this objective, they serve the public interest. In addition, performance measurements can help to redefine which public services are desired and may help to shape the community's perceptions of the scope and depth of public services in the future. In this regard every cycle of performance management and budgeting gives rise to the next cycle of data collection, analysis, interpretation, and reporting, thus returning the public manager to Step 2.

# PERFORMANCE MEASUREMENT OPTION: THE SCORECARD

Benchmarking is one approach to performance management but is by no means the only approach. The balanced scorecard is also widely employed. The balanced scorecard treats an organization's vision and strategy as central to the development of its analytical framework but views the vision from four perspectives:

- the customer's view;
- the employees' view, sometimes called the internal process;
- the financial view, which is the perspective of shareholders and taxpayers; and
- the learning and growth view, which is the assessment of the organization's ability to adapt, grow, and improve.

From each of these perspectives, scorecards are developed that identify the objective, its metric, the specified goal (target), and the tasks or necessary actions (initiatives) needed to improve performance. Scorecards are a set of key indicators drawn from a longer list of performance measures. They serve to focus the attention of government officials and managers on accomplishments in mission-critical areas.

For example, Community Alpha is concerned with rising vandalism and the declining care of homes and landscaping in the community. Its scorecard might look like Table 18.6.

**Table 18.6   Scorecard: Neighborhood Improvement**

| Perspective | Objective | Metric | Target | Initiative | Percent Achieved |
|---|---|---|---|---|---|
| Resident | Strengthen neighborhoods | Quality-of-life index | 102 communities | Neighborhood councils | 72% |
| Public works | Strengthen areas | Graffiti removal | Within four days of call | Revised follow-up system | 83% |

Organizations then track the consequences of each initiative as it constitutes a share of the overall objective as seen from each perspective.

Each approach has advantages and disadvantages, and the choice of strategy should be based on what best fits the organization's circumstances and resources.

# ETHICS, EQUITY, AND PERFORMANCE MEASUREMENT

Performance measurement seeks to hold government accountable by making performance transparent. Thus, it serves the cause of ethics. But the practice of performance measurement may get sidetracked. As discussed in this chapter, sometimes measures are selected because they are easy—data are available and understandable. It is more difficult to develop and use measures that reflect the goals and objectives of a strategic plan and help to inform the public, policy makers, and government staff about how well these efforts meet or exceed goals and objectives. The ethical considerations are complex. Measuring systems that provide the greatest accuracy may be costly and difficult to administer. Whichever measurement approach is taken introduces a bias that may favor one view of the public interest, or one sector of the public, over others. Consequently, the very tools that performance advocates claim will provide greater accountability and transparency in government may serve only to obfuscate and distort public efforts.

Let's assume a community's vision is to provide its youth with a quality education. How shall quality be understood and measured? If quality is measured by graduation rates, there will be a rise in the number of students graduating. If quality is measured by standardized test scores, then higher scores will be a measure of successful performance, and teaching will focus on preparing students for the test rather than mastery of the subject matter. If quality is measured by participating in scholarly competitions and gaining recognition, administrators will expand participation efforts and coach students to be successful competitors, and thus the success of a few students may become a measure for the quality of education. Is the public recognition of and competition by a few students a measurement for the quality of education in general? It is often required that students, employees, and program participants be informed as to how their efforts will be assessed. It is human nature to want to demonstrate the best outcomes and skew efforts to serve the assessment tool rather than let the tool measure the program's performance.

The greatest ethical challenges are determining what a feasible, comprehensive metric is and whose definition of quality will be employed: educators', parents', taxpayers', or elected officials'? Perhaps quality is arrived at by an assessment team of educators, psychologists, and child development specialists who interview students, engage them in interactive experiential exercises, and review homework, course projects, portfolios, and standardized tests. Such an approach would be very costly. A less costly option would be a reliance on only a standardized test. This option is biased in favor of those who are more successful with structured tests and may not adequately measure the competency of those who are less affluent or from homes where English is a second language and where private tutors and costly preparation courses are not available.

As with most ethical considerations, there is no simple or single solution to this challenge. Instead, communities continue to experiment with numerous tools and means for observing and measuring their efforts, the results they produce, and the consequences or outcomes realized.

## CONCLUSION

Since the establishment of the Republic in 1789, scholars and practitioners have sought to develop systems that would hold administrators responsible for and accountable to the legislature and the public for their use of public resources and authority. Early attempts were tied to budget reforms in the mid-1950s and 1970s.

The more recent approach has been to borrow performance measurement techniques from the private sector. These efforts potentially can bolster and derail public service programs. In this chapter we looked specifically at one performance management effort: benchmarking. This approach is similar to other performance measurement efforts such as gap analysis and the balanced scorecard.

Whatever the performance measurement framework might be, the core challenge is interpreting and linking the data to outputs and outcomes in a meaningful way for decision makers and the public.

## PRACTICING PUBLIC ADMINISTRATION

1. You have been asked to develop metrics for the town's (45,200 population) fire department. What is it you want a fire department to do, and how would you measure its process and productivity?

2. Which factors need to be taken into account in identifying jurisdictions that are comparable to your town's fire services for the purposes of developing appropriate benchmark comparisons?

3. How might a focus on efficiency undermine a fire department's effectiveness and responsibility to operate in the public interest?

4. Below is a list of rankings of California cities based on the California Crime Index:

| City | CA Crime Index |
|------|----------------|
| A | 1,205.4 |
| B | 1,700.9 |
| C | 1,785.0 |
| D | 1,916.8 |
| E | 2,356.6 |
| F | 1,905.8 |
| G | 1,374.3 |

What is the median crime rate for these seven communities?

5. When might a manager determine that the balanced scorecard is preferable to benchmarking when establishing performance measures for their organization?

# BIBLIOGRAPHY

Ammons, D. N. (1999). A proper mentality for benchmarking. *Public Administration Review 59*(2): 105–109.

———. (2001). *Municipal benchmarks.* (2nd ed.). Thousand Oaks, CA: Sage.

Ammons, D. N. (2019). *Performance measurement for managing local government.* Irvine, CA: Melvin and Leigh Publishers.

Ammons, D. N., & Roenigk, D. J. (2015). Benchmarking and interorganizational learning in local government. *Journal of Public Administration Research and Theory 25*(1): 309–335. https://doi.org/10.1093/jopart/muu014

Center for Performance Measurement. (2008). *What works: How local governments have made the leap from measurement to management.* Washington, D.C.: ICMA.

Evergreen, S. (2019). *Effective data visualization: The right chart for the right data.* (2nd ed.). Thousand Oaks, CA: Sage.

Hatry, H. P. (1999). *Performance measurement: Getting results.* Washington, D.C.: Urban Institute Press.

Hatry, H., & Allison, M. (2002). Good, better, best? Inter-organizational learning in a network of local authorities. *Public Management Review 4*(1): 101–118.

Howard, D., & Marney, D. (2007). What is the balanced scorecard and what can it do for your library? *PNLA Quarterly 72*(1): 23, 26.

Huddleston, M., & Dresang, D. (2007). *The public administration workbook.* (5th ed.). New York, NY: Pearson Longman.

Kaplan, R. (2002). The balanced scorecard and nonprofit organizations. *Balanced Scorecard Report,* November–December: 1–4.

Kearney, R., & Berman, E., Eds. (2019). *Public sector performance: Management, motivation, and measurement.* New York, NY: Routledge.

Keehley, P., Medlin, S., & Longmire, L. (1996). *Best practices in the public sector: Benchmarking for performance improvement.* San Francisco, CA: Jossey-Bass.

Kitchell C. E. M. (2021). *Park Amenity Condition Assessment: Final Report.* https://www.sandiego.gov/sites/default/files/prbr210715a-item202a.pdf.

The KPI Institute, smartKPIs.com, & Brudan, A., Ed. (2015). *The local government KPI dictionary: 660+ key performance indicator definitions.* Melbourne, Australia: The KPI Institute.

Lang, R. E., & Sohmere, R. R. (2000). Legacy of the Housing Act of 1949: The past, present, and future of federal housing and urban policy. *Housing Policy Debate 11*(2): 291–298.

Lenhard, C. (2007). Achieving success through a balanced scorecard. *FBI Law Enforcement Bulletin 76*(7): 24.

Niven, P. (2003). *Balanced scorecard: Step by step for government and nonprofit agencies.* Hoboken, NJ: John Wiley.

O'Malley, M. (2019). *Smarter government: How to govern for results in the information age.* Redlands, CA: Esri Press.

O'Malley, M. (2020). *Smarter government workbook: A 14-week implementation guide to governing for results.* Redlands, CA: Esri Press.

Speklé, R. F., & Verbeeten, F. H. M. (2014). The use of performance measurement systems in the public sector: Effects on performance. *Management Accounting Research 25*(2): 131–146. https://doi.org/10.1016/j.mar.2013.07.004

Stupack, R., & Leitner, P., Eds. (2001). *Handbook of public quality management.* New York, NY: Marcel Dekker.

# 19 ───◆───◆───◆

# Leadership for Administrators

Leadership is a critical component of public governance, but what is leadership? How are leaders different from managers and supervisors? How can leaders affect overall organizational performance? How do people become leaders? Academic researchers and practitioners have struggled to understand these questions for more than a century and have developed many answers which are still evolving.

Leadership theorist Peter Northouse (2013) defined leadership as "a process whereby an individual influences a group of individuals to achieve a common goal" (p. 5). There are many facets to leadership, however. Northouse states that leadership primarily involves influence that occurs in groups where the attention is on common goals.

The terms manager and leader are often used interchangeably. However, there are key differences. One key difference is the manager's focus is often relatively narrow with primary emphasis on short-term goals and tasks; while a leader's focus is on people, the organization's vision, and long-term planning. Both are responsible for providing direction, creating stability, and guidance. While there is a clear distinction between the two, there are times when a manager will step into the role of a leader or when a leader will assume more of a managerial role, depending on the organization and its immediate needs. Managers and their positions appear on organization charts. Leaders can be anywhere in the organization and their influence may extend beyond the span of control implied by where they appear on the organization chart.

> One thing that has become clearer than ever to me is that integrity is the most important characteristic of a leader, and one that he or she must be prepared to demonstrate again and again. Too many . . . forget that something's being legal doesn't mean it's right. And they forget that what the public giveth, it can take away. (Bennis, 2009, p. 42)

Table 19.1    Leader Versus Manager Characteristics (Bennis, 2009)

| Leader | Manager |
| --- | --- |
| Innovates | Administers |
| Develops | Maintains |
| Focuses on people | Focuses on systems and structure |
| Inspires trust | Relies on control |
| Long-range perspective | Short-range view |
| Asks what and why | Asks how and when |
| Eye is on the horizon | Eye is always on the bottom line |
| Originates | Imitates |
| Challenges the status quo | Accepts the status quo |
| Is their own person | Is the classic *good soldier* |
| Does the right thing | Does things right |
| Reduction of complaints against officers | Cases before Internal Affairs |
| Other services | Get cat from tree, give directions, find lost child, assist disabled pedestrian, and so forth |

From *On Becoming a Leader* by Warren G. Bennis, copyright © 1989. Reprinted by permission of Basic Books, an imprint of Hachette Book Group, Inc.

We share Warren Bennis's view in the quote above, that leadership is a repetitive behavior that propels members to act collectively for the greater good of the organization and its community. We trust that leadership is learned through several mechanisms which are described below under the subheading, *Leadership and Management Development*. However, over the past 120 years there have been a plethora of theories and approaches regarding leadership. Some deviate significantly from that of Bennis while others do not. This chapter discuss some of these conflicting approaches and is an overview rather than an exhaustive discussion of the history or approaches to leadership that have dominated over the past century. The chapter concludes with a discussion of ethics and its influence on leadership.

## LEADERSHIP IMPACT ON ORGANIZATION AND OTHERS

Leaders have a tremendous impact on employees and the organizational culture. Organizational culture is defined as the beliefs, values, and norms established within an organization. Strong leaders, as well as ineffective or unethical leaders, provide a vision, sense of purpose, and motivation for those they lead, and therefore, can drive an organization in either a positive or negative direction. It is essential to understand that there is a direct correlation between organizational culture, leadership, and the job satisfaction of employees.

## EXPLORING WHAT LEADERSHIP IS
## AND HOW LEADERS ARE MADE

Leadership approaches and theories have evolved over the last 125 years. This section discusses five views of leadership that emerged since Woodrow Wilson's *Study of Public Administration* in 1888 during the Progressive/good-government era. In the early 1900s the concept of leadership emphasized control and power. The 1930s reflected a shift to trait-focused leadership and the leader's influence rather than their role. This attention on "traits" prevailed until the 1960s which was influenced by the cultural shift occurring in the world and manifested in a new behavioral view of leadership. By the 1980s, largely due to scholarly work, students of leadership were grappling with various definitions and competing leadership styles. In the 21st century leadership scholars agreed that there was no single definition of leadership, but a continuum of styles.

The discussion about leadership evolved over time as the workplace changed and as more was known about how to achieve desired results (e.g., profits in the private sector and other goals in the public and nonprofit sectors). All the approaches attempted to help organizations and their members determine how leaders should interact with followers (staff) in different situations to achieve long-term objectives.

## THE LEADER-FOCUS APPROACH TO LEADERSHIP

The earliest research on leadership saw leadership through the eyes of the leader. There are a few beliefs associated with this perspective including: *traits, skills, style, situation, and convergence.* The underlying assumption of these approaches is that leadership is fundamentally the leader's traits, competencies, behaviors, and suitability for the organization's tasks and/or the organization's evolving demands (the contingency approach). Leadership was *unique* to the individual, like one's eye color, gender, or height. These approaches might guide attempts to identify persons with preferred traits, skills, etc., but offered little to no remedy for organizations unable to revitalize their workforce, take on new challenges, or build more productive working relationships.

### Trait, Skills, and Style

The *trait* approach focused on the leader and maintained certain people were born with special traits. This approach was one of the first systematic attempts to study leadership and categorized leaders versus non-leaders. It identified eight traits: intelligence, alertness, insight, responsibility, initiative, persistence, self-confidence, and sociability. Having these traits did not mean someone was poised to be a leader, but these traits enabled leaders to handle challenging situations

(Stogdill, 1948). A follow-up study in 1974 added personality factors like risk taking, ease in social situations, drive, managing stress, and tolerance for frustration to an ever-growing list of attributes. The trait approach sees leaders at the forefront of organizations by virtue of their attributes, many of which were viewed as innate. They serve as a behavioral benchmark for others. The approach, however, is based on a subjective list of attributes, does not consider how leadership might be expressed in specific situations and implies that traits are not learned and fundamentally do not change over time.

The *skills* approach, like the trait approach, emphasizes a leader-centered perspective of competencies found in leaders. The difference in this approach was that the focus shifted from attributes of one's personality to a focus on discrete skills and abilities. While personality plays a role, the skills approach suggested that knowledge along with traits are essential for effective leadership. A 1955 *Harvard Business Review* article identified a three-skill approach to effective leadership: *technical, human, and conceptual*. It was noted that all three were important to managing (Katz, 1955).

Bennis (2009), Deming (1982) and others fundamentally challenged these assumptions. They maintained that leaders, and leadership traits, can be developed. These traits were not innate in some people and unachievable by others. Leaders are made, not born.

In 2000 the *skills* approach was updated and divided into two parts. The first part retained the basics of technical, human, and conceptual while the second part added a list of components needed for effective performance: outcomes, career experiences, and environmental influences. The skills approach has continued to evolve and now stresses that a needed skill may be learned, is not innate, and may be fostered by leadership and developmental programs. However, this approach neither predicts nor explains how the competencies produce effective leadership or desired outcomes.

The *style* approach emphasizes the behavior of the leader, rather than their skills and traits. The emphasis here is on what leaders do and how they act, rather than who they are. The major contribution of this approach has been the development of training tools (questionnaires) that measure leadership behavior and describe these behaviors along a grid enables one to map leadership behaviors (Blake and Mouton, 1964). However, like the approaches noted above, it does not enable one to identify how a set of behaviors produces an effective leader. Neither does it provide a paradigm to modify the style once the individual is plotted on the map.

Another key development in the exploration of leadership was the importance of context or the leaders/members' circumstances. Among the approaches that focused on these factors were the *situational* and *contingency* approaches.

## Situational Approach

The situational approach is the first approach to suggest how leaders might become most effective in different organizations with varying tasks. Central to this model are concepts of directing the behavior of others rather than motivating (supporting) others. A leader who provides instruction, clear explanations, and supervision is categorized as *high directive*. A leader who delegates tasks to those who are skilled and able to operate independently is categorized as *highly supportive*. Situational Leadership classifies leadership within those two parameters: degree of direction required and degree of support required. The leader can identify the appropriate leadership style and skills needed for a particular situation by identifying where the subordinates' needs and abilities appear within the grid.

**Figure 19.1    Situational Leadership Grid**

**Degree of Direction Required**

The extremes are (1) high directive – low supportive, (2) high directive – high supportive, (3) low directive – high supportive, and (4) low directive – low supportive. The approach describes how each style relates to a range of abilities and sense of commitment of subordinates. This approach suggests that leadership is a very different matter if one is encouraging physicists to develop an atomic bomb at the end World War II versus trying to get a chain gain to complete repairs on a highway. This approach outlines the most effective leadership style to be employed after diagnosing the subordinates' task situation. Leadership is measured using a questionnaire regarding a leader's abilities, flexibility, and effectiveness. This approach is widely recognized as providing clear rules for how leaders should act, having practical applications for organizations, providing a tool for training, and identifying there is no one best style for leadership. However, there is a lack of information on the subordinates' preference for leadership, and/or how a leaders use tools in a large scale setting as opposed to a one-on-one setting.

## Contingency Approach

Finally, the contingency approach shifted leadership research by examining the leader in particular situations. It is defined by its emphasis on how well the leader's style matches the situation. Effective leadership is seen as dependent on the fit between the situation and the leader's style. To measure situations, a tool is used to assess three factors: the leader-member relations, the structure of the task, and position power (authority). Taken together these factors serve to illustrate which leaders are expected to be the most effective. This approach emphasizes the situation's impact on the leader's success, predicts effectiveness, acknowledges that a leader's efforts will not always be effective, and provides the leader with critical information. However, this approach does not explain how the leader may use the results to adapt to changing situations. Nor is there information on the subordinates' preference for leadership, and/or how a leader uses these tools in a large-scale setting rather than a one-to-one interaction (Fiedler 1964, 1967; Field & Garcia, 1987).

# LEADERSHIP: THE FOLLOWER'S PERSPECTIVE

The persistent orientation on the leader and the leader's view had limitations. In John Kennedy's 1961 inauguration address, he said, "the torch has been passed to a new generation of Americans." This phrase recognized a younger, diverse, impatient, and idealistic population entering the workforce and residing in the nation's cities and towns. The leader-centered approaches ignored that leadership was a relationship and that the subordinates/followers were a key to defining what leadership was and how best to diagnose and behave in a range of situations. The shift away from the leader focus to the joint view of leader and followers gave rise to new approaches to tools, training, and measures of performance. These approaches are referred to here as the leadership relationship from *the follower's perspective*. What these approaches share is the realization that followers and subordinates, along with leaders, define what leadership is as well as what is effective behavior and results. As described in more detail below, the *path-goal* approach assumes that what is most needed from the leader is information while the *leadership-member exchange* (LMX) approach asserts that there are two key components of a leadership-follower relationship: the expectations that arise out of their relationship and the obligations and support that arises from these expectations. Like LMX, the *transformational leadership* approach held that the relationship between leader and follower was less about a need for information and more about a need for insight and inspiration. Leaders took on the role of coach as opposed to instructor or commander. The *servant leader* upended the leadership-follower perspective and saw the leader as servant or subordinate to the follower. While the *servant leader* was a new concept for the study of leadership it was an old concept dating back to the 1st century of the Common Era. Finally, *authentic leadership* provided the follower with unencumbered access to the leader and *team leadership* tore down any remaining barriers between the leader and follower. Roles, responsibilities, expectations, obligations arise out of the phases and stages of the team's life cycles (described below) and the concept of leadership-follower becomes fluid and distinctions between who is the leader and who is the follower becomes virtually indistinguishable.

## Members' Need for Direction, Motivation, Inspiration

Path-goal was among the first approaches to leadership that perceived the leader-follower relationship as what was needed from leaders by the followers. Path-goal assumes that a leader's behavior is dependent on the satisfaction, motivation, and performance of employees (a.k.a., followers). The leader guides others to take the optimum path to reach their goal while promoting the organization's objectives. Results of this approach have been mixed. In some studies, this approach is correlated with successful results but not in others. More recently the path-goal approach is seen as effective to the extent that the leader/subordinate relationships complement the followers' environment. To the extent the environment does not provide clear causal linkages between effort and goal, it becomes the leaders' function to arrange and/or explain linkages and clarify the subordinates' perceptions. Also, it is the leader's role to provide information, support, and resources to ensure the subordinate's satisfaction and effective performance (House, R.J., 1996). Central to the application of path-goal was the fit between the leader-subordinate relationship and their environment.

Leadership-Member Exchange (LMX) is also a relationship-based approach to leadership that is considered both *transactional* and *transformational*. Transactional is an exchange between two people. Market transactions are the most familiar transactions where customers get a good or service in exchange for paying a fee. Transformational is behavior that arises out of a relationship such as is found in families, professional associations, or social gatherings. In these cases, behavior arises out of expectations about the relationship that give rise to obligations and/or to unsolicited support or nurturing. LMX is centered on the reciprocal relationship that develops between leaders and followers. In LMX, leaders are labeled as *leaders* or *supervisors*, and followers are referred to interchangeably as *followers, members, employees,* or *subordinates.* (Notgrass, 2014; Scandura & Lankau, 1996; Graen, 1976; Graen and Cashman, 1975)

LMX examines the leadership relationship within groups (group-level effect) and within dyads (dyad-level effect or relationship between a leader and follower). While leader-focused approaches assume leaders treat subordinates similarly, LMX focuses on the relationship that specifically exists and grows between the leader and each subordinate, believing that leaders act differently and develop varying levels of bonds with individual subordinates (Lunenburg, 2010; Graen & Uhl-Bien, 1995; Lunenburg, 2010).

LMX approach is grounded in role theory and social exchange theory of social psychologists, R. Linton and G. Mead. Role theory explains the tasks and expectations of both leader and the follower while social exchange theory emphasizes the relational interactions between leader and follower (Kahn, Wolfe, Quinn, Snoek, & Rosenthal, 1964; Blau, 1964). The approach linked perceived relationships to interactions.

Path-goal and LMX viewed the need for leadership from the member's perspective. Other approaches emphasized the same perspective but defined the need of members as a need for inspiration and/or motivation. When rewards and punishments were the prime motivations, then a leader remained a leader as long as one served in a position that enabled them to manipulate rewards. However, practitioners and scholars were aware of persons who influenced behavior, promoted objectives, and realized outcomes but were not those who had control over rewards. This latter type of leadership was called **transformational** and was characterized by persons who were inspirational, charismatic, and encouraged followers. The transformational leader can motivate others by showing them the significance of the task, the greater good that was served by performing the task, and the significant relationship between the importance of the task to the individual as well as to the team. The behavior of the transformational leaders was less about providing instructions and direction and more about coaching and spurring others to realizing their personal best. This emphasis on inspiring or urging another to their best was echoed in the servant leadership approach.

A servant leader utilizes emotional intelligence to encourage passion in others. The servant leader cares for others and sets a standard of behavior and care for others that is motivational. The core values expressed by servant leaders are to prioritize resources to those most in need, to share power so all have an appropriate voice in decision making, to demonstrate care or show empathy, to develop the knowledge and skills of others, to work for the greater good, to build trust, and to create a workplace where mistakes may occur and yet individuals feel safe to share wins and losses. While there are many who gravitate toward the servant leadership approach in some fields (education and health care), there are many criticisms of this method. Among the concerns is that the inner qualities and/or inner journey of leaders and followers is difficult to define or to test empirically. A key concern is that it may depend on specific organizational or cultural contexts. Finally, there is not yet sufficient evidence of cause and effect to link the servant leadership with results.

The *authentic leader* is sometimes best known for being "down-to-earth," genuine, an all-around-good person. Platitudes aside, there are four components associated with the authentic leader: (1) self-awareness or an understanding of how their behavior and actions influence others; (2) transparency or good communication skills in working with others; (3) balance or the ability to identify and navigate the dynamics of teams, the task, and project's needs; (4) strong sense that decisions made in the workplace must be fair and equitable. The consequences of this approach are employee job satisfaction, clear expectations, collaboration over individualism, innovation, and high-performance ratings. Obstacles that separate leader from follower seem to dissolve.

## Teams and Leadership Inside and Outside of Organizations

Participants in team efforts have long recognized that teams go through phases and stages. As early as 1964, Tuckerman identified five distinct stages of teamwork: forming, storming, norming, performing, and adjourning. While there may be little need for leadership when groups are *forming* and everyone is on their best behavior, this stage is followed by stress, strain, and conflict. Now members of the team need to listen to all sides, move forward where possible, communicate, collaborate, and facilitate ways and means to resolving concerns. Based on this shared experience during *storming*, everyone's contribution is recognized, and roles, responsibilities and expectations get defined. This practice is referred to as *norming*. High *performing* teams recognize that while task assignments are part of the organization's scaffolding (metaphorically speaking), team members will mix up roles from time to time to assure performance and to share ideas. Consequently, team leadership is fundamentally the contributions of all team members, a focus on collaboration and on meeting or exceeding performance standards. Team leadership is diffuse by design and there is a need for ongoing research on its limitations and contributions to organizational success.

## Leaders in Different Circumstances

With the advent of the team member as a participator and as a leader, the gap between leader and follower all but disappeared. Organizations maintained administrative structures with identifiable points for accountability but relied operationally on the accountability of the team. In this regard public administrative systems did not differ from their private-sector counterparts. However, unlike the private sector, public employees might find themselves in leadership roles separate from the scaffolding of an administrative system. A police officer may need to take on a leadership role for a few hours to divert traffic from a road hazard. A recreation coordinator may need to take on a leadership role for days to enable athletic teams to go through *elimination rounds* to determine the league's finalists. A director for neighborhood revitalization may need to take on a leadership role for decades to promote cooperation, coordination, and mutual regard among stakeholders transforming a declining neighborhood into a robust and vibrant residential and commercial community. Consequently, leadership is seen as skills needed across a wide range of roles and tasks provided by the public sector. Leadership approaches share three enduring emphases: (1) the relationships among members in a group; (2) the context, environment, or situation; and (3) the effect or results.

There are volumes of texts and journals dedicated to how leaders behave in different situations and circumstances. A full discussion is beyond the scope of this text. Readers are encouraged to avail themselves of the resources noted in the bibliography below.

# LEADERSHIP AND MANAGEMENT DEVELOPMENT

## Ongoing Employee Development

Leadership development can use many methods. One method is the formal employee evaluations. However, leadership should extend beyond the formal evaluation. Indeed, W. Edwards Deming (Walton, 1990) says that the formal performance evaluation should be completely eliminated because it has nothing to do with improving an employee's performance, increases workplace stress, and decreases morale. The growth of managers and leaders should not be left to chance. Discussions with aspiring leaders and managers should include ongoing candid reviews of career objectives and opportunities within the organization. A clearer picture of which specific actions need to be taken can then be developed. Much as a tree is watered and fertilized periodically, aspiring leaders should meet periodically with their supervisors or mentors to monitor progress and plan how to improve. Some organizations maintain formal leadership development programs, including the U.S. Office of Personnel Management Federal Executive Institute and management development centers. However, many governmental organizations have strict civil service rules that make it difficult to single out individuals who can be groomed for leadership positions. In this case, organizations may make leadership development programs widely available to employees who meet certain qualifications.

Fortunately, similar leadership development opportunities exist for ambitious individuals who may not have access to such formal organization-specific leadership programs. Professional organizations are a gateway to deeper involvement and visibility. In the public sector, professional organizations can be found for everything from finance to law to communications. Benefits of membership in professional organizations include opportunities to network with peers (developing what some call the "golden Rolodex"), ongoing professional education, and timely profession-specific information via newsletters, emails, and organization internet websites as well as the occasional meeting, conference, or social gathering. The leadership maxim "It's lonely at the top" is made less true by actively building a healthy list of contacts, allies, and supporters to whom one can turn for information and guidance. Table 19.2 includes a representative list of professional organizations.

**Table 19.2    Professional Organizations in Public Administration**

| Professional Organizations | Website |
| --- | --- |
| American Society for Public Administration | www.aspanet.org |
| International Public Management Association for Human Resources (IPMA-HR) | www.ipma-hr.org |
| Society for Human Resource Management (SHRM) | www.shrm.org |
| Government Finance Officers Association | www.gfoa.org |
| Institute for Public Procurement | www.nigp.org |
| National Contract Management Association | www.ncmahq.org |

While public speaking to strangers ranks near the top of commonly held fears, reaching out to other professionals through informational phone calls, meetings, or lunches is a skill that can be developed. This sort of colleague contact should be an active part of the life of any professional. This is particularly true in the public sector where stakeholders may include other departments scattered across a large geographical area, other public-sector organizations, and publicly elected officials, and where people can frequently move from one organization to another. Social contact and networking opportunities may not occur naturally as one walks through a department or building. Reaching out to colleagues can improve the flow of information and communication to support one's work.

Supervisors are coaches who should encourage employee development in a variety of ways. Encouraging employees to attend training or seek advanced education is an obvious approach. However, on a day-to-day basis supervisors can enhance opportunities for growth by redesigning and expanding work to include greater levels of responsibility as employees are ready. For example, junior staff can be invited to attend high-level policy meetings where they will glean substantive information as well as develop interpersonal skills and self-confidence. In public agencies, aspiring leaders should consider attending public governing board meetings and public hearings for their organizations. Observing board meetings and public hearings provides the opportunity for exposure to the political and policy issues that impact organizations. Culture and practice vary across organizations. An aspiring leader who visits board meetings outside their own organization improves their exposure to different leadership styles and public-sector issues. Reading board agendas and minutes can lend insights into leadership issues and challenges those aspiring leaders may one day face.

Communication is a key element of employee mentoring and development. Explaining the reasons for assignments and providing clear instructions both ensures a better work product and enhances morale. Supervisors must ensure that they are accessible and approachable so that employees can obtain feedback to questions. Teamwork and cross training are valuable development techniques as well. Employees who have an opportunity to take on new challenges, learn the jobs of their colleagues, and those who are encouraged to share information develop more quickly and add more value to their organizations. Encouraging employees to participate in community service activities outside of the job is another development tool. Appendices A and B provide detailed descriptions of tools and techniques for developing written and oral communication skills.

## Resources for Understanding Individual Styles and Group Dynamics

The goal of employee development is to cultivate talent and groom future organization leaders. Self-awareness and independent thinking are crucial as one makes the transition to the role of leading others. A keen understanding of self is a first step in understanding others. Diagnostic tools are available to provide feedback for leadership development. One of these feedback tools is the Myers-Briggs Type Indicator (MBTI). The MBTI provides some systematic insights about oneself and how one's style may differ from others. This feedback may provide the foundation for individual leadership growth discussions, an understanding of teams and culture, and an understanding of how to approach improving performance and conflict management. Since leadership is contextual, the benefits of understanding different personal styles and applying the related insights to effective leadership are useful. There are several online personality diagnostic instruments to explore what type of personality one is (see https://www.16personalities.com/free-personality-test).

The Strength Deployment Inventory (SDI) by Personal Strengths provides leaders and their teams feedback about how to choose behaviors that will produce productive working relationships. Relationship awareness, motivation, and understanding conflict are key elements in the SDI. The SDI provides a foundation for leaders to understand themselves and the people they lead.

Both the MBTI and SDI have their roots in research by psychologists including Carl Rogers, Elias Porter, and Carl Jung. A primary challenge for the individual is understanding how to apply the results of either the MBTI or SDI to any particular situation.

## Approaches to Nurturing Talent: Mentoring and Coaching

Mentoring is an informal method in which a senior and/or experienced person—usually other than the employee's immediate supervisor—acts as a role model and guides the employee in improving their skills and functioning successfully in the organization's culture. Its success is based on how well the mentor is matched with a protégé as well as the mentor's willingness to engage and explore areas of interest and importance and to provide an ongoing time commitment to confer with the protégé. The mentor-mentee relationship often continues for many years, usually at varying levels of intensity, and may continue even when they are in different organizations.

Coaching is similar to mentoring except that in the coaching situation there is less interaction, and the coach observes the protégé in a work situation and provides feedback, using a consistent format, on a regular basis. Coaching tends to be more job-specific than mentoring and is successful when it creates an environment that is supportive, nurturing, and challenging. The understudies, or those being coached, become coaches for others, creating networks of communication and talent within an organization. These approaches may help encourage openness and foster learning, independence, flexibility, and accountability.

Leadership is an activity that is best learned by practicing. Aspiring leaders and managers must be wary of copying other leaders. The most accomplished leaders develop their own styles. What works for one leader may not be comfortable or appropriate for another. Leadership styles develop through the practice of leadership in multiple contexts. If opportunities for leadership do not formally exist, aspiring leaders should seek out opportunities to lead projects or take on special assignments. They should critically assess their capabilities, often with the aid of a mentor or coach, and focus efforts on projects they are best prepared to complete successfully. By taking on leadership responsibility, no matter how small, one sharpens leadership skills, connects with others, and increases visibility in an organization.

## Team Building

In addition to requiring individual development, effective organizations require that employees work well in groups. Rarely do employees work alone, and the dynamics of groups can be constructive or destructive. In this context, a team or group is any collection of people one works with, regardless of the frequency of the association. Sometimes a single individual can poison a group, while in other instances the entire group may become dysfunctional. When leaders (including both managers and supervisors) observe unproductive groups or become aware of deficiencies through complaints from inside or outside a team, they need to act, whether through informal meetings or by calling in professionals who specialize in analyzing and facilitating group interactions. This process can spark new life in a group. To sustain team spirit, leaders need to consistently model the behavior of effective team members in their interactions with colleagues. A common set of departmental or organizational goals provides a framework and direction for teams. The leader shapes the culture, emphasizes the mission and goals, communicates purpose, and consequently is valued by the team. Metrics and measurements for success are important for evaluating team progress toward goals and support of the mission (see Chapter 18, "Performance Measures"). Not to be overlooked are the rituals, ceremonies, and symbols that hold cultures and organizations together. Acknowledgments might include team shirts, recognition celebrations, or personal notes of appreciation.

## Task Forces and Special Projects

Along with cross training and teamwork within work units, opportunities in which employees from various units work together for temporary assignments (such as establishing innovative programs, troubleshooting problem issues, or serving on ad hoc committees) develop employees as well as organizations. This approach gives rank-and-file employees, supervisors, and managers exposure to other people in the organization and to different styles and perspectives. Interaction between work units can take several forms. The most formal could be a leadership-academy type class in which a cohort of aspiring leaders in the organization meets regularly to hear from each department and function. A more in-depth interaction is an exchange program wherein participants job shadow or work in another department for a period of time or for several hours a week. Participating in other departments' meetings gives one insight into the inner workings and issues of those departments. Some public agencies hold periodic public town meetings. These are also venues for leadership development, even if one's initial role is to take notes or lead a small discussion group. Also at an informal level, taking time to lunch with peers and managers in other areas of the organization may provide opportunities for greater understanding of organizational issues and connecting professionally with others. Participating in organization-sponsored volunteer activities can also broaden networks and relationships.

## Executive Development

All the approaches previously discussed help develop executives and staff at all levels. However, there are some characteristics that agencies look for in their top executives. Agency leaders (e.g., department heads) are expected to shape and maintain a culture in an organization and/or to facilitate change in a manner that serves its clients well and makes employees feel confident and empowered to handle the challenges ahead. Expectations of leaders at the executive levels of public-sector organizations are weighted heavily toward managing the message and results. Executive public-sector leaders are the public face of the organization, and as such, they must be adept at the skills required for this, particularly communicating with the public (see also Chapter 5 and Appendix A and B). Managing the image of the organization includes ensuring that good positive stories about the results being delivered are shared. Part of the challenge for the public-sector executive within the organization is finding these stories. Sharing positive stories can be done through press conferences, press releases, organizations' internet sites, and good relationships with the local print, radio, and television media. Perhaps the greatest challenge for an executive is when negative stories about the organization appear. Only those persons specifically tasked with representing the organization to the public should discuss negative stories with the public, press, or on any media, including all social media; everyone else in the organization should refer questions to the senior executive or Public Relations department. This centralization of communication helps ensure that all of the relevant information is gathered and incorporated into the response. Aspiring public-sector executives who wish to avoid the limelight may not enjoy being an executive. Executive public-sector leaders extend their influence and ability to influence by participating in external organizations. These may include local nonprofits; service clubs such as Rotary, Kiwanis, or Lions; the chamber of commerce; or public volunteer agencies such as United Way.

Executives may find themselves making presentations to the public or responding to questions from the media. Public-sector executives must ensure they are prepared and minimize the probability of appearing flustered or caught off guard. Decisions are often made in public with the media present. Public-sector executives are accountable to the public, taxpayers, their governing boards, and the people who work for them. Public-sector organizations, be they in education, safety, or health, can shape lives. The building and maintaining of public support are crucial if a public agency wishes to keep serving the public.

The changing demographic composition of communities should, ideally, mean having a changing public sector workforce and political input that reflects the diversity of the community. Executives need to be aware of these changing circumstances and proactively include a diversity of perspectives, inputs, and interests in the decision-making process and the staffing and operations of public services. The issue of diversity in public administration practice is not well settled and we are not prepared to delve into the subject in any significant detail; we only caution leaders in public administration be aware of the issue of diversity and develop their skills in recognizing the changing environment and methods to deal with it.

## ETHICS AND LEADERSHIP

### Ethical Leadership Defined

The elements of ethical leadership are defined as:

- respect for others,
- service to others,
- a focus on equity and justice,
- honesty (transparency), and
- building community.

*Ethical Theories.* Chapter 4 describes ethical decision making and introduces readers to three normative models: utilitarianism, deontology (duty), and virtue. However, there are also practical or applied concerns when discussing ethics in leadership. Among the components of applied ethical leadership are (1) internal uniformity, (2) proactive perspective, and (3) an ongoing agenda for improvement, sometimes referred to as vigor. The first objective is for the organization and the leadership which directs it should be internally consistent. This does not mean rigid but that ethical contradictions are resolved. Proactive means that the ethical framework of the organization ascribes what persons are to do rather than being a list of don'ts. Finally, there is the understanding that organizations are dynamic and in flux. Consequently, the affirmation and reaffirmation of the organization's ethical standards and behaviors are dynamic and should regularly be reviewed and upheld.

## CONCLUSION

This chapter defined leadership as the influence that occurs in groups where the attention is on realizing common goals. The issue of organizational leadership has been a primary concern of scholars and practitioners for over a hundred years. This chapter identified and critiqued both leader-focused and follower-focused approaches to leadership. Specifically, it sought to determine how leadership was defined, what perspective (leader, follower, other) was employed by each approach, the importance of context (environment), and the empirical evidence that the relationship correlated with goals or outcomes. These underlying criteria served to highlight the advantages and disadvantages of each approach. The findings are mixed; however, it is clear that leadership is a complex phenomenon that incorporates the relationship among members in a group in an array of circumstances.

The practical implications are discussed here as well. Because leadership is such an integral part of organizational success, agencies seek to engage in programs and policies that continue to develop, nurture, and promote leadership competencies in managers and staff. Finally, a key component of leadership is establishing and sustaining ethical decision making throughout the organization. The clear, unambiguous link between leadership and organizational success in the short and long term is discussed.

## PRACTICING PUBLIC ADMINISTRATION

1. How are leaders different than managers or supervisors?
2. Distinguish between the *traits, skills,* and *styles* approaches to describing or identifying leaders.
3. How does the *situational approach* help a leader select the appropriate leadership style?
4. What approaches share the realization that followers and subordinates, along with leaders, define what leadership is as well as what is effective behavior and results?
5. What are the key elements of the Strength Deployment Inventory (SDI)?
6. What are some of the benefits of membership and participation in professional organizations?
7. What are the five elements of ethical leadership?

## BIBLIOGRAPHY

Bennis, W. (2009). *On becoming a leader.* New York, NY: Basic Books.

Blake, R., & Mouton, J. (1964). *The managerial grid: The key to leadership excellence.* Houston, TX: Gulf Publishing Company.

Blanchard, A. L., Welbourne, J., Gilmore, D., & Bullock, A. (2009). Followership styles and employee attachment to the organization. *The Psychologist-Manager Journal 12*(2): 111–131. doi:10.1080/10887150902888718

Blanchard, K. H., & Blanchard, K. H. (1985). *SL II: A situational approach to managing people.* Escondido, CA: Blanchard Training and Development.

Blanchard, K. H., & Johnson, S. (1981). *The one minute manager.* New York, NY: Berkley Books.

Blanchard, K. H., Zigarmi, P., & Zigarmi, D. (1985). *Leadership and the one-minute manager: Increasing effectiveness through situational leadership.* New York, NY: Morrow.

Blau, P. M. (1964). *Exchange and power in social life.* New York, NY: Jossey-Bass.

Chen, Y., Wen, Z., Peng, J., & Liu, X. (2016). Leader-follower congruence in loneliness, LMX and turnover intention. *Journal of Managerial Psychology 31*(4): 864–879.

Dansereau, F., Graen, G., & Haga, W. (1975). A vertical dyad linkage approach to leadership within formal organizations. *Organizational Behavior and Human Performance 13*: 46–78. doi:10.1016/0030-5073(75)90005-7

Deming, W. E. (1982). *Out of the crisis.* Cambridge, MA: MIT Press.

Fiedler, F. (1964). A contingency model of leadership effectiveness. In Berkowitz, L. (Ed.), *Advances in experimental social psychology*, Vol. 1 (149–190). New York, NY: Academic Press.

Fiedler, F. (1967). *A theory of leadership effectiveness.* New York, NY: McGraw-Hill.

Fiedler, F., & Garcia, J. (1987) *New approaches to leadership, cognitive resources, and organizational performance.* New York, NY: John Wiley and Sons.

Graen, G. (1976). Role-making processes within complex organizations. In Dunnette, M. D. (Ed.), *Handbook of industrial organizational psychology* (1201–1245). Chicago, IL: Rand McNally.

Graen, G., & Cashman, J. (1975). A role-making model of leadership in formal organizations: A developmental approach. In Hunt, J. G. & Larson, L. L. (Eds.), *Leadership frontiers* (143–166). Kent, OH: Kent State University Press.

Graen, G., & Uhl-Bien, M. (1995). Relationship-based approach to leadership: Development of leader-member exchange (LMX) theory of leadership over 25 years: Applying a multi-level multi-domain perspective. *The Leadership Quarterly 6*(2): 219–247. doi:10.1016/1048-9843(95)90036-5

House. (1996). Path-goal theory of leadership: Lessons, legacy, and a reformulated theory. *The Leadership Quarterly 7*(3): 323–352. https://doi.org/10.1016/S1048-9843(96)90024-7

Kahn, R. L., Wolfe, D. M., Quinn, R. P., Snoek, J. D., & Rosenthal, R. A. (1964). *Organizational stress.* New York, NY: Wiley.

Kang, D., & Stewart, J. (2007). Leader-member exchange (LMX) theory of leadership and HRD. *Leadership & Organization Development Journal 28*(6): 531–551.

Katz, R. L. (1955). Skills of an effective administrator. *Harvard Business Review 33*(1): 33–42.

Lundy, J. (1986). *Lead, follow, or get out of the way.* San Diego, CA: Avant Books.

Lunenburg, F. C. (2010). Leader-member exchange theory: Another perspective on the leadership process. *International Journal of Management, Business, and Administration 13*(1): 1–5.

Mumford, M. D., Zaccaro, S. J., Connelly, M. S., & Marks, M. A. (2000). Leadership skills: Conclusions and future directions. *Leadership Quarterly 11*(1): 155–170.

Notgrass, D. (2014). The relationship between followers' perceived quality of relationship and preferred leadership style. *Leadership & Organization Development Journal 35*(7): 605–621.

Northouse, P. G. (2013). *Leadership: Theory and practice* (4th ed.). Thousand Oaks, CA: Sage.

Roberts, W. (1985). *Leadership skills of Atilla the Hun.* New York, NY: Warner Books, Inc.

Scandura, T., & Lankau, M. (1996). Developing diverse leaders: A leader-member exchange approach. *The Leadership Quarterly 7*(2): 243–263. doi:10.1016/S1048-9843(96)90043-0

Stogdill, R. (1948) Personal factors associated with leadership: A survey of the literature. *The Journal of Psychology 25*(1): 35–71. DOI: 10.1080/00223980.1948.9917362

Stogdill, R. M. (1974). *Handbook of leadership: A survey of the literature.* New York, NY: Free Press.

Walton, M. (1986). *The Deming management method.* New York, NY: Perigee Books.

Walton, M. (1990. *Deming management at work.* New York, NY: Perigee Books.

Yammarino, F. J. (2000). Leadership skills: Introduction and overview. *Leadership Quarterly 11*(1): 5–9. https://coek.info/queue/pdf-leadership-skills-introduction-and-overview-.html

# Appendix

## A

## Writing Reports and Speaking Effectively

Effective writing and speaking are the two most important skills for public administrators. As the above example demonstrates, even the simplest communication may not send the message intended by the writer.

There are many functions of written communications. Writing is used to provide information, give instructions, and make recommendations. Some of these uses are highlighted in Chapter 5, "Informing and Involving the Public," which focuses on media and public relations.

Business writing used in the government sector has some style characteristics that differ from casual writing used in everyday communications or academic writing used by students or professors. Writing effectively is a learned skill that takes considerable practice, and understanding some of the basics is a first step.

Similarly, administrators should learn the skills of effective verbal communication While we have all been speaking with others most of our lives, effective verbal interactions in the world of public administration do take some important skills to enhance clarity, ensure effective transmission of information, and promote interpersonal relationships.

This appendix covers some of the basic principles of effective report writing and of verbal communication.

Appendix B covers the special skills of preparing and making effective presentations both internally and to the public. A presentation in this context is an oral report that is often augmented by visual aids and/ or written materials. Presentations are often recorded and archived for future reference or distribution.

## WHO WRITES?

Almost everyone writes something, although some jobs require writing as their primary function, particularly analyst jobs. Beginner analysts write, as do most senior analysts. Senior managers may or may not write but certainly do review and edit, drawing on their past experience in writing. Technical staff such as engineers and maintenance supervisors may write technical reports and memos in the normal course of their work. As they move up the career ladder, they may write more frequently for governing bodies. Most supervisors write employee evaluations, and just about everyone in a civil service position fills out forms and writes portions of examinations used for promotion.

## CREATION, TRANSMISSION, AND STORAGE

The methods used to create, transmit, and store information change over time; however, the basic processes and uses of writing change little. In the late 20th century, electronics dramatically changed the mechanics of writing, transmitting of writing, and storage of what is written, and those changes continue in the 21st century. More and more people have never used a typewriter or carbon paper to make a copy of a document (the origin of the term "cc" for "carbon copy"). Most writing is now done on computers and the writing is transmitted and stored electronically; less and less writing is printed on paper and stored in filing cabinets. Most of the documents created and used by public administrators have not changed all that much over the past 50 years, but now they are accessed and transmitted electronically and virtually instantaneously. The documents must still be created with care to ensure they communicate effectively and clearly.

Both how long and the physical format in which a particular document must be stored may be set either by law or the practical needs of the organization. Some documents must be maintained on paper for a fixed time period after which they may be stored on some other media (e.g., microfiche or electronically) and/or destroyed. Other documents may be stored only electronically and printed only when necessary. The organization's attorney is the primary source for legal requirements for document retention (storage) and destruction. The organization's chief administrative officer or other senior manager specifies retention and destruction protocols for documents that do not have specific statutory requirements.

Digital (electronic) files are not indestructible; over time they will degrade and some data bits will change or be lost. A good practice is to duplicate digital files at least every 5 years, depending on the digital media. A curator at the Getty Museum once commented that, "We're making digital photographs of 4,000-year-old papyri and storing them on magnetic tapes that might last for 10 years."

## TYPES OF WRITTEN COMMUNICATION

Any of the documents described below may be created and transmitted electronically (most commonly by some form of email). However, some documents may require physical printing on paper with a "wet ink" signature to verify that they are properly reviewed and authenticated by a responsible manager or official.

### Internal Memos/Intradepartmental Correspondence

The example at the beginning of this appendix is an internal memo which is written between staff members within a department or organizational unit. It is the least formal form of written communication. Nonetheless it should communicate effectively, even if only a few sentences in length. Internal memos may be as simple as the one above or span multiple pages if they are intended to describe more complex topics. A subordinate who is preparing information requested by a supervisor for internal use would use this type of format or, alternatively, a similar format titled "intradepartmental correspondence." Any employee can normally send a memo. Informal memos of this type often do not include recommendations but can do so if it is appropriate.

### Interdepartmental Correspondence

More formal than internal memos, interdepartmental correspondence is correspondence that is sent between departments in a government agency. Although written by a staff member, it may require the signature of a division or department head because it represents a point of view of the department. Therefore, it may require several levels of review within the organization. It may or may not include formal recommendations. The length of the correspondence dictates whether it is divided into sections such as Background, Findings, and Recommendations or uses a narrative format.

## Reports

Reports are types of formal correspondence typically between departments, boards of directors, or elected officials in response to specific requests, such as a council request, and they address more complex and lengthy subjects. Reports are the mechanism by which departments provide staff recommendations to elected policy makers. They often have an Executive Summary of a page or two, which may include Recommendations either before or after the summary. While formats vary from organization to organization, it is typical that the detail is included in a lengthier Findings section, which may also be preceded by a Background or Request section and formal headings with file references noting who requested the report. Reports often become part of an agency's permanent public record and are therefore subject to the greatest amount of review before being released.

## Manuals

Policy and procedures manuals are common forms of written communication that analysts often prepare. Manuals range from desk procedures or departmental procedures to agency-wide practices (e.g., civil service or contracting procedures). They usually have a set format and are based on a standard template. The most important element is that they convey the information intended and are understandable by a diverse audience. Manuals often undergo many levels of review to ensure their accuracy. Because they are intended for long-term use, they are often bound and/or uploaded to a website for distribution throughout an organization and/or made available to the public.

## Transmittals

Transmittals, which may go by various names in an organization, are very short documents (normally only one page or less) used as cover memos for larger documents sent between departments, usually indicating authorization or approval. Frequently the transmittal sheet lists all of the people who should see and review the larger document and has a place for each to sign that they have seen it. For example, a department authorized to review and/or approve expenditures of funds or filling of positions might send a short transmittal to the requesting department indicating that "the attached request is approved for further processing" or is "returned without action," with a signature of the appropriate official.

## Forms

Forms collect information in a consistent format making analysis and review easier. More and more forms are available and can be filled out and submitted electronically. Some forms may be completed electronically but require printing and a "wet ink" signature. Secure electronic signatures are becoming more widespread. Everyone is familiar with forms and has experienced the frustration of filling them out when they are unclear or have insufficient space to provide the required information. Since government agencies are often the source of forms and many public administrators are assigned to develop them, the author should put themself in the position of the reader and see if they understand the instructions. It is also a good idea to circulate forms to several people for review to test their accuracy and clarity.

## Email

Electronic mail, or email, is not actually a type of written communication: it is a method of transmitting written communications. Prior to the 1990s almost all written communication was transmitted by the postal service or couriers. Today email is the most common means of transmitting written communication. It is used for sending all types of documents and often in lieu of telephone calls.

Email in its most basic form is a transmittal sheet or memo which may also have other documents attached to it. Recipients may reply to only the sender or may send the same reply to all who received the email. Two primary advantages of email over "snail mail" (sending paper by postal service) are the ability to easily send several documents at the same time to multiple recipients, and the ability to easily view the sequence of conversations on the topic.

Because so many people use email for personal use and are accustomed to sending text messages, they may not be aware of the guidelines for its use in the workplace and some of the risks associated with email. Below are some guidelines for email:

- Email is not confidential. Email is very difficult to delete once it has been sent, and there is no control over whom an email may be forwarded to. Even if the user deletes an email from their own computer, it is probably stored on a computer network server accessible by systems technology staff or hackers. This means that if one does not want to see the local newspaper print an embarrassing email sent to a supervisor, one should not send it. Be careful about sending personal information.

- Offices have varying policies regarding the use of email for personal reasons. Organizations often require employees to sign an internet use policy before they can get internet access. Organizations can also block access to certain sites and to pop-ups.

This applies mostly to external email. Although many organizations have policies stating that email is for official use only, occasional personal computer use is usually tolerated as long as it does not interfere with employees' work and/or reduce productivity. As a practical matter, enforcement of restrictions is very difficult since employees use email regularly for official use and supervisors are not aware of all the recipients of employee mail. The tolerated use of email may include a brief message to a spouse or child or a message regarding a personal appointment. Email has replaced the quick telephone call. Also, email may be used to announce anything from office events to food in the refrigerator. Some places may have a zero-tolerance policy, particularly regarding public contact offices. When one is hired it is important to inquire about and understand the email policy of the office.

- Email used to communicate government business should be created and treated like the documents described above. It should be professional looking with correct capitalization, punctuation, grammar, and spelling. Sloppy email suggests sloppy writing and/ or work habits and reflects unfavorably on the sender and the sender's organization.

- Keep the body of the email short but complete. If there are several questions or topics, either send them as separate messages or indicate at the very beginning the number of questions or topics in the message.

- Email is an easy way to distribute information to many recipients, and setting up groups to receive routine emails is very effective. It is also easy to send blind copies when appropriate (i.e., copies to persons whom other copied recipients do not see). However, it is also easy to make mistakes such as sending replies to the wrong person (when an email has been forwarded) or to "Reply All" by mistake and send items to an entire office. These errors can be quite embarrassing, and therefore one must be very cautious in an office environment.

## Social Media

New platforms of electronic communication are constantly evolving. Most of them are intended for short personal messages and informal communications among individuals, groups, or segments of the general public. Social media, which includes SMS (short message service) or texting, deserves special attention primarily because it is relatively new and its proper place in business communication is not well established. Like email, social media communications are fraught with the likelihood of misinterpretation and of misrepresenting an individual's opinions as an official position. Misinterpretation is caused partly through the lack of non-verbal signals we see during face-to-face talk; these signals modify the meanings of words and whole sentences and are not always adequately replaced by emoticons. The very nature of SMS is that it is short, often abbreviated (e.g., LOL, FWIW, IMO, etc.), and often emphasizes speed of response over considered content in the response.

At the present, use of social media by an organization is typically limited to a very few gatekeepers who make the official posts and replies. Administrators and employees at all levels are on the safest ground when they do not use social media for any aspect of their work unless it is assigned as part of their job.

# WRITING EFFECTIVELY

## Basic Principles

While this book is not intended as a writing course, there are some basic principles to keep in mind.

- Know your audience. Is the recipient a supervisor, an executive or governing board, a group of well-educated professionals or technical employees, a group of unskilled employees, or the general public? The level of writing should keep the audience in mind; that is, whether simpler vocabulary and sentence structure are appropriate. If the audience is elected officials, it is important to provide the message up front and in a direct manner. In this case, beginning with an executive summary is a good approach, as this audience frequently must review many documents and may need to quickly review the first couple of pages

- Organize your thoughts—outline the basic ideas before you start writing, particularly long reports.

- Begin each paragraph with a topic sentence, and make sure the balance of each paragraph is related. Start with general statements and work down to details.

- Read as you write to make sure the writing is relevant, is logical, and says what you mean.

- Short sentences with only one or two thoughts and relatively simple words are better; do not use complex sentences or flowery vocabulary to try to impress your audience.

- The report summary, while often placed at the beginning, is usually the last section written. Make sure it covers all the major points in the body of the report. There should be no information in the summary that is not in the body.

- Make sure the recommendations are clear and follow from the findings.

- Determine whether data are better suited to the body of a report or an appendix. Short tables or illustrations tend to work within a report, but longer ones are usually better in an appendix.
- Proofread carefully for typographical and grammatical errors.
- If possible, ask someone to review your communication for clarity and grammar.
- For reports with numerical data, cross-check totals to verify accuracy, and if you are using computer-generated spreadsheets, verify the formulas and data support all calculated values.
- Be tactful, even when writing something with a negative message (e.g., describing an inefficient organization or incompetent staff person). Business writing should be professional, not emotional.
- Avoid slang terminology unless it is used to quote someone or when it is appropriate within the context of the written material (e.g., in describing someone else's reaction). Be sure to indicate quotations with quotation marks.
- Avoid acronyms and abbreviations. When necessary, explain them at the beginning of the text and use the acronym or abbreviation consistently throughout the document.

## Style Manual

A style manual, or style guide, is a set of standards for the writing and design of documents, either for general use or for a specific publication, organization, or field. Common style guides include the *Chicago Manual of Style* (CMOS) and the *Publication Manual of the American Psychological Association* (APA). The former is a general style guide used for many types of writing; the latter is widely used for academic and scientific writing. The larger the government agency, the more likely it is to have its own style guide to address its particular field and publication needs. The *United Nations Editorial Manual*, for example, is the "compendium of rules and directives on United Nations editorial style, publication policies, procedures and practice" which specifies, among many other things, that "'United Nations' should not be abbreviated in English." Style guides commonly include tables of abbreviations, language usage, and punctuation in addition to physical layout guidelines for text, tables, figures, citations, and bibliographies.

## SPEAKING EFFECTIVELY

Many of the hints described for effective writing also apply to speaking. Knowing the audience, using proper grammar, communicating tactfully, and communicating professionally are good pieces of advice for speakers as well as writers.

## Oral Communications Hints

- Be organized and prepared. If speaking to a supervisor or the governing board about a report, make sure the backup information for the report is readily available. Highlight the points in the report you want to cover.

- When making a formal presentation, whether to a group in an office or at a public meeting, outline the speaking points beforehand. Whenever possible, write out and practice the speech aloud—this will identify words and phrases that are difficult to say so you can change them. Attempt to be prepared for the unexpected question by checking additional facts or doing research before the meeting.

- Speak slowly and use short phrases. This makes enunciation of words easier, reduces the tendency to run words together, and increases the sense that you are confident about what you are saying. President Kennedy's inaugural address is a good example of pacing and phrasing (Kennedy, 1961).

- Minimize using contractions. Their endings are often difficult to hear or distinguish, and greater emphasis is made when each word is spoken (e.g., "don't" versus "do not").

- Be aware of verbal and nonverbal cues from audience members. Do not put them to sleep, talk down to them, or overwhelm them with unwanted details. Be flexible enough to respond to comments or body language that suggests a presentation is too long and losing the audience. On the other hand, be alert to inquiries or comments that suggest the need to provide further explanation.

- When speaking at a public meeting, particularly before a legislative body, it is always a good idea to introduce yourself and identify your organization at the beginning of the presentation. If you are speaking from a podium or a table across from the audience, try to make eye contact with the committee members.

- Microphones are often used at public meetings both to amplify sound and to record the meetings. They can be intimidating.

  » Remember to hold the microphone close to your face, adjust the height if necessary, and speak directly into the microphone rather than turn away when responding to questions from people to the side or behind the podium. Pivot around the microphone so it is between you and the person you are talking to.

  » Speak loudly enough so a person 15 feet away can hear you without the microphone.

  » Always assume that the microphone is turned on and people will hear whatever you say under your breath.

- Remember that if the meeting is being recorded, many people may be listening live through speakerphones in offices or will listen later to the tape—which emphasizes the need to be prepared and professional. Some meetings are recorded or streamed live over the internet. Some meetings, such as regular meetings of a city council or board of education, are recorded routinely and shown regularly on local cable television. In these cases, speakers may not be aware of the recording equipment in the background. The press may show up with one or more portable cameras to record all or part of a meeting about a subject of interest or controversy. These latter meetings may also generate a large public audience.

- Be careful when dealing with news media representatives who may attend the meeting. Many organizations have public relations or public information officers who give training about working with the media, as described in Chapter 5, "Informing and Involving the Public." Let the public information officer deal with the press. Your statements or responses may seem very different than what you thought you said when they are edited for publication or broadcast.

- If you do not know an answer to a question, do not guess at a response because it will usually get you in trouble. Always volunteer to obtain the information and get back to the individual with the request or concern.

- Never contradict an official who makes an incorrect statement in public. The misstatement may be inadvertent, based on ignorance, or intentional. If unintentional, calling it out will be an embarrassment. In other situations, misstatements, exaggerations, or omissions may be for political reasons either to calm a hostile audience or to pander to a friendly one to gain support. Experience is the only way to recognize which situation applies.

- If an elected official attacks you verbally, particularly in a public meeting, try to remain calm and not react or become defensive or emotional. The best approach is to end the presentation as quickly as possible and indicate you will get back to the official with a response to his or her concern. A brief apology that you are not able to answer the question might be appropriate, depending on the situation. Remember that the elected official may be directing comments to the audience; however, also recognize that their displeasure could be the result of your lack of preparation or poor presentation. Whatever the reason, this experience can occur to the most experienced and prepared speaker. As upsetting as it may be, one must be prepared for the next time and try to take whatever steps are necessary to avoid reenacting the public exchange.

- When speaking to members of the public in a public meeting, particularly to a hostile group, the same rules apply as when speaking before elected officials. Be polite, try to be informative, and when appropriate admit to not having information and promise to follow up—then do it in most instances. However, be aware of gadflies and the occasional disturbed individual who attend meetings regularly but may ramble incoherently. If they are available, consult with other staff members who may be familiar with these individuals, but in all cases remain professional and respectful.

- Dealing with members of the public either over the phone or at a public counter may be another challenging situation. Citizens who have been transferred from one office to another may be frustrated by the time they get to you. Listen intently. Allowing them to vent is important, along with expressing understanding and trying to be as helpful as possible.

- In preparation for speaking before a legislative committee or to an official in a private meeting, try to develop a relationship with the committee's or official's staff and determine before the meeting whether there are any questions or concerns that may arise during the meeting. Oftentimes when these are anticipated and resolved, the presentation will be much smoother, and there will be fewer surprise questions.

- Use conversation fillers such as "you know" or "like" very sparingly if at all.

- A cardinal rule in all communications, whether written or spoken, is to avoid any words or phrases that may be interpreted as discriminatory, insulting, or harassing toward any group of individuals, whether they are present or not.

## Listening

It may seem counterintuitive, but an effective speaker is also carefully listening to and observing the audience, whether it be a single person or a group of any size. By listening to and watching the audience you can determine if they are understanding what you are saying. Nodding up and down often shows they are agreeing with what you are saying; quizzical looks usually indicate they are lost and you should ask them what you should clarify.

During person-to-person or small group conversations, backchannel communication helps keep you on track. Positive backchannel communication (such as, "uh-huh," "I see," etc.) is the feedback from listeners that lets you know that they are engaged and following your line of thought. Negative backchannel communication (such as looking away or wrinkled brows) lets you know the listener is not interested or not following or not understanding.

# CONCLUSION

The above discussion points out that there is a common theme that applies to all forms of communication. Be accurate, professional, and prepared when writing all types of documents, and when speaking in both informal and formal settings. Regardless of people's knowledge or intelligence, others judge them by how well they communicate. Good writing and speaking skills are keys to success in any organization.

---

### Box A-1 PLAIN LANGUAGE

The federal government has a goal of improving its communications to the public. The website www.plainlanguage.gov is a valuable resource for practitioners looking for hints to make correspondence and government documents more readable. The following are some examples from the website that illustrate wording that is ambiguous or overly complex and redundant:

---

**Before:**
This regulation governs disaster assistance for services to prevent hardship caused by fire, flood, or acts of nature that are not provided by FEMA or the Red Cross.

**After:**
This regulation governs disaster assistance that:
 (a) consists of services to prevent hardship caused by fire, flood or acts of nature; and
 (b) is furnished by a provider other than FEMA or the Red Cross.

---

**Before:**
This rule proposes the Spring/Summer subsistence harvest regulations in Alaska for migratory birds that expire on August 31, 2003.

**After:**
This rule proposes the Spring/Summer subsistence harvest regulations for migratory birds in Alaska. The regulations expire on August 31, 2003.

---

**Before:**
A number of various available applicable studies have generally identified the fact that additional appropriate nocturnal employment could usually keep juvenile adolescents off thoroughfares.

**After:**
Studies have shown that more night jobs would keep youths off the streets.

## PRACTICING PUBLIC ADMINISTRATION

1. Review the website www.plainlanguage.gov for further examples.

2. Review a report you have written and identify sentences that could be rewritten to be clearer and more understandable.

3. Review three email conversations that you have sent. Identify how each could be rewritten to improve clarity or professionalism.

# BIBLIOGRAPHY

Adler, M. J. (1983). *How to speak, how to listen.* New York, NY: Touchstone.

American Psychological Association. (2020). *Publication manual of the American Psychological Association* (7th ed.). https://doi.org/10.1037/0000165-000

Curzan, A. (2020). *How conversation works: 6 lessons for better communication.* Video course. Chantilly, VA: The Teaching Company, LLC.

Friederichs, A. (2020). *Written communications. Being heard and understood. Course guidebook.* Chantilly, VA: The Teaching Company, LLC.

Garner, B. (2012). *HBR Guide to better business writing.* Boston, MA: Harvard Business School Publishing.

Kehoe, D. (2011). *Effective communication skills.* Chantilly, VA: The Great Courses, LLC.

Kennedy, J. F. (1961). Inaugural address. https://www.youtube.com/watch?v=PEC1C4p0k3E

O'Conner, P. (2009). *Woe is I: The grammarphobe's guide to better English in plain English.* New York, NY: Riverhead.

Truss, L. (2003). *Eats, shoots, and leaves: The zero-tolerance approach to punctuation.* New York, NY: Penguin.

United Nations Department for General Assembly and Conference Management. (2021). *United Nations editorial manual.* New York, NY: United Nations. https://www.un.org/dgacm/en/content/editorial-manual

The University of Chicago. (2017). *The Chicago manual of style* (17th ed.). Chicago, IL: University of Chicago Press.

# Appendix

# B

# Preparing and
# Making Presentations

This appendix discusses both formal and informal presentations to others, both within and external to the organization. Administrators, managers, and staff at all levels of organizations make presentations as a normal and integral part of their job. Preparing and making presentations that are informative, succinct, and interesting often distinguishes someone who is an authority from someone who is not.

Formal presentations are often given in a meeting environment to other departments, senior management, the public, or some combination. Usually the formal presentation has a single presenter or a small team of presenters and an audience. The audience and venue may be small, such as a conference room, or large, such as an auditorium or live broadcast. Typical formal presentations for public administrators include proposals or status reports to city council, commissioners, other legislative bodies, or other policy makers.

Informal presentations are usually given within a department and may involve only the presenter and one or two others. An informal presentation may even be just an off-the-cuff meeting with a more senior person or other staff.

The process of preparing and making both formal and informal presentations is essentially the same. The primary difference is the amount of time and other resources used. Informal off-the-cuff presentations often skip Step 3. Understanding the process of preparing and making an impactful formal presentation makes the astute administrator more able to quickly and effectively make short, informal, off-the-cuff presentations.

There are four major steps to prepare and deliver a presentation:

1. Define the story.
2. Identify appropriate visual aids.
3. Practice the presentation.
4. Deliver the presentation.

## DEFINE THE STORY

A presentation tells the story about what a report or proposal says, including its impact and important points. It is not reading the report or proposal, which is usually sent before the presentation is made. Think of the presentation as a book report on "War and Peace" by Leo Tolstoy; you wouldn't read all 1,200 or so pages to the audience. There are four primary steps to define the story.

### Step 1: Identify the Audience

> Designing a presentation without an audience in mind is like writing a love letter and addressing it 'to whom it may concern.
>
> —Ken Haemer, Presentation Research Manager, AT&T

As the presenter, you are the subject matter expert. Your audience, typically policy makers of one sort or another, usually are not. Many policy makers do not have college degrees, and if they do it is likely not in the topic you are presenting, so they may not understand the jargon or acronyms. Policy makers receive information from conflicting sources, so they want your information presented clearly, concisely, without long-winded explanations, and without a lot of prevarication, but with clear arguments for or against a particular course of action.

If your audience is your own department personnel, you may assume they are more familiar with the topic and jargon. Your presentation is still a story about the report or proposal, it is not reading or duplicating the report or proposal.

In the case of informal and off-the-cuff presentations, the audience is rather easily identified allowing you to tailor your presentation to their technical expertise and familiarity with the subject.

### Step 2: Identify Time Limits

Formal presentations in the world of public administration are typically expected to last no more than 20 minutes or so with an undefined period for questions and answers. It is best to verify the expected duration with the person requesting the presentation.

## Step 3: Draft the Presentation Text

Write out the text of your presentation, keeping in mind the audience, their familiarity with the topic and its jargon, and the time allotted for your presentation. At this point, do not worry about slides or other visual aids; concentrate on the information you want to present. It is good to remember that most TED Talks use no visual aids. (TED Talks are presentations made at the Technology, Entertainment, Design conference or one of its many satellite events, and are limited to 18 minutes.) Your story should be engaging by itself.

A common method for drafting the presentation is beginning with an outline and then filling in the text. If there is a standard outline that your organization uses for particular presentations, by all means use it. The outline lets you identify the major points to cover and each of the minor points and details to include. It also lets you quickly and easily sequence the information into a good story.

Some presentations, especially in a training or educational setting, benefit from the "tell, tell, tell" approach. Tell them what you're going to tell them. Tell them. Then tell them what you told them. The first telling is the general outline of major points you will cover. The second telling is each of the major points along with all necessary detail. The third telling is a short summary of what was covered.

Many presentations should end with a call to action. Identify what action the audience should take. Approve a draft ordinance? Deny a conditional use permit? Purchase specific software? The call to action should be strongly supported by the rest of the presentation.

## Step 4: Read the Presentation Aloud

Read the draft presentation aloud. It is critical that you actually speak the words out loud and not just read them in your head or use the "Read Aloud" function in the word processor program. This will let you know how long it takes to present and will let you find words and phrases that are difficult to say (e.g., "She sells seashells by the seashore"). If a word cannot be changed, practice saying it until you are fluent. Edit the text until you can speak it clearly and within the time allowed.

The audience will rarely be upset with a presentation that is shorter than expected as long as it contains the necessary information and is clear, concise, and interesting. If the audience expects a 20-minute presentation, they will start losing attention at 21 minutes unless the story is exceptionally interesting. Don't rely on your story being exceptionally interesting.

# IDENTIFY APPROPRIATE AUDIO/VISUAL AIDS

## Function of A/V Aids

Audio/Visual (A/V) aids assist or augment the oral presentation of the story to the audience. Like a cane assists walking, A/V aids assist presenting the story; the cane does not walk by itself, and A/V aids are not the presentation.

## Selecting A/V Aids

The first check is identifying what must be used in addition to the presenter's voice to make the information clear. If the spoken story is clear and adequate, then A/V aids may be eliminated altogether, as is the case with most TED talks. If A/V aids will amplify the story, then you need to verify the availability of the appropriate aids both while you are creating them and at the presentation venue. For example, planning a presentation using a whiteboard when no whiteboard is available at the presentation venue will be an exercise in frustration.

Most agencies have style guides and defined layouts for A/V materials used with presentations; these guidelines are usually maintained in the public relations or similar department.

All copyrighted material that appears in A/V aids must be properly cited and, if necessary, permission obtained to use it.

The following paragraphs discuss many of the A/V elements that may or may not be appropriate.

### PowerPoint/Slides

PowerPoint has become perhaps the most widely used and abused A/V aid, largely replacing overhead transparencies and slides. Each PowerPoint screen image is called a slide. Your story determines the number of slides needed to augment your presentation; there is no maximum number of slides, there is only the right number for the presentation.

Remember that each slide must augment the presentation and help clarify the point being made while the slide is displayed. Multiple slides may be needed in sequence to help develop a point (such as a list or graph), with each slide adding one item to a previous slide.

As long as there is a slide displayed, the audience will be reading it and paying less attention to what the presenter is saying. Any errors on the slide will detract from the presentation. Anything on a slide that is not discussed in the presentation will be a distraction.

Let's discuss some of the most common elements on slides.

*Text.* Text is the most common element. The text should generally show key words/phrases or short bullet points. A text slide might contain only the major point being discussed at the time. Text should generally not be the same as what the presenter says, unless the exact phrasing is critical (e.g., a definition or the wording of an ordinance). Since slides are often shown at some distance from the viewer, the text size should be no smaller than 28 point. If it's too small for the audience to read, it's just a wasted slide.

The font used should be simple and consistent throughout the presentation. Georgia, Times New Roman, and Arial are commonly used. Font colors should show good contrast with the background and should be consistent throughout the presentation. Again, check for agency or departmental style guidelines.

How much text should be on one slide? As little as necessary, and it should be synchronized with the verbal presentation. A bullet list of five items, for instance, can be most effectively shown by five cumulative slides, with each successive slide adding the new item as it is discussed, with the final slide showing all five items. This technique keeps the audience synchronized to the story and keeps them from getting ahead of the speaker.

*Check spelling.* Re-check every slide for typos or incorrect words. Every typo or incorrect word can make the audience lose confidence in the presentation.

*Photographs/Pictures.* Pictures should be very relevant to what is being discussed at the moment, and should only include relevant elements. When possible, crop out distracting items. Pictures should be high quality and not fuzzy. If text is used on the same slide, follow the guideline for text described above and ensure that it can be easily read over the image.

The agency may have a library of stock photos available to use.

*Graphs.* Graphs are an excellent means to summarize data and show trends. It is good practice to introduce the elements or axes of the graph, including the units and the scale. As with other elements, the audience must be able to read the graph, including the legend, if any. In many cases, it will be helpful to display the elements of the graph on successive slides as the graph is discussed, especially if the graph has several elements.

*Tables.* When introducing a table, a best practice is to first summarize what it contains and then highlight what is displayed in the columns and rows as well as how calculations are made. It is best to limit the amount of data shown in a table on a slide and to talk about everything shown in the table. Any data displayed but not mentioned in the discussion distracts from your story. The audience will divide their attention between reading the data on the table and listening to your story. Any errors in the data or ambiguities in how calculations are made will decrease the credibility of the analysis.

*Maps.* Maps should have North at the top of the graphic; when this is not possible, be certain to point out the orientation immediately after introducing the map. As with other A/V aids, keep the map as simple as possible and eliminate unnecessary details.

*Animation.* Animation can help illustrate change over time or movement through a sequence of steps. However, animation can easily distract from the story that is the heart of the presentation, so it should be used very carefully or not at all.

*Recordings.* Incorporating a video or audio recording into a presentation requires careful planning. Among other things, the venue must be capable of displaying the video and/or audio recording, and the time taken for the recording counts as part of the presentation time. Recordings should be of the highest quality available, and should be introduced so the audience knows (1) what they are about to see or hear, (2) why the recording is included in the presentation, and (3) what they should be looking for in the recording.

### *Whiteboard/Blackboard*

Whiteboards (and blackboards) are commonly used in less formal and small group presentations such as staff meetings, classes, and workshops. Pre-plan what to put on the whiteboard and where to put it so that at the end of the presentation the whiteboard summarizes the important points in a logical order. The whiteboard should not have doodles or unnecessary writing on it; erase these immediately when their utility is over.

Ensure that all writing is legible and that colors are used for appropriate emphasis. Yellow, for instance, is nearly impossible to read on a whiteboard, but is very readable on a blackboard; while black is impossible to read on a blackboard but is very readable on a whiteboard.

### *Flip Charts*

Flip charts, especially paper pads and giant Post-It® notes on easels, are also used, primarily in less formal and small group presentations such as staff meeting, classes, and workshops. In a workshop presentation, ideas are often developed and listed on individual sheets and then posted around the room for the group to review and revise as the workshop progresses. As with a whiteboard, the presenter should pre-plan what will go on each flip chart. Some pages may be made beforehand while others may be left blank or incomplete to be filled in during the presentation. A handy way to develop a graphic is to draw it lightly in pencil before the presentation and use markers to make it visible during the presentation.

### *Handouts*

Anything that is provided to the audience before, during, or after the presentation is a handout. Any handout provided before or during the presentation can easily become a distraction during the presentation, so their use must be carefully integrated and controlled. Any handout may also be provided via a link to a website.

Common handouts include:

- **Written reports:** Written reports are commonly distributed well before the presentation itself, although it can be very effective to give the presentation first, especially if the report is lengthy. Expect at least some of the audience to go to the report itself if you include a page reference in your presentation story. Ensure that all report copies are complete, and that any page references you make are accurate.

- **Objects:** Objects typically include a product or part that the presentation highlights or discusses and may be distributed to each person or a single object (like a car or airplane) may be presented to everyone. Objects are rarely handed out in the world of public administration, although small objects such as body cameras, electronic tablets, or uniforms may be appropriate handouts for a presentation about the object.

- **Copy of the presentation:** Providing a copy of the presentation, or at least the slides used, is common practice. If it is handed out at the start of the presentation, expect some of the audience to leaf through the pages throughout the presentation and miss much of what you say. Often attendees are electronically sent a copy of the presentation after it is over.

## Integrate Aids Into the Presentation

Return to the written script of the presentation and mark cues for when to introduce each A/V aid. The cues may include adding words to the script to introduce the aid or highlight marks that indicate when to display the next aid. Review the script and what the A/V aid contains to ensure the aid supports the script; remembering that it is the story in the script that is paramount, not the aid. Revise or eliminate each A/V aid as necessary.

# PRACTICE

Practice is the key to delivering a memorable presentation with impact and confidence. Practice is over when the presentation is concise, delivered smoothly both aurally and technically, and within the time limit. Practice must be done aloud and in real time.

It can be very helpful to have someone from your target audience sit in on your practice sessions to critique it and prepare some questions that may come up during the question-and-answer period. This can help identify weak parts of the presentation as well as prepare you for questions that may arise from the audience.

## Equipment Operation

Practice efficiently setting up, connecting, and using every piece of equipment and technology that is needed for the presentation.

*Computer.* The chances are that you have prepared your presentation using a computer. Ensure you know how to find and open the presentation file. Good practice is to copy your presentation to a thumb drive as a backup.

If you are using Microsoft PowerPoint, there is a feature called "Use Presenter View" under the "Monitors" section of the "Slide Show" tab. This requires using two screens, the computer screen and a second one for the audience. Using this feature, the presenter's computer screen displays the current slide seen by the audience, the next slide to be displayed, thumbnail images of several slides, and notes that can be attached to each slide. When the slide show is running, there are additional options available in the lower left corner including a pointer dot, enlarging part of the slide, and making the audience image blank (this is handy when you do not want a slide showing for part of your presentation).

Become very familiar with how to go from one slide to the next using the computer controls, just in case the slide clicker doesn't work.

*Projector and Slide Clicker.* Connecting the computer to a projector is normally done by either an HDMI or a VGA connection, while some use other interface systems such as DisplayPort or Thunderbolt. You may need an adapter to go from one to the other; it's best to be prepared. Become familiar with connecting your computer to a projector or second monitor.

A slide clicker is a remote device that connects to your computer and lets you change slides without using the computer keys. Some clickers also include a pointer light beam; however, the pointer light beam can only be seen on a projected image such as a wall—it cannot be seen on a monitor or LED display (here is where the pointer dot on the PowerPoint system comes in handy).

*Microphone.* A sound system amplifies whatever sounds enter the microphone. The microphone does not select the sounds it receives, that is the job of the user. General rules for effective use are:

- Speak directly into a microphone from a constant distance (usually no more than a few inches).

- Speak loudly enough that a person can hear you from 10 feet away without the microphone.

All microphones amplify whatever sound enters them. The high-pitched squeal you can hear happens when a microphone picks up the output of a speaker connected to the microphone; this is called feedback. Learn where the speakers are that are fed by the microphone and avoid having the microphone facing the speaker.

Always assume that a microphone is turned on and will pick up remarks you do not want others to hear. When in doubt, cover the microphone or ensure that it is turned off.

Microphones come in three general styles: fixed position, hand-held, and lapel or clip-on. Each require some particular attention from the user.

*Fixed-position* microphones are mounted to a podium, dais, or microphone stand. Position yourself comfortably near the microphone and when you look around the room, move so that the microphone is always directly between your mouth and where you are looking. Do not turn your head to one side; pivot around the microphone. If you tilt your head up or down, the sound will diminish.

There may be multiple microphones installed on a podium. Sometimes all are connected to the same sound system, allowing the speaker to turn their head and one of the microphones will pick up their voice. At other times, different microphones go to different sound systems or different recorders, so turning your head will reduce the sound to some of the microphones.

*Hand-held* microphones are, as the name implies, held in one's hand. We have all seen singers using microphones, and when they are singing the microphone is less than two inches from their lips, and sometimes they seem to be swallowing the mic. There is a reason for this: to keep other sounds from entering the microphone. Generally, the microphone should be no more than about the width of your hand from your lips, or three or four inches, and it should be pointing directly at your lips. Put the microphone in one hand, position it properly, and lock that hand in position. Turn your body when you face a different direction or person.

*Lapel* (or clip-on) microphones are attached to a lapel or other article of clothing, which automatically keeps the microphone a constant distance from the lips. These are generally used where there are few background sounds. This gives the user the greatest freedom of movement, but turning your head to one side may still greatly reduce the volume to the audience.

**Internet Connection.** Remote presentations using internet connections have become more common. Establishing and maintaining a connection with sufficient bandwidth to transmit the data to all of the users in a remote presentation can be difficult. If the presentation itself includes connecting over the internet, the problems may escalate.

**Lighting.** Understand how to turn off and on lights as needed for the presentation.

**Whiteboard.** Clean the whiteboard before your presentation. If there are multiple sliding whiteboards, ensure you know how to operate them. Check that you have the proper colors of markers, that they are the proper type for the whiteboard you will use, and that you have an eraser. Practice writing on the board and placing the information so that when complete it summarizes the important points.

*Flip Charts/Pads.* Practice setting up the easel, attaching and flipping the flip charts. If you will be developing graphs or charts during the presentation, practice filling in the pre-penciled lines to make a clear and legible display.

*Handouts.* Practice getting, distributing, and talking about anything that will be handed out during the presentation. When handling an object, ensure that the audience can clearly see what you are doing or what you are pointing at.

## Speaking

Practice out loud and at a comfortable pace for the listener, using simple language and short sentences. Do not rush; you are telling a story. Vary your pitch and tone as necessary to convey meaning and enhance the conversation with the audience. This is a story the audience has not heard before, let them enjoy the experience. Practice any hand or body motions you want to employ at the appropriate times that will enhance the presentation.

If there are multiple presenters, practice transitioning from one to the next so the flow of information is smooth and the storyline is not interrupted. Generally it is less disruptive to introduce the speakers at the beginning of the presentation, rather than as they appear during it.

## Revise

After the first and each successive practice run, revise the presentation script and A/V aids as necessary. Eliminate discontinuities or rough transitions in the script. Critically evaluate each A/V aide to ensure it supports the story being told at the time and does not distract in any way.

Practice everything until every part of the presentation is:

* concise,
* delivered smoothly both aurally and technically, and
* within the time limit.

Then practice at least two more times to become perfectly comfortable with every aspect of the presentation.

> Amateurs practice until they get it right. Professionals practice until they cannot get it wrong.
>
> —Unknown

# PRESENT

Having properly drafted the script, identified and developed the appropriate audio and visual aids, and practiced making the presentation until it is concise and you can deliver it smoothly and within the time limit, you are now almost ready to make the actual presentation. First make certain that everything is prepared; then make the presentation as you practiced it.

## Preparation

- **Clothing:** Verify that you are properly attired and groomed. Your clothing and accessories should help convey your professionalism and competence with the topic; you are not trying to seduce the audience or dazzle them with your sartorial selections. Check buttons, collars, and zippers. This is not the time for a wardrobe malfunction.

- **Equipment:** Verify that every single piece of equipment needed for the presentation is present, properly connected and powered, and working. Make a checklist if that will help ensure nothing is missed.

  » your computer and presentation script
  » projector and clicker (install fresh batteries in the clicker)
  » microphone (do a sound check and verify the microphone is where it should be; when doing the sound check, be certain to speak as loudly as you will during the presentation)
  » internet connection
  » lighting
  » whiteboard and markers
  » flip charts/pads and markers
  » handouts
  » other

## Make the Presentation

Present the story as you practiced it. This is not the time to change your mind about what to say or how to say it.

## Q&A

Let the audience know at the very beginning of the presentation if you will not be open to taking questions at the end.

Normally at the end of the presentation, you should thank the audience for their attention, let those attending know how they can get a copy of the presentation, and open the floor for Q&A.

When fielding a question, it is a good idea to first ensure that you understand the question. This may involve rephrasing or repeating the question. When you have finished answering a question, verify with the questioner that you have answered it. If you cannot immediately answer the question, get the questioner's contact information and let them know you will get the answer to them later—and do it.

## BIBLIOGRAPHY

Anderson, C. (2013). How to give a killer presentation. *Harvard Business Review*, June. https://hbr.org/2013/06/how-to-give-a-killer-presentation

Bergman, E. (2020). *One bucket at a time: Presentation secrets to inform, educate, influence, persuade.* Petticoat Creek Press, Inc.

Donovan, J. (2013). *How to deliver a TED talk: Secrets of the world's most inspiring presentations.* McGraw-Hill Professional Publishing.

Duarte, N. (2012). *HBR guide to persuasive presentations.* Boston, MA: Harvard Business Review Press.

Etherington, B. (2019). *Presentation skills for quivering wrecks.* Singapore: Marshall Cavendish International (Asia).

Garmston, R. J., & Wellman, B. M. (1992). *How to make presentations that teach and transform: ASCD.* ASCD.

Hoogterp, B. (2014). *Your perfect presentation: Speak in front of any audience anytine anywhere and never be nervous again.* New York, NY: McGraw-Hill Professional Publshing.

Hopkins, C. (2013). Help! I've got a presentation coming up. https://www.lulu.com/shop/caroline-hopkins/help-ive-got-a-presentation-coming-up/paperback/product-1mwy6wv6.html?page=1&pageSize=4

Keyes, J. M. (2011). *Carpe audience: Give better presentations despite PowerPoint.* North Charleston, SC: CreateSpace Independent Publishing Platform.

May, G. (2013). *Persuasive business presentations: Using the problem-solution method to influence decision makers to take action.* Hampton, NJ: Business Expert Press.

Pollard, T. (2016). *The compelling communicator: Mastering the art and science of exceptional presentation design.* Billings, MT: Ministrat LLC.

Provan, D. (2009). *Giving great presentations in easy steps.* Leamington Spa, UK: In Easy Steps Limited.

Reynolds, G. (2010). *The naked presenter: Delivering powerful presentations with or without slides.* Pearson Education. (NOOK Book).

Tracy, L. (2013). *The shortcut to persuasive presentations.* North Charleston, SC: Booksurge, LLC.

Treasure, J. (2022). *How to speak so that people want to listen.* Chantilly, VA: The Teaching Company.

# Appendix

# C

# Hiring in
# Government

This is a summary of practical information about how to get a job in local government and how to select and interview applicants, with emphasis on administrative and professional jobs. It covers topics such as the application and testing process, interviews, and promotions. It is intended for college students applying for their first professional positions; for people changing to careers in local government; and for current government supervisors and managers wanting to refresh their knowledge about interviewing and selecting applicants. This is decidedly not a comprehensive text or guide on all the details and legal requirements and restrictions on hiring in government. In every case, the wise public administrator will follow the dictates and details of their specific department and agency.

## GENERAL INFORMATION

### The Local Government Job Market

There are many job markets in local government. There are regional job markets for different parts of the country and for large metropolitan areas. Big cities are able to create more job opportunities for new and current employees. An employee of a larger local government may move up the career ladder without leaving his or her employer. Larger governments tend to hire from the outside for entry-level positions and at senior levels. Supervisor and middle-level jobs are often for internal candidates only. Smaller cities and counties have fewer internal promotional opportunities, and people tend to move between agencies in search of career opportunities. Fortunately, these governments are often members of statewide pension and benefits agencies, so job and employer changes do not necessarily mean major disruptions in benefits.

## Civil Service or Non-Civil Service Jobs

Many governments hire using the civil service system, described in Chapter 11, "Managing Human Resources." The civil service system generally is used for positions that have a large potential applicant pool; the regimentation of the civil service system helps eliminate or minimize political or personal influence in filling common positions. This appendix describes the civil service system as it relates to job seekers. Some governments designate some jobs as non–civil service. These may be trades jobs (plumbers, mechanical helpers, etc.), or higher level managerial and executive jobs.

Hiring for non–civil service jobs closely resembles private-sector hiring. Jobs are advertised, interviews held, and a person selected. Civil service hiring is more complex, more regimented, and is a major focus of this appendix.

# APPLICANT/CANDIDATE PERSPECTIVE

## Finding Government Jobs

Local government jobs are advertised on governments' own websites, on general websites such as www.governmentjobs.com, and may also be advertised on websites operated by professional organizations (which may limit access to its members and/or charge a fee to access). Interested applicants may often do research on the types of positions a government has by looking at its website. Complete position descriptions are usually available online. Budgets, which are usually available on government websites, show the number of people employed by the government and can indicate if the position is permanent or linked to special funding; look for *position counts*, *staffing*, and similar terms.

While the position description and/or the advertisement should indicate the position's status within the civil service system, it may not always be stated. In such circumstances, it may be best to ask about how the position fits into the general employment system and/or the long-term status of the position if linked to special funding from grants from the state or federal government.

The opening describes the position in general, the minimum qualifications, the testing and evaluation procedures, and due dates for applications. Local governments generally have a policy of advertising positions for some period of time (maybe a week or longer) before closing the application process. Some positions are advertised as "open until filled" or "open until a sufficient number of applications are received" (this may be five to 10 applications). Filing dates for applications often cannot be changed, and late applications are usually not accepted. Very occasionally an exception is made if an applicant was unable to submit an application during the application period due to circumstances beyond their control—but do not rely on being granted the exception.

Local governments generally will not accept applications for positions for which they are not currently recruiting. Interested persons may be able to request notification via postcard or email when the government is accepting applications for a particular position.

*Entry-Level Positions.* Entry-level jobs are most frequently, although not exclusively, filled through the civil service system. Governments hire people for a number of entry-level jobs in general administration, engineering, planning, information technology, clerical areas, unskilled labor, and skilled trades with titles such as management assistant, information technology aide, maintenance laborer, mechanical helper, or clerk typist. There are also many entry-level public safety jobs such as police officer and firefighter. Although many of the processes are similar for applicants for all civil service jobs, this chapter will focus on administrative and professional jobs since there are unique processes for some positions (e.g., public safety jobs) as noted in Chapter 11, "Managing Human Resources."

An applicant for an administrative job who has a college degree and less than two years' experience typically starts as an analyst of some type. Analysts help with such tasks as budget preparation and monitoring, contract management, personnel administration, and special events. They may supervise clerical employees who staff a public desk and issue permits to the public, collect payments from the public, and so forth. Applicants with degrees in accounting, engineering, and so forth have other options. There are a number of entry-level job classifications and career paths in these more technical areas.

Applicants without college degrees often start as clerks or assistants. An employee in one of these classes may have the opportunity to move into the analyst classes with a few years' experience and after passing an exam in a "bridge" classification (often a training classification such as aide that gives an employee a chance to learn other duties and qualify for analyst and other related exams). Alternatively, a clerk or assistant can pursue an undergraduate college degree and take a higher level exam when he or she has completed the degree. If there are few openings for jobs requiring degrees, it is sometimes a good strategy to take a clerical job as a starting point. This may provide an advantage to someone competing for an administrative/professional job because the applicant will have gained experience and knowledge about an agency and may be able to compete on a promotional basis. Another good way to learn about local government and gain an advantage in an entry-level exam is by taking a paid or unpaid internship while in college or after graduation.

Jobs at all levels of government are usually organized in "series." Progressing up a series from lower to higher levels or moving to a closely related series is a career path. Within the class, there may be pay grades (I, II, etc.) representing different levels of responsibility, amounts of supervision, and pay scales. Employees move up the path by taking competitive exams or by some other process, such as competitive applications and hiring interviews without exams. The following is an example of a series:

**Table C-1   Position Series Example**

| | |
|---|---|
| Budget Analyst | Helps with budget preparation |
| Senior Budget Analyst | Supervises analysts who work on the budget |
| Principal or Chief Budget Analyst | Supervises the administration of a department budget, including preparation and management |

*Middle-Management Positions.* Many, although certainly not all, middle management positions are filled internally through promotions. This helps preserve "institutional memory" and provides a career path for employees. Advancement to a more responsible position often requires additional training; for example, eligibility to advance from "Budget Analyst" to "Senior Budget Analyst" may require specific training in supervisory skills.

*Senior-Level Positions.* The most senior-level positions are often filled from outside the agency and often involve recruiting agencies ("headhunters") rather than the civil service system. Information about these positions is normally found in the same places as other positions are listed, but the initial processing of applications, including screening and often the first interview, is handled by the recruiting agency as directed by the hiring government.

## Understanding the Hiring Process

Although there are common elements in the hiring process, each government agency and department will have its own unique attributes. Check directly with the agency to confirm the details of its process; failing to follow its directions will often, at best, prolong the process or, at worst, end consideration of your application.

*Time Frames.* Understand when each step of the process must be completed; the deadlines for submitting information is normally not flexible. This helps ensure an equal opportunity for all applicants and also gives the agency information on your ability to follow directions and meet deadlines.

*Contacting Agency Personnel.* There are normally limits of who and when an applicant can contact agency personnel concerning their application. This helps ensure that all applicants are treated equally and that agency personnel are not inappropriately dealing with applicants. The position announcement will typically specify the contact person. Contacting other people at the agency may result in your application being summarily denied.

*Sequence of Events.* Confirm the sequence of events in the agency's process as well as the deadlines and time frames. There may be strict deadlines for some events, such as submitting the initial application, but more flexible time frames for other events, such as the agency letting you know if and when you will be scheduled for a screening test. Typical events include:

• submission of application
• submission of official transcripts
• submission of references
• submission of licenses and/or certificates
• initial screening tests
• interviews
• interview follow-up

*Recruiting Firms.* Recruiting firms are often used for senior-level positions and when the hiring government wants to recruit from a very broad geographic area. This saves the government the time and expense of sending its personnel to many cities to conduct interviews. Recruiting firms also have expertise in identifying viable candidates for specific positions, such as airport operations director or city manager, and in recruiting minority candidates.

From the perspective of the applicant, the recruiting firm simply stands in for the government agency for some of the steps in the hiring process. The final job offer and final negotiation of employment terms will almost always be with the government agency, not the recruiting firm.

*Hiring Freezes.* Occasionally a hiring freeze is imposed for any of a number of reasons. When a hiring freeze is set, all hiring activity stops. All applications, tests, interviews, etc., are simply suspended and no further steps can be taken until the freeze is lifted. Applicants who are somewhere in the hiring process will typically be notified that a hiring freeze is in place; applicants may or may not be notified when the freeze is lifted.

When the hiring freeze is lifted, applications that had been in process may resume where they left off (with new deadlines and time frames) or the entire process may begin anew for everyone. You can normally check with the contact person at the agency to see which is the case for your pending application.

## Completing and Submitting the Application

When an application period is open, a government website shows the job announcement and frequently provides an online application process. Alternatively, there may be downloadable forms that the applicant fills out, signs, and mails in. (Many governments like to have original signatures on forms.)

The following are some guidelines when applying for a job:

- Read the application instructions and follow them exactly. Do not be creative. Not following the instructions could lead to the rejection of an application.

- For application forms, note the following in the job history section:

  » Note whether it is possible to summarize all positions with a single employer (e.g., different assignments with the same job title) or if each position should be listed separately.

  » Note whether all jobs ever held should be listed or just jobs held in the past "x" number of years. Most forms will require that applicants account for all time in the past "x" number of years, showing periods of unemployment, full-time study, and so forth.

  » Note whether the form requires the position duties to be entered on the form or permits entering "see attached resume."

  » If there is a section about criminal convictions on the application form, be sure to fill it out. Having a conviction does not necessarily disqualify an applicant. But if an applicant has a conviction and fails to fill out this section, it will be considered lying by omission. This often will be discovered during a background check and will prevent an applicant from getting a job offer or will lead to the rescinding of an offer or to termination if discovered after hiring.

- Be sure to sign and date the application.

- Follow the instructions in the job history section. Forms may allow a very brief to a long description of duties in this section for each position, or they may allow applicants to "refer to the attached resume." If a resume is allowed, be sure to provide the required information (name of employer, dates of employment, salary [often optional], supervisor's name, etc.) with a brief description of duties.

- Attach a cover letter or email, if it is allowed. This is important, but the application and resume (and answers to supplemental questions, if required) are more important. The cover letter might be misplaced or moved to the back of an application packet.

- Some positions require a resume (and cover letter) only, without an application form. The person hired may still need to fill out an application form later so the government's personnel department has a complete file.

- Answering supplemental questions may be required in addition to submitting an application form and/or resume; the answers are usually submitted on a separate sheet of paper or papers. These questions usually ask for information about the applicant's experience in some specific areas. Be sure to follow the instructions closely, particularly those on page limits.

- Do not provide more than is required. Do not, for example, submit letters of reference until requested; these are usually not required with the application. The government will contact references later in the process. Do not provide samples of work; these may be requested later. An applicant may be asked for proof of their academic degree(s) in the form of official or unofficial transcripts or copies of the degree(s) itself.

- Be sure that contact information, especially email addresses and telephone numbers, are correct. Many local governments ask that applicants keep them updated about changes.

- Ensure that all of the required items are included in the application packet and in the sequence specified.

- Ensure that the application packet is submitted to the proper person and will be received before the deadline. Assume there will be delays in postal and electronic deliveries.

- Keep a copy of everything you submit. Paper and electronic files do get lost.

What happens with the application? In some cases, all the application packets are simply logged when they are received and not processed at all until the submission deadline. In other cases, applications packets are processed as they are received. One or more people will review the material submitted to see if (1) all required items are included, and (2) an applicant meets the minimum requirements for the position and will document when the complete application packet was received. Sometimes only the applicants with the most experience (the "best qualified") will be invited to the next step for the position. Other times, everyone meeting the minimum requirements will be advanced to the next step.

Once you have submitted the application packet, you can check with the contact person to verify that it has been received.

## Selection Overview

The selection process, or testing, can mean anything from a formal written test to a review of applications, resumes, and supplemental questions.

Generally, there are two phases to the process:

1. The government develops a list of eligible candidates. Most of this work is done in a Personnel or Human Resources department. Applications are reviewed to exclude applicants who do not meet the minimum requirements for the position or who have not submitted all required information. Criteria are then applied to rank candidates. The list of ranked applicants becomes the *list of eligible candidates*.

2. The list of eligible candidates is given to departments with vacancies to fill, and department staff schedule and conduct screening tests or assessments, conduct hiring interviews, and make job offers. The specifics associated with these steps are discussed below.

*Screening Test.* In its simplest form, the test entails resumes and answers to supplemental questions, if applicable, being scored and applicants judged to be the best qualified getting the highest scores.

Written tests may be conducted for a variety of positions. Tests may be in the form of multiple-choice, short-answer, and/or essay questions. Questions may be validated for job-related content by the government's specialists or by outside consultants. The government may develop its own tests, purchase tests from a research organization, or use some combination of testing resources. Multiple-choice questions are usually scored electronically. Short-answer and essay questions are usually scored by experts, people who have held the position, and/or who supervise people in the position.

Written tests for entry-level jobs do not typically require knowledge of the local government. They may have vocabulary, reading comprehension, basic math (percentages, interpretation of graphs, trends, averages), and logic sections. Exams for higher level positions may require more knowledge of the government's structure, policies, and processes. The applicant's score on the written exam may be part (perhaps 40% to 60%) of the total score, with the remainder coming from the score on an oral interview. A certain score on the written test (maybe 60% to 70%) may be required to advance in the process and be interviewed.

The following are some guidelines about essay questions:

- These questions may test your analytic abilities by including identifying irrelevant information. Do not assume that all information provided must be included in the answer. Be selective and stick to the basics. Recognizing irrelevant information is part of the test.

- Be sure to read the questions and instructions carefully. Not following instructions closely may result in a lower score.
- If the question has multiple parts, it is good practice to label them clearly in your answer to make it easier for the reviewer to follow.
- The test may be administered online or in person. Online tests may require procedures to verify that the person taking the test is not aided. An in-person test may require using pen and paper or allow use of a personal computer. If you handwrite the essay, be sure that it is written legibly and organized neatly so the reviewer can easily read it.
- Plan your time carefully. The test administrator will announce the maximum time. Be sure to plan the work and save time for proofreading and revision.
- Reviewers are looking for the ability to follow instructions and write clearly with proper grammar. Do not worry about being too creative. Even though a question may mention the government and its operations, the reviewers will not expect that everyone knows the details, especially in entry-level exams. When answering essay questions, it is good to remember standard essay form, including an introductory paragraph, a topic sentence and conclusion for each paragraph, and a summary or overall conclusion.

Some positions, such as clerk typist and truck driver, may have a performance test (typing or driving) as part of the testing. This test may be scheduled at the same time as the written test or later, for only those applicants who passed the written test.

*Assessment Centers.* Some entry- and higher-level positions use assessment centers to evaluate candidates. These centers may be run by outside recruiting and testing firms with participation and observation by local government Human Resources staff. They attempt to place candidates in real work situations, setting up simulations such as giving impromptu presentations (with one hour or less to prepare) and participating in or leading discussions. Assessment centers generally supplement traditional interviews and take the place of written tests.

*Results of the Test.* The results will be mailed to applicants several weeks after the test is completed. The score will generally be a numerical score (such as 90) plus the applicant's rank on the list of eligible candidates (such as number 2). The rank might be stated as a number or a letter (A, B, etc.). A higher rank means that the applicant's name is more likely to be forwarded to departments that have vacancies soon after the testing, although placing in the lower ranks may result in an interview at a later time. Those making the final hiring decision will often set a limit on how many of the completed and ranked files they wish to review in the next phase of the hiring process. The written notification of the score may also have information about the list, such as the number of applicants with the same score or with higher scores. The notification will tell applicants how to get more information, which may require a visit to the government's personnel office to see the list of eligible candidates and possibly the interview panel's comments about the applicant. Applicants may be given only a narrow window of time, perhaps a few days, to visit the personnel office.

The notification letter will include instructions for making a protest, including the time limit for doing so. Applicants may protest testing procedures to the personnel department or a civil service commission. The questions themselves cannot be protested if the government has validated them using testing research. Personnel departments try to treat everyone equally and fairly, but there may be instances when applicants do not get enough time to complete a written test because the clock stopped or interviewers asked inappropriate questions that appeared to the candidate to be biased or discriminatory, for example. A protest will result in an investigation that will often delay the results of the exam.

*The List of Eligible Candidates.* Before the list can be used for hiring, it may have to be approved by a governing board, such as a civil service or personnel commission and/or the city council or board of supervisors. After it is approved, the head of the personnel department can certify the list and allow operating departments to hire from it.

Once the list is official, it is sent to departments that have available positions and approval to hire people in the particular classification. Departments are given the names in a rank-order list, with the highest ranks first. In some governments, departments may be required to interview only a small number of candidates, perhaps five to 10. Lists for many job classifications can be much longer than this, so the departments may receive an abbreviated list showing only the first few ranks of eligible candidates. Names of applicants who are interviewed but not hired remain on the list and can be interviewed many times.

These lists are valid for specific time periods, perhaps 6 months to 2 years. Lists for positions that have relatively few openings and little turnover may be extended past the original expiration date. Lists for positions with significant turnover may be renewed by testing more frequently. Names on the lists go to many departments with vacancies during the life of the list.

## The Initial Interview

Because of the wide use of essay questions on screening tests, it may take 1 month or more for a panel of experts to score exams and for applicants to be notified of the results. The notification may be in the form of an interview appointment or notification that the applicant did not score high enough on the written exam to be granted an interview.

Applicants selected for initial interviews will likely be interviewed by a panel of two or more individuals. Educational institutions are particularly inclusive and may have panels of nine or more to include faculty, staff, and others in interviews for administrative positions. Panel members will include people who work for the local government and may also include people with expertise who are employed by other public agencies or private companies. The names of the panel members will usually be posted near the interview room or otherwise given to applicants. The names are provided so that applicants have an opportunity to object to anyone on the panel prior to the interview. Applicants can ask that someone on the panel not participate in the interview if the panelist might be biased or if an applicant is uncomfortable because they supervised or worked for a panel member.

The panel should have a structured list of questions to ask applicants. Compared to interviews in the private sector, civil service interviews are generally short, maybe 20 to 30 minutes in length. This is not much time to impress the panel. Because of the time restriction and because the panel needs to ask everyone the same set of questions to ensure fairness, the panel appreciates applicants who are succinct in their answers.

The civil service or initial interview panel is not normally the panel that will hire the applicants. This panel helps refine the list of eligible candidates. The panel members rate the applicants' backgrounds and their answers to questions that are related to the civil service classification, but not necessarily to specific job openings. Their ratings plus applicants' scores on the written exam will determine the applicants' final scores and their places on the final list forwarded to departments with unfilled job openings.

Because this panel does not make hiring decisions and may not even know the details of the open positions, they probably cannot answer many questions about specific jobs. If they are interviewing for entry-level jobs, the jobs may exist in many departments and have varied duties.

The following are some typical questions:

- "Please tell us how your education and experience prepare you for this position." There could be a variation of this question. It is best to study the position description and prepare a one- to 2-minute statement linking your background to the key requirements of the position. Try not to memorize the statement; be flexible and prepared to respond to unexpected follow-up questions.
- "What experience do you have using [software name]?" Be able to tell in detail the extent of your knowledge and skills, especially

in software specified in the job announcement. Applicants are generally expected to know basic use of common word-processing and spreadsheet software.

- "Suppose you are working at a public counter and a citizen is loudly complaining about services. What would you do?" There may be a question like this about dealing with the public. A good way to answer this question is to state that you would let the person vent, listen to the complaint, promise a response, and isolate the person in a private office, if possible, so that the general office is not disrupted. This is a good time to describe any customer service training and experience.

- "What are your strengths and weaknesses?" This question, while not actually very useful in determining a candidate's qualifications, is occasionally asked. Keep your response limited to those to strengths and weaknesses that are specifically related to the position (for example, having a 15-golf handicap is probably not a relevant strength). Instead of dwelling on weaknesses, describe them in a positive light and emphasize strategies to overcome them (for example, "I have little experience using R, but have used SPSS for 4 years for statistical analysis").

- "What are you proudest of?" Make sure the examples are related to the job.

- "If you are hired for this position, what would be your role in equal employment opportunity?" In some governments, all interviews include a question of this type. Research the government's policies regarding equal employment opportunity, non-discrimination, sexual harassment, and similar topics.

- "Is there anything that you would like to add?" Frequently this is the final question. It is a good idea to have a very short statement in mind. You can also use this as an opportunity to elaborate on something you may have forgotten, recognizing that the interviewers are expecting to end the interview soon.

When being interviewed, be aware of verbal and nonverbal cues from the panel members that they are bored or not quite satisfied with a response and interested in hearing more. Respond accordingly. If the panel members start looking at their watches, it usually means it is time to start wrapping up a response.

## Interview Follow-up

It is important not to attempt to contact the members of a civil service interview panel. For private-sector interviews it is customary to send thank-you notes to the panel members. In the public sector, any attempts to contact the panel members may result in the disqualification of the applicant.

## The Hiring Interview

Hiring departments may be permitted to screen candidates and may not interview all candidates, especially if the list of eligible candidates contains many candidates. Screening can take many forms. Generally, it involves requesting resumes, applications, writing samples, and/or other material from candidates and using criteria to evaluate this material to decide whom to invite to interview. It is important for candidates to respond quickly to these requests for material and to follow instructions carefully since it is easy to disqualify late or incomplete applications.

Some information and advice on test and interview appointments:

- Tests are usually given in groups on specific days and at set times or by a certain date.

- An applicant may be given a set interview date and time, or may be offered a choice. Interview panels are difficult to organize, so interviews are usually scheduled back-to-back, in 30- to 60-minute time periods, during one or more days. Generally, the appointment for the civil service interview is set at the time of the initial interview notice, and there is little opportunity to reschedule, but there may be flexibility if the candidate is ill or has an emergency. Although hiring departments may be more flexible in terms of setting an appointment, it is always a good idea to accommodate their schedules.

The hiring interview is the applicant's chance to learn more about a specific job. The interview panel is probably made up of employees of the department and may include the supervisor. Surprisingly, applicants can be hired without meeting the supervisor. The interview will probably be short, and the process can include another exam, often an essay to test writing ability (see Appendix A).

The hiring department and its interview panel always appreciate interviewing candidates who are interested in a department. While they will not expect detailed knowledge, they will be more likely to rate a candidate higher who has researched the agency. The following are some ways to do research on a government in preparation for an interview:

- Look at the government's website for information about programs, services, and issues.

- Look at the budget for the size (dollars of expenses) and trends from previous years. Look at the introductory material, often a letter from the mayor or city manager. This material will include a discussion of issues, goals, and priorities. Look also at the revenue sources, especially those funding the position you are seeking.

- Look at organization charts to see how this job fits into the whole.

- Look at agendas for council or other public meetings to learn about the types of issues handled and the amount of detail. Some councils handle more general policies while others approve lists of expenditures of fairly low dollar value.

After doing this research, it is best to see how one's own experience relates to these issues and goals. For example, if the government indicates that a recent study found poor customer service and the mayor is making improvement a top priority, candidates can emphasize their training and experience in this area.

Unlike the panel in the first interview that cannot be contacted after the interview, applicants can usually send the hiring panel thank-you notes via email or mail. Again, it is best to check to see if thank-yous are allowed.

Since there are usually deadlines for making hiring decisions, this panel will act relatively quickly when evaluating applicants. The applicant selected may receive an offer within 1 or 2 weeks.

It may be possible to find out more about the job and office through informal channels. Local chapters of professional organizations such as the American Society for Public Administration and the Government Finance Officers Association are good sources of contacts. It is also possible to telephone or email people who currently work for the department to get their perspectives.

## Accepting an Offer

The offer itself will probably be in the form of a telephone call from the supervisor or a personnel manager followed by an email or letter with the details. Applicants should be sure that they understand their offers in detail, especially the following:

*Start Date.* When and where you should first show up. Often the first stop will be with the Personnel Department to sign documents, get an ID badge, etc. before reporting to your new department.

*Pay.* The job announcement may show a range of salaries, with perhaps five to seven steps. The local government's website or budget may have more information about the salary range, along with the ranges of other positions. Normally, a new employee is hired at the lowest salary step, unless they can demonstrate that that rate would result in a significant pay cut and they have unique experience compared to other candidates. Confirm each of the following:

- starting pay
- whether pay is hourly or salary
- what the pay period is (e.g., weekly, on the 15th and 30th of each month, monthly)
- initial work schedule

Bonuses are rare in the public sector, although some jobs may have special salary provisions for credentials of higher education exceeding those required by the job. For example, an employee hired into an accounting job may receive additional pay for being a CPA; an entry-level engineer who is licensed or a police officer with a college degree may start at a higher step or have a pay adjustment. End-of-the-year performance and profit-sharing bonuses are generally not part of public-sector compensation.

There is usually very little room for negotiating pay and work schedules at the entry-level positions, but flexibility increases as positions become more difficult to fill.

*Benefits.* Benefits are often generous compared to benefits in the private sector. The following are some considerations and questions to ask (see also Chapter 12, "Benefits"):

- Does the employee pay the entire retirement contribution, or does the government pay all or part of it? The government may pay some portion, up to 100%. The employee's share is often in the range of 5% to 7% of his or her salary.
- Does the government participate in Social Security? All governments participate in Medicare, but some do not participate in Social Security. Thus, ask if there will be deductions for Medicare and Social Security.
- Is there a car allowance or mileage reimbursement? These may be offered in lieu of providing government cars for official business, so employees are expected to drive their own cars to meetings, site visits, and so forth.
- What is the subsidy for health benefits? Governments generally subsidize part of the premium and often the entire premium for a single employee. Employees often must pay a part of the premium for family members or if they select a more expensive employee-only plan.
- Does the government offer a cafeteria benefits plan? This plan gives employees a certain amount of money to use to buy benefits (health, dental, and disability insurance, etc.)
- Does the government offer other benefits such as tuition reimbursement or, if required for the position, costs of uniforms and equipment?
- What holidays are observed?
- What is the vacation policy, including accrual rates and vesting?
- What is the sick leave policy?

Some agencies use Personal Paid Time Off (PPTO) instead of vacation and/or sick days. The difference can be significant financially when you leave the organization. Unused PPTO often does not have to be paid when you leave the organization; accrued and vested vacation time and sick leave usually must be paid when you leave.

*Perquisites.* Perquisites (or "perks") are special rights or privileges enjoyed as a part of one's position. There are few perks available at the entry level, but become more available as you move up the organization. Perks may include such things as designated or free parking, use of athletic club facilities, life insurance, financial counseling, etc. The cost of perks is paid by the employer but is added to wages and other cash payments when reporting total compensation to the IRS.

## Preparing for Promotion

Like private-sector workers, government workers want to progress in their careers. Applying for a promotion in government means going through the same or similar type of testing and review process as do entry-level workers.

The following are some pointers:

- Learn as much as possible about the government.
  » Look for training to increase skills and find out about how the government works. Some governments have organized training programs for entry-level employees.
  » Read the charter, administrative code, civil service rules, agendas, and so forth. These should all be on the government's website.
- Participate in employee activities, such as office-sponsored events and sports leagues, to meet people and learn about the organization.
- Understand the career ladder for the position. Start preparing for promotions:
  » Ask people who have taken the next level exam what to expect.
  » Organize and participate in a study group with others who will be taking the exam.
- Learn from evaluations, particularly during the probationary period, which is an on-the-job test. Ask supervisors to explain the basis for evaluations and for suggestions about how to improve work performance and skills. Also seek advice about preparing for a promotion.
- It is advisable to stay in a position long enough to learn the job and not be considered a "job hopper." At the entry level, 2 years is a reasonable time period, although promotional opportunities may come up sooner. Employees are not penalized for taking promotional opportunities whenever they arise.

- Take as many promotional exams as possible, even those for jobs in which you do not have an interest. Doing well on promotional exams is the chief way to promote in many governments, and the more practice one has in exam taking, the better.
- The stereotype of a public servant is someone who does the bare minimum of work and is resistant to change. The best way to be promoted is to not fit this stereotype.
  - » Be productive, ask questions, work quickly and efficiently, ask for feedback, and be flexible.
  - » Be responsive to others. Return telephone calls and emails. Provide requested information.
  - » Be willing to change. Process improvement is becoming increasingly important in government. Look for opportunities to make improvements. Volunteer for process improvement teams.
  - » Keep up to date. Find out what other governments and the private sector are doing. Join professional organizations.
  - » Be respectful and nice to everyone at all levels in the organization. People tend to stay in government employment for long periods of time. Some people will progress from clerk typist to senior manager during a career. It is not uncommon for colleagues or subordinates to become supervisors. They will remember how they were treated by their co-workers.
- Seek out valuable experiences. It is good to know something about each of these areas:
  - » budget preparation and monitoring;
  - » bill payment, which can be complex in governments;
  - » contracting and contract administration;
  - » personnel, especially how the civil service system works and what the equal employment opportunity policies and programs are; and
  - » general government policies.

*Professional Organizations.* Membership and participation in professional organizations is an excellent way to stay up to date as well as to become acquainted with others in your field. Refer to Chapter 19 for more information about professional organizations.

*Networking.* Networking is a very effective way to prepare for promotions and become known in your field. This may involve membership in service clubs such as Rotary International or Kiwanis or it may involve volunteering with a nongovernmental organization (nonprofit) with a mission you personally embrace. Networking also includes judicious and professional use of social media, being very careful to not give the impression that your comments represent the position of the agency or department you work for.

# AGENCY/EMPLOYER PERSPECTIVE

Every manager and most supervisors will at some time be involved in hiring people. This section provides a brief introduction to important aspects of that process.

## Job Description

The first step in filling an open (or new) position is to review (or create) the job description. An accurate, comprehensive, and up-to-date job description is essential to searching for and identifying candidates who are capable of filling a position. This starting point is, unfortunately, often overlooked or is given only a cursory review. The useful job description will help guide the selection process away from replacing an individual (who may have had many years' of experience in the position) and toward identifying viable candidates who can perform the job. The last person in the position did not have as much experience when they were hired as they did when they left; the new hire should have only as much experience as is needed to execute the job adequately. The good job description will also indicate how this position fits into the overall operational and compensation structure.

***Essential Elements*** A good job description contains several elements, each serving a specific purpose.

***Development Process.*** Human Resources is typically primarily responsible for developing and maintaining comprehensive and useful job descriptions, but they require input from several other areas, including the job manager, incumbents, and legal. Before starting the search for a new hire, the job manager should carefully review the current job description and have it updated as necessary.

## Searching for Candidates

Human Resources usually does the primary work in advertising an open position and recruiting applicants. Entry-level positions typically receive the least specialized advertising, although there may be extra efforts to locate minority candidates who are not currently well represented in the department. Mid-level openings often are primarily open to internal candidates, although outside recruiting may also occur. Senior-level openings tend to require more extended experience in government; recruiting may include specialized recruiting firms. Searching for senior-level candidates may also require a certain amount of secrecy to minimize disrupting the organization during the search process.

## Table C-2  Job Description Elements

| | |
|---|---|
| **Title:** | This should very briefly indicate the type and level of work to be done using concise descriptive words that are consistent with other job titles in the organization and the field. |
| **Exempt/ Non-exempt Status:** | Identify if this position is exempt or not exempt from overtime requirements. |
| **Reporting Structure:** | Describe where this position fits in the organization, including direct and indirect reporting relationships and titles of direct reports. |
| **Summary:** | A brief overview of the job, including its purpose and responsibility level. This summary is often used in advertising the position. |
| **Duties and Responsibilities:** | List each duty and responsibility which accounts for more than 5% of the incumbent's time or is critical to successful job performance. List items in sequence of most time consuming to least. |
| **Requirements:** | Describe the minimum requirements that are essential to perform the job. These should be legally defensible and should not be things that would be nice to have. For example, if a certificate or license is listed, it should be actually required to perform the job. When a minimum number of years of experience is specified, there should be backup documentation of how that number was determined. This section should also include how much time is spent traveling and well as the geographic extent of the travel. |
| **Bona Fide Occupational Qualification:** | Bona Fide Occupational Qualifications (BFOQs) allow hiring based on race, sex, age, or national origin if it relates to an essential job duty and is absolutely necessary for the position. For example, a women's clothes designer may be permitted to hire only female models to show the clothing line; however, the designer would not be allowed to hire an accountant based on sex because being female is not necessary to doing accounting. Refer also to Bona Fide Occupational Qualification Law & Legal Definition http://definitions.uslegal.com/b/bona-fide-occupational-qualification/ Any BFOQ should be reviewed and specifically authorized by an agency attorney. |
| **Working Conditions:** | Describe the general and any abnormal physical working environment (e.g., exposure to hazardous materials or chemicals) or working conditions (e.g., work is often done standing on ladders). Details are usually not required in job descriptions where the work will be performed in a normal office environment. |
| **Disclaimer:** | The disclaimer indicates that not every possible job duty or responsibility is included in the job description. Typically, this is a statement such as "May be required to perform other related duties as assigned." |
| **Salary Grade:** | The salary range or grade is often included for an internal job posting, but may not be included in a public announcement. This information helps in the recruiting and screening process. |
| **Authorization:** | A signed and dated job description indicates when it has last been reviewed and approved. It is typically reviewed by Human Resources, line management, and legal to assure that it accurately describes the position and complies with legal requirements. |
| **Company Overview (optional):** | This helps potential candidates understand what the organization does and its culture. This is mostly used in general public job postings and is rarely seen for government jobs. |

## Reviewing Applications and Resumes

The application packet provides historical and technical data about the candidates; the interview process provides information about the person and how they may fit with the organization. Human Resources usually conducts the first review of applications, primarily to ensure that they are logged in, are received within the allowable dates, have all the necessary parts and signatures, and may also screen out those that clearly do not meet the minimum qualifications for the position. If there is a closing date for applications, Human Resources will typically hold all the applications until the day after the closing date before the next step in the process. See also the Selection Process section earlier in this appendix which describes screening tests, assessment centers, and other steps candidates may go through.

If the application form includes a page containing demographic (e.g., age, sex, ethnicity) and other possibly discriminatory information, it should be kept by Human Resources and neither forwarded to nor considered by others in the organization. This "protected data" is usually used to document the breadth of applications received and the extent of the agency's recruiting process.

Review the application packet (cover letter, resume, application form, etc.) to get an overall impression of the candidate. The application form helps quickly locate specific pieces of information about the candidate. This helps to begin ranking the candidates from best to worst. Among things to look for are:

- unexplained gaps in employment history
- prior positions' applicability to the position sought
- additional education or training
- length of time in each position
- why the candidate left prior positions

Review the resume (if any) to refine your impression of the candidate. Among things to look for:

- consistency with data on the application form
- description of job duties and responsibilities (probably will be more detailed in the resume than on the application form)
- description of accomplishments

Review the answers to any supplemental questions for:
- writing and thinking clarity
- technical approach to the issue posed
- ability to eliminate unnecessary information
- ability to communicate effectively in writing

Reviewing the application packets, including resumes, supplemental questions, etc., often requires an iterative approach. With each pass, your impression of each candidate relative to the other candidates and the position requirements and how well the candidate might fit with the rest of the staff will be refined. Creating a system for ranking the candidates with each review will help. For instance, on the first round you might rank each candidate A, B, or C with As being people you clearly think could do the job; Bs those who could possibly could do the job; and Cs being those you have some serious doubts about. With each successive round of reviews, rank sequence the candidates in each group, possibly moving a candidate from one group to another as well.

## Interviewing Candidates

You might interview candidates at any stage in the hiring process. The successive interviews serve to refine the organization's understanding of the candidate and their likelihood of succeeding in the position and with the organization. Interviews should be designed and conducted to elicit a greater understanding of the candidate and how well they will fit in the organization and with their coworkers.

*Questions.* All questions should be relevant to identifying qualifying or disqualifying traits or experience of the candidates. Questions should be properly phrased to elicit the type of answer desired. To confirm information, the question should elicit "Yes" or "No" as the answer (e.g., "Have you worked with C++?"); to elicit information, the question should not be able to be answered "Yes" or "No" (e.g., "How many years have you used C++?"). That is, ask the question you want answered.

When there is a panel of interviewers, each should have specific questions to pose, avoiding duplication unless necessary to confirm critical data. It is best at all levels of interviewing to enter the interview with specific questions for the candidate; off-the-cuff questions should be asked when an answer provokes them.

There are some questions, or types of questions, that cannot be asked during an interview unless they relate directly to a bona fide occupational qualification. These prohibited questions are those that ask about any of the following:

- race
- color
- sex or sexual orientation
- gender identity
- sexual orientation
- marital status
- age
- national origin

- religion
- medical conditions not directly related to the job (e.g., pregnancy, breastfeeding, etc.)

Virtually any other question may be legally allowable, but the purpose of the interview is to learn how likely the candidate is to succeed in the position and with the organization. While some questions are legally allowable, it is important to eliminate questions that will primarily embarrass the candidate or provide little useful information (e.g., "What is your greatest weakness?" or "Why should we hire you?"). A good question to include at the end of the interview is "What else do you want us to know about you?"

All candidates should be asked the same questions, especially in the initial stages of the hiring process, even if the answer may seem obvious (e.g., asking a person in a wheelchair if they will need any ADA accommodation).

## Making the Job Offer

The formal job offer may be made by either Human Resources or the manager, depending on the agency and the level of the position. The offer is often first made by a telephone call and should always be followed up in writing.

The job offer should include:

- position/job title
- start date
- pay
- benefits
- perquisites

Whoever presents the offer to the candidate must be ready to discuss each item in detail and, in some cases, be authorized to make minor changes to the offer. The person presenting the job offer should also make it clear exactly where the candidate should go and who to see on their first day.

## First Day on the Job

Most of the first day on the job usually involves "onboarding" activities, many of which are done at Human Resources. These include formal signing of various documents (IRS Form W-4, USCIS Form I-9, etc.), issuing an employee ID badge, etc.

Once the new employee is released to their new department, the manager should welcome them; introduce them to their new co-workers, subordinates, and indirect reports; and review the position and the job offer to ensure that it is clearly understood.

## BIBLIOGRAPHY

Axelrod-Contrata, J. (2008). *Career opportunities in politics, government and activism*. (2d ed.). New York, NY: Checkmark Books.

Collins, A. (2016). HR interview secrets. SuccessInHR.com

Gallo, A. (2020, June 22). How to nail a job interview—remotely. *Harvard Business Review*. https://hbr.org/2020/06/how-to-nail-a-job-interview-remotely

Gordon, R. L. (1998). *Basic interviewing skills*. Long Grove, IL: Waveland Press, Inc.

Guilford, H. (2018). *How to interview people*. Self-published: CreateSpace Publishing.

Knight, R. (2015, January 23). How to conduct an effective job interview. *Harvard Business Review*. https://hbr.org/2015/01/how-to-conduct-an-effective-job-interview

Leanne, S. (2003). *How to interview like a top MBA*. New York, NY: McGraw-Hill.

Liff, S. (2008). *Managing your government career*. New York, NY: Amacom.

Ringel, R. (2021, October 5). 8 tips for conducting and excellent remote interview. *Harvard Business Review*. https://hbr.org/2021/10/8-tips-for-conducting-an-excellent-remote-interview

Smalley, L. R. (1999). *Interviewing and selecting high performers*. Hoboken, NJ: Wiley.

Trull, S. G. (1964, January). Strategies of effective interviewing. *Harvard Business Review*. https://hbr.org/1964/01/strategies-of-effective-interviewing

U.S. Department of Labor Occupational Network. https://www.onetonline.org/

# Index

*Note:* Page numbers followed by *b, f, t* denote boxes, figures, and tables, respectively.